FinTech Revolution

Sofie Blakstad · Robert Allen

FinTech Revolution

Universal Inclusion in the New Financial
Ecosystem

Sofie Blakstad
hiveonline
Copenhagen, Denmark

Robert Allen
hiveonline
Copenhagen, Denmark

ISBN 978-3-319-76013-1   ISBN 978-3-319-76014-8   (eBook)
https://doi.org/10.1007/978-3-319-76014-8

Library of Congress Control Number: 2018938315

This Palgrave Macmillan imprint is published by the registered company Springer International Publishing AG part of Springer Nature
The registered company address is: Gewerbestrasse 11, 6330 Cham, Switzerland

Preface: Level the Field

We've spent most of our careers building banks, delivering business structures and technology to make them work better. As we did so, we observed the industry, the technology, customers and economic changes both as insiders and as customers of banks.

This book is about the future of finance, but it's also about its immediate past, and the things many people, including us, have done and are doing to make finance fairer and more inclusive. It's about the opportunities that are now emerging for the billions of people who lack access to traditional financial services, to participate and thrive in the new financial ecosystem.

Financial services companies are trying to become more customer focused, but struggling to help huge customer segments, particularly in developing economies. Alternative financial models and tools are emerging, which are being embraced by consumers and incumbents. In large parts of the developing world, alternative services are leapfrogging traditional finance, meaning more and more people have access to finance without ever needing a bank. Since we left the world of traditional banking to develop new business models based on emerging technology, we've become deeply involved with the effort to implement the United Nations' Sustainable Development Goals[1] (SDGs), 17 targets we must meet as a species to create a sustainable home for ourselves by 2030.

The SDGs are a broad-reaching set of goals covering everything from poverty to water safety, gender equality to financial inclusion. Emerging financial technology offers unprecedented opportunities for underserved customers in both developed and developing economies, enabling them to collaborate in global communities and rewrite global capital markets. The way markets, work, supply and money works is changing fundamentally, empowering smaller and traditionally underserved small and micro-businesses, alongside ordinary consumers.

Meanwhile, the barriers around financial services companies are crumbling, as they become more reliant on integration with new providers and alternative types of service. Financial products can no longer be viewed in isolation, but as part of a service landscape that supports how people "do life". This means rethinking how our businesses are designed, motivated and organised, and letting go of the old ways of thinking about supply and demand. There's a new world on the horizon where mobile wallets, disintermediated payments, trustless trust, ecosystem identity and community finance will transform the way we perceive and use value and trust.

We offer a practical guide to the evolving landscape of finance, highlighting how it's changing our relationship with money and how financial technology, together with macroeconomic and societal change, is rewriting the story of how business is done in developing economies. We present the practical steps businesses and, in particular, financial services organisations, need to take to participate in a global service ecosystem, and how both customers and staff will benefit from this. We show the critical role that many technologies, especially blockchain, will have in contributing to these developments, drawing on our experience in both the old world of major international banks and the new world of Fintech, where, through our company hiveonline, we're building some of the solutions that will drive the Fintech Revolution.

There's a joke circulating on the internet: *The world is full of two types of people: 1. Those who can extrapolate from incomplete data.* The joke is, of course, that the data are always incomplete. The future is unknown, messy and full of "no shit" moments. In *Back to the Future*, Doc asked Marty in 1955, who the POTUS was, and got the answer "Ronald Reagan"—everyone laughs, it's funny viewed from 1955. Today, we have Donald Trump, flying delivery vehicles (although no flying cars yet) and the sum of all human knowledge accessed through your phone. Nobody knows what's around the corner, and however smart or expert you are, the future is too messy and full of surprises to predict fully.

However, history also teaches us lessons, if we are humble enough to read it with open eyes. Looking back over our lifetimes, there are very few occasions when the world has been truly taken by surprise; there are, though, many more where the signs and predictions were made, but ignored, for short-term political, reputational or financial reasons or, more commonly, because the people with the knowledge weren't the people making the decisions.

People making decisions are often ill-equipped to do so and surround themselves by people who are equally poorly equipped. The nature of politics means that expertise isn't that valuable an asset, while many experts choose to avoid involvement in politics, so that they can get on with developing solutions. Human behaviour is often motivated by purpose and value rather than by money; classical models of economics and society fail to account for this and are proving terrible at predicting how our world evolves, while evolving technology supports new types of interaction, leading to more "new normals" every few years.

For people like us at the leading edge of technology developments, it's very easy to appear to cross the line into the "tin-foil hat" brigade for some observers, while appearing mainstream to others; what seems obvious and the natural order of things to others looks crazy and suicidal to us. It's a matter of perspective.

We are living in many stories. The ones we tell in this book are the story of how financial services have evolved following the 2008 crash, how technology has helped change people's interaction with financial services, how global economic and societal change is needed and can be supported by these changes, and how business and work is moving from a pyramid culture to an ecosystem, with the struggles that movement entails. We tell parts of our own story of how we've both experienced and participated in these changes, but they are everyone's story today.

We've anchored our story in the observations we've made working in 12 of the world's largest financial institutions, and the research we're living as we build a new sort of financial institution for the future. But the book isn't about banks. We tell the story of financial institutions, but we also tell the story of an evolving world, where billions of people can grasp the opportunity to rise out of poverty thanks to social and technological developments, while at the same time trust in traditional institutions and nations is eroded by scandals, spread by social media and the rise of fundamentalism of all flavours.

We've arranged the book in two sections: the first half looks at how financial institutions and Fintechs are evolving, together with the opportunities technology can present for sustainability, and especially for the many underserved and unbanked people and businesses in the world, and the second half explores broader societal trends in consumer behaviour, what this means for consumers and financial institutions, and finally how financial institutions can realign their business and service models towards the resulting eco-system economy.

But we hope you will engage with the sections or chapters that interest you, as you choose: treat it as a how-to guide to building a bank, or as a guide to the evolution of alternative finance, or as a commentary on global socio-economic change driven by technology. Each chapter is cross-referenced with relevant chapters, so you're not tied to a linear narrative; we've found that life doesn't work that way, so why should a book?

Copenhagen, Denmark   Sofie Blakstad
January 2018   Robert Allen

Note

1. Sustainable Development Goals homepage (UN). https://sustainabledevelopment.un.org/?menu=1300. Accessed 11 January 2017.

Contents

Future Business, Part VI   Services for the Ecosystem Economy

Building the Future

List of Figures

List of Tables

The Un-bank, Part I

Fintech for Financial Inclusion *What's Behind It?*

Financial services are changing. Following the 2008 crisis, new services have evolved to challenge, supplement and supplant banks.

The first half of this book explores the evolution of financial services away from the monoliths into the ecosystem, and the implications for underserved customers—the unbanked, largely (but not exclusively) in developing economies, and small businesses everywhere, who have been suffering from limited availability and high cost of banking services, while larger corporations continue to grow and benefit from economies of scale, often transcending national boundaries and taxation. We describe both how emerging solutions, exploiting but not driven by technology, are already having an impact, and the further, greater impact that will follow.

We show how these solutions are helping to fuel the growing drive towards finding sustainable business solutions, in support of the UN's Sustainable Development Goals and enabling communities everywhere to be self-supporting and sustainable.

This half focuses, necessarily, on exploring the technologies that will support and partially drive the evolution. A key technology is blockchain and its many potential applications, together with the enormous implications it has for disrupting traditional notions of money, value and transactions. But this isn't a book about blockchain so much as the ecosystem economy that it will enable, which is already emerging around us, despite all the technical limitations in our legacy systems.

And that gives us good reason to state with confidence that the Fintech Revolution is already happening; the nascent ecosystem economy is already here, and the new financial ecosystem is beginning to emerge.

What's Behind It?

In developed economies, most people see banks as a necessity; like schools, transport or food shops, they're part of the familiar infrastructure of modern capitalism, and we would struggle to function normally without them. But banks as we know them, and the traditional financial system, are changing. Following the crash of 2008, governments and regulators have encouraged greater competition in the financial system to mitigate the "too big to fail" risks that contributed to the crisis; but banks are struggling to change, while alternate financial services are gaining ground.

In this part we examine the challenges banks are facing in moving into the new ecosystem economy, the alternate services that will replace many of their current offerings, and the impact this is likely to have on the financial services industry, its customers, and the wider economy.

1

Ecosystem vs Egosystem and Revolution vs Evolution

Banks need to move into the ecosystem to participate in the new economy, but it's not easy.

In this chapter, we consider the forces driving us from traditional financial services to the emerging financial ecosystem. We examine the way financial services organisations have been structured to date, and the binding forces that are keeping them that way, despite efforts to change. We discuss the factors that have allowed the ecosystem economy to emerge, and how the transition is happening—with some examples of organisations that are successfully bridging the gap.

The change is radical, fundamental, holistic and impacts all aspects of financial services; we consider the level of disruption that will be required or result from the transition, and ask whether relatively pain-free evolution will be overcome by a more compromising, dramatic and painful revolution.

Dinosaurs and Dynasties: The Financial Services Egosystem

Banks evolved from individuals holding big buckets of money. The guy holding the purse strings (literally, at first) called the shots. Banks grew as balance sheets and customer numbers grew and became giants at a time when labour was cheap, computing was in its infancy, and popular management theory held that hierarchical organisations were the lifeblood of the economy. Corporate pyramids, beloved by American organisations of the

© The Author(s) 2018
S. Blakstad and R. Allen, *FinTech Revolution*,
https://doi.org/10.1007/978-3-319-76014-8_1

1950s to 1970s, were still maintaining their apparently unassailable position as the ideal business model, riding on the back of the US's relative economic prosperity following World War II, and subsequently adopted by the world as the cause, rather than a correlation, of that prosperity.

Banks also went through a period of rapid growth and consolidation[1] from the 1980s to the 2000s,[2] in parallel with the development of many new products and services, facilitated by relaxing regulations and greater technical opportunities. As banks grew and rewards skyrocketed, they ceased to be boring, safe workplaces and became attractive to ambitious individuals seeking to make their fortune. And those individuals were rewarded; their creativity and hard work supported the sales of a broader range of products to more lucrative markets, and profitability headed skywards too.

Banks were locked into a cycle of making money, attracting talent so that they could make more money, increasing their value and attracting more talent. Regular culls at most institutions cut out any underperformers, ensuring teams were composed of the brightest and most ambitious people. Leaders, however, were rewarded for two key metrics: building bigger teams and making more money. And it worked: as banking practice expanded to previously untapped areas of the market, a growing consumer acceptance of credit and creative secondary products expanded the mortgage books and made gambling on capital markets an increasingly profitable activity; balance sheets grew, salaries continued to escalate and shareholders were happy.

Out of the Crisis?

Then in 2008 the bubble burst, and things changed—but not everything. After the crisis, banks recognised the need to scale back, but the consolidation continued. They were still locked into trying to deliver value for shareholders; even though valuations were in the toilet, they couldn't see a way to reduce their costs by losing key individuals without losing the ability to generate value, so those salaries stayed high, while lower-cost people were let go to bring the numbers down, and people were rewarded for the same old metrics. Because large teams selling products at volume to large numbers of customers require consistency and aggressive selling to make lots of money, originality was discouraged in favour of aggression.

The large team/volume sales approach built generations of leaders who have learned that success is earned by building large teams and making lots of money against aggressive, quarterly targets. It also selected for leaders who were good at these two things. Consequently, most of the leadership teams of banks today are still pretty homogenous; despite the recognition that aggressive, sales-oriented "groupthink" directly led to the crisis in the first place,[3] it has been challenging for firms to edit out the profile of people that have formed both their leadership teams and their leadership pipelines for decades.

Banks have recognised the cultural challenge and, especially as it becomes increasingly apparent that customers are demanding greater transparency and accountability, are making committed efforts to change. However, despite widespread reform, groupthink and the underlying culture are proving difficult to shift.[4] Why is it so hard?

Cultural Barriers to Transforming for the Ecosystem Economy

Most banks' rewards systems are still at least partially focused on quarterly sales, so while many have now included metrics supporting customer-centricity and longer-horizon decision making, an underlying culture in many institutions persists which is driven, at least partially, by short-term, aggressive sales. So the people who rise to senior positions are still those who can meet the sales targets and build large teams.

This creates a challenge for banks when it comes to selecting diverse leadership teams; if the talent pool is homogenous, they're struggling to find leaders from a spectrum of attitudes and backgrounds, because those new leaders just aren't rising through the pipeline. Bringing different types of leaders through the pipeline requires the existing leaders to recognise the values organisations are looking for when selecting new leaders, which is hard when the existing leader doesn't share those values.

While a focus on more rigorous recruitment screening has vastly improved selection processes for senior roles over the last two decades, at senior levels relationships are built on common values, which is likely to lead to self-perpetuating culture on the executive team and the board. And even when new types of leaders make it through and are selected, we've seen outliers (often women), brought in at least partially for the diversity they can bring to the team, only to be managed out after 12–18 months because they can't agree common ground with the pre-existing team. Studies have shown that any minority group needs representation of 30%[5] to have an effective voice in a group; so bringing alternative views to the table in dribs and drabs is also setting them up to fail.

This problem persists, despite some enlightened leaders who fully understand the need for culture to change; these leaders are driving culture change programmes, often forcing the education top-down and expecting their executive teams to enforce them. Top-down is the most effective way to drive cultural transformation, as role modelling is key to changing values and behaviours, but it's also tough to implement when the majority of the senior people in an organisation have long-learned values and behaviours which support the hierarchy and pressure selling approach, often over decades.

Moving from a hierarchical focus to a service aligned, capability oriented organisation takes more than cultural transformation; it requires a fundamental change to how the organisation is structured, how people are rewarded and how power structures work, and the last section of this book is dedicated to how those organisations look. Asking your homogenous leadership team, for whom managing a large hierarchy has been a foundational career goal, to drive this change is not just asking turkeys to vote for Christmas; it's also asking them to become different people.

Cultural training can help to move the needle, but the chances of building a team with a majority hit rate, or even that 30% figure needed to be effectively represented, in changed attitudes is small. Together with structural change, a key driver for cultural transformation is a change to rewards metrics, which is something that not just executive committees, but especially boards, struggle with, while performance is already impacted by flatlining interest rates, the cost of implementing regulatory changes and reduced customer growth. Boards and executive committees are responsible to shareholders, who have in good faith invested in a profitable enterprise; while they can see a future where things need to change, it's very hard to justify turning off the tap in the short term, to achieve longer-term survival.

So we've seen many banks and financial institutions making serious efforts to transform, often recognising how critical cultural change is in driving transformation, but falling at the point where they try to make those changes structural and drive the business towards a flatter, ecosystem ready structure. As we discuss in the last section of the book, it's difficult to provide customer-focused services in a traditional hierarchy; cultural change will only survive if leaders are seen to walk the talk, while if workers' experience is that nothing really changes, the cultural transformation initiative is perceived as lip service and a waste of time and money, leading to workers becoming disillusioned with the idea of change.

Values driven cultural transformations like these in banks have, therefore, frequently failed, as they fail to address the hierarchical structure of banks.

Only in a small number of examples have they been successful—ING[6] is a good example of a bank that has embraced a values driven transformation to the extent that leaders are required to adopt not just the values, but the (IT in this case) skills that are central to delivery of the bank's vision. This has meant restructuring the organisation, changing the way people are rewarded and letting a large number of people go—changes that, as ING has demonstrated, can be made with determination and the willingness to transform from top down, but are proving too much of a challenge for many banks, even with the looming crisis coming visibly closer.

If Not Banks, What?

And that crisis surrounds the banks today. As we examine throughout this book, there is a growing ecosystem of non-bank financial services emerging outside the banks, attracting growing customer numbers and seeing mainstream adoption by the banks' traditional customer base. Alipay, the Chinese digital wallet sensation, and M-PESA, the West African mobile money solution which has transformed financial inclusion in Kenya and elsewhere, are both examples of this. It's easy to identify the technology that has enabled some of these services to emerge, but it's also important to acknowledge that the growth of this ecosystem has not been driven so much by technology innovation as by customer need—necessity, as usual, being the mother of invention.

Non-bank financial services have always been with us; since before banks even existed there were money lenders and alternative structures, such as guilds and less formal community groups, supporting business growth and sharing financial risks, and these have persisted in parallel with the formal banking system—some becoming regulated under the same rules as banking and others, particularly lenders, managing to dodge inconvenient regulations and consumer protection rules. Because banks have been able to build large customer bases through their unique relationship with central bank-issued currencies, fractional reserve lending and strong regulatory protection, they have continued to dominate financial services, while non-bank financial services have been offered at often prohibitive premiums, to customers who, in many cases, are least able to afford them because they fail to meet the high standards of identity and credit history required by the banks.

But alternative financial services have exploded over the last ten years, driven by consumer behaviours and lower costs; M-PESA[7] in Kenya originated as Safaricom, the telco provider, observed that consumers were using phone credit instead of cash to exchange value; the business model which emerged then changed how consumers interfaced with finance. In developed economies, meanwhile, wide adoption of mobile apps driven by the iPhone and Android smartphones led to consumers experiencing, and then expecting, a fragmented, app-based and partially gamified interface with their service providers, opening the door for widespread adoption of payments services providers and mobile wallets.

While these new services could not have emerged without the availability of the relevant technology which enables low-cost scale and distribution, it's important to acknowledge that they were not driven by the technology but by a combination of behavioural changes and novel operating models, and that they have not resulted from banks, Fintechs or other providers driving the change in behaviour; rather, that smart providers have observed and then exploited changes in consumer behaviour that were already happening and filled them with novel service models.

In rare cases, business models can drive that change rather than responding to an existing change in behaviour; Alipay has been largely responsible for driving Chinese customer behaviour away from a cash-based economy towards an almost cashless economy in population centres, in less than a decade. Like M-PESA, Alipay[8] adopted a completely new business model to exploit consumer behaviours at scale and changed the way an economy operates in a very short space of time. Unlike M-PESA, which exploited a growing trend to transact mobile credit, Alipay emerged to fill a need for frictionless transactions which wasn't yet being filled, by innovative customer behaviours, but the speed of adoption proves that the need was there, and with the opportunity to observe M-PESA and other wallet adoption, the opportunity could be well understood.

Cases of pure technology driving changes consumer behaviour, in finance or elsewhere, however, are vanishingly small; the iPhone and some other Apple products are examples of game changers, but the rest of us are simply using the opportunity created by the behaviours they have created. We have seen many more examples where innovative business and service models have built on emerging behaviour change.

Apple and Alipay have shown us that consumer behaviour can, and will, evolve rapidly under the right circumstances—a combination of need (the opportunity) and low adoption barriers (the technology or the business model) creating the shift towards a new normal of behaviour. This is antithetical to one of the key underlying assumptions inherent to banks' traditional sales models: that the banks create the customer behaviour changes through creation of new products. Product-driven sales models are fundamental to the structure and business model of the dinosaur dynasties, and it's hard to acknowledge that customers are now driving changes to your competitive environment when coming from this mindset.

Digitising Banks

Banks have been making attempts to adapt to changed customer behaviours, not by identifying unsupported problems and creating genuinely new services, but by adopting interfaces to their traditional products that mimic the new types of services customers demand—every bank has an app now, but by funnelling customers through traditional products and processes, they score low in customer satisfaction and fail to exploit opportunities created by the changes in how customers interact with business models. The contrast is obvious when you consider the way in which many other apps deliver services, in comparison to banks.

It's rare for any organisation, other than a bank, to create an app which simply replicates its online service (although some apps have created online services which replicate the app) for good reasons—the reasons people use them, and the way they use them, are different; metro and bus apps will sell you tickets while you plan the route, while the BBC weather app is GPS sensitive. Successful apps are fragmented, agile, offering services at the point of delivery, location sensitive and highly interactive. Most deliver services in a completely different way to the website, if one exists, or deliver services which are not available via a website. And banking apps are, in general, mimicking services that existed long before web interfaces; in many cases, following an almost identical process to the bricks-and-mortar service of old.

The Transition Is Beginning to Happen

Some banks are now moving to adopt more ecosystem services, with a growing level of partnership and integration with smaller, or large platform providers who can provide these more intuitive, differentiated services. The year 2017 saw a large number of partnerships announced between banks and Fintechs, particularly in AI, robotics and blockchain. The integration is often a tense relationship, as a move from direct competition to cooperation (or "coopetition") requires changes not just to business strategy, but to fundamental practices within banks—and, in most cases, a steep learning curve for the ecosystem providers in how to deal with the banks, as well as for the banks—some have ridden it more successfully than others.

While it's impossible to generalise across all institutions, most have followed a process transitioning through stages of maturity:

First, observing the changes coming and attempting to build competitive services internally; often hiring teams of specialists in AI, robotics, blockchain, etc., who find adjustment to corporate life challenging, or, worse, appointing internal high fliers (or misfits) to create functions internally tasked with tackling the issues. We've met a few "heads of blockchain" who have transitioned from not always technical banking roles, who are then left to build teams to deliver some undefined strategy with unknown tools.

It's unsurprising that this approach didn't go well.

Secondly, most banks learned from their early mistakes and started to hire entrepreneurs and technologists with direct experience in building more agile teams. In some cases, this has worked very well, while others struggle to attract budget or senior level airtime. A common mistake is to put the head of innovation into a hierarchical reporting line, such as Retail Banking or IT, where they are forced to compete for budget for projects which will support strategies reducing the cost base and influence of their boss.

Thirdly, and often in parallel, banks have set up Innovation labs—internally focused initiatives, designed to harvest and nurture innovation ideas from their own staff, or Accelerators, externally focused mentoring programmes for Fintech startups, usually run as a competition. The internal labs, which usually run very popular innovation days, often struggle for resources and cash and fail to secure headcount needed to realise ideas as practical solutions. Banks' accelerators also struggle; in a competitive environment where hundreds of accelerators are competing for the top startups, they don't always attract the best ones, who are tempted elsewhere by higher rewards and don't want to put all their eggs in a single bank's basket, especially where the reputation of the accelerator is poor.

Both these innovation lab models sit awkwardly within banks; their pace is necessarily different, and instead of creating synergies, they often just bring the problems small, young organisations have when dealing with banks, of procurement, timescales and integration, in-house, without solving the problems. There's a lifecycle to these activities, which usually start badly, build enthusiasm as the quality of initiatives increases, and then end badly as the people involved and the wider organisation recognise that initiatives started in the lab have low chances of gaining traction in the wider organisation.

More recently, banks are starting to partner with Fintech Hubs, which takes the innovation teams and models outside of their walls, and some of these initiatives are looking promising. Partnering the Hubs, whose stock and trade is helping innovative new businesses to grow, with the banks' innovation teams, is starting to result in some strong partnerships. Other partnerships are evolving as the Fintechs themselves mature and get better at dealing with large corporates; it's a learning curve on both sides. But these relationships are still peripheral, and while the business partnerships are starting to work better, the transformation to culture and fundamental services is still struggling to mature.

Many banks have partnered with firms which promise to solve the problem of emerging disintermediated technology, by providing a SWIFT equivalent version of DLT platforms,[9,10] giving them the illusion that they have "done" blockchain and potentially leaving these institutions high and dry as the ecosystem evolves around them. Others are collaborating on research initiatives with more promise, particularly in areas such as trade finance[11] and structured products.

A few banks are addressing the problem by fundamentally questioning their operating model, their strategy and how they fit with the new competitive environment. We've been following banks like ING,[12] which have rebranded themselves as technology companies and are driving ecosystem interactions throughout their businesses, and others like Triodos[13] who are engaging customers in ecosystem communities with reward currencies and other ecosystem economy activities. Even some of the larger banks are making radical root and branch changes that are likely to result in changed operating models, a transformed approach to collaboration and partnership and, ultimately, survival as a new type of organism in the ecosystem economy.

Most banks that we've observed are struggling to embrace the new economy or provide an effective response to customer behaviour changes. Often, this is despite a leadership imperative to change; even the clearest direction is hampered by embedded culture and a lack of execution ability, which is exacerbated by the embedded structural constraints described earlier in this chapter.

What's Next for Financial Services?

Chapter 2 describes the services that banks offer and the alternatives that are emerging as direct competition or partnership opportunities. Banks need to decide which services they want to provide, and how to remain competitive, but before they can do this, they also need to identify who their customers are and what problems they're solving. It's time for a lot of soul-searching about how they provide existing services, but, more importantly, where they want to play and who their customers are.

Banking the Unbanked?

Much of this book is dedicated to discussing opportunities for supporting the 40% of adults globally who currently lack access to basic financial services.[14] Most of those 2 billion people are financially active, and many are entrepreneurs. While most currently live in developing economies, a significant number of unbanked people live in developed economies—7% of US households[15] were unbanked in 2015, for example. As well as presenting a significant opportunity to increase the wealth, living standards and productivity of these 2 billion people, the world's unbanked population present a massive market opportunity for financial service providers, who should be able to share in the increased prosperity opportunities of these customers offered by financial inclusion.

The reasons for lack of access to financial services are not complex; in nearly all cases it's a lack of accessability or lack of credit history, combined with challenges proving formal identity, which leads banks to treat these customers as high risk, pushing the cost of conventional banking services beyond their reach. The main reason cited is "not enough money", but usually in combination with other reasons.[16] This is true from Derby to Dakar, and non-bank financial services fill the gap offering loans with interest rates of up to 500% or more, exploiting the lack of access. This perpetuates individual poverty and, more significantly, the credit ceiling that prevents small and micro-entrepreneurs from growing their businesses, which has the effect of maintaining and, over time, increasing the wealth gap between smaller and larger businesses, and therefore, the poor and the rich.

Fintech offers significant opportunities to address these barriers, and as M-PESA has shown, can act as a gateway to inclusion in the traditional financial system, particularly for women and other groups who have been underrepresented for cultural reasons. Banks can benefit from these developments; in Kenya, where M-PESA originated ten years ago, one of the major commercial banks has grown its customer base from half a million to six million customers, thanks to a credit history from M-PESA enabling customers to show banks their financial history. But many more people in Kenya who could now get a bank account are choosing not to, despite this opportunity—with a population of over 180 million and nearly every adult having used M-PESA, its customer numbers outstrip those of the banks.

M-PESA isn't a sophisticated or particularly easy to use service, and many users are occasional rather than regular, but it fills the need; Fintech isn't going to wait for the traditional players to catch up, and banks need to evolve rapidly to survive. And as Fintech services become more user friendly, the adoption barriers fall down. M-PESA hasn't seen the flyaway success of Kenya in some of the other markets it has entered, because of the relatively low ease of use, but other services are rapidly taking up the slack and presenting attractive, non-bank payments and wallet offerings which are easy and convenient, Alipay and WeChat Pay being shining examples of this. They both integrate with traditional banks for now, but could operate independently or with alternative providers if they choose to.

Small, Medium and Micro-Businesses

Small businesses (or SMEs, as we'll refer to them throughout this book) have a tough time. They face many challenges which result from their scale and lack of volume—cash flow is a huge problem for most, as customers typically pay them last, while they can't benefit from delayed invoicing themselves. Bank services offered to SMEs are basic, because there's no margin in offering any kind of sophisticated service at that scale, whereas the smaller businesses lack specialist departments and skills, so actually need more help managing their finances than larger businesses; a small business like a builder or a farm has complex supply chains and customer management, in some cases more complex than a larger business would have.

And yet SMEs form over half of the economy in the developed world, and up to 60% of the economy in the developing world,[17] where many small and micro-businesses form the backbone of how the economy runs. With average employee numbers of 4.1 in Europe, the vast majority don't have the scale to make even a visit to the bank convenient, and many use services like accountants to manage basic financial functions because they lack the skills. Fintech solutions are emerging, with many being successfully used by large numbers of businesses (QuickBooks, Xero, etc.) and these have been very successful with largely office-based and medium-sized businesses. Others, such as hiveonline, with integrated contracts, payments and reputation system bundled into a mobile app, are now helping the majority of small businesses who don't work in offices and find these packages daunting. While they started with accounting, these packages are now aggregating financial records and adopting wallet solutions; it won't be long before they can help customers operate independently of banks.

Investors

Exchanges, underwriters and brokers are needed because capital markets are opaque and complex. Investors need security which they can offer. However, investors are now demanding greater transparency and Fintech is beginning to fill this gap, with blockchain-based bond and trading products springing up, while ICOs, once the hype has died down and regulation has caught up, will offer normal people opportunities for direct investment in a growing number of businesses and diverse business types. Meanwhile, the shifting nature of value and publicity about cryptocurrency is waking investors and the general public up to alternative currencies, which, as we'll discuss, present one of the biggest disruption opportunities for the way markets, and the global economy, work in the future, with increased transparency and reduced, or zero, need for intermediaries.

Evolution or Revolution?

Up to 2017, banks were reassuring themselves that they have the customer numbers, the brand recognition and the trust of customers. These are all powerful and important customer retention (also referred to as "stickiness") factors, but the key element of trust is now being attacked by other services, as we discuss throughout the book. And customers are no longer as passive as they used to be; customer inertia used to be a very powerful factor, with customers rarely switching banks in their lifetimes, but thanks to evolving customer behaviours and regulatory changes, the inertia is also being overcome.

The image of banks has changed irreversibly since 2008. Customers don't like banks and they don't trust the industry. Banks are portrayed in the press as greedy and exploitative, while the publicity around publicly funded bailouts has left people angry and resentful. Banks are seen as a necessary evil and, as with other necessary evils, viable alternatives look attractive.

Fintech solutions to date—whether it's M-PESA for the unbanked, Alipay for China, QuickBooks for small business or Robo-advisors for investors—have started to eat away at traditional financial services, at first taking small bites, but now increasingly large chunks. Alipay has 520 million customers, while WeChat Pay is starting to encroach on Alipay with its nearly 1 billion WeChat users rapidly adopting their payments service. And this was using relatively unsophisticated technology—Alipay introduced face recognition recently and is using more advanced behavioural analysis, but all of these services replicate traditional services in a recognisable way, and none are using cutting-edge technology like blockchain at the time of writing.

Blockchain technology is still developing, but blockchain applications moved from proof of concept to live in 2017, and this is heralding a rapidly increasing acceleration in the evolution of Fintech services offered by alternative providers. Despite the lack of maturity, and the well-publicised challenges, cryptocurrency valuations exceeded the market cap of Goldman Sachs and several economies in 2017. 2018 is the year of blockchain applied to non-cash transactions—primarily provenance, which will encroach on identity, authentication, supply chain, insurance and capital markets; it is the year when the ecosystem economy starts to mature, with more services joining up across IoT, AI, blockchain and novel business models.

Fintechs are maturing too; beyond cool but sometimes not very useful applications of technology, a growing number of players are entering the market led by mature teams concerned with solving customer problems, including problems that banks haven't even tried to address. As the ecosystem economy emerges, the opportunity to cross-pollinate services, supported by the growing interaction between different technology families, will boost the growth of "life tech", where your devices and apps support you without clear distinctions between them. HSBC coined the term "invisible banking", but if your bank is invisible, do you care whether it's a bank or something else?

So, is this evolution or revolution? Consider that:

- Alipay has more customers than the adult population of Europe and has moved China from a cash economy towards majority cashless in less than 10 years.
- QuickBooks processes 1/3 of the USA's GDP through its software and has more customers than any US bank.
- M-PESA has moved the needle of financial inclusion in Kenya from 17% to nearly 100% in 10 years.
- In 2017, UNDP used blockchain to distribute aid to 10,000 refugees without any money changing hands.

None of these innovations were initiated or driven by banks. All of these developments have brought great benefits to customers the banks have ignored. And we, with other providers, are building services that will launch in 2018 and beyond, reshaping tranches of financial services even further.

Conclusion

In this chapter, we've presented the challenges banks are facing in supporting customers in a rapidly evolving financial ecosystem. We've shown how emerging services are helping solve problems for unserved or underserved groups, and how the gap is being filled by non-bank service providers.

We've discussed how banks are hampered from evolving by their own self-perception and the structures that have grown up over years. We'll break this down further in subsequent chapters and present some opportunities for banks and other organisations to support their transition into the ecosystem in the last section.

If banks are to participate in this accelerated activity, they need to move fast and change fast. Evolution will no longer help them keep pace. The revolution is already happening.

Notes

1. Rhoades, S. A. (2000). Bank Mergers and Banking Structure in the United States, 1980–98. Board of Governors of the Federal Reserve System, 174; Adams, R. M. (2012, August 8). Consolidation and Merger Activity in the United States Banking Industry from 2000 Through 2010. Federal Reserve Bank. https://www.federalreserve.gov/pubs/feds/2012/201251/201251pap.pdf. Accessed 7 January 2018.
2. Greenwood, R., & Scharfstein, D. (2013). The Growth of Finance†. *Journal of Economic Perspectives, 27* (2) (Spring). Harvard Business School. http://www.people.hbs.edu/dscharfstein/growth_of_finance_jep.pdf. Accessed 7 January 2018.
3. Boyle, C. (2015, January 6). Bank of England "Groupthink" During Credit Crisis. *CNBC.* https://www.cnbc.com/2015/01/06/released-bank-of-england-minutes-show-groupthink-during-credit-crisis.html; Shiller, R. J. (2008, November 1). Challenging the Crowd in Whispers, Not Shouts. *The New York Times.* http://www.nytimes.com/2008/11/02/business/02view.html. Accessed 7 January 2018; Schneider, H. (2011, February 10). "Groupthink" Blocked

IMF's Foresight of Crisis. *The Washington Post*. http://www.washingtonpost.com/wp-dyn/content/article/2011/02/09/AR2011020906222.html.

4. Davis, J. (2012, March 4). Group-Think Continues to Lead to Losses. *Financial Times*. https://www.ft.com/content/d58c5738-63a4-11e1-9686-00144feabdc0. Accessed 7 January 2018; Goodhart, C. (2013). Group-Think and the Current Financial Crisis (Springer Link). https://link.springer.com/chapter/10.1057/9781137302953_5. Accessed 7 January 2018; Carney, M. (2017, February 10). Central Banks Need "The Spirit of the Millennial", Oscar Williams-Grut. *Business Insider*. http://nordic.businessinsider.com/bank-of-england-governor-mark-carney-diversity-the-spirit-of-the-millennial-2017-2?r=UK&IR=T. Accessed 7 January 2018.

5. Nadkarni, S., Oon Nee E. Y., Dr., & Chu, J., Dr. (2016, July 15). Looking Beyond Corporate Boards: Drivers of Female Representation in Executive Roles. Cambridge Judge Business School. https://30percentclub.org/assets/uploads/UK/30__Club_Reports/CJBS_white_paper_v8_web_version.pdf. Accessed 7 January 2018.

6. ING's Agile Transformation. *McKinsey Quarterly*, January 2017. https://www.mckinsey.com/industries/financial-services/our-insights/ings-agile-transformation. Accessed 7 January 2018.

7. M-PESA Home Site. https://www.safaricom.co.ke/personal/M-PESA. Accessed 28 December 2017.

8. Alipay International Home Site. https://global.alipay.com/. Accessed 28 December 2017.

9. R3 Home Site. https://www.r3.com/. Accessed 28 December 2017.

10. Ripple Home Site. https://ripple.com/. Accessed 28 December 2017.

11. Manders, S. (2017, October 24). Banks Unveil Roadmap for We.trade Blockchain Platform. *Global Trade Review*. https://www.gtreview.com/news/Fintech/banks-unveil-roadmap-for-we-trade-blockchain-platform/. Accessed 28 December 2017.

12. ING Homepage. https://www.ing.com/Home.htm. Accessed 28 December 2017.

13. Triodos Impact Bank Homepage. https://www.triodos.com/en/about-triodos-bank/. Accessed 28 December 2017.

14. World Bank Findex. http://www.worldbank.org/en/programs/globalfindex. Accessed 28 December 2017.

15. Federal Deposit Insurance Corporation Survey, 29 June 2017. https://www.fdic.gov/householdsurvey/. Accessed 28 December 2017.

16. Hodgson, C. (2017, August 30). *Business Insider*. http://www.businessinsider.com/the-worlds-unbanked-population-in-6-charts-2017-8?r=UK&IR=T&IR=T. Accessed 31 December 2017.

17. Small and Medium Enterprises (SME) Finance, World Bank. http://www.worldbank.org/en/topic/smefinance. Accessed 27 December 2017.

2

What's the Point of Banks?

In this chapter, we review the alternative financial solutions emerging to challenge the services offered by traditional banks and question whether the utility of banks is waning, or whether banking as a concept needs to change. Later in the book, we examine various models for banking in the related Chapter 9 and applications of Fintech which can remove the need for banks as intermediaries in a wide range of applications.

In Section II, we also address the changing nature of customer loyalty and drivers for changed customer behaviour which are influencing customers' perception of banks and their utility.

What Are Banks[1] for?

The answer you get to this question will depend on who you're asking, but fundamentally a bank is somewhere safe to keep your money and an institution that will lend you money when you need it, so it's about pots of money (positive or negative). Further, it provides the ability to transfer value from one pot of money to another (payments). To some, it's an advisor, a portfolio manager, a market maker, trader or broker and we'll briefly cover these disciplines and the major emerging disruption below, before expanding in the next chapter on the future of capital markets.

Of course, you're not just giving the bank wads of cash to sit in a vault with a big round iron door; the bank can use your money to create "new" money in the shape of loans and take a profit from lending, whether as a

© The Author(s) 2018
S. Blakstad and R. Allen, *FinTech Revolution*,
https://doi.org/10.1007/978-3-319-76014-8_2

mortgage, or trade finance, or other types of credit. It may also use it to buy bonds and equities, either on behalf of customers or on their own behalf (proprietary trading). Lending and trading activities both carry risks, and these are mitigated by capital reserves (your money), the bank's strategy (hedging), internal risk controls (customer due diligence, credit and market risk) and by regulatory limits to what banks and in particular trading divisions are allowed to do.

Since 2008, in addition to fulfilling risk compliance obligations, banks are required to keep a balance of cash in reserve to offset the risk of lending (fractional reserve),[2] an amount which varies from country to country and bank to bank, depending on their risk profile and the regulator's risk appetite, to hedge against potential market collapses, so there's an inbuilt inefficiency in the way that money is used—this figure is around 10% or more of the amount a bank can lend in most jurisdictions. Banks also build credit risk into their profit model, so that all borrowers are paying extra for the borrowers who won't be able to, or choose not to, pay back their loan as well as for the complex risk management systems and liquidity balances.

So far, so inefficient. We'll get onto regulators in a moment. Managing that credit risk also requires banks to do very thorough customer due diligence to ensure they're not lending to people who are unlikely to pay lent money back, as that would push the risk profile, and the cost of lending, up. That means there's a high barrier to entry for customers, who have to prove lots of things about their history and who they are before they can be given a loan. They also usually need to provide some additional security in the form of guarantees or collateral, of which the most obvious example is a mortgage. This high bar to entry means that many people can't get a bank account at all, *even if they don't want to borrow any money*, so we're also excluding a significant chunk of the world's population. This is important because those people are not able to access credit, which, in the case of small producers and merchants, is the most important thing they need to climb out of poverty.

Then, there are the regulations. Because banks are so big and so important to how the system works, to guarantee our safety, governments have mandated stringent regulations via Financial Services Authorities, Central Banks and other regulatory bodies. These regulations control restrictions such as the capital reserve ratio mentioned above, whose banks are allowed to lend to (more customer due diligence) and on top of that, how well they're managing their businesses and their risk profiles. All of this is critical while banks are the custodians of our cash, and especially in the light of 2008 and more recent high-profile failures, but again it means that running a bank is both costly and extremely complicated. Guess who pays for it?

Alongside money markets and capital markets trading, many also offer corporate finance, or the issuance of equities and bonds, which are then traded on the secondary markets, either for clients or on the bank's own behalf; as we saw vividly in the financial crisis, these secondary markets including derivative products, such as the mortgage-backed securities of 2008 fame, can be a source of significant losses, as well as significant profits. In order to support these complex markets, banks have specialist divisions of advisors, analysts, product and market specialists, all of whom are paid well to use their significant expertise in advising companies and governments on issuance, or predicting market movements and creating products attractive to investors. Basically, it's very sophisticated betting.

Several important factors are behind the system:

Size = **Security**. Everyone is familiar with "too big to fail", but even at the smaller end of banking, regulations require institutions to have significant, diversified backing, to guarantee security. Maintenance of balances is further guaranteed by capital ratios, as described above. Higher barriers to entry apply to banks issuing or trading on capital markets so the number of banks able to support an issuance is relatively low.

Regulation = **Security**. Customers have guarantees that regulated institutions will be meeting the standards expected of them, or face censure if they don't. While there continue to be scandals of various sorts which receive wide exposure, in reality the reliability and security of banks is extremely good.

Guarantee of **identity**: banks historically have been the primary means of guaranteeing many critical aspects of our identity, such as our creditworthiness, and in many cases, guarantees of who we are. Being unbanked restricts access not just to banking accounts, but a whole range of financial services, accommodation and even jobs, because these checks cannot be performed.

Financial **Products**: the most familiar of these are the current (or checking to the US customer) account, the loan including the mortgage and payments. Key to this is maintenance of guarantees against what you put in and what you get out, whether that's instant access to your cash via an ATM, electronic transfers, etc., associated with current accounts, fixed rates associated with mortgages or loans, or fixed interest associated with deposits; all of these products come with inbuilt guarantees, so you know what you will be getting. This is further underwritten by central banks and regulation, so you can trust that you'll get what you've been promised. We go into more detail on financial products and their alternatives in the service analysis below.

Monopoly on **Access** to certain facilities, such as central bank currencies and payments transfers, etc. While alternatives are emerging, the vast majority of transactions are constrained to run over central infrastructure between banks because they (a) require the funds to originate from and end up in recognised, secure, validated accounts, (b) use recognised currencies, which are backed by central bank ledgers, to which the banks have access, but ordinary companies and customers don't, and (c) have authorisation and the infrastructure to pass payments over centrally managed payments transmission systems.

Familiarity: what's known as the "power of inertia"[3] describes a negative type of customer loyalty, which is based on two psychological phenomena—first, familiarity bias,[4] or the underlying assumption that the thing you know is automatically better than unknown things, which helps to build society, but is unhelpful when you're trying to make a reasoned judgement between competing products; the second is the disproportionate perceived effort vs actual effort of actually changing. When Current Account Switching[5] came into the regulations in 2012, governments and banks assumed mass exodus would follow, but in fact not that many people did switch at the time. This is, however, changing.

We'll discuss these factors as we consider the alternatives, and for simplicity, we'll break it down to service types.

Banking Services and Emerging Alternatives

There are some services offered by banks today that we're not addressing below; credit cards and insurance are not included as these are not generally services operated by banks, but by third parties on behalf of organisations, including banks, so we're excluding those services from this section.

Storing Your Money and Letting You Spend It When You Want to

The obvious place to start is with the current account (or checking account). A current account has the following features:

- Retains balance including current actual balance, future or virtual balances based on forward payments and remittances, payments in clearing, etc.

- Linked to bank maintained customer ID via bank's systems
- Linked to transactions, processed by the bank
- May be linked to cards (e.g. debit card) or e-wallet
- May be linked to parallel accounts, usually held by the same bank
- May attract interest payments or remittances depending on balance
- Can have positive or negative balance
- Protected by government guarantees, which vary from country to country

It's important to consider that the bank account is not just a pile of notes in a vault, but a "bucket of money" that can be in several states at the same time:

- the state of actual money that is in the account, i.e. money that has been cleared and paid
- the state of balances in clearing (in and out)
- various balances based on payments that have been agreed but not yet reached clearing, such as direct debits and standing orders

Interest on the account will also be a factor, and all these in/out payments contribute to a variety of balances on any one account at any one time.

There are a few alternative ways of storing your money for instant access in the old system; manufacturers and shops have taken advance deposits, and it has been possible to buy prepaid cards or tokens for use as future payment, but these have mostly been issued by individual stores. In some cases, multiple stores and manufacturers have signed up to schemes; virtual currencies such as air miles or store points have been around for a long time, used as a loyalty incentive and in some cases allowing customers to spend the virtual currency with other stores (such as the Green Shield Stamp scheme for those old enough to remember it, or the Nectar loyalty card[6]), but these had limited reach, and therefore, it's questionable whether they could be described as truly liquid.

The currently available alternative, the digital wallet or e-wallet, operates on similar lines, but with significantly more reach, offering the following features:

- Payments, C2B, C2C or B2B, usually via mobile or internet
- Retains balances including current actual balance, future or virtual balance based on payments
- One-time customer authentication linked to trusted source (usually a bank but increasingly other sources)

- Linked to transactions, processed by e-wallet infrastructure
- May be linked to cards, bank account, mobile app and cash top-up
- Usually doesn't incur interest charges for consumer; merchants pay
- Balances cannot go below zero (unless in special circumstances, e.g. managed e-wallets)
- Usually not protected from hosting company failure

The e-wallet is an increasingly popular alternative to current accounts today, with three distinct markets: merchants, who benefit from a reduction in margin over card transactions; (largely) banked customers, who can seamlessly pay for internet purchases, and both unbanked and banked customers who want to make peer-to-peer transfers with their mobile phones. The obvious disadvantage is the lack of access to automatic credit, but the advantages are significant, particularly for merchants and unbanked customers. The most common vehicles for e-wallets are mobile phones and online; for the unbanked, this is a very significant development because while nearly half of the world's population are unbanked, 80% of the population in developing countries owns a mobile phone (women are 14% less likely to own one). Many mobile wallets are linked to a bank account, but it is also possible to hold them via the mobile provider, removing the need for a bank altogether.

A further development is the evolution of cryptocurrencies, which are necessarily held in an e-wallet and independent of sovereign currencies (so far). While cryptocurrencies have been relatively low in actual value compared to traditional currencies in circulation, 2017 saw that changing. There is no theoretical limit to how much value could be transferred to cryptocurrencies, which has led to many central banks seriously contemplating the issuance of their own Central Bank Digital Currencies (CDBC). When this happens, the implications for bank accounting as we know it will be enormous, as the e-wallet could be held independently of a traditional bank, with customers able to make direct peer-to-peer payments in a secure digital currency, backed directly by central banks, without the need for a banking intermediary. This will significantly reshape the way that banks are supported by deposits today and leave a hole in their reserve, which would have to be filled in other ways, as explored by the BoE's BankUnderground.[7] CBDC are the subject of Chapter 5.

The other challenge which particularly impacts the unbanked is that these types of account have not been historically accepted as guarantees of credit history; however, this is now changing, thanks to alternative approaches to evaluating creditworthiness which are now emerging, as described below.

Storing Your Money for Longer with Restricted Access

Savings deposits of various sorts are the second type of deposit account held with banks; these can be fixed term—maturing on a certain date—or with restrictions to access, so that the bank can forecast more effectively how much of your money it will have at a given time, and use it more efficiently (or get a fee if you choose to invoke a break clause), or instant access, which is a sort of hybrid between a current account and a deposit account. The main difference with these accounts is that you can't go below a zero balance, and they will all give some sort of interest, either applied based on balances at agreed intervals, or at the end of a maturation period. In many cases, you are able to make and receive payments directly into these accounts, but it varies depending on the terms of the agreement.

Partially equivalent to savings accounts are bonds, which are government- or company-issued debt instruments (i.e. you lend the issuer money) with agreed, fixed rates of return. Unlike savings accounts, they don't have the flexibility of changes to agreed terms, but they can be traded on secondary markets, so capital can be realised in this way if the bondholder chooses to do so. Equities are more flexible investment instruments where instead of lending money, the investor buys a portion of the company; however, unlike bonds, the value of equities changes with fluctuations in the issuing organisation's perceived value, so they lack the security of either a deposit account with a bank or a bond, although returns can be significantly higher if companies grow. And both equities and bonds as financial instruments are moving away from the "saving money" service towards "buying stuff"; for a really illiquid asset example, many of us have one in the shape of bricks and mortar property.

Giving You Money for General Purposes, That You Promise to Pay Back

As described above, there's no point in a bank just hanging onto your cash, especially since they're (usually) either not charging you for the service, or indeed paying you for the privilege of holding onto it. Exceptions such as premium accounts and corporate accounts do attract fees, but at a net loss to the bank, and while banks may charge savers in negative interest economies, again this usually doesn't reflect the true loss to the bank. So to make money out of your money, they also lend money out and charge borrowers for the privilege. And the money they lend isn't the money on deposit—banks can lend many times what they have on deposit, as long as they hold the pre-scribed currency reserve (fractional reserve) to meet their regulatory obliga-tions. This means that they effectively control how much money is in the system, although the limit is set by the reserve ratio.

One form of credit is the overdraft, as mentioned above, but banks will also give you personal unsecured loans on the basis of a guarantee of repay-ment, usually based on your creditworthiness (secured loans are discussed below). While banks will usually want to know what you're going to do with the money, the key restriction is whether they think you're able and willing to pay it back, or, as Bob Hope memorably said, "*A bank is a place that will lend you money if you can prove that you don't need it*".

Loans, like deposits, can be and more often are fixed term, but they can also be open-ended, with interest paid on a regular basis for both types. Open-ended credit, the overdraft being the most common example, typ-ically attracts much higher interest rates than fixed term, because there is a much higher statistical risk of default, while unplanned overdrafts, as a warning sign to banks, attract notoriously high charges.

In deciding whether to issue a loan, a bank is usually in a strong posi-tion to evaluate your creditworthiness; they already know who you are and have access both to your historical transaction behaviour with them and with trust authorities such as credit bureaux. They can therefore perform extremely robust checks when deciding whether to give you the money, which means they're able to offer relatively low rates of interest.

However, banks have never had a monopoly on extending credit. Credit cards are a contemporary familiar form of lending with huge saturation. Merchants were extending credit long before banking had been invented. People have also always lent each other money, either person to person through trust relationships or, as we know, the seedier side where loan sharks exploit unbanked or vulnerable people by personal loans and extortionate interest rates, through to more respectable organisations on a sliding scale from more to less seedy, and there's some regulation imposed on these organisations.

Banks also are big lenders to businesses, with business and corporate banking core to many large banks. This ranges from small-scale loans to small businesses, usually at relatively high interest rates, to tailored loans for larger customers; what is risky at the SME end (with 8 out of 10 SMEs fail-ing in the first 18 months) becomes a way of making your money work at the more robust, global corporation end.

For business customers, again, banks have never been the sole source of capital; venture capitalists, Angel investors and government-backed funding schemes are all well-established sources of funding for businesses, although VCs and Angels typically form a very small percentage and focus on high-growth potential companies. Microfinance lending has also been available to micro-businesses, but traditionally at disproportionate or extortionate rates (e.g. up to 500% APR in parts of Africa), partly to cover risks and administration costs but also exploiting the lack of alternative providers. As with lending to individuals, the most vulnerable and poorest business owners typically have the fewest and most expensive options, leaving a huge number of unbanked microbusinesses, especially in the developing world, without access to affordable growth capital.

But emerging lending paradigms are also opening out opportunities for credit, both for businesses and for individuals. Peer-to-peer lending is now flourishing both for business and, to a lesser extent, private individuals. The growth in platforms offering individuals and larger investors the opportunity to invest in business ventures has dramatically reshaped startup investment. Peer-to-peer lending, and particularly crowdlending, is also causing disruption to the traditional VC/Angel/bank investment of more conventional ventures. Entrepreneurs present their ideas, usually via a competitive voting system on the host's platform, to attract small investment from individuals. This is presenting several interesting trends:

- The lower cost of evaluation of ideas and lower stakes mean that more risky or smaller ventures are likely to attract some interest, so the barriers to attracting investment are lower than in the traditional model and more small businesses can attract investment.
- Fashion and peer reviews may have an even stronger influence than before—and this may be a good thing! Traditionally, investors have assessed the market worthiness of a business venture, which, despite significant research and ample data, is often still invalidated by market forces. Going direct to the market and cutting out the middleman has its risks, as investors are relatively uneducated, but are as likely, if not more likely, to be in touch with market trends, because they *identify* with the idea.
- Clearly, this means that investors are exposing themselves to potentially greater risks, but given the relatively small amounts invested in this model by individuals, it's mainly important to ensure investors understand the risks, rather than worrying about systemic collapse, as when a larger investor makes an unwise decision.

Some unsecured personal loans are also facilitated in this way, again over websites. Because of the low expense of maintaining the websites, in general the cost of borrowing is lower than via a traditional bank; in most cases, investment is at the risk of the investor, mitigated by hedging across multiple investments, although some platforms now ring-fence funding to recompense victims of bad debt. However, where platforms fail, as TrustBuddy did in 2015, investors' money is at risk and not protected in the way that a savings account with a bank is, by government or other guarantees. The problem of unregulated or less regulated lending has historically been ignored or minimised by politicians, as the major impact has been on the poorest and least influential groups of society. But as alternative lending rises and, to be cynical, more vocal groups are affected, regulators are exploring additional options to protect consumers and lenders.

ICOs are a new form of investment in alternative currencies issued by businesses seeking to raise money, which we discuss in some depth later in the book, which have potential to reshape how lending and investment work. And as with current accounts, the issuance of central bank cryptocurrencies could significantly disrupt the traditional bank lending model, cutting out the intermediary between the central bank and the borrower and therefore removing the banks' ability to control the level of money in the system; if more lending moves outside of the bank system because of reduced capital ratios, alternative lending could explode to fill this gap, while more loans would have to be backed by deposits, instead of just a portion, as in today's models.

Giving You Money for Specific Purposes, That You Promise to Pay Back

In addition to unsecured loans, which are guaranteed against your creditworthiness as an individual or a business, some specific loans are guaranteed against collateral, usually the thing that you are using the capital to buy. For individuals, it's the mortgage or the car loan, where the guarantee of payment is linked to the property being financed. These types of loans have varying levels of risk, and there's a risk that the value of the collateral will fall below the value of the loan, but generally they are lower risk than other types of loan and so can attract lower interest rates; they often have a longer payback period too, which means that the bank creates a long-term income stream, and this is usually reflected in the rates. In contrast to the unsecured loans described above, these are "secured" by documentation promising that you will give the collateral to the bank if something goes wrong and you fail to pay them back.

Even more than unsecured loans, merchants have long been providing secured loans, in the shape of HP, buy-now-pay-in-12-months and various other models. Manufacturers have introduced creative ways to build the price of an item into reusables, meaning that you're effectively getting the original item at a discount that will be recouped via usage costs (think Nespresso).

Mortgages, more than other debt products, can be complex, because rates may be fixed for a while, followed by a flexible, index-linked period; there are arrangement fees and buyout clauses, and the customer can renegotiate the term within certain parameters. There is also usually some linkage to insurance, and in Denmark, this is also built into the structure of the mortgage, making these even more complicated. Mortgages are typically accompanied by a long list of clauses, which can be confusing for the customer.

For businesses, trade finance is an extremely important form of lending, as well as being one of the oldest, and one that has changed the least over the years. Like a retail secured loan, the bank lends the company money based on certain guarantees, but these will be guarantees that goods have been shipped, such as an invoice or a bill of lading, for example, rather than deeds to a house. Trade finance[8] is key to businesses managing cash flow, because there is a mismatch between the date when materials are shipped and when the value of those goods can be realised by the seller, and again between the receipt of goods and when the manufacturer can sell them. Conversely, for exporters of manufactured goods, there is a time lag between shipping the goods and receiving payment. Banks have historically been critical in helping companies manage this hole in their expenses, giving them the capital they need to keep producing while their own capital is tied up in supply chains. Currently, half of world trade runs thanks to trade finance and demand is growing due to uncertainty in international trade markets.

To date, growth of businesses would not have been possible without commercial lending from banks, especially trade finance; unbanked micro-producers are stuck under the barrier to entry to this system, which leaves them unable to grow. Trade finance is also subject to a high degree of fraud, for example with fraudulent individuals raising multiple finances based on a single set of paperwork, which pushes up the cost for businesses as risks increase. While an estimated USD 4 trillion is supplied in trade finance annually, a further estimated USD 1.5–3 trillion opportunity exists, where organisations are not able to access financing due to the high level of risk.

But this is changing with the introduction of smart contracts over blockchain. Smart contracts themselves aren't particularly new; the concept is that you set up a chain of contracts that are pre-agreed between parties, programmatically, so the terms are bound with the execution of the contract. However, as described in subsequent chapters, through the application of smart contracts to blockchain platforms, these agreements can now be made and validated without the need for banks or financial institutions to become involved; blockchain traceability and transparency remove opportunities for fraud, and transfer of value is also managed in the same way. Once agreed, smart contracts are irreversible and so form an upfront guarantee that transactions will be executed on certain dates or on meeting certain conditions, so rather than waiting for a bill of lading to be produced post-shipment, liquidity can be released on the basis of the contract being agreed upfront by all parties.

The same technology can be applied to mortgages and other types of secured loan; instead of paper documents being validated by banks as escrow agents, transfer of funds can be guaranteed and executed almost instantly via smart contract over blockchain platforms. Cash flow becomes less of a problem, and alternative funding sources become available, secured by the guarantees of the contract but not relying on banking intermediaries. Smart contracts reduce the risk of multiple invoices fraud, where a supplier issues the same invoice as proof to multiple trades; where banks maintain their own ledgers, there's no opportunity to spot this in reconciliation, but with the full ledger visible at every node, over the blockchain, this type of fraud is not possible.

This, along with central bank cryptocurrencies, represents one of the biggest potential disruptions to the traditional role of bank lending by new technology; many institutions and governments are exploring the concept, with Sweden the first country to trial putting its land registry on blockchain smart contracts. Scale is still a challenge, as we discuss elsewhere. And while smart contracts can speed up and validate the value chain, there is still a need to involve a source of funding, which is still today, in most cases, a bank. This will change further, with the introduction of central bank-issued cryptocurrencies, while with the application of crowdfunding principles to smart contract-based trade finance in a peer-to-peer system, small- and medium-size enterprises, or individuals, could lend to support each others' trade finance, without the need for a bank to intermediate at all.

Crowdfunding has promoted the concept of prepaid goods as fractional ownership: thanks to the ability of the internet to broadcast unrealised products through plans, visuals and mock-ups to a global audience, the opportunity to presell before manufacturing, which had previously been restricted to a few sectors such as construction and specialist small manufacturers, has exploded. Customers worldwide can sign up in advance to buy bamboo bicycles or cool new gadgets before the manufacturers have invested in raw materials, completely reversing the cash flow challenge faced by traditional manufacturers and importers, so removing the need for trade finance and, in extreme cases, for VC, bank or Angel investment.

Another example of this is the common "design your own t-shirt" model, where the customer pays upfront before goods are created, and another truly disruptive business model is threadless.com,[9] who invite customers to submit t-shirt designs which are then presented in a voting process, with winning designs being printed. This not only creates a strong sales pull, but removes the need for design, distribution channels and much of the marketing challenge, while integrating up to the minute market research into the value chain. ICOs have taken this approach to the next logical level, issuing coins for investors based on the business model (often nothing more than a white paper describing the idea), allowing entrepreneurs to raise large amounts of cash before a product is in the market.

Transferring Your Money Between People or Businesses

Payments—between individuals, companies and governments—are one of the mainstays of banking. Banks are authorised to make payments on your behalf and, conveniently, as they hold your money, are also able to extract the funds from your account. They can accept payments into accounts and set up regular payments on your behalf (direct debit or standing order payments). All payments other than physical currency payments are electronic transfers, usually between banks, and we cover the mechanics in more detail elsewhere, but essentially there are central bank currency accounts held by each bank (nostros and loros) between which value is exchanged by a series of electronic messages, and the value is transferred by the bank between these central bank accounts and the originator's or receiver's accounts.

The differentiating utility of central bank currency is the ability to pay taxes in that currency, which leads to it being widely accepted as the primary transaction currency of the jurisdiction in which those taxes are due. As only certain banks can hold these central bank currency accounts, larger banks will also maintain loros and nostros on behalf of other, smaller banks, increasing the number of intermediaries. It's important to note that the central bank issuing the currency needs to be involved in every single payment—either as issuing that currency in note or coin format, or by holding the currency accounts and validating the payment between the banks. As this ledger validation is restricted by central bank issued licence to certain banks, this is the main reason payments must go through banks today.

Credit card payments are a form of liquid credit issued as payments via a card, and the mechanism is essentially the same, with value being transferred via a receiving bank (the merchant's) and added to the merchant's account. The issuing card company, which may be a bank but is more likely to be a credit card company, carries the risk of default and charges fees for late payment accordingly, while settlement of the debt is again paid from the carrier's bank account, in another normal payment. Cheques, however, are not actually payments; they are a form of contract between the purchaser and the merchant, who can choose to refuse the cheque, which then need to be cleared by the bank (or clearing house on behalf of the bank) before the payment is made.

Debit card payments, by contrast, are more directly linked to a bank account and will usually be settled in a bank's standard overnight processing; reversing a debit card transaction means creating a new, reverse transaction, which may not always be possible; in this case, the account holder (usually a bank) carries the risk of default. International payments between different currencies are more complicated, because the central banks don't guarantee each other's currencies and so additional checks need to be introduced. On top of this, banks also monitor payment activity to detect fraud and misuse of funds (e.g. for terrorism).

All this costs money, and of course it's the customer who pays, usually via the merchant, who passes on charges at aggregate into the price of goods. That means that selling goods for low amounts of electronic money is not usually economically viable for merchants, because there's a lower bound to transaction fees (usually around $0.1, although it can be lower, depending on the type of transaction and the country). In other cases, the customer is charged directly, for example CHAPS payments and international transfers usually attract high fees. So, if, for example, you make a payment in a different currency to the one your bank account is held in because you're buying off a foreign website, you'll be paying exchange fees (usually about 3%) and the merchant will be paying a fee for the payment to be processed at their end. That's before you've even paid for shipping!

Mobile payments are the main movement currently disrupting the traditional payments model. The great strength of mobile payments is the ability to unlink the payment from a bank as intermediary; in the model popular in Asia and parts of Africa, the price of the purchase is underwritten by the mobile operator or an e-wallet provider such as mHITS in Australia, rather than by a bank, in a model similar to a credit card purchase. The big difference is that unlike a credit card, you don't need a bank account to get a mobile phone, and e-wallets can be topped up via cash payments to agents.

Of course, many mobile payments *are* linked to bank accounts, and this model is growing in popularity wherever it's launched, with China leading the payments revolution, as even fully banked people are more likely to have their phone than their debit card to hand.

Mobile payments, while growing in maturity and popularity, are still finding their feet in some countries; while Alipay's implementation using QR codes is extremely reliable and efficient, in other implementations the e-wallet paradigm is still not completely reliable, while there can be challenges in fulfilment, lost or hacked data and a high cost overhead, which is passed on to the customer or merchant, or both. Mobile payments linked to bank accounts follow a variety of pricing models, with merchants currently picking up the bill, although as noted above, the cost is generally lower than for traditional payments.

The other big disruptor is blockchain. The scaling challenges associated with first-generation cryptocurrencies such as Bitcoin and high-profile hacks (or poorly coded smart contract exploitation depending on your perspective) on Ethereum have shown that the platforms and technology need to undergo some significant changes before becoming a universal paradigm for payments. While the applications of smart contracts over blockchain are already presenting a major change opportunity in trade finance and other banking use cases, the code base for Ethereum, the most widely used smart contract platform, is evolving. Competitors, such as Neo,[10] Cardano,[11] WanChain,[12] are appearing with new features, quickly driven by the hundreds of millions of dollars raised through ICOs. In the enterprise space, R3's Corda,[13] Hyperledger[14] and Digital Asset[15] are all working on distributed ledger technology alternatives.

Blockchain for B2B/P2B/P2P payments is likely to reach saturation slowly, partly because of the scaling issues on public blockchains but also because of trust challenges; the image of blockchains as a vehicle for subversion of trusted currencies is falling away as their use becomes more mainstream, and financial institutions are investing in more secure uses of the paradigm, but there are still raging debates about regulation, bubble-like behaviours reaching mainstream news headlines and as with all new developments, has yet to reach commonly agreed standards. Very public failures, such as the Distributed Autonomous Organisation (DAO) hack in 2016 and its impact on Ethereum, are not preventing institutions from moving forward, but illustrate the risks inherent at this stage in a new paradigm's development.

Despite this, 2017 saw a broader acceptance of Bitcoin and especially Ethereum in mainstream trading, many more smart contract applications and, of course, the ICO explosion, much of which use Ethereum smart contracts—along with the emergence of CBDC starting in 2018. While there's been a backlash against Bitcoin and ICOs following a spate of negative publicity, regulators and traditional capital markets players are beginning to recognise their potential; a period of regulation and restriction on scams will inevitably follow, while China is the first major economy to declare its intention of issuing a state cryptocurrency. We anticipate that the use of blockchain platforms for peer-to-peer disintermediated payments will also rise steadily, especially in the cross-border space, and will soon present a significant challenge to existing payments services—as do the banks, hence their sharp rise in interest in the opportunities presented by the technology.

ID Authentication and Validation

As with holding accounts and managing payments, historically banks have been the key holders of information about who you are, whether you're an individual or a company. Holding a bank account still gives you an entry to many opportunities, such as many types of employment or housing, that are closed to the unbanked. As with access to credit, this creates a sharp divide between banked and unbanked customers; even if you are able to build your business up, without a bank account you are still a non-person in the eyes of many organisations.

Banks provide validation of your financial history, but they also provide other validation, including being used to authenticate your address. That model worked fine when people generally had a single bank account, held at a local branch, which was responsible for looking after all of your finances, but it breaks down in a world where people are likely to have two or more bank accounts with different institutions, on different ledgers. Your transaction history with one may be very different to another. For example, we currently hold several accounts with five banks in different countries, some of which we just use for payments and the occasional international transfer, whereas others are used for salary and personal day-to-day payments. Reviewing the first might tell you a bit about our tastes in culture and charities, but it wouldn't give you an idea of our spending power or creditworthiness.

Of course, this problem is addressed by data aggregators such as credit ratings agencies like Experian, who take information from a number of different bodies including banks, credit card providers, mortgage providers, etc. With the introduction of PSD2 and open data, it is also easier for additional authorised entities to access this information, but with the growth of all the other products and financial opportunities we've discussed here, it no longer makes sense for a bank to be central to that validation in all cases. We are already seeing the use of mobile records to validate behavioural[16] patterns, which are a much stronger indicator of creditworthiness than transaction records.

Mobile data are much richer than pure transaction history, because it can include physical movements and of course communication history, which in turn leads to the opportunity for network-based validation. This could present personal information (PI) challenges, as behaviour patterns are likely to be as unique as thumbprints, and with the availability of data today, that means it's possible to identify individuals from their aggregated data, but that is not the concern of this chapter. There's also a growing number of blockchain-enabled authentication protocols that could threaten banks' position in this niche, as well as the traditional providers such as Experian. Many banks are now taking advantage of these third-party authentication providers, who can help to reduce costs, although regulations generally stipulate that banks need to manage their own KYC, which leads to a variety of interpretations including keeping the whole process (usually very inefficiently) in-house.

Managing Your Portfolio and Placing Your Bets

For corporations, wealthy individuals and governments, many banks have long provided additional services including managing investment portfolios, investment advice and a more person-to-person service than to their general customers. This interaction is usually strongly based on personal relationships either between the wealthy individual and family members, or senior executives for the corporate market and the bank. Banks with trading divisions can also offer brokerage on behalf of corporate and personal clients, as well as on their own behalf. These disciplines are known as Asset Management, Wealth Management and Brokerage.

Banks also offer different tiers of financial planning advice to their customers, depending on the value of the customer and their needs. The financial advice offered by banks to customers is, however, restricted by anti-trust laws, which means that they are not able to recommend specific products under most circumstances. Financial planning is most used by individuals when planning major investments or lifestyle changes, such as buying a house, marriage or retirement, while businesses and wealthy individuals will have a more regular, personalised service, depending on their value and the size of the challenges they face.

Portfolio management, brokerage services and advice have always been available from other organisations, and many independent wealth management institutions exist. They are now being joined by a growing number of "robo-advisors" which use automatic intelligence, usually combined with human expertise, to create a variety of bundled products for investors and execution, at much lower fees than would typically be charged by an investment advisor. We have seen more and less automated versions arising; to date customer numbers, while high, are not yet sufficient to balance the cost of customer acquisition and running these firms. However, as they mature, they are starting to capture a greater share of banks' traditional investment customers. Some banks are now partnering with these new businesses, while others have, with varying degrees of success, built additional intelligence into existing systems.

Cash Management and Payroll

In addition to managing accounts and payments on behalf of governments, businesses and individuals, banks typically offer larger corporate customers and some wealthy individuals services such as cash pooling/concentration, where money from various accounts is consolidated for better liquidity, or managing automated clearing on remittances, physical bulk clearing, for example cheque processing, and regular bulk payments such as real time gross settlements, payroll or pensions payouts.

Pooling and sweeping of corporate accounts help companies to move money from multiple accounts to central accounts and to use excess liquidity in other ways, such as investing in mutual funds overnight to earn interest, which is then returned the next day.

So far, we haven't seen any new entrants in this market, and there's a good reason for that; the management of companies' bank accounts is intrinsically linked to cash management. In addition, this is an area which requires significant trust in the institution's expertise and robustness. However, secure cryptobanks platforms like NodL are emerging which can provide these services, while central banks have been experimenting with cryptocurrency alternatives for real time gross settlement, and if some of the developments described above start to emerge, such as the growth of non-bank held accounts following the issuance of CBDC, this is another area where new entrants could apply automation and business logic to address customer needs, particularly by applying structured blockchain applications such as nested contracts in a DAO.

Increasing Shareholder Value

Finally, banks with investment banking divisions are also engaged with supporting corporate clients in the issuance of equity (shares) or debt (bonds) to finance expansion, and helping them to manage the balance of financing for their firms. These and secondary markets are covered in more detail in the next chapter. Corporate Financiers also advise on mergers & acquisitions (M&A) and demergers, management buyouts, takeovers and joint venture financing. This role is largely advisory and, while strongly related to the trading activities, is ring-fenced from trading via a "Chinese wall" to avoid insider information about upcoming deals reaching the trading floor.

While in theory much corporate finance advisory could be automated or taken out of the hands of banks, we believe that the low maturity of relevant algorithms in comparison with the complexity of the activity means it will be some time before a viable alternative to human intelligence-driven advice is likely to emerge. While cryptocurrency alternatives are being explored for trade settlement, this experimentation is being done within banks and centralised mechanisms, rather than being the purview of third parties today. The main existential threat to corporate finance is in product issuance, market operations and trading, as covered in the next chapter, together with increasing regulation, which may eventually lead to the need to spin off advisory activity and ring-fence it more effectively from trading divisions.

Conclusion

So, in summary, we don't think banks are dead yet, but there are several areas where significant disruption is likely to soon affect the industry, some others where the emerging competition requires significant maturity development, and others where the competition is yet to emerge. Based on recent movements and developments, we anticipate that the first wave will emerge sooner than many incumbents are currently anticipating:

Enemies at the Gate

- Trade Finance/Smart Contracts
- Smart Contracts for mortgages and secured loans
- Peer-to-peer lending
- Mobile payments and e-wallets

- Identity authentication

Developing Threats

- Blockchain-enabled payments
- Core bank-issued digital currencies/current accounts
- CBDC/payments
- Robo-advisors/online brokers
- Securities issuance and exchanges
- ID validation
- Cash management

Long Horizon

- Corporate Finance advisory
- Brokerage
- Market making

So, while payments, account management and trading will continue to underpin traditional banking for some time, the medium-term horizon looks threatening. Banks are developing strategies to respond to these threats, which we'll cover in future chapters, but we believe that if responses are not made quickly, these threats will quickly become existential.

Notes

1. We are including Building Societies and Credit Unions under this broad bracket for this analysis; comments applying to Banking Products and services also apply to these.
2. How Fractional Reserve Banking Works. *Quickonomics.* https://quickonomics.com/fractional-reserve-banking/. Accessed 7 January 2018.
3. Ochs, S. (2011, October 27). Banking on Inertia: Not a Customer Retention Strategy. *American Banker.* https://www.americanbanker.com/opinion/banking-on-inertia-not-a-customer-retention-strategy. Accessed 7 January 2018.
4. Robert Stammers, CFA. (2011, December 21). Three Behavioral Biases That Can Affect Your Investment Performance. *Forbes.* https://www.forbes.com/sites/cfainstitute/2011/12/21/three-behavioral-biases-that-can-affect-your-investment-performance/#19dc08773786. Accessed 7 January 2018.

5. Current Account Switch Service (Payments UK). https://www.paymentsuk. org.uk/projects/current-account-switch-service. Accessed 7 January 2018.
6. Nectar Loyalty Card Homepage. https://www.nectar.com/. Accessed 7 January 2018.
7. *Bank of England Blog.* 25 July 2016. https://bankunderground. co.uk/2016/07/25/central-bank-digital-currency-the-end-of-monetary-poli-cy-as-we-know-it/. Accessed 23 December 2017.
8. International Chamber of Commerce Trade Finance Survey 2017. https:// iccwbo.org/publication/2017-rethinking-trade-finance/. Accessed 24 December 2017.
9. https://www.threadless.com/. Accessed 24 December 2017.
10. Neo Homepage. https://neo.org/. Accessed 14 January 2018.
11. Cardano Hub Homepage. https://www.cardanohub.org/en/home/. Accessed 14 January 2018.
12. WanChain Homepage. https://wanchain.org/. Accessed 14 January 2018.
13. Brown, R. G. (2016, April 5). Introducing R3 Corda™: A Distributed Ledger Designed for Financial Services. *R3.* http://www.r3cev.com/ blog/2016/4/4/introducing-r3-corda-a-distributed-ledger-designed-for-fi-nancial-services. Accessed 14 January 2018.
14. Hyperledger Homepage. https://www.hyperledger.org/. Accessed 14 January 2018.
15. Digital Asset Homepage. http://www.digitalasset.com/. Accessed 14 January 2018.
16. *The Wall Street Journal.* (2015, November 30). https://www.wsj.com/arti-cles/lending-startups-look-at-borrowers-phone-usage-to-assess-creditworthi-ness-1448933308. Accessed 24 December 2017.

3

The Death and Resurrection
of Capital Markets

In this chapter, we examine how capital markets have evolved, how they have contributed to the growth of global trade and international currency stability. We describe how the structure of capital markets, increasing complexity and lack of transparency has contributed to various crises, growing inequality and a lack of accountability in large corporations, which are becoming more powerful (and less accountable) than nations in the twenty-first century.

We posit that today's capital markets structures are flawed and favour exaggerated growth of already large corporations, at the expense of smaller businesses. Meanwhile, governments are losing their grip on corporations and platforms, as these become ever more powerful and borderless.

We also consider how technology, platform and ecosystem economics are likely to impact capital markets, as banks lose their stranglehold, and participation in the benefits is no longer restricted to larger companies.

A Capital Markets Primer

Capital markets move money from people and organisations that have it to companies that need it, so that the companies can be productive and (hopefully) grow. The provision of capital beyond margins on sales is essential to the growth and smooth running of most organisations. Suppliers of capital try to achieve the greatest possible return at the lowest possible risk, while users of capital want to raise it at the lowest possible cost.

© The Author(s) 2018
S. Blakstad and R. Allen, *FinTech Revolution*,
https://doi.org/10.1007/978-3-319-76014-8_3

A Very Short History of Capital Markets

Capital markets in some form have been with us since the early money-lenders, but became increasingly sophisticated as the Industrial Revolution gave rise to large, ambitious infrastructure projects and factories, requiring significant injections of capital to fund high build costs before they could become profitable. Investments in many such schemes, starting in Western Europe and in particular the (then spectacularly wealthy) UK—especially overseas schemes in "the Empire" and other developing economies such as the USA—made many eighteenth- and nineteenth-century financiers rich. More importantly, they allowed the foundations of capitalism to become cemented in what are now most of the world's most prosperous economies.

Capital markets converted the wealth gained from sheep, trade and war to factories and infrastructure that transformed, and accelerated development in, much of the rest of the world; they fuelled scientific discoveries and resulted in unprecedented social change, but at a risk. An eighteenth-century speculator in a far-away railway had nothing more than an attractive prospectus and the promises of plausible salesmen to guarantee whether the investment was genuine, or had any hope of generating returns.

Throughout the nineteenth and twentieth centuries, the complexity of capital markets instruments increased from simple loans and share purchases to include complex instruments traded on secondary markets, created to allow financiers to hedge portfolios against risk caused by uncertain returns and volatile economies. As markets expanded and information technology progressed, these instruments became more complex, and trading more automated, resulting today in a proliferation of electronic trading—and trading floors, that previously bustled with shouting (and often profane) traders, replaced with floors of computer systems.

Debt and Equity

Capital markets are made up of two types of transfers of value from money owner to organisation, in the shape of debt and equity. Debt is a loan, which is subject to interest, whereas equity is ownership of part of the company (stock/shares). Debt is safer, with guaranteed repayment and pre-agreed payments of interest, although subject to default risk, whereas equity, while riskier, presents a greater potential return, as the value and return relates to the value of the company, which can increase significantly or even exponentially.

Primary and Secondary Markets

Primary markets allow companies to raise capital by issuing debt or equity products, the most basic and oldest type of investments, without running an initial public offering (IPO). These represent investors directly transferring value to the company in exchange for stocks (shares) with an ownership value in the company, or bonds, with a redeemable cash value and pre-agreed interest (coupons), to be paid at agreed periods.

In an IPO, the company can issue a large number of shares to large institutional buyers, exposing them to secondary markets. In secondary markets, institutional and private investors can resell their equity and debt to investors via the stock market or the bond market. More complex products (derivatives), such as Exchange-traded Funds (ETFs), allow investors to purchase fractional holdings in a portfolio of products over secondary markets, and further derivatives are created under structures allowing for hedging across multiple types of products, or by tracking their yields.

While the original sellers profit from this sale, and may continue to hold a stake in the underlying company, the company doesn't benefit directly from the sale of these new products. However, the company's performance on the secondary market will continue to influence their price/risk and saleability.

Participants

Many participants can issue debt on primary markets; however, stock (equity) can only be issued by companies. Bonds (debt) can be issued by governments, municipalities and organisations as well as companies. Meanwhile, companies, municipalities, governments and organisations can also act as investors in capital markets, as can institutional investors such as pension funds and mutual funds. In addition, private investors participate directly or via funds.

There is a growing trend for smaller investors, who would traditionally have invested via funds, or not at all, to invest directly, following the growing sophistication of automatic trading and advisory services.

Regulation

While efforts are being made to harmonise regulation globally, driven by the G20 group of countries and initiatives such as the Basel Accords,[1] capital markets regulation is still defined by national financial regulators as part of national regulation. Given the variable maturity of markets in different countries, the close dependency of capital and money markets and the relationship to national economies and monetary policy, local regulation is essential in most countries, but differences between countries create complexity, loopholes and a lack of transparency in the system.

Many institutions choose to adopt international regulatory standards, based on Basel 3, Dodd/Frank, etc., above their local regulations, to trade on global markets, while issuers wishing to trade globally are likely to choose one of the exchanges with a higher standard of regulation, such as the US or European markets, to reach the broadest possible markets. High standards of regulation therefore benefit sales; however, they also limit the type and size of company that can issue products on exchanges.

Capital Markets and the Economy

The size of capital markets in any country is normally directly related to the size of the economy of that country, while the maturity of capital markets is also reflected in the health and maturity of the economy. Capital markets' size and maturity are not just indicators, but drivers for a successful economy in capitalism, as it ensures the smooth flow of cash from people who have it to organisations that need it. Capital markets enable and drive the growth of companies through the release of cash into the economy.

While this has resulted in tremendous growth in major economies, and is helping the growth of developing economies, it has created an uneven playing field, where companies that are able to achieve a certain scale and are able to participate in capital markets have much lower barriers to liquidity, than smaller companies. This in turn creates a ceiling for smaller companies, who find it hard to achieve that scale due to liquidity challenges.

Typically, smaller companies can issue limited securities (debt and equity) depending on the appetite for stocks and bonds in that type of company and the possibility for growth, but outside of innovation companies with significant (and obvious) growth potential, investors tend to be limited to "friends and family", as there are limited channels for the exchange at this scale. The smallest companies, including more traditional small businesses, are limited to bank and personal loans, and even these are only available to a minority in many economies.

This has resulted in economies that are unevenly weighted in favour of larger companies, that in turn benefit from their scale to achieve more growth, through greater liquidity, while the vast majority of companies (99%+) suffer from disproportionately higher costs of borrowing, and lack access to capital.

Meanwhile, although the value of capital markets is directly linked to the value of the real economy, capital market growth can create or reflect unrealistic market capitalisation for companies, unrelated to their current earning potential and, in some cases, unrelated to future earning potential. This can make good sense for investors where a company sale or divestiture is likely to generate high returns, but divorces economic performance and the real economy from the perceived value of an organisation. This, then, can lead to wage inflation for senior leaders, who are rewarded for the increased value of their company rather than for its actual performance, while real wages contract as profits decline. Meanwhile, investors see increased returns, so at an aggregate level, the disparity between rich and poor, including the lower-waged, tends to increase over time.

Capital vs Money Markets

It's important to distinguish capital markets from money markets; capital markets are concerned with the flow of capital into businesses (and governments, municipalities, etc.) with the goal of creating long-term growth, whereas money markets are concerned with short-term, often unsecured loans, with a goal of making more money. Money markets products include deposits, collateral loans, acceptances and bills of exchange, where the gamble is on the relative value of the debt. Critically, money markets, while they're useful for risk reduction and can be used to generate significant profits, don't create economic growth in the same way as capital markets.

The Death of Capital Markets—The Paradigm Shift After the Next Crash

Without capital markets, modern industrial society could not have evolved. It is reasonable to argue that in the absence of capital markets, we'd still be bartering in local markets, growing our own vegetables, weaving our own cloth and dying of horrible diseases at an early age; living in pre-industrial conditions, as we still witness in some of the least developed parts of the modern world.

However, capital markets have also evolved to support and perpetuate some fundamental capitalist principles that, in today's broadly industrialised world, are undermining their primary function, in particular, the growth of wealth and economies. While there is plenty of wealth creation still happening, as the potential for ground level development is increasingly realised, there is an increasing concentration of growth in wealth and value at the top of the pyramid, at the expense of organisations and people lower down.

The Problem with Capitalism

One of the fundamental challenges of modern capitalism is that it's based on a theoretically infinite potential for growth; this was a reasonable position when the world was resource-rich and relatively people poor, but we're now living in a world where natural resources can't keep up[2] with the growth of the appetites of our global population, fuelled by both population growth and increasing growth in developing economies leading to a growing global middle class. Modern corporate and individual wealth has been built on the industrialisation of developed nations, but that industrialisation was itself fuelled by wealth created by ransacking natural resources and populations, first in their own, and then in less developed countries. Three centuries ago, most of the modern USA and Europe were developing economies by the standards of their own metropolitan populations; as these developed, other OECD countries and, now, Tiger economies, BRICS (Brazil, Russia, India, China and South Africa) countries are industrialising rapidly and becoming fully developed economies.

So today, that opportunity has shrunk; corporations are still creating wealth by exploiting cheaper labour and natural resources in developing economies, but as those economies develop their middle class grows, increasing domestic demand for those same resources and increasing both standards of living and wages. This depresses the differential and therefore advantage of overseas production for developed economy corporations and consumers. Increased visibility of working conditions in developing economies and consequent public scrutiny are forcing global companies to demonstrate their overseas production facilities are responsibly operated, again increasing costs. Companies are still offshoring labour, but for different reasons—as Tim Cook observed[3]—Apple's operations in China are there because of the availability of highly skilled knowledge workers, rather than purely for cost reasons.

Meanwhile, it is no longer acceptable to openly send your army to "civilise" another nation into letting you have all its resources at little or no cost to yourself. In the near future, population movements caused by global warming will further augment the competition for shrinking natural resources, as those (generally) poorer countries most impacted simultaneously become unsuitable for further asset-stripping by overseas corporations, as their environments collapse.

Added to this, classical capitalism requires a general upward trend in personal wealth, to allow for continued growth and development; wealth is a relative concept, and markets reflect this, so while everyone in developed countries today is "wealthier" than their ancestors in pre-industrial society, growing inequality[4] means that many of the population are actually getting poorer in relative terms, and quality of life for the majority of people in developed nations is reaching the tipping point where it's starting to decline, rather than improving, particularly in countries run on more capitalist principles, where wage disparity is greatest.

Globally, there is clearly an opportunity for great economic growth in developing economies, which are the fastest growing today and likely to remain so for many years. An increasing number of analysts are, however, starting to question whether growth is reaching a plateau in more developed economies. As Kate Raworth observes in *Doughnut Economics: Seven Ways to Think Like a 21st Century Economist*,[5] challenging one of the key principles of capitalism doesn't go down well with governments, economists or central banks, because continuous growth is so fundamental to capitalism, however, we may now be forced to rethink what an economy without growth could look like, in many of the world's most developed economies. It would mean flattening of or reduction of value across many of the key economic indicators, such as aggregated wages, stock market values, property, trade and consumer sales. And some influential economic commentators are now publicly saying that this scenario is something we need to consider.

Wealth of Communities vs Wealth of Markets

We also must consider that, while capital markets have been critical for the growth of corporations, they aren't generally that great at fostering innovation and research; capital tends to follow ideas that have been tested and found a market, by which time they're lower risk than investing in pure ideas or research. Most original research, including most of the research that has led to breakthroughs such as the internet, originated from state-funded institutions (particularly the military and academia), while very nearly all research is conducted by people who've been educated to a high level, in many cases partially at the expense of the state. On top of this, many companies are eligible for state support, to encourage them to create wealth and stimulate trade, so states further support them in the shape of rebates, tax relief and grants.

State institutions and education systems are designed to foster experimentation, failure and learning. Universities and the military enable the establishment of long-term discovery focused research; salaries and research grants are paid whether results are positive or negative, which is an important precondition for transformational discovery. Private companies are under pressure to make a profit, particularly those with a high injection of capital from investors, and typically need to show results quarterly. There's a natural progression of researchers from academic to private institutions, while the discoveries of the academic and military communities typically become commercialised by private companies. Private investors reap the rewards of public spending through state-funded research and education, as well as important wealth creation factors such as infrastructure, public health and security, all of which are funded by the state in nearly all developed economies.

Of course, the state also benefits from the growth of economies, in the shape of taxes, creating employment and trade. But as companies grow and become global, their obligations to the national tax systems in their country of origin cease to be directly relevant, while shareholders can and do profit from the investments made by states which make high contributions to public education and defence through returns on their investments; these contribute tax revenues to different states, or not at all. Ultimately, countries with a high concentration of shareholders may be benefitting from investments made by other states, including public services, research institutions and the military. This can lead to a disincentive for contributor states to subsidise education and research, which in turn perpetuates wealth inequality within populations and further reduces the scope for innovation in those countries where this applies.

There are some exceptions; big pharma and some big technology companies have a strong history of R&D and still invest heavily in development, but these, too, rely on a supply of highly educated workers. And while they can, and do, invest in research institutions or individual scholarships, the field is narrowed to furthering the goals of those organisations, reducing opportunity for the type of transformational innovation that might challenge their scale and growth.

The Problem with Megacompanies

Apart from their ability to avoid paying tax, megacompanies, created by the favourable conditions in the current capital market economy, have power that is already outstripping that of the states which seek to benefit from their presence (and, in many cases, justify low corporation taxes in an attempt to woo them). This means that they can avoid re-injecting much of their wealth into national exchequers in the shape of corporation taxes, while countries are under increasing pressure to reduce the tax burden even further, to avoid losing their presence and the job creation that it leads to. Corporate tax cuts are expected, in classical economic models, to increase wages, however, in markets with plentiful labour supply, the tendency is for corporations to pass on the benefits to shareholders, rather than employees, as we're seeing in the USA following corporate tax cuts; the elevation in value of US companies reflects an expectation of greater profits, not higher wages.

And while megacompanies do, indeed, create employment, that job creation isn't as supportive of local economies as job creation by local or smaller companies; large corporations and particularly large international corporations typically create proportionally more lower-paid jobs than smaller, local companies, because they can benefit from economies of scale to reduce expensive manpower in middle and senior management roles. With increased automation, larger companies can also afford to automate more roles, and while much automation has replaced the lower-paid roles, increasingly robots are replacing skilled workers in engineering and manufacturing, while the lowest paid jobs are often harder, or less cost-effective, to automate.

These lower-paid workers are again a burden on their state, especially in countries where minimum wages are low, non-existent or not imposed, and state subsidies are needed to support their subsistence through more tax rebates, grants, subsidised housing, food stamps and state supported healthcare. Even in countries where public support systems are not comprehensive, the burden of support is transferred from companies to the state or to NGOs by lower wages, particularly in rich economies.

A higher proportion of lower-waged employees is also bad for the economy and political stability; they spend less money, so there's less capital going into the system, while growing wealth gaps cause political discontent, leading to the rise of extremism, nationalism and polarised politics. Workers living in poverty, or doing multiple jobs to afford a basic standard of living, are more vulnerable to falling into a cycle of debt, or skimping on basic needs, which can lead to health issues and social problems. The children of lower-paid workers are also statistically less likely to continue education, reducing the pool of people available to drive future innovation through research (NB while we know first-hand that further education is not always a prerequisite to academic research, it is statistically important at a population level).

Politicians exploit frustration and the increased tribalism that is a direct result of polarisation, by corralling voters to find scapegoats for their inability to succeed. Optimism bias—the belief that regardless of statistical probability, your own outcome will be better than average—fuels this resentment and blame. The American dream, in particular, is built on the popular perception that individual poverty is a self-imposed condition, which belief is perpetuated by poorer individuals—who see themselves as temporarily embarrassed millionaires, with a bright future if only the perceived obstacles can be removed. Few politicians will point the finger at the system that creates the situation, because this is unlikely to win many votes.

We've seen the results of this in growing wealth inequality in developed economies, the emergence of popular nationalism, demonisation of easy scapegoats such as immigrants or homeless people, which usually escalates to other groups including ethnic minorities, women, LBGQT people, religious minorities and single parents, and the consequent increasing divide between the urban, educated, young population and the (usually) older, non-metropolitan population, who feel growing isolation as they perceive the concerns of the "elites" do not include their needs, and force populist, usually nationalist and isolationist agendas in an attempt to regain the control of their lives that has been lost, thanks to increasingly precarious living standards or employment status. It's a scenario that's played out in many countries in economic crisis in the past, especially in South America, *but we're now seeing it playing out in some of the richest countries in the world.*

The Problem with Capital Market Economics

Capital market economics also relies on a surplus of untapped value, to support the continuation of upward trends in the overall value of the markets. This, again, works fine where there is growth in global economies, but when those economies stop growing in real terms, capital markets can react in two ways: classical recession can result in markets contracting, but because of the way markets are structured, it's possible to make money out of betting on the value of assets reducing, so the relationship is not simple, and it's also possible to increase some areas of wealth as real values fall. Some investors get richer by "shorting", i.e. betting against growth, and where investment products are structured and hedged, can result in capital market growth while real economies shrink.

A reduction of growth in overall value can also lead to bubbles, where a concentration of investors gambles on potential future growth sectors. A bubble can occur at any time, based on hype and overconfidence in a market sector (the dot.com boom is a good example), but such bubbles, when they burst, typically have the greatest impact on the sector concerned and don't have as much impact across other market segments. Market corrections, which can look like a bubble bursting or a recession, occur during any growth period but usually only impact markets or segments of markets by up to 10%, and are followed by recovery. A bubble that's a symptom of overconfidence alongside a shrinking or stagnating real economy can have much wider reaching consequences when it bursts.

And there are also crashes associated with overconfidence combined with other factors, such as lack of transparency, unintended consequences of market automation, or, notoriously, group-think culture, which has been identified as one of the key elements leading to 2008s credit bubble and subsequent crash.

Growth, as we've observed above, is often based on perceived rather than actual value, and all investments are a gamble against value increasing (or decreasing in the case of shorts). What's unusual about today's capital markets is that we're seeing continued growth with no notable corrections, over the course of two years, across all sectors, despite the lack of equivalent real growth—markets have been outstripping the growth of real economies. February 2018 saw a slight correction, ironically in response to better than expected GDP projections from the USA, which in turn pushed investors back to sovereign bonds and impacted the over-inflated equity prices, but markets globally dipped less than 10%, and markets remain over-valued in comparison with real economic output. As markets typically expand in parallel with real economies, the trend since 2015 is unusual; commentators are speculating about another potential crash. Multiple inflationary bubbles occurring at once, or unrealistic growth across sectors with strong interdependency, have the inevitable effect of eventually depressing the entire market when they burst.

Today, we are seeing sharp growth in some probably overhyped areas (cryptocurrencies being a good example) in parallel with a rise in unrealistic market capitalisation for the most successful or prominent technology companies. Tesla, for example, had a market cap of USD 58.26 billion at the time of writing, a phenomenal figure for an organisation that has sold fewer than 250,000 vehicles in its entire history, which amounts to a market cap of over USD 750,000 for every unit sold in 2016. While Tesla is working on some extremely ambitious and potentially very lucrative projects, it is valued as though there is no real competition, whereas it's clear that a number of new and existing rival companies are moving into the sector which, backed by regulation and emissions targets, is bound to be a strong performer, but consequently, likely to become crowded.

Flat and negative interest rates, meanwhile, have led to a rise in negative yield government bonds, with price outstripping returns, and this in turn leads to a combination of unusual behaviours, including a flight to equities, which are further exacerbating the bubble-like behaviour. Investors are treating "safe" equities, especially the big tech firms, as a bond equivalent, again increasing the concentration of value in a small number of firms representing an unrealistic percentage of overall market capitalisation. Add to that growing consumer credit, particularly in auto loans, a resurgence of credit in housing, falling real wages and spending with the move towards the gig economy, and the outcome looks worrying. The credit bubble is particularly unsettling in developing economies, notably China and sub-Saharan Africa, where microloans at astronomical rates are perpetuating, rather than resolving, poverty.

As interest rates start to creep up, borrowers will be hit hard, while as we have seen in the February 18 correction, it will cause a reversal in the flight to equities, removing much of the artificial valuation from the market. This will lead to further corrections, which should not be confused with crashes caused by systemic collapses such as that of the credit bubble. By the time you read this that bubble may have already burst.

Meanwhile, other parts of the market, particularly cryptocurrencies, are behaving in ways that are unpredictable and unprecedented, due to the novel nature of the asset; Bitcoin in particular regularly loses up to a third of its value, before recovering even more strongly; it follows seasonal patterns, typically growing exponentially towards the end of the year, then dipping in January, before recovering strongly in February/March as City bonuses are paid and Chinese New Year celebrations take place. Although most commentators have been predicting a crash of cryptocurrencies, it's impossible to predict what will really happen with an asset that behaves in such an unusual way. They also, at time of writing, represent a tiny fraction of money supply, capital markets value or any other significant economic indicator, so while they may grab headlines, we believe their valuation is unlikely to have a large direct impact on the wider economy; the global credit bubble is the real worry.

The Problem with the Real Economy

We've used the term "real economy" above, and it's useful to distinguish sale of products and services, assets, lending, ownership and transactions, from market economics; there is a distinction between making money out of, for example, selling toasters, to making money on derivatives. However, there are shades of grey in-between, and, depending on your perspective, both, or neither, could be described as the "real" economy.

You could argue that capital markets, as the largest generator of wealth, are more important to the economy than the "real" economy, while, as we've said above, the real economy can't function effectively without the movement of capital that capital markets provide. At the other end of the scale, you're exchanging a toaster for money; money is in itself a construct of the economy rather than something "real" (NB for anyone who still thinks money represents assets, please see Chapter 10 on the subject). The toaster's value is determined by market forces in the economy in which it's sold, including the value of labour and materials, together with the availability of liquid capital in the form of personal wealth, and other factors such as utility, novelty and fashion.

Value of labour and services is in turn determined by a complex relationship between resource availability, economic factors such as wealth and stability, and demand. The value of labour is also influenced by supply and demand to a very granular level, which in turn is influenced by educational policies, social security and other government policies in the countries where the components of the toaster are produced, which are in turn impacted by availability of tax revenues and of capital.

Flow of capital is what allows organisations to scale beyond micro-businesses to larger, more efficient and more productive organisations. It also allows organisations to make longer-term plans and develop new products, thanks to that scale allowing for specialisations such as research and development, as well as the ability to absorb large investment in building future products.

So, while it is important to separate capital markets conceptually from the real economy, it's also very important to acknowledge that one cannot function without the other in the way that money, organisations, labour and value are structured today. The challenge we see with the growing division between producers and beneficiaries created by the structure of today's capital markets is that the mutual interdependency is becoming less obvious to both sides; with some justification, as derivatives markets are increasingly detached from the underlying producers.

Bringing It Together

Considering all of these factors, it's not surprising that many experts are forecasting a crash and further corrections. In the next section, we consider how the next crash will be set against a different background, not only the rising instability, wealth inequality and dissociation between corporations and states, but also the emerging trends in technology which will shape the financial ecosystem of the future.

The Resurrection of Capital Markets—Death of the Dinosaurs and Rise of the Mammals

What's Next for Capital Markets?

Anyone with a reasonably functional crystal ball could use the information in the market to predict another crash, and many commentators are. Whether the crash has already happened by the time you read this, whether it comes sooner, later, or not at all, a major correction is likely. It's impossible to predict what will spark it, although credit is likely to be one of the major drivers, as confidence in lending is demonstrated to have been overly optimistic.

But the next capital markets correction—or collapse—is not going to happen in a "normal" capital markets environment. Lending, securitisation and currencies have all been evolving rapidly and chipping away at the edges of traditional capital markets; these new paradigms will not just influence the shape of the correction and recovery, but fundamentally alter the future structure of capital markets and how they perform.

ICOs, Crowdfunding, Microfinance, Community Coin, Direct Investment and the Evolution of Traded Products

Elsewhere, we discuss the ICO (or token sale) boom riding on the cryptocurrency explosion, together with evolving paradigms for direct investment in new and smaller businesses. Despite the current noise and negative publicity around volatility, "Pump and Dump" and fraudulent activities in this evolving area, we see this development as a pivotal change which will offer opportunities to change both financing, as we demonstrate in Chapters 10 and 12, and the nature of currency, as we discuss in Chapter 8. Here, we offer a brief summary of the characteristics of these paradigms, as they relate to investment. For further details on the instruments, please refer to the relevant chapters.

Community currency has been with us for a while in various formats, aimed at keeping capital within a (usually geographical) community, and is now moving into more interoperable, crypto versions. These models share many characteristics that, while not completely novel in capital markets, are exposing investment opportunities to both issuers and investors in new ways.

- Multiparty contracts: ICOs, token sales, crowdfunding and microfinance all involve large number of small players, either as investors or beneficiaries of the investment and sometimes both.
- Off-exchange: these investment approaches operate outside of the traditional listed equity paradigm, meaning that issuing companies don't have to qualify for listing on a stock exchange in order to attract investment.
- Peer to peer: although an intermediary is involved in crowdfunding and microfinance, there's more of a direct investor/investee relationship than in traditional exchange-traded equity investments; it is closer to the relationship between Angel or VC investors in a small business, but with smaller amounts. There is a personal element to the investment, based on a desire to progress the business or person involved, usually outweighing the need for returns.
- Community-based: in ICO and token sales, investor motivation is generally more directly financial but again based on the faith of the investor in the strength of the underlying proposition, outside the usual structure of stock exchanges, advisors and brokers. Today, ICOs tend to attract an investor community that is strongly emotionally invested in cryptocurrencies as a concept, although many investors are worryingly ignorant about both the technology and potential economic outcomes. Token sales, being associated with underlying assets or behaviours, may attract an investor community with differing ideological motivations, but often similarly ignorant of the factors influencing likely returns.
- Low stakes: like micro-investments, most investors don't stake a significant amount of money in ICO/Token sales, so they're not exposed to significant risk: "caveat emptor". But the two areas differ: because investors in micro-investments tend to be ideologically motivated and because the intermediary is regulated, investors are prepared for negative returns and able to weigh up the risks rationally. Investors in ICOs and token sales may also be aware that there are risks, but without intermediaries, they are more likely to make rash decisions and have unrealistic expectations.
- Crypto whales: the nature of the new crypto token markets, and the relatively low liquidity of the exchanges, has led to the rise of the crypto whales—individuals or organisations who hold large quantities of cryptocurrencies and have the ability to move markets in directions from which

they can profit. For altcoins (non-Bitcoin cryptocurrencies and tokens), the smaller the market and the less the liquidity, the greater the damage a whale can do. Often the markets move in unexpected and unexplainable ways, and whale activity is often blamed for this.

Sometimes whales don't purchase or sell on traditional crypto exchanges because the large orders could create panic in the market. For cryptocurrencies, over the counter trading (OTC) or "dark pools" are where big buyers and institutional traders can purchase large quantities of crypto without being detected by the public. Dark pools[6] are similar to OTC trading as they are usually found on exchanges that enable 'off the record' trades ensuring a whale's moves are more private.

However, whether accepting risk or having unrealistic expectations, investors are now able to invest small stakes en masse in small or large ventures, directly and without having to participate in formal exchanges. This is also happening with more traditional traded products, thanks to the growth of robo-advisors, that enable small investors to invest in ETFs in relatively small amounts, but with the assurance of professional structure and regulated products.

All these evolutions are eating away at the market, and while the bites are tiny today, they are likely to grow as consumer awareness grows, and the paradigms become perceived as normal, while evolving technology will make these, and other investment vehicles, more accessible to ordinary consumers.

These types of investments could go a long way towards freeing up capital currently held as savings; today, it's a footnote in the investment landscape, but as these investment paradigms start to scale, they could start to impact both the availability of capital to smaller enterprises and early-stage enterprises, radically changing the flow of capital, and reduce the balance of deposits, affecting fractional reserve lending for commercial banks.

As alternative investment products with greater assurance and provenance start to scale investment opportunities, particularly in developing economies, the confidence for smaller investors to put stakes in smaller and riskier companies will also increase, which could radically scale investment in SMEs and infrastructure in developing economies, funded by private investors in developed economies. Clearly, the flow of capital wouldn't be exclusively from developed to developing economy; within economies and ecosystems, the same flow of capital from cash surplus to cash need could also be facilitated at a local scale.

What's an investment footnote today will likely become a norm; technology is evolving to support the construction of alternative financial products as we write—alongside other providers, at hiveonline we are developing a range of cryptocurrency-based investment products; while the regulators are currently struggling with classification of ICOs and token sales, there is growing collaboration between issuers and regulators, and we're confident this will also give rise to new standards driving private participation in direct investments. The balance of capital will move from deposits to micro-investments, probably quite rapidly, over the next few years, and this will impact the foundations of the flow of capital as it grows.

Cryptocurrencies, Evolving Transactability of Value, Behaviour and Assets and the Move into the Ecosystem Economy

As we'll expand on in the next section, the nature of value and how we perceive it is evolving; representations of value are transforming, while new technology and alternative business models are facilitating transactability in non-traditional units of value. Or to put it another way, are enabling transactability in *traditional* forms of value that hitherto were not represented as transactable units. This includes forms of value such as assets, which are familiar to us in terms of value—shares and commodity products have traditionally been used as transactable representations of assets—but also, forms of value associated with behaviours.

Behaviours have always been fundamental to the most important value we hold in society, which is trust, but they've hitherto been hard to quantify or measure, and not used in transactions. Community currencies, at a community network level, have explored the use of behaviour as transactable value in some instances.

These behaviours have always influenced, and in many cases controlled, our personal interactions, because they shape the level of trust we have in individuals who are known to us. But hitherto, the mechanisms for communication have been clunky, to say the least—our credit rating gives some sort of insight into our financial reliability, but it's limited and relatively easy to fake. Our online presence is easy to curate and sway; even reviews can be influenced by fashion, information bubbles and volume (see Chapter 18). And none of these reputations has allowed a direct level of transactability associated with behaviours we've personally performed.

Now, with cryptocurrencies and tokens, we're able to codify behaviours in a standardised way, into borderless tokens, which can be programmed to behave in different ways depending on the strength of the underlying behaviour. Cryptocurrencies and tokens allow us to tokenise and give full provenance to behaviours, and allow us to combine behaviours with assets based on rules which give us a rich type of value associated with a spectrum of the things that are important to us in that transaction.

This lifts the trust in behaviours from communities to a global level, as we now have a clear line of sight to behaviour, linked to assets, even when we don't know a person; in translating behaviour to the coin or token, we know that it has only been created and transacted within the desired behavioural rules, wherever in the world the coin or token originates. And that means that we can now transact between different units of value associated with behaviour and assets, in different combinations, without the need to translate these units into traditional currencies. *Effectively, by transacting in the value-based ecosystem, we don't need money any more.*

If that sounds at odds with the release of capital we described above, it's not. The micro-investments we're describing can equally use any transactable value outside the traditional financial system, especially if the beneficiaries are not included in the traditional financial system. The only constraint today is the exchange between crypto and fiat, and that's only a necessary part of the system until the proliferation of value-based currencies makes interoperability and transactability between value-based currencies a standard means of exchange, much as today we exchange fiat currencies. The fact that these value-based currencies exist outside the traditional financial system opens up their use as a means of value exchange, and as a source of capital, accessible to both smaller businesses in developed economies unable to raise capital through listing and to the millions of unbanked businesses in the developing world. We expand on this in Chapter 8.

Platform Economies and the Dissolution of Bordered Value

We discussed earlier in this chapter how global corporations are no longer constrained by national boundaries for tax purposes, and how investors derive value globally from state investment that has been input locally. Within current asset-based structures, the only available recourse of the state to try to recoup its investment is to levy taxes on corporations and investors to the best of its ability; as we've discussed, the bigger and more influential the corporation, the less constrained it is by state control and taxation, while investors will normally pay taxes locally. States can, and do, invite industry to fund services, as we have shown, with some level of payback. But what happens when a level of education and research also becomes global?

As we've seen in the previous section, there's an important link between state-funded research and the development of private businesses, which may be threatened by an imbalance in research funding. However, we're now seeing global developments in research; online education[7] enables institutions to scale their educational offerings to thousands, instead of hundreds, of students, allowing economies of scale and reduced unit costs. Research and development conducted by global communities, as we've seen with open source software, can result in high-quality innovation. Open source software, while mature and pervasive (Linux is now in most large businesses), represents a relatively small area of R&D, while online learning is still developing a market share, but both paradigms sit naturally with the global nature of academic research and scholarly collaboration.

What has not been resolved is how this will be funded in the future; today open source development is fairly limited because it requires talented people to provide work for nothing—as we explore elsewhere, this is likely to grow, but in order to achieve stability some sort of community reward is needed, University-funded online learning is working as a model and could benefit hugely from further private investment if fund-raising were easier.

With the rise of behavioural tokens and the community activity they represent, it's reasonable to assume that some research currently conducted and funded at state level could move into the global research ecosystem in a more formalised way, capturing and regularising some of this activity for dedicated communities. Where national businesses previously supported national institutions (Tate gallery, etc.) will we now see Google's academy and research move out into the global ecosystem, and start to support and interact with the global academic community?

R&D is a clear opportunity to move prosumer value into the global ecosystem—after all, it has been happening for decades in some sectors, without the support of an underlying value mechanism. And with the availability of behaviour-linked assets, a whole range of transactable developments, services and goods can be supported by global ecosystem communities without the need for state intervention. We're seeing it today in the negative example of the "dark web", where a global community has built a range of services, value exchange and goods outside of national boundaries. Using a similar approach, but with the benefit of regulation, more beneficial communities are arising. Apart from open source, which has been with us for some time, we are now seeing the emergence of renewable energy coins and their communities, forestry and agriculture. These communities are maturing, and others will follow.

So does this mean that states lose control of regulation? Well, to an extent, yes. States are already hanging on by their fingernails to regulation in some sectors, and as we've discussed elsewhere, borderless currencies will require greater regulatory collaboration. Financial regulators are already building bridges, and we believe this is an opportunity for more consumer bodies to collaborate. Ultimately, though, we will need to accept a new paradigm where much regulation is global. Will that be controlled by the platforms? Independence has always been an important characteristic of state control, holding institutions and corporations to account. Without independent regulation, there's a risk that the worst characteristics will dominate these new marketplaces, as we've seen with the dark web, so we believe there's a significant need for global collaboration to create independent bodies with the authority to regulate these markets.

And as we've seen in economies where there's a close collaboration between state and commerce, such as China and Singapore, that close relationship does not preclude the development of innovation, transformational technology and new paradigms in community finance. States are accountable to citizens while corporations are accountable to customers; however, states can control their citizens more easily than corporations can control their customers, and as we've discussed, more transparency leads to greater accountability for corporations. With transparency comes a greater incentive to be seen to be compliant, whether it's in funding research or not exploiting slavery, and customers everywhere will expect stronger standards.

Global regulation and a more direct "taxation" in the form of support for research and development provides an opportunity to make platforms more accountable, and to ensure value is returned to the community in a way that is beneficial to platforms, governments and populations. A platform based global community could be influential in overcoming disparity such as access to education or research facilities, accelerating development and equality.

And how will this impact capital markets? It's likely to change the status of global corporations; conferring some obligations usually associated with statehood comes with baggage—we would argue these corporations are already acting with the autonomy of states, so this transition would consolidate that status and build in obligations to the community. There would be a need to hedge against corporate collapse, to ensure the continuity of development communities; behaviour coins would need to form a part of their value proposition to maintain this equilibrium. And it would mean increased traceability, with research moving into the public domain and greater ecosystem collaboration and contribution to the development of corporations.

The borders around corporations would necessarily be flexible; we believe this is a natural progression as we move towards the ecosystem economy, but this has profound implications for shareholders, who derive value from the private and proprietary nature of development by corporations. A transition towards hybrid ownership structures, supported in part by private equity, and in part by behaviour/asset-based tokens, may be the medium term outcome.

The New Transparency

Later in this book, we present many examples of the traceability that can be achieved through cryptocurrencies and smart contracts. Equities, bonds and secondary products today lack much of that traceability; you know which company you're investing in, but there's little or no traceability to what that investment is funding. As we've seen with sustainable investments, applying that traceability to a full value chain exposes underlying activities. What happens when this is applied to the wider market? Will investors want to hold issuers to account more? It's unlikely they will want to do so at a granular level, but again the assurance given by behaviour coins is likely to be attractive to many investors, and to issuers who can present a premium product guaranteeing their accountability to investors.

And tokenisation also offers further opportunities to develop new portfolio models. Derivatives were originally developed to allow investors to hedge across portfolios of products, to avoid undue exposure to potential losses. But what happens when you can hold coins that effectively represent a type of min-ETF in your wallet? Will consumers start to structure their own portfolios without thinking about it?

The day when the average person is carrying around a portfolio of equity style coins in their digital wallet is probably some way off, but we are already happily carrying around portfolios of digital cash—some more useful than others—in the form of prepaid apps, air miles, store points and, of course, money, without paying it too much attention. When we describe a world where you're carrying around treeCoin, energyCoin and CowCoin that may seem far-fetched, until you think about the contents of your digital wallet today.

Enabling consumers to participate directly in targeted investments in this way must further help the flow of capital, but clearly, this will evolve in parallel with a reduction in the "real" money supply, as behaviour/asset coins are fundamentally transactable in a way that, say, shares in a supermarket aren't. We cover the likely impact of cryptocurrencies on the money supply elsewhere, and we think that this change will also impact much, if not all, of the current equity market, and secondary products, eventually. It's hard to foresee how derivatives will evolve, but with a hedge portfolio of transactable ETFs in your wallet, secondary markets are likely to flatten and become more efficient. It's also likely that pricing will remain centralised to some extent, but as the distribution of value is subsumed into ecosystem-based value systems, and organisations transact value towards behaviours, valuations should become more reflective of markets, rather than individual corporations.

Conclusion

Moving money around is critical to business and to society, and capital markets have enabled the growth we've seen to date. But today's capital markets structures are flawed and favour exaggerated growth of already large corporations, at the expense of smaller businesses. Meanwhile, governments are losing their grip on corporations and platforms, as these become ever more powerful and borderless.

We see a fork in the road offered by the emergence of both the ecosystem economy and blockchain technology; the movement of value into behaviour and asset-based systems could supplement and augment the current private equity structure, while enabling corporations to participate in social development and research progress at a global scale. While we are convinced this will require changes to regulations, we're already seeing symptoms of the changes, or the developments leading to these changes, emerging, in the shape of transactable behaviour coins, ICOs, peer-to-peer investment vehicles and increasing investor demand for transparency. The more worrying recent developments, such as the immunity of global corporations to national boundaries, could also be symptoms of a move towards a positive change with a combination of technology advances and regulatory collaboration.

Capital markets have been through many evolutions; the next evolution looks very like democratisation and a move into the ecosystem, in parallel with the democratisation and move into the ecosystem of commercial financial services. We think this will have a positive, stabilising effect and, most importantly, give capital access to the millions of small businesses who struggle with the credit ceiling today. An evolution this significant will not happen overnight; it will mean a gradual recalibration of valuation and value in traditional equities. Debt markets will open up to more participants, freeing capital held in private deposits and, in parallel with the money revolution, moving debt from the fractional reserve lending system currently underpinning commercial banking towards private, ecosystem markets.

Most profound is the potential impact on national capital, fiscal balances, taxation and regulations—by acknowledging organisations and communities are global ecosystem players, more control of both capital and social support moves into the borderless economy. This could be the solution to the current challenges we're seeing in state relationships with global platforms and corporations; it could also be the answer to redirecting wealth and value to where it's needed the most, and to ensure these megacorps participate in supporting the development of future generations.

The alternative is to attempt to regulate at national level that which is already borderless; to somehow hold corporations, which are more powerful than countries, to account; to perpetuate increasing inequality and detachment between producers, and those profiting from them, in a world with diminishing resources and diminishing means of increasing real wealth.

Notes

1. Basel III: International Regulatory Framework for Banks, Bank for International Settlements. https://www.bis.org/bcbs/basel3.htm. Accessed 12 January 2018.
2. https://www.overshootday.org/. Accessed 25 December 2017.
3. Apple CEO Tim Cook: This Is the Number 1 Reason We Make iPhones in China (It's Not What You Think). Glenn Leibowitz (Inc.), 21 December 2017. https://www.inc.com/glenn-leibowitz/apple-ceo-tim-cook-this-is-number-1-reason-we-make-iphones-in-china-its-not-what-you-think.html. Accessed 24 February 2018.
4. *The New York Times*, 7 August 2017. https://www.nytimes.com/interactive/2017/08/07/opinion/leonhardt-income-inequality.html. Accessed 25 December 2017.
5. Raworth, K. (2017, March 22). *Doughnut Economics: Seven Ways to Think Like a 21st Century Economist*. White River Junction: Chelsea Green Publishing.

6. Redman, J. (2016, August 11). Former Tradehill Founder Starts Another Bitcoin Dark Pool. *Bitcoin.com*. https://news.bitcoin.com/former-trade-hill-founder-dark-pool/. Accessed 12 January 2018.

7. *Times Higher Education Supplement*, 19 October 2017. https://www.timeshighereducation.com/blog/where-will-online-education-be-five-years#-survey-answer. Accessed 15 December 2017.

The Un-bank, Part II
Fintech for Financial Inclusion *What's Going on?*

As we've shown, the financial services industry is undergoing significant change, with implications for the banks, the Challengers and customers—especially the unbanked, and the wider economy. In the next section, we examine some of the technical and economic changes that are happening in the world of money and payments; how we have moved from a straightforward notion of cash to new and more complex types of payments, and how money is now evolving further.

Central banks have traditionally controlled the flow of money and are engaging with new types of money; we describe the opportunities and challenges that this presents. We look at how the changing nature of value is impacting, and being impacted by, evolving trends such as global connectedness, shifting notions of reward and expectations.

Finally, we describe how emerging alternative finance providers are helping to reshape the financial services ecosystem, augmenting, replacing or bypassing traditional banks, especially in underserved populations.

4

New Payments Landscape

In this chapter, we examine how payments have evolved in recent years, from cash-based to digital and from batch to instant. We present the commercial landscape of payments today, with central banks, centralised infrastructure, distributed commercial banks and payments services, together with some of the technical challenges in adapting to new standards, such as instant payments. We show how alternative methods of moving value, including non-bank payments and blockchain-based transactions, are bypassing payments infrastructure and the banking system.

We show how balances in bank accounts are no longer based on units of currency and how fractional reserve lending has abstracted value from "real money", with implications for a move towards ownership-based units such as cryptocurrency. We explore the risks to individuals and businesses in moving to payments outside of the traditional banking system, and how this transition is likely to impact the banking sector. We discuss how regulations designed for bordered currencies are failing to adapt to evolving payments, both from a currency and from a payment management perspective, and the changes that will be needed. Finally, we show how payments are likely to evolve and the implications for individuals and organisations.

The Old World

To many, a payment is the core utility of money. The word "payment" means different things to people depending on context and perspective. Consumer, merchant, business, retail banker, commercial banker, central

© The Author(s) 2018
S. Blakstad and R. Allen, *FinTech Revolution*,
https://doi.org/10.1007/978-3-319-76014-8_4

banker—all actors in a complex global ecosystem that transfers hundreds of billions of dollars of value around the planet every year using a multitude of payment instruments, schemes, networks and systems.

Today, we are still interacting with the Old World infrastructures, supported by computerised edifices that have been built over the last five decades based on centuries-old processes of centralised trust organisations. Consumers and merchants exchange money for goods and services; facilitated by card networks, banks extend credit and reconcile balances between themselves, ultimately being settled at their national central bank or using counter-party processes via archaic global messaging systems between global commercial banks. There are many interdependent actors in an ecosystem with many intermediaries, all of whom are profiting from the movement of the value in payment.

The world of payments isn't complicated, and we'll provide a brief outline here. For interested readers, there are some excellent sources of information with far more detail than we have the space to provide here, but the Bank for International Settlement,[1] the Bank of England Payment and Settlement[2] and the US Federal Reserve Payment Systems[3] are good places to start. Below is a quick primer on the key Old World structures and participants.

Payment Systems

Payment systems are a set of common rules and procedures, which support the transfer of funds between people, businesses and financial institutions. Most payment systems are managed by operators and supported by one or more infrastructure providers of hardware, software and communication networks. Some financial institutions have direct access to each payment system and provide payment services to their customers.

Many payment systems employ a two-stage deferred net settlement process. Payments are initially made in commercial bank money, often between different banks; this creates net obligations between these banks, which are settled in central bank money at a later point in time (i.e. settlement is deferred). Features such as the netting of payments can have liquidity saving benefits in systems where participants make multiple offsetting payments between each other in a short space of time (e.g. payments between banks).

Payment Instruments

Payment instruments are the things that end users of payment systems use to transfer funds between accounts at banks or other financial institutions.

Cards, credit transfers, direct debits and e-money are examples of non-cash payment instruments.

Payment Schemes

A payment scheme is a professional body that sets the rules and technical standards for the execution of payment transactions using the underlying payment systems. Payment schemes manage the day-to-day operations of the payment systems and processes and ensure any regulatory requirements associated with the processing of payments are met.

Characteristics of a payment scheme (based on the UK Payments definition) are as follows:

- offers a service to move money between parties
- has a governance structure that includes independent directors with a mandate to represent the views of all service users, together with directors appointed from the members of the scheme
- custodians of the payment scheme rules and technical standards for operation of the payment schemes
- responsible for the operation of the underlying payment systems
- complies with regulatory aspects governing payment schemes and systems
- has access criteria and an application process for joining.

Card Schemes

Card **schemes** are **payment** networks linked to **payment** cards, such as debit or credit cards, of which a bank or any other eligible financial institution can become a member. By becoming a member of the **scheme**, the member then gets the ability to issue or acquire cards operating on the network of that card **scheme**.

SWIFT

The Society for Worldwide Interbank Financial Telecommunication, or SWIFT,[4] is a global network that enables over 11,000 financial institutions to send and receive information about financial transactions in a secure and standardised way.

SWIFT does not facilitate funds transfer and does not perform any form of clearing[5] or settlement.[6] It allows payment orders to be transmitted around its network, which must be settled by correspondent accounts that the institutions have with each other.

The New World

Fintechs were the pioneers that entered this Old World with disruption and innovation in their hearts. Building a new type of bank is hard; it takes time, regulatory support and lots of capital, but tackling one of banking's pain points for customers—the "payments use case"—was far easier. Whether the pain each addressed was real or perceived, those startups focused on a single, simple problem and, armed with growing consumer expectation, mobile-fetishism and other rapidly emerging new tech, focus they did. Whether supporting international money transfer (TransferWise, AirWallex, etc.), remittance (Azimo, WorldRemit, Coins.Ph, etc.) or social network payments (WeChat, Venmo and Braintree), legions of payment-focused Fintechs and mobile apps emerged with their world-changing plans, lean startup ideology and new technology.

These Fintechs were unencumbered by most of the regulation and archaic legacy computer systems that make banks such slow movers into innovative new product areas. To add insult to injury, Fintechs were even encouraged in some jurisdictions by friendly regulators keen to bring some competition into the stuffy and stitched-up global retail banking market. This strategy has been successful executed across the world in the Fintech hotspots of San Francisco, New York, London, Singapore, Tel Aviv and Hong Kong, with many other countries now seeking to build their own Fintech ecosystem.

While banks have been forced to focus on regulatory initiatives, and the avoidance of massive fines, as the main driver for structural change in the industry, the Fintechs are focused on changing customer expectations for value-added services and emerging technology as the most important drivers.

The technology giants: Apple, Google, Samsung, Alibaba, etc.,—all with access to huge numbers of customers and able to put mobile technology into their hands—are also in this new payments mix. Native payment apps, tied to their devices: Apple Pay, Android (now Google) Pay, Samsung Pay, Alipay, etc., were a natural next step. If not particularly imaginatively named, and not even very feature rich, the "Pays" do have the advantage of native payment functionality in our beloved mobile phones. For now, these "Pays" have only attempted to replace card payments on merchant terminals, by loading the app with the customer's card or cards of choice. Rationally, it makes sense given customer behaviour: our mobile phones are always in our hands, whereas that pesky bit of plastic is lost in some forgotten crevice in a purse or wallet and far more difficult to find.

The uptake in mobile payments, however, has been slow so whether this is the killer app that the mobile manufacturers had hoped for remains to be seen. What is clear to us, though, is that it is a very small step from here to the widespread provision of mobile to mobile payments: payments that are free, cross-border, instant, integrated seamlessly with social messaging and need no involvement from banks, as the tech companies could control the liquidity within the ecosystem that they create. Pay apps drive device sales for the tech giants; development costs that would cripple a Fintech startup present little more than a miscellaneous line on their business development department's P&L. With a little imagination, they could be so much more inventive in developing features.

Millennials are the largest adopters of mobile banking and in-app banking services in preference to bank branches, as well as the largest group of online shoppers. Increasingly, consumers are demanding personalised offerings and agile payment solutions from their payment providers. With more people than ever wanting to access their money and friction-free banking services at the push of a button, the Fintechs and banks with the best digital offerings can claim the biggest market share.

Responding to the threat, banks and payment providers are looking to improved data capabilities to help reduce their reliance on profits from retail payment transaction fees. In 2017, the payments landscape saw continued consolidation, largely driven by the need for payment processors to expand coverage of both new regions and card-not-present transactions. Venture capital funding in the payments space is also coalescing, with just three gateways—Stripe, Adyen and iZettle—collectively raising nearly $1 billion in funding. With rising competitive pressure from Fintechs, payments providers will need to invest further in improving their understanding of customer needs to pave the way for bold new strategies. New revenue models may then emerge such as the brokerage of non-payment data, engagement tools or platform fees.

By 2020, it is highly likely that emerging economies will be the powerhouses of global electronic payment growth, with China possibly challenging the USA as the leader in this market. Chinese tech giants have aggressive expansion strategies and are eyeing up other regional markets with Alibaba's Ant Financial seeking to buy Moneygram and Tencent making a move into the Indian market.

In emerging markets, initiatives to promote cashless societies, technological innovation and financial inclusion have been key drivers for the significant growth rates. The World Payments Report also states that financial inclusion measures will fuel continued high growth rates of non-cash transactions, particularly in India, Indonesia and Vietnam, as mobile and other forms of digital payments are rolled out. Examples of these innovations are the Indonesian Government's National Strategy for Financial Inclusion (SNKI), which aims to increase the proportion of citizens who are banked from 36 to 75% by 2019, and Peru's BIM, which enables peer-to-peer mobile payments with cash in/out and mobile top-ups.

The Movement of Whose Money?

As we have described elsewhere in this book, balances in bank accounts are no longer based on units of currency and fractional reserve lending has abstracted value from "real money", with significant implications for a move towards ownership-based units such as cryptocurrency. However, there are many risks to individuals and businesses in moving to payments outside of the traditional banking system: from the heavily regulated world in which consumers are protected to the Wild West where there is scant protection.

Near Future Trends: Exponential Payment Growth

According to the BNP Paribas and Cap Gemini World Payments Report for 2017,[7] global electronic transactions broke a decade-long record for growth in 2014–2015, with volumes exceeding 11% growth to reach more than 433 billion. In 2017, they estimate that global non-cash transaction volumes will record a CAGR of 10.9% during the period 2015–2020 reaching 725 billion in 2020. Developing markets are expected to boost the global growth rate of transaction volumes with a sustained CAGR of 19.6% during this period, while mature markets are expected to grow by a modest 5.6% over the next five years.

There are several key convergent payments trends to watch:

- Internet of Things (IoT) device payments. The Internet of Things will change the way businesses and consumers, even whole cities, interact through connected devices. Forecasts show that 20.4 billion connected devices[8] will reach the market by 2020 with 90% expected to be connected. Visa has responded to this opportunity and now certifies IoT devices for technology companies and device manufacturers who want to offer secure and seamless payment solutions via its Visa Ready[9] Program.

Soon, our fridges will be ordering and paying for our milk resupply, our smart home systems will be calculating and paying for power and light, and our connected driverless cars will be negotiating the cost of overtaking on the highway with other connected cars.

- Micropayments. Today, we can't make or receive micropayments (fractions of pennies or cents) for tiny units of service, such as paying to read a single online news page or receiving a financial reward for clicking on a website advert, mostly because the Old World transactions cost too much. Money itself is divisible, but there's no point paying 0.05 of a cent for something if processing the payment costs many times more than that. Thanks to emerging technology and new payments systems, this constraint may soon be a thing of the past, with entirely new business models rapidly developing.

- Peer-to-peer and social payments. Roommates and colleagues are using social media platforms to split bills, rent and utilities, supported by innovative peer-to-peer payments platforms such as Venmo and Braintree. Social contexts give platforms an opportunity to build on emotions and personal bonds and social reinforcement to gain traction. In 2017, WeChat, China's favourite messaging app, had over 980 million monthly active users. There's a Chinese tradition of exchanging packets of money among friends and family members during holidays, and in 2014, for Chinese New Year, WeChat introduced a feature for distributing these virtual "red envelopes", allowing customers to send money to contacts and groups as gifts. A month after its launch, WeChat Pay's customer numbers expanded from 30 million to 100 million. Two years later, in 2016, 3.2 billion red envelopes were sent over the holiday period.

- New digital payment channels. Mobile payments have become ubiquitous; a big driver of commerce lies in enabling consumers and merchants to connect at new points of discovery. Businesses can reimagine business models and how they interact with their customers thanks to new technology, especially integration with social and lifestyle platforms. As the platforms provided by Facebook, WeChat, Amazon, Google, Alibaba and others continue to lower the barriers of participation, opportunities arise for payments providers to differentiate consumers' and merchants' experience, and allow select financial services to fit more naturally into their customer's lives. The key to success will be identifying which account features (balances, payments, account opening, etc.) are best handled through which channels, including voice, messaging and even augmented reality. Augmented reality, for example, can provide new payment channel opportunities through customers' devices, such as selecting and paying for a food

item from an in-app store through an in-app camera, or by reserving a seat in a cinema while scanning the "Screening Now" board in the street.
- Transparent payments. Much has been made of the so-called Uberisation of payments where payments are so low friction you hardly know they're happening. Although it can be necessary and serve a purpose, especially for a merchant or service provider, payment friction can get in the way of customer experience, so new interaction models are evolving where friction is removed or diminished.

All these trends point to an exponential growth in the number of payments being made globally in the very near future.

The New Payments Landscape and Its Enablers

Regulators are driving a global push to increase the adoption of open banking—allowing customers more options to select providers who can manage payments for them, and Europe is leading the efforts with a Payments Service Directive[10] (PSD2) forcing banks to open out their data, and with the UK's Open Banking Initiative.

In July 2016, the Australian Government also announced an independent review into an Open Banking regime for Australia.

> Open Banking is about giving Australians greater access to their own banking data and has the potential to transform the way in which Australians interact with the banking system,

> Greater consumer access to their own banking data and data on banking products will allow consumers to seek out products that better suit their circumstances, saving them money and allowing them to better achieve their financial goals. It will also create further opportunities for innovative business models to drive greater competition in banking and contribute to productivity growth.
> Treasurer Scott Morrison[11]

Third parties, such as payments providers or data aggregators, can access banking systems in a controlled, permissioned and secure way via open Application Programming Interfaces (APIs). APIs are used by leading digital companies like Amazon and Google to transform customer experiences; regulators, and the Fintech industry as a whole, are keen to see this extended across the banking industry—both to stimulate competition and to encourage the development of innovative new products for customers.

Progress outside Europe, however, is slow. Banks are the most vocal in citing costs and potential security or operational risks as reasons. Meanwhile, Visa has published more than 40 APIs "for every payment need" on its developer platform with their head of product Rob Walls, saying financial institutions that fail to make their APIs openly available were "doomed".

Payments Standards

As in the early days of the internet, broad agreement on standards is needed for mass adoption within a healthy and thriving ecosystem. So, for the new payments landscape to thrive, regulators and operators need to agree on international standards. Despite efforts to harmonise in the past few years, competitive forces such as the lack of consistency in the interpretation of European regulations, coupled with a lack of accountability in how the collaboration is governed.

Many regions across the globe are driving standardisation, including:

- W3C's PaymentRequest API. W3C has introduced a standard[12] candidate for Payment Requests that seeks to improve interactions during the online purchase process, reducing the risk of customers abandoning payments due to a broken or idiosyncratic form, providing a more consistent experience and enabling web merchants to use different payment methods.
- Single Euro Payment Area (SEPA).[13] The European Payments Council introduced SEPA in collaboration with member states, to harmonise electronic payments in the EU. SEPA provides rulebooks and guidelines for each of the electronic payment instrument to standardise payments processing across EU.
- ISO 20022[14]: This standard has gained momentum with many payment schemes using it: for example, SEPA and the Australian New Payments Platform. There are, however, still challenges related to regional differences that need to be addressed to achieve full harmonisation.
- Fast Identity Online (FIDO) Alliance[15]: The specifications and certifications developed by the Alliance enable an interoperable ecosystem of hardware-, mobile- and biometrics-based authenticators that can be used with many apps and websites.
- Open Banking Working Group (OBWG)[16]: The UK-based group has recommended the creation of standards for banks to share data securely with other stakeholders. The standard is expected to enter into force in 2019.

- Banking Industry Architecture Network (BIAN)[17]: This member-led group collaborates with different stakeholders to develop standards across banking domains including operations and execution, risk management and compliance.
- R3[18]: Corda is an open source, distributed ledger technology (DLT) that has been developed by a consortium of banks developing standards for DLT in financial services.

Crypto Payments and Blockchains

Bitcoin

Bitcoin, famously, was designed as a "peer-to-peer electronic cash system", that is, a system that provides a means for parties to transfer value between themselves without knowing (or trusting) one another and where a third party (i.e. a government or bank) cannot intercede to prevent that transaction happening.

A transfer of value is not a payment per se. Anyone can hand over legal tender to another, transferring legal ownership of that value, without goods or services in return. So it was with Bitcoin. By design, a Bitcoin wallet holder can send or receive some multiple/fraction of Bitcoin to another wallet holder, just by knowing their wallet address (i.e. their public key)—for now, let's ignore the fact that the user experience was (and still is) mostly terrible and prone to fat finger errors, confusion and "man in the middle" security threats.

This is not a familiar payments experience and won't entice mass adoption by millions of consumers wanting to use their Bitcoin to pay for coffee/beer/pizza, etc. So two Bitcoin Improvement Proposals, or BIPs, were proposed, called BIP70[19] (authored by Gavin Andresen and R3'S Mike Hearn) and BIP75[20] (authored by Netki's Justin Newton et al.). The BIPs, collectively, are how the developer community debate proposed changes to the Bitcoin protocol and network. These two BIPs are of particular interest, because they explain how a cryptocurrency (not just Bitcoin) can be turned into a legitimate payment network.

BIP70 and BIP75 describe protocols for communication between a merchant and their customer, giving both a better customer experience and better security against man-in-the-middle attacks, by extending Bitcoin to include Payment Request and acknowledgement messages.

1. Human-readable, secure payment destinations—customers will be asked to authorise payment to "example.com" instead of an inscrutable, 34-character Bitcoin address.
2. Secure proof of payment, which the customer can use in case of a dispute with the merchant.
3. Resistance from man-in-the-middle attacks that replace a merchant's Bitcoin address with an attacker's address before a transaction is authorised with a hardware wallet.
4. Payment received messages, so the customer knows immediately that the merchant has received and has processed (or is processing) their payment.
5. Refund addresses, automatically given to the merchant by the customer's wallet software, so merchants do not have to contact customers before refunding overpayments or orders that cannot be fulfilled for some reason.
6. BIP75 allows the requester (Sender) of a Payment Request to voluntarily sign the original request and provide a certificate to allow the payee to know the identity of who they are transacting with. This ensures that the payment details can only be seen by the participants in the transaction, and not by any third party; allows for store and forward servers to allow, for example, mobile wallets to sign and serve Payment Requests; and allows a sender of funds the option of sharing their identity with the receiver. This information could then be used to, among other things, allow for an open standards-based way for businesses to keep verifiable records of their financial transactions, to better meet the needs of accounting practices or other reporting and statutory requirements.

Many of the crypto community who have advocated Bitcoin and other public, permissionless DLT technology hold strong beliefs about the right to anonymity on the network. BIP75 received much criticism from them for daring to introduce the concept of digital identity, which some believed compromised this right. Finding a consistent, portable and secure way for users of online systems to maintain control over attributes of their identity without putting themselves at risk of identity theft, however, is key to the future success of many world-improving Fintech use cases, and as we'll see, does not actually compromise anonymity.

The Bitcoin scaling issues, increasing transaction fees, and the subsequent hard-fork cloning into numerous wannabe alt-coins have quashed much of Satoshi Nakamoto's original Bitcoin dream. The laws of unintended consequences have overtaken Bitcoin, turning it into a speculative new asset class, but not one with which anyone sane would want to pay for their coffee. In fact, many businesses that initially took Bitcoin in payments have stopped doing so, because of its volatility.

Bitcoin's blockchain has become a speculative instrument: digital gold, reserve currency for other cryptos—everything but a "peer-to-peer electronic cash system". A commonly quoted statistic is that Bitcoin processes approximately 7 transactions per second (the average is closer to 3.5), whereas Visa processes up to 20,000 transactions (average 7,000) per second, so Bitcoin itself could never compete with the card networks even at today's levels of use—let alone support micropayments and the anticipated exponential growth in global electronic transactions. This has made Bitcoin unlikely to ever be a near-real-time peer-to-peer international payment system, but the collective Bitcoin developer hive mind is addressing this, through additional layers and what are known as sidechains; for Bitcoin, the Lightning network is being positioned as the solution.

The Lightning network[21] is based on the premise that not all transactions need be recorded on the Bitcoin blockchain. In simplest terms, it's a payment channel between transacting parties that records its opening on the blockchain. The parties can then transact any number of times through this payment channel over any period from hours to decades. Then, when the parties decide that they don't want to transact any more, the final status of the transactions is written to the blockchain and the payment channel is closed.

So what of Bitcoin's much vaunted ability to make cross-border payments in real time very cheaply? Coins.ph[22] has made very good business from using Bitcoin as payment rails in the Philippines and Thailand. With a focus on financial inclusion, Coins has the admirable mission of bringing financial services to Southeast Asia's 300+ million unbanked.

Coins.ph enables customers, including those without bank accounts, to access financial services such as remittances, mobile air-time, bill payments and even game credits from their mobile phone. With 2 million customers, their platform processes thousands of transactions a day and uses existing retailers (such as 7-Eleven) for deposits and withdrawals.

This approach appears to work well for Coins.ph. However, many of the real costs for banks in cross-border money transfers lie in meeting both domestic and international regulatory requirements and in the identifying and compliant onboarding of customers. Currently, Bitcoin and similar cryptocurrencies only address a small fraction of these real costs, such as the actual transaction cost, and don't provide savings over newer, completely digital money transfer schemes. In fact, with Bitcoin transaction fees climbing ever higher it's unlikely that soon, this approach will be competitive at all—although other cryptocurrencies, such as Bitcoin Cash, Ethereum or Litecoin, could potentially be a replacement for Bitcoin.

International money transfers need local sources of liquidity, but Bitcoin (or any other cryptocurrency) is not the world's reserve currency—and won't be dethroning USD for that honour any time soon. Bitcoin transactions are still too slow to execute in and out of fiat currencies, and a final exchange rate (and the ultimate cost) is often not known until up to 30 minutes or more after the trade has been executed. In a world of extreme cryptocurrency volatility, this adds additional risk and potentially cost.

This, of course, is only relevant when you withdraw the cryptocurrency into fiat cash. If there is an option to hold (or "hodl" in the crypto vernacular) the crypto in the wallet or even use it to purchase goods directly, then the risk to the recipient diminishes. Sadly, most developing nations do not yet have the opportunity to buy their staple foods in Bitcoin or their public transport in Dogecoin. However, Bitcoin's underlying technologies—blockchain and distributed ledgers—do have the potential to revolutionise financial services and we are already seeing applications of blockchain as an alternative to traditional payment rails, in illiquid, difficult and non-cost-effective corridors—and especially so with crypto-exchange controlled currencies.

Mojaloop

The Bill & Melinda Gates Foundation[23] has, since 2015 through its Level One Project, been working on ways to create a playbook to establishing national digital financial services systems, enabled by shared, open, standards-based components, and governed by its direct participants.[24] In October 2017, the Foundation launched Mojaloop,[25] an open source payment platform designed to encourage the development of interoperable payments networks for the world's unbanked.

Mojaloop's mobile payment software includes the Interledger Protocol (ILP) technology built by payments startup Ripple.[26] Interoperability is one of the holy grails of DLT, now that it is widely agreed that there will not be a single global blockchain, but many, possibly thousands with specific purposes. Mojaloop wants to link financial institutions, payment providers and other companies that provide payment services and share information with the ILP being used as a solution to the interoperability barriers that banks and providers have traditionally faced. Perhaps the ILP will be the first step in enabling interoperability between traditional payments, mobile payments and blockchain-based systems. Mojaloop is an exciting project and may become the platform of choice for developers focusing on financial inclusion use cases.

Other Cryptocurrency Payment Solutions

Other "top 10" public cryptocurrencies specifically offering payments use cases are Ethereum, Ripple and Stellar:

Ethereum

Ethereum[27] has a similar problem to Bitcoin in that its network gets congested and its Proof of Work consensus protocol can be slow. Its equivalent to Bitcoin's Lightning is Raiden[28] which, when delivered, claims it will enable near-instant, low-fee and scalable payments and will be compatible with any ERC20 compatible token (those tokens generally issued in ICOs and then traded on secondary markets via crypto trading platforms).

Ripple

Ripple has targeted the slow and opaque international money transfer process via SWIFT and built a blockchain-based system that banks use to issue IOUs and settle debts. The Ripple token, XRP, is used to pay fees on the Ripple network and as a "bridge currency" for value transfers between any two institutions that don't have a trusted relationship. There is much debate in the community about quite how many banks are actually using Ripple, and whether XRP is needed at all, other than as a speculative asset beloved of crypto traders.

Stellar

Stellar is an open source blockchain-based protocol and infrastructure for payments, designed to make it easy for financial institutions to issue tokens representing fiat currencies. It has a stated focus on financial inclusion and applications in developing economies. Stellar also features a built-in distributed exchange which allows people to seamlessly convert from one currency to another during cross-border or cross-currency transactions.

These blockchain-based cryptocurrencies can all, to a greater or lesser degree, trace their heritage back to Bitcoin; they have similar scaling and performance issues and similar second-layer sidechain-like workarounds to the problem. However, blockchains are not the only game in the Fintech town, and there are alternate crypto-technology proposals such as the

Swirlds[29] HashGraph or IOTA's Tangle[30] that could very well resolve the scaling and performance issues in the very near future.

A Convergence of Old and New

The typical user experience of a crypto wallet owner is not good. Buying crypto through exchanges is frustratingly inconsistent, and with the recent demand from speculative investors, there's a long lead time for processing accounts. Once you have an account on an exchange, then buying Bitcoin (or some other token which the exchange offers) is relatively straightforward, but trying to exchange it back to fiat and transfer to a bank account is often not easy. Coupled with the intricacies of personal key management and entirely new conceptual models for financial services, it can all leave your head spinning.

Entrepreneurs often find it easier to take new products to consumers if they look familiar, and we are now seeing this happen in the crypto space. Many Fintechs are offering debit cards onto which you can load your crypto (via a crypto wallet) and then spend it normally in retail outlets. In the background, the crypto is converted to fiat at the time of transaction, so the card sales interaction is normal. These crypto card services are offered by a number of organisations including Monaco, TokenCard and TenX.

Rumours of Their Demise Are Exaggerated

The incumbent international card networks and SWIFT will not, however, go down without a fight and have responded to the threat as follows:

- **Visa** has made multiple patent applications for blockchain-based technology and has launched the trial phase of its business-to-business payments system built with blockchain startup chain.
- **Mastercard** has similarly applied for many blockchain patents showing that they are looking at the technology for uses from easing payment settlement times to building refund-capable services for cryptocurrency users. Mastercard has joined the Ethereum Enterprise Alliance and opened access to its blockchain APIs, indicating it wants to focus on business-to-business and cross-border payments.
- **American Express**, by contrast, has joined the Linux Foundation-led Hyperledger blockchain project and has run a pilot using Ripple's blockchain to connect Santander clients in Europe and the USA.

- **SWIFT** has had something of an on/off relationship with blockchain, and there was some confusion in 2017 about whether their Global Payments Initiative (GPI) was actually a blockchain project or not. The first phase of this has now been launched with 120 transaction banks from Europe, Asia Pacific, Africa and the Americas, and SWIFT claims that GPI dramatically improves the customer experience in cross-border payments by increasing the speed, transparency and end-to-end tracking of cross-border payments—all on a blockchain... perhaps.

Conclusion: Future (Im)Perfect

The future is near, but is it as simple as stating the future of payments will be mobile, peer-to-peer payments on a blockchain? Well, no, it isn't.

Payments technology has evolved rapidly in recent years, from cash-based to digital and from batch to instant. From the commercial landscape of payments of the Old World, with central banks, centralised infrastructure, distributed commercial banks and payments services, together with some of the technical challenges in adapting to new standards, such as instant payments, and growing customer expectations in an instant and mobile world.

A new payments ecosystem is emerging, created by higher corporate and consumer expectations of value-added services, the ever-changing regulatory landscape, the emergence of Fintechs, and an increase in payments-enabling technologies that has provided alternative methods of moving value, including non-bank payments and blockchain-based transactions, and these are bypassing payments infrastructure and the banking system.

Open APIs, instant payments, blockchain technology and regulatory standardisation are key enablers of the new payments ecosystem. However, there are still issues, such as a lack of harmonisation and standardisation as well as ever-growing cyber security risks and scaling the platforms to meet the expected exponential growth in demand, which are slowing ecosystem development.

The ability for Fintechs to differentiate is amplified as technology, and friendly regulators lower the hurdles into financial services. Banks and payments companies must increasingly focus on improving customer interactions, particularly in an environment where they have limited opportunities to connect with consumers. To stay in the game, payments providers will need to invest in Machine Learning-based fraud management techniques, robotic process automation (RPA) tools, new customer engagement strategies, alternative risk models in an attempt to innovate and differentiate on consumer interaction. Time to market will also be key and will continue to be heavily dependent on the agility and cost with which they can update or replace their legacy infrastructure.

Balances in bank accounts are no longer based on units of currency, and fractional reserve lending has abstracted value from "real money", with implications for a move towards ownership-based units such as cryptocurrency.

Regulations designed for bordered, national currencies are failing to adapt to evolving payments, both from a currency and from a payment management perspective, and the changes that will be needed. However, there are risks to individuals and businesses in moving to payments outside of the traditional banking system, as well as this transition's likely impact to the banking sector.

Payments in the new payments landscape will continue to evolve and must stay relevant to consumers, be built on modern digital systems and offer experience-based rewards and insights such as budgeting and analysis.

The near future is a Utopian/"Black Mirror" world where IoT devices working on your behalf, controlled by an AI brain that you have delegated your identity to, make micropayments to other devices all for the betterment of the lives of you and your loved ones. Your toaster, FitBit and Tesla will be part of your web of devices ensuring you have everything you need, constantly negotiating best prices and executing the agreed payments for (respectively) artisan bread deliveries, health insurance and highway overtaking rights on your behalf!

Notes

1. Bank for International Settlements. https://www.bis.org/. Accessed 10 January 2018.
2. Bank of England Payments and Settlements (BoE). https://www.bankofengland.co.uk/payment-and-settlement. Accessed 10 January 2018.
3. US Federal Reserve Payments Systems (Federal Reserve). https://www.federalreserve.gov/paymentsystems.htm. Accessed 10 January 2018.
4. SWIFT (Society for Worldwide Interbank Financial Telecommunication) Homepage. https://www.swift.com. Accessed 12 January 2018.
5. Clearing, Investopedia. https://www.investopedia.com/terms/c/clearing.asp. Accessed 12 January 2018.
6. Settlement of Transactions and Delivery of Securities, Investopedia. https://www.investopedia.com/exam-guide/series-26/recordkeeping-rules/settlement-delivery.asp. Accessed 12 January 2018.

7. World Payments Report 2017. https://www.worldpaymentsreport.com. Accessed 10 January 2018.
8. Gartner Says 8.4 Billion Connected "Things" Will Be in Use in 2017, up 31% from 2016. *Gartner*, 7 February 2017. https://www.gartner.com/newsroom/id/3598917. Accessed 12 January 2018.
9. Visa Ready Homepage. https://visaready.visa.com/. Accessed 12 January 2018.
10. Payment Services (PSD2)—Directive (EU). https://ec.europa.eu/info/law/payment-services-psd-2-directive-eu-2015-2366_en. Accessed 12 January 2018.
11. Empowering Consumers Through Open Banking, the Hon Scott Morrison MP, Treasurer of the Commonwealth of Australia, 20 July 2017. http://sjm.ministers.treasury.gov.au/media-release/065-2017/. Accessed 12 January 2018.
12. Payment Request API Standard (W3). https://www.w3.org/TR/payment-request/. Accessed 12 January 2018.
13. SEPA Homepage (European Commission). https://ec.europa.eu/info/business-economy-euro/banking-and-finance/consumer-finance-and-payments/payment-services/single-euro-payments-area-sepa_en. Accessed 12 January 2018.
14. ISO 20022 Homepage. https://www.iso20022.org/. Accessed 12 January 2018.
15. FIDO Alliance Homepage. https://fidoalliance.org/. Accessed 12 January 2018.
16. Open Banking Working Group Homepage (Payments UK). https://www.paymentsuk.org.uk/policy/european-and-uk-developments/payments-uk-help-ensure-best-outcomes-uk-customers-multi. Accessed 12 January 2018.
17. BIAN Homepage. https://www.bian.org/. Accessed 12 January 2018.
18. R3 Homepage. https://www.r3.com/. Accessed 12 January 2018.
19. Bitcoin Improvement Proposal 70: Payment Protocol. https://github.com/bitcoin/bips/blob/master/bip-0070.mediawiki. Accessed 12 January 2018.
20. Bitcoin Improvement Proposal 75: Payment Protocol Extension. https://github.com/bitcoin/bips/blob/master/bip-0075.mediawiki. Accessed 12 January 2018.
21. Lightning network Homepage. https://lightning.network/. Accessed 12 January 2018.
22. Coins.ph Homepage. https://coins.ph/. Accessed 12 January 2018.
23. Bill and Melinda Gates Foundation Homepage. https://www.gatesfoundation.org/. Accessed 12 January 2018.
24. Level One Project (Bill and Melinda Gates Foundation). https://levelone-project.org/. Accessed 12 January 2018.
25. Mojaloop Homepage (Bill and Melinda Gates Foundation). https://leveloneproject.org/mojaloop/. Accessed 12 January 2018.

26. Ripple Homepage. https://ripple.com/. Accessed 12 January 2018.
27. Ethereum Homepage. https://www.ethereum.org/. Accessed 12 January 2018.
28. Radien Homepage. https://raiden.network/. Accessed 12 January 2018.
29. Swirlds Homepage. http://www.swirlds.com/. Accessed 12 January 2018.
30. Popov, S. (2017, October 1). The Tangle. IOTA. https://iota.org/IOTA_Whitepaper.pdf. Accessed 12 January 2018.

Further Reading

European Central Bank Market Infrastructure and Payments Page (ECB). https://www.ecb.europa.eu/paym/html/index.en.html. Accessed 12 January 2018.

Payments UK's Introduction to Payment Systems and Schemes (Payments UK). http://www.accesstopaymentsystems.co.uk/introduction-payment-systems. Accessed 12 January 2018.

5

Central Bank Digital Currencies and Cryptocurrencies

We briefly described the potential impact of Central Bank issued crypto-currencies in Chapter 2. In this chapter, we explore the emerging trend for central banks to experiment with digital versions of fiat currencies and cryptocurrencies. We discuss the opportunities presented by cryptocurrencies for central banks and individuals, together with the risks. We explore the possible impacts to existing commercial banking systems and why the structure of government, central banks, regulators and commercial banking in different countries creates more or less challenging environments for the issuance of Central Bank Cryptocurrencies/Digital Currencies (CBCCs, or CBDCs as we use in this book). We examine the opportunities and risks in countries suffering from political or financial instability, and with a large unbanked population. We present alternative models with greater or lesser involvement of central and commercial banks and discuss the pros and cons. Finally, we discuss the countries already moving towards digital currency issuance and the implications for the near future.

Note: there is an increasing trend to make "cryptocurrency" and "digital currency" synonymous terms. This is not strictly correct; "cryptocurrency" refers to types of currency underpinned by crypto-technology (though not only distributed ledger technology), while "digital currency" is a superset of digital value which includes cryptocurrencies, but also other types of digital exchange of value based on other technologies. However, many of the banks are using "CBDC" to cover a variety of potential digital or crypto options, and the term is now used by many to mean Central Bank Cryptocurrency,

© The Author(s) 2018
S. Blakstad and R. Allen, *FinTech Revolution*,
https://doi.org/10.1007/978-3-319-76014-8_5

so for the purposes of this book and for simplicity, we have assumed that CBDC is a type of cryptocurrency issued by a central bank.[1]

Central Banks and Cryptocurrencies

On the surface, central banks and cryptocurrencies belong to different worlds. Why would a central bank want to get involved with something like Bitcoin, that exists thanks to its properties of being anonymous, disintermediated and unregulated? Before explaining this growing trend, let's use Bitcoin as an example and consider its characteristics in comparison with central bank currencies.

- No intermediary is needed; all transactions are peer to peer
- Units of value are owned by the holders—one's holding of Bitcoin is for specific units and is based on the transaction history of those units
- Transactions themselves are transparent to all parties, though the parties themselves are (pseudo) anonymous
- Transactions cannot be altered or changed (they are immutable in a public, distributed ledger) because each block containing the transactions relies on the previous block not changing
- Transaction throughput is low, although processing is fast compared to some traditional batch-based payments networks
- Transaction fees are determined by the network using "Dutch auction" techniques—the higher the fee you attach to your transaction the greater the chance of it being included in a block
- The value is not pinned to any country's economic policy (as with fiat currencies), asset or index, so volatility, driven by the market, is high and speculative
- Anyone can set up a wallet and participate with no entry requirements

Central banks, by contrast, are responsible for currencies that are national and controlled, and typically are issued in both physical and digital format, with different characteristics, i.e.:

- Underpinned by, and delimited by, national or regional monetary policy—increases or decreases to volume or value usually determined by national governments
- Value fluctuations often controlled by international agreements

- Exchange rates aggregated across multiple financial institutions and exchanges
- Identified as the currency in which taxes for a nation or region must be paid
- Issued as physical currency, which has no customer ownership barriers
- Issued in electronic form through trusted agents (usually banks) which have high barriers to entry for account ownership
- Carry the risk of physical fraud (counterfeiting)
- Carry the risk of double spending of electronic money when using slow batch settlement systems and complicated reconciliation processes

Despite these differences, and because of some of them, many central banks are exploring the merits of issuing a central bank, government controlled, digital version of their national fiat currency. This has grown from early experimental research and speculation started in 2014, to assertions by some central banks and important international bodies such as the IMF, that cryptocurrencies will form part of their strategy in the future; a future which is likely to become a reality in 2018.

CBDC Opportunities

CBDCs issued by central banks would inherit some properties of borderless currencies like Bitcoin, while other characteristics will be determined by the banks and have more in common with a traditional fiat currency; the obvious one being the value of the currency, which would be pegged to a fiat currency or national monetary policy in some way, to make it a useful tool for transactions. The key advantage for central banks is that digital money is programmable, meaning that its behaviour can be controlled so that it operates in predictable ways under predefined conditions; major differences to Bitcoin are likely to be:

- Pegged to a local fiat currency in value
- Can be used for paying national or regional taxes
- Availability set by central bank and government (although a number of potential models are options, explored below)
- Money supply can be controlled by the central bank according to its purpose, use and fiscal/monetary policies of the government
- Exchange rates match existing fiat exchange rates

- Issuance controlled to central banks and authorised nominees (most likely commercial banks)
- Citizens would be able to have accounts at the central bank

While the differences to physical fiat currencies (cash) are:

- Cannot be forged or "photocopied"
- Transactions are traceable/auditable
- Value can be controlled, e.g. interest can be imposed
- Transfer of value can be based on predetermined conditions, e.g. distribution of welfare benefits
- Beneficiaries can be controlled—certain parties could be prevented from receiving the currency

Conversely, the differences between existing digital currency such as the electronic dollars or pounds in your bank account (the most common form of currency in use today) and a central bank cryptocurrency (i.e. a CBDC) are:

- Transactions are peer to peer without the need for an intermediary
- Currency is ownership based—you own specific units of the currency, rather than just a balance which can be made up of an arbitrary set of units
- Settlement is instant rather than having to wait for a bank batch run, and irreversible, like physical currency
- Deposits do not need to be held with a commercial bank
- Double spending is prevented

CBDC Benefits

Many central banks have already been experimenting with blockchain technology to replace ageing real time gross settlement and trade settlement systems[2] and several central banks have published papers or statements of intent regarding issuance, but the models vary and to date we haven't seen a consistent approach emerging. Some of the fundamental problems regarding ownership and privacy are political hot potatoes, while the risk to fractional reserves is taken more seriously in some countries than others; conversely, reduced transaction cost, greater availability and reduced collateral requirements may all present macroeconomic benefits.

Central banks stand to benefit from CBDCs in several ways:

- Greater control of the relationship between monetary policy and implementation such as interest rates, and in particular negative interest rates, the flow of cash through quantitative easing (QE) and imposition of policy directly into the value of currency.

  Today, central banks are prevented from imposing negative interest rates below a certain level (presumed to be around—0.5%) because of the risk that people will withdraw money in physical cash, which is not subject to interest rate penalties, rather than leaving it on deposit in accounts where they are charged. To date, while some banks have charged negative interest on deposits, so far this has only been attempted on commercial deposits, as the common assumption is that individual savers would be incentivised to withdraw cash and put capital ratios at risk. In a scenario where the "cash" is a digital currency, then these penalties could be charged against any currency holding, reducing this risk (although flight to alternative currencies would remain a risk).

  Quantitative easing is the governmental strategy of choice to impact relative interest rates in an economic environment where interest rates cannot fall far below zero, but today this involves transferring government bonds to the central banks' balance sheet, which in turn relies on the commercial banking system to translate this to a transfer of cash into the real economy; while incentives are in place for them to do so, historically there has been a tendency for commercial banks to increase their own balance sheets in times of quantitative easing. Issuance of a CBDC as QE would directly increase the money supply without the need to rely on commercial banks to play their part.

  Positive interest could also be added directly to CBDCs via automated rules, encouraging savers directly rather than relying on banks to provide incentives to savers. Most proposals set the automated rates of interest lower than central bank policy, to keep commercial bank deposits competitive and attractive to savers, but again this could reduce the reliance on commercial banks' good behaviour to incentivise savers.
- Traceability and taxation opportunities

  One of the major opportunities offered by CBDCs over standard digital balances is the traceability of transaction history, which instead of being maintained within individual banks' ledgers, is available (in a model like Bitcoin) on all nodes of a shared ledger. This would allow central banks and other authorised institutions, such as tax authorities, full visibility of transactions at an aggregate level, enabling better understanding of cash flow for individuals and corporations. This would also allow for much better detection of fraud and the ability to prevent money laundering.

Another key benefit for central banks is better understanding of money movements, providing rich data for determining policy, and in particular for taxation.

Governments would have a new opportunity to use this traceability to reconcile tax records for individuals and corporations, and possibly to levy taxes at source in more efficient ways than the current centralised system, which requires coordination of multiple ledgers across many parties including individuals, employers, businesses, banks and government, with expensive and lengthy reconciliation processes representing major cost to economies. This traceability also represents a major opportunity to reduce tax avoidance, given sufficient use of CBDCs proportionately to the money supply.

- Greater utility of money supply

   Reductions in transaction costs and the reduced need for intermediaries in applying fiscal policy are predicted to increase the usability of money in the system significantly, allowing for greater liquidity which, in turn, reduces cost of both spending and borrowing, leading to greater deposits and lending. Increased guarantees of tax revenues, reduced cost of reconciliation and a higher proportion of tax at source would also increase the supply and therefore utility of money in the general economy, reducing costs and stimulating overall GDP.

For individuals, the benefits and risks are more nuanced:

- Reduced need for traditional bank accounts

   With CBDCs, ownership is based on a store of units of currency held in a digital wallet, so individuals could hold a store of central bank currency outside of the traditional banking system. This means an opportunity for unbanked individuals to maintain a store of central bank currency, without having to qualify for a bank account, which would reduce the risk of theft and offer greater convenience and utility to people over using cash. For users of alternate, parallel currencies such as M-PESA, it offers greater fungibility, taking away the need to exchange (usually via a booth) to physical fiat cash. And for customers who have grown up as digital natives, or for those who are disillusioned with banks, it removes the need to open an account with a traditional bank.

   Central banks could provide an account as part of any individual's citizenship and verified using their national identity credentials (such as passport, national identity number, national insurance number)—this would be made even more frictionless if the country has adopted a digital identity trust framework.

The disadvantage of holding deposits outside of banks is that savings are not protected today by national deposit guarantees; central banks will need to address this issue before non-bank deposits can become a significant store of value.

- Reduced transaction costs and increased speeds
Peer-to-peer spending between individuals and from individuals to merchants would allow value to be transferred directly without the need for processing through a bank's ledgers, credit card network, central bank systems, etc. as they are today. While instant payments systems exist today, these still involve the traditional bank ledger system. A peer-to-peer system outside of bank ledgers would reduce the cost of transactions and take the need for reconciliation away, meaning that even high-value transactions could be performed swiftly and without intermediaries. Much bank reconciliation against transactions today is designed to ensure money can legitimately be transferred, and to reverse any errors caused by fraud or double spending. Using CBDCs, like cash, value can only be transferred once, and if it is valid in the first place, removing much of the need for reconciliation. The downside for consumers is that transactions, once made, cannot be reversed—however, presumably this would be addressed through existing consumer protection legislation with refunds being available via "equal and opposite" transactions between the parties.

- Reduced cost of borrowing
While the realignment of a portion of national value towards CBDCs would impact commercial banks' capital ratios and therefore their capacity for lending, the direct availability of CBDCs for non-bank lenders, together with reduced reversibility of transactions, cryptocurrency traceability and the opportunity to provide full automated platforms, would allow non-bank lenders to reduce their rates below that of commercial banks and, even for high-risk borrowers, make the cost of borrowing more affordable.

- Greater potential for social control
In addition to traceability meaning nowhere to hide for potential tax evaders, impacting large parts of many economies which currently run on a cash basis, cryptocurrencies can be parameterised so that only trusted parties can use them. While this has benefits for governments, it creates a risk of unethical social control, for example by excluding certain groups from using it, creating social and economic divisions between the "haves" and "have nots". This parameterisation is likely to vary from country to country, depending on social attitudes and level of government intervention.

- More marketplace and circular economy opportunities
  The general availability of CBDCs and the ability to manage with fully accountable, sovereign currency outside of standard banking and payments systems, will allow for the growth of alternative marketplace models, including peer-to-peer retail and lending, while the wallet providers becoming integrated into normal retail and commercial financial management will allow for more peer-to-peer and circular marketplace models, transacting behaviours and other types of asset in exchange for sovereign cryptocurrency, as we explore in greater detail in later chapters.

The possible impacts to existing commercial banking systems depend largely on which model is adopted, and how far commercial banks are embedded into the operation of the CBDC, but implications could be more negative, including:

- Reduction in capital ratios leading to greater cost of lending
  If, as is both implied by relevant studies and by our own observations of trends towards non-bank wallets, the issuance of central bank cryptocurrencies results in more individuals and organisations holding deposits in non-bank accounts, this could have a significant impact on the level of deposits held by commercial banks and, therefore, their capital reserves. As there is a direct relationship between the capital reserves and the amount they can issue in loans, this would both reduce their capacity for commercial lending and push cost of lending banks up for banks, with a greater reliance on wholesale business.
  Barrdear and Kumhof[3] of the BoE (2016) hold that this reduction in deposits would be more than offset by the stimulation offered by greater utility of money and that commercial bank deposits would actually increase. They present some compelling arguments, although their model assumes efficient markets and a sovereign bond backed currency.
  Increased costs of bank lending and the direct availability of CBDCs to non-bank lenders would also allow the cost of non-bank lending to reduce, potentially increasing the availability of non-bank and non-traditional lenders, particularly peer-to-peer lenders.
- Collapse of traditional commercial payments models
  As observed above, bank payments systems are complex and rely on a system of reconciliation with central banks to validate customer transactions, based on the current centralised ledger system. This has led to the development of robust but expensive to run systems within banks and in

national payments infrastructure, which is currently supported by banks charging for making payments. The introduction of a peer-to-peer payments network, which would significantly reduce the cost for consumers, would almost certainly reduce the volumes of commercial bank payments to a level which threatens their financial viability.

Although the introduction of CBDCs can be seen as an opportunity to replace legacy payments systems, for the banks this would be a painful and expensive transition, as they will be required to maintain existing systems for as long as customers need them, at increasing cost. A clear transitional plan would be required for countries with the more mature and sophisticated payments infrastructures.

The main challenge for analysts in all central banks is that there is no existing model on which they can base their predictions; all agree that CBDCs will not behave like Bitcoin, and all agree that they aren't the same as existing bank digital money or cash, but beyond that there are many different models and motivations.

Why Would Central Banks Issue Cryptocurrencies?

While the opportunities described above are significant, the risks are also great—one of the biggest risks is imposing an untried system onto a financial system that is in delicate equilibrium, the workings of which are not fully understood by anyone. Models are based on assumptions, many of which are known to be approximations, because modelling the real-world economy is too hard. Much of the best modelling and analysis has also been done with a strong classical economics flavour, which focuses on the behaviour of markets but less on the behaviour of individuals; with a new technology and new form of currency, the behaviour of individuals will be critical to understanding its implications, and that is why several countries are now running pilots, to understand real-world implications of the new models.

As we observed above, the introduction of CBDCs has implications for the entire banking system and for individuals, while it will fundamentally change the role of the central bank in any economy that issues it. Different parties in the economy have different needs and motivations, and these will vary from country to country due to cultural and regulatory drivers; here, we present a few considerations for those parties:

- **Central banks** are concerned with maintaining stability in the economy. In most countries, as well as directly issuing currency notes, they authorise the supply of money through the commercial banking system, as well as managing policy including interest rates.
- **Governments** are responsible for fiscal policy, usually in collaboration with central banks, and seek to achieve political goals through how the financial system works, while they are concerned with maintaining financial stability and a healthy economy.
- **Regulators** often run as a subset of central banks, governments or both, are responsible for overseeing commercial operations to ensure consumers are not exploited; they set and agree rules for operations of commercial banks and are responsible for inspecting them. In their role as guardians of customer rights, they are also concerned with encouraging competition in the banking sector.
- **Commercial banks** have to act within the law and regulations set by the government, regulator and central bank, but their primary goal is to create wealth and growth for their shareholders. Banks are heavily regulated, largely because of the scale and impact of their operations. As banks are also authorised to create money under the fractional reserve system, they are subject to additional regulations regarding competition and control of money supply.
- **Non-bank financial players** are also motivated by profit, however, because they're not able to issue money and perform other higher-risk activities that require a banking licence, are operating under much less stringent regulations than full-service banks.
- **Corporate customers** are corporations and other organisations such as charities, NGOs, educational establishments and government departments who handle large amounts of money and need banks to manage it for them in wholesale banking operations. Corporate customers are generally regarded as "sticky" because they are integrated with a large range of banks' services, however, this is changing as more services beyond the traditional banks become available.
- **Retail and business banking customers** are individuals and small businesses with access to a simpler range of banking services. Retail and business customers have been targets of many non-bank financial players and new banks, largely due to the limited services offered to them by traditional banks.
- **Investors** (financial or corporate) may invest in government debt (bonds) and banks for a stable return on investment.

All of these players will influence how CBDCs are implemented in different jurisdictions and will behave in different ways in different places, so there is no standard blueprint for what will succeed.

Developed Economies and CBDCs

Many mature, democratic economies have a significant share of the economy in commercial banking: in some key economies, for example, the UK and the USA, commercial banking represents up to 10% of GDP and tax revenues. Clearly, putting the sector at risk through a significant injection of CBDCs is something that central banks, with their responsibility to economic stability, would be unwilling to do without strong political backing, and this is unlikely to come unless politicians are very confident of a positive outcome, or otherwise persuaded of the necessity of the change.

Democratic countries with clear segregation of central bank, regulator and governments are often characterised by politicians with a strong public agenda but lacking expert knowledge. In these democracies, highly complex economic arguments are necessarily presented in more black and white terms, which can lead to partisan politics having an unnecessarily high degree of influence, and this can also delay decisions or lead to misguided decisions. Politicians lacking expert knowledge will normally, sensibly, err on the side of caution with untried technologies.

Countries with a high level of collaboration between the commercial banking system and central banks, regulators and governments are also more likely to encourage regular dialogue and expert knowledge in elected officials. The downside of this is that public opinion may have relatively little voice; however, from a CBDC perspective, a close collaboration between central and commercial banks presents an opportunity to exert greater control over such a system, allowing for adjustments and reducing the risk somewhat.

Countries with less mature markets, or smaller countries with a flatter banking system, may also be able to exert a greater level of control than larger countries, again allowing them to experiment and adjust, de-risking the exercise to an extent.

Countries with a very high incidence of digital payments today will see relatively low adoption barriers for consumers and banks (depending on their level of participation), together with an already high compliance in filing taxes, so may see less impact than other countries.

Countries where consumers have access to a large number of alternative providers, and where customers are suspicious of banks, are already seeing a movement towards non-traditional financial services; this could be accelerated by the move, putting commercial banks at risk.

Developing Economies and CBDCs

Countries with large unbanked populations, highly unstable currencies or very immature markets, may see the greatest benefits from the issuance of CBDCs. In countries with high proportions of unbanked people, cash is a critical commodity but also subject to fraud, corruption and theft, which makes it a high-risk commodity. Most workers are paid in cash, creating risk to managing payroll as large amounts have to be transported, while large sections of the economy exist below the taxation radar.

Unbanked people can be vulnerable to exploitation by unscrupulous middle men and unable to build identity or financial records, preventing them from breaking out of poverty. Women are disproportionately disadvantaged as they typically have proportionally less access to finance, especially in developing economies. As we'll discuss in more detail in Chapter 7, with M-PESA in Kenya and other countries, giving the unbanked access to basic financial services can empower entrepreneurs, especially women, to grow businesses and rise through the credit ceiling. Changing payroll from a lorry-load of cash shipped weekly to a plantation, to payments paid electronically to a secure digital wallet, would significantly help the poorest workers in those circumstances, reducing the opportunity for fraud and exploitation—as well as reducing operating costs of businesses.

The benefits to currencies with extreme inflation or volatility are also clear from a government and central bank perspective, as are opportunities to reduce cartel, government or mafia corruption by monitoring and controlling payments.

Many of the world's developing nations are the ones most severely impacted by crises—natural disasters, war and other humanitarian catastrophes. At these times, national infrastructures break down while citizens lose access to bank accounts or any other store of wealth, along with identity credentials, leaving them with nothing at the time when it is most needed. Anything they can physically take with them is vulnerable to theft and unscrupulous parties seeking to gain from the chaos. Although not a panacea for strife, in a nation with a CBDC, money could be distributed easily and quickly via basic mobile phones, that could be distributed by government or humanitarian relief organisations. We expand on this idea in Chapter 7.

Developing economies typically have less mature capital markets and less powerful regulation, which creates an opportunity for CBDCs to achieve rapid adoption; as with most emerging financial paradigms, we are likely to see some of the earliest CBDCs being issued in countries with some of the most extreme needs. However, the combination of low barriers and burning platform also means there is a risk that they could be implemented without sufficient research, piloting or due diligence.

The other risk in unregulated or less regulated markets is the element of social control, especially in countries where central government has a distant relationship with democracy. CBDCs could present a powerful tool for governments to impose political control, use currency as a tool for coercion and exclude "undesirables" from access to basic financial inclusion. This would be as far away from the original libertarian dream of the Bitcoin founders as one can get—a centrally controlled, government-manipulated cryptocurrency being used to subvert democracy and control populations.

So, while the potential benefits to people in developing economies are significant, so are the risks. As we've seen with the rapid adoption of mobile money, developing economies may be both early movers and rapid adopters of CBDCs, even if the solution is imperfect.

Options for CBDC Implementation

As we've discussed, there are many different models open to central banks; from a reserve of fiat currency held in a kind of giant escrow, with equivalent value being issued as CBDC tokens, to the Bank of England recommendation of issuing against government debt; hub and spoke or centralised models; use of different actors (commercial banks, Fintechs, etc.) in the financial system; and a huge variety of models regarding control, auditability, interest rates, automated taxation and the other things we have covered above.

The use of commercial banks in a hub and spoke model for issuance of cryptocurrencies both for commercial and personal use is a feature of many of the proposed national examples that we describe below; this model partially mitigates the risks associated with CBDCs drawing funds away from fractional reserve deposits, although this mitigation is subject to design considerations.

Cryptocurrency-based value systems, instead of being pinned directly to national fiat currencies, could also be based on a variety of alternative underlying assets/indices, and span different geographies to traditional fiat currencies. For example, a currency based on the International Monetary Fund's special drawing rights basket of five major currencies, which is currently a reserve currency equivalent used to stabilise global values post-Bretton Woods, would represent an international, stable and globally transactable fiat.[4] Alternatively, CBDCs backed by internationally transactable commodities such as gold or other commodities may lack the stability of economically significant fiat currencies in the short term, but would represent a globally recognised asset. We explore asset-backed cryptocurrencies in greater depth in Chapter 8, and we anticipate there will be a convergence of use cases across asset based and behavioural coins over time, which should provide an opportunity for national currencies to benefit from some of their strengths.

Another alternative approach would be for countries to collaborate on regional cryptocurrencies—e.g. an alliance of West or East African nations, Caribbean states or South Pacific Islands. These could be issued in parallel with their individual fiat currencies, reducing trade friction and, over time, less reliance on the post-Bretton Woods dependence on the US dollar. This regional cryptocurrency approach is likely to arise over time, either in parallel with, or as the result of collaboration between, national fiat CBDCs; while other blocs, such as the EURO/EEA, which already exist in today's fiat system, would be natural candidates for regional CBDCs.

Technological Considerations

If we put the selection of actual technology (e.g. blockchain) aside and, like IT systems engineers, consider the needs for CBDCs, what are the actual requirements that need to be met?

For these purposes, let us consider a CBDC to be universally accessible, and widely used by individuals as well as businesses—rather than institutional investors and commercial banks. The high level technology requirements for such a system were presented by Simon Scorer of the Bank of England[5] and are summarised below (Fig. 5.1).

Resilience

A widely used CBDC would likely be considered critical national infrastructure.[6] Any unexpected downtime could have a major impact on the functioning of the financial system and on the real economy. It would need to be operational across the country, 24 hours a day, 365 days a year and require extraordinary levels of resilience. A minimum operational availability of 99.999% might not be unreasonable for the core settlement engine—equating to a downtime of approximately 5 minutes during a year.

Requirement	Summary
Resilience	High operational availability (>99.999%), 24/7/365
Security	Secure against cyber attacks
Scalability	Potential for several thousand transactions per second
Transaction processing	Near-instantaneous, real-time, with settlement finality
Confidentiality	Private, but not anonymous
Interoperability	Interoperable with existing systems and other CBDCs
Innovation	Enable the overlay of innovative features/services
Future proofing	Ability to upgrade and enhance, without impacting service

Fig. 5.1 Technology requirements for a CBDC system

Security

A CBDC would need to be designed to protect against any unauthorised access to, and alteration of, data, as well as disruption to operation (e.g. DDoS attacks[7]). Potential attackers will have many varied motivations in addition to theft, including simply disrupting or undermining confidence in the system, as well as significant capabilities and resources (potentially including state-sponsored attacks).

Scalability

The actual requirement will be dependent on many factors, but it is likely that a successful implementation will need to scale many magnitudes beyond its original purpose. Consider, for example, the payments infrastructure of the UK: Figures from Payments UK[8] show around 1200 transactions per second (includes electronic, cash and cheques) based on average annual volumes. Transactions during peak times will be significantly higher, so a reasonable estimate of a peak figure may be in the region of several thousand transactions per second between a national population of nearly 70 million.

The actual requirement might be much higher than this, as a CBDC might be used internationally, or drive payments demand in new growth areas such as micropayments or between Internet of Things[9] devices.

Transaction Processing

In order to be useful for retail payments, CBDC transactions will need to be confirmed near-instantaneously and it will be vital that settlement finality[10] is established.

Payments in CBDC would, by definition, be in central bank money from the outset without the need for commercial banks to be involved so the underlying transactions in CBDC would likely be real time gross settled[11] rather than the deferred settlement systems used widely today.

Confidentiality

Levels of financial privacy at least equivalent to those in place today would be needed: the system must be *private* (i.e. transaction details are only visible to the counterparties of that transaction, except perhaps in the case of infrastructure operators) but not *anonymous* (i.e. participants must be identifiable and relatable to real-world identities, to enable applicable regulations, e.g. Anti-Money Laundering and Know Your Customer).

Depending on the legal environment, certain authorities (e.g. law enforcement[12]) might also require the ability to view the transactions of particular parties under the appropriate circumstances.

Interoperability

A CBDC would need to coexist with the current financial system, and potentially with multiple other national CBDCs, to enable simplified and faster cross-border payments. Synchronisation of payments between these systems should ensure that the final transfer of CBDC only occurs if the final transfer of an asset in the corresponding system also occurs (i.e. Delivery versus Payment[13] or Payment versus Payment[14]).

Innovation

A CBDC could act as an enabler of further innovation. Key to this is the programmability of payments; for example, the automation of tax payments, the distribution of welfare benefits, or parents being able to restrict their children's spending to trusted stores or websites. Micropayments between IOT devices and cross-border payments are other potential innovations.

These innovations would most likely be enabled as overlay layers to the core infrastructure allowing a CBDC and private innovation to coexist. A CBDC would therefore need to be implemented by technology in such a way that enables this overlaying of innovative features.

Future Proofing

A CBDC would need to be able to adapt to a changing environment over a long period of time—potentially decades—with ever-evolving user demands and security threats. The ability to continually upgrade and enhance both functional and security attributes of any system would be critical.

Global Response to CBDCs

The central banks of many countries have stated that they are moving towards digital currency issuance, with some even moving back from initially stated opposite positions as they realise the implications. By the time you read this, it's likely that some of these will have announced their CBDCs to be launched in 2018.

China: China has announced that it will be issuing its own state cryptocurrency in 2019, meaning it is likely to be the first major country to launch a CBDC. Strategically, it is in line with the Belt and Road Initiative, an integrated upgrade of China's international cooperation with the Eurasian Economic Union, China-Japan-South Korea Free Trade Area and other areas. It enables China to exert its geopolitical advantages and is an important platform for cooperation.

Despite the crackdown in 2017 and 2018 on cryptocurrency exchanges, ICOs and associated Fintech businesses attempting to create and use cryptocurrencies, the country has historically taken a positive attitude towards CDBCs and blockchain technology. In February 2016, People's Bank of China (PBOC) president Mr. Zhou Xiaochun first admitted that the Chinese government has been investigating the adoption of CBDCs and on 27 December 2016, blockchain was written into the "13th Five-Year Plan for National Informatization", affirming the value of blockchain technology and including it in the national science and technology strategy.

In January 2017, China's central bank successfully tested the digital notes exchange platform where a digital currency was used to exchange notes between commercial banks and in July 2017, the Central Bank Digital Currency Research Institution officially began operating as a separate business unit within PBOC.

We have long expected China to be one of the first movers in the CBDC space, although probably initially through a pilot programme to manage the risk and public expectation. While details are still emerging at time of going to press, the Chinese CBDC is likely to first be limited to banks for intra-bank transactions so that existing foreign exchange and capital controls can be maintained, but the People's Bank of China has clearly expressed the opportunity for its currency to support China's majority digital transaction-using consumers.

United Kingdom: The Bank of England[15] set up a research unit in early 2015 to investigate the introduction of a sterling-linked digital currency based on blockchain technology. A number of proofs of concept have been run to experiment with the use of distributed ledger technology as applied to the issuance of digital currencies—in particular, central bank custody of retail accounts, the distribution of welfare benefits to claimants and the replacement of the UK's legacy Real Time Gross Settlement System, CHAPS. According to a Bank spokesman, the research unit is expected to report back in 2018.

Singapore: The Monetary Authority of Singapore (MAS) has been putting significant money and policy behind Fintech developments under its chief Fintech officer, Sopnendu Mohanty, and in doing so has become one of the driving forces in global Fintech.

Project Ubin[16] was set up in 2016 to explore the use of distributed ledger technology and better understand the benefits for clearing and settlement of payments and securities. This is with the goal of developing simpler-to-use and more efficient alternatives to today's systems based on digital central bank issued tokens.

The first phase completed successfully in March 2017 and focused on developing a prototype solution for domestic inter-bank payments using a central bank-issued Singapore Dollar (SGD) equivalent. On 5 October 2017,[17] MAS announced[18] the second phase, that the consortium has successfully developed software prototypes of three different models for decentralised inter-bank payment and settlements with liquidity savings mechanisms. The technologies used for these prototypes are R3's Corda, IBM's Hyperledger Fabric and J. P. Morgan's Quorum.

MAS now intends to launch spin-off projects that will leverage the lessons of the prototypes, one of which focuses on new methods to conduct cross-border payments using central bank digital currency.

Canada: The Bank of Canada was one of the first central banks to run a proof of concept on CBDCs and has since then been considering the societal benefits of digital currencies. In a research paper[19] released by the central bank in November 2017, it concluded that there are merits to creating a Central Bank Digital Currency as society moves away from cash.

The staff discussion paper said a CBDC could become a cheaper alternative to debit and credit cards and other forms of payment, making it easier for competition to emerge in the retail and large-value payment sectors. While supporting the view that there are potential cost savings, the report discounted some of the other proposed benefits of a digital currency such as reducing criminal activity and believed that there would be increased operational risk. It concludes that, given the complexity and uncertainty around the potential for CBDCs, central banks should proceed incrementally and cautiously.

Dubai: The city of Dubai[20] has been working on becoming the "world's first economy that's built on the blockchain", and with it its own digital currency, dubbed emCash, launched in September 2017. emCredit, the city's credit bureau, partnered with UK-based Object Tech Group to create emCash, which works as part of a payment system called emWallet. emWallet handles various transaction types with a near-field communication (NFC) support through a smartphone.

Dubai Economy deputy director general Ali Ibrahim acknowledged the benefits of a digital currency to Dubai's citizens, namely faster processing, improved delivery time, less complexity and cost. He goes on to state that "It will change the way people live and do business in Dubai and mark a giant leap for the city in harnessing game-changing innovations to improve ease of business and quality of life". It remains to be seen how game-changing a city-based digital currency actually is, whether there's sufficient uptake to achieve critical mass, if it will interoperate with the other UAE states, and most importantly, whether it changes the lives of the huge migrant workforce who desperately need cheaper ways of remitting funds home.

Sweden: Sweden, like the other Nordic countries, is close to becoming a cashless society and the Riksbank of Sweden has an eKrona project under way to determine whether it should supply digital central bank money to the general public. The project is considering different technical solutions, but no decision has been taken on the solution with the project expecting to be finalised in late 2019.

Russia: Vladimir Putin is reportedly fully behind the launch of a "CryptoRouble" which, unsurprisingly, is designed be centrally controlled, taxed and regulated, and to have "traceable encryption" (which presumably means the government holds the keys). It also appears that Putin and his government see a CryptoRouble as a way of avoiding western sanctions. This would appear to be as far from the core tenets of cryptocurrency as it is possible to go, but is somewhat expected since the totalitarian crackdown on Bitcoin and other cryptocurrencies. "Regulators of all countries agree that it's essential to develop a national digital currency, that it is the future", said Olga Skorobogatova, the deputy governor of the central bank. "Each country will decide on specific timeframes for itself. Based on the pilot projects [that] we are conducting, we will understand which system we could use in our case for our national currency".

In 2017, it was reported that the country's central bank was testing out several digital currency schemes to determine which would work best for Russia and a launch is expected in early 2018.

Oleg Fomichev, Russia's deputy minister of economic development said, "This mustn't be a private currency, but the one which is issued by the state, controlled by the state and [able] to provide circulation of digital money in light of the digital economy".

Further, according to Artem Duvanov, the director of Moscow Exchange Group's National Settlement Depository, "Cryptocurrencies combine convenience and freedom of cash with the potential of total control of all operations, If the government wants to introduce some control on operations done via crypto on its territory, it does make a lot of sense to issue its own cryptocurrency", he said. Understandably, this has led to concerns about an Orwellian level of state control.

According to reports from the Russian Communications ministry, there is a belief that Russia must issue a CryptoRouble soon or else be overtaken by their neighbours in the Eurasian Economic Community. Interestingly, the report also suggests that a 13% tax rate will be charged when converting CryptoRoubles back to Roubles, indicating the digital currency may be receivable from outside the state-controlled area.

Ecuador: The small Latin American country of Ecuador became one of the first to issue a digital currency in 2014. Ecuador has certainly seen a few currencies during its history. Pesos, francos, sucre, reales, dollars, some based on silver, some on gold and even the Moby Dick coin (an 8 Escudos doubloon)! The Ecuador Sucre had been relatively stable for most of the twentieth century until, in 1999, its value plummeted, resulting in the country officially adopting the US dollar as its own currency.

As technology advanced, however, the country created its own digital currency—the Sistema de Dinero Electrónico. The currency is stored in digital wallets and can be used on public transport and within the country's tax and invoicing systems, but has had a very slow uptake from the public and extreme resistance from the country's banks.

In preparing to launch its digital currency, perhaps following a similar pattern to what we're seeing in China and Russia, Ecuador banned Bitcoin and all other cryptocurrencies. However, the Bitcoin Community of Ecuador remains strong despite the ban on the cryptocurrency. Bitcoin trades at a premium in Ecuador, and the number of users is growing, and so is the small number of brave businesses accepting it in payment.

The 5-year goal for the digital currency was to reach over 4 million users registering around $80-million. In 2016, a year and a half into this plan, the digital currency had reached only 70,000 users registering close to $763,000—representing only 0.002% of the money supply within the economy. Despite this relative rejection from the public, the Ecuadorian government is still pushing the Sistema de Dinero Electrónico. A reformation of the digital currency, announced in late August 2017, removes the Central Bank from the system reportedly due to the cost of cash—importing and replacing money can be particularly expensive for countries that do not mint their own currency.

The country's reform of its digital money system is set to launch by October which could act as a new beginning for the troubled system. The Association of Private Banks of Ecuador estimates that the use of cash will be reduced by $800-million within one year, and by $1.6-billion within two.

Japan: Japan is one of the world's biggest crypto-cheerleaders having recognised Bitcoin as legal tender and approving several companies as operators of cryptocurrency exchanges.

The Bank of Japan last year set up a department in charge of Fintech to offer guidance to banks seeking new business opportunities, and joined up with the European Central Bank to study distributed ledger technology (DLT) like blockchain. But the BOJ and ECB said in September they had judged that blockchain was not mature enough to power the world's biggest payment systems—though not ruling it out in future.

In spite of this, Japanese banks are planning to introduce a digital currency for the 2020 Tokyo Olympics called the JCoin which will be used to pay for goods via smartphones. The JCoin will be convertible into yen on a one-to-one basis in the app and payments will be made using QR codes that are scanned in stores. Banks will offer the service for free, and be paid in the data they will collect on consumer spending patterns.

Estonia: The small Baltic state of Estonia is well known for its progressive technology focus and blockchain-based e-residency programme. It is therefore no surprise that it is planning to launch its own digital currency.

Kaspar Korjus, the managing director of Estonia's e-residency programme, announced in December 2017, that Estonia is considering three different models for a digital currency, nicknamed "estcoin". This initiative has received criticism from the European Central Bank as eurozone member states cannot introduce their own currency under European rules. Because of this, Korjus has responded that the estcoin would not be an alternative currency to the euro, but that one of the approaches was an estcoin pegged to the euro and made available to Estonia's digital residents. The other two options for estcoin are a "community estcoin" to reward volunteers who help improve Estonia's e-residency programme, and an "identity estcoin" tied to a person's digital identity. It is proposed that these could be used to pay for government services or to pay fines.

Senegal: In 2017, the Senegalese central bank, Banque Regionale de Marches (BRM) in collaboration with eCurrency Mint, following neighbour Tunisia's example, launched its version of a national digital currency, the eCFA. It has the same value as the country's currency, the CFA franc, and can be stored in e-money wallets, is based on blockchain technology and has been designed to be compatible with other African digital currencies.

A statement from BRM and eCurrency Mint said: "The eCFA is a high-security digital instrument that can be held in all mobile money and e-money wallets. It will secure universal liquidity, enable interoperability, and provide transparency to the entire digital ecosystem in WAEMU (West African Economy and Money Union)".

Venezuela: In November 2017, Venezuelan President Nicolas Maduro announced that his nation's collapsed economy is to be shored up by a digital currency called a "petro" backed by oil reserves; it would be followed, he stated, by equivalents backed by other gas, gold and diamond reserves. The petro and its siblings, Maduro said, would help Venezuela "advance in issues of monetary sovereignty, to make financial transactions and overcome the financial blockade". On 20 February 2018, the petro was launched as the world's first national cryptocurrency, however, at the time of writing, few specifics have been announced although supposedly $735 million was raised on the first day of its pre-sale and there are reports that the petro has been built on top of the NEM blockchain (although the whitepaper states Ethereum would be used).

The primary driver for this initiative appears to be to circumvent US-led financial sanctions and its ability to move money through international banks and to distract from the freefall of the country's national currency, the bolivar. In a country that is lacking in basic needs like food and medicine, one must wonder how a government that cannot manage its economy "traditionally" will be able to implement both a digital currency infrastructure and its economic consequences. It remains to be seen, therefore, whether the plan has any credibility at all.

Conclusion

Implementing a CBDC is far from just a simple question of implementing technology; any central bank contemplating CBDC will need to answer a host of fundamental economic questions,[21] as well as considering the feasible and viability of achieving all the required features. A great deal of further research is required before making CBDC a reality.

And although the technology behind blockchain is evolving rapidly, greater maturity and fully scaled production references will be needed before it is usable in the volumes anticipated in a cashless, borderless, micropayment and IoT-enabled society. Blockchain has advantages of security, resilience and availability, depending on how the network is architected, but there are trade-offs between resilience and control, which still need to be resolved. One of the biggest challenges for central banks, even assuming technical suitability, will be the big one between privacy, anonymity and the potential to control characteristics of the currency, such as who can use it or whether to tax at source. While these are technical considerations, the answers will be decided politically or even societally.

So it is not surprising that countries with different political agendas are pursuing very different approaches. Looking at the landscape, there appears to be a trend for countries with a high degree of collaboration between governments, central banks and the commercial banking system to be making early moves, supported by their ability to suspend or control cryptocurrency trading as a precursor to launching a CBDC. While some of the most mature research teams are in countries such as the UK, Japan and Canada, it is likely that early movers will come from China or other more directly controlled regimes, where a lot of research has clearly been done in the background.

Countries under sanctions can use the same technology to circumvent international law as well as find new ways to oppress their population and even if Venezuela's efforts to avoid sanctions end up failing, other countries will be watching and learning how to adapt the model to succeed.

Already, a number of nations who have recently been issued sanctions have begun to explore state-backed cryptocurrencies. A senior member of the Iranian government[22] floated the same idea, following the Russian deputy prime minister[23] announcing similar endeavours.

Between political and technical challenges, commercial bulk settlements seem to be a good place to start and many pilots have been in this area. We think that early CBDCs will focus on RTGS before expanding to general use, but much will also depend on the country and their ability or desire to control their financial system. The benefits to the general population are not yet as clear, and any significant rebalancing towards a generally available CBDC may put the fractional reserve lending system and payments industry at risk, potentially disrupting national commercial banking industries.

However, the benefits to developing economies, together with lighter regulations and less mature markets, may also form conditions for early release of a CBDC, particularly where it offers an opportunity to stabilise volatile national fiat currencies. By the time you read this, we may already have seen the answers emerge.

Notes

1. Bech, M. L., & Garatt, R. (2017, September 17). Central Bank Cryptocurrencies. *Bank for International Settlements*. https://www.bis.org/publ/qtrpdf/r_qt1709f.htm. Accessed 3 January 2018.
2. Bech, M. L., & Garatt, R. (2017, September 17). Central Bank Cryptocurrencies. *BIS*. https://papers.ssrn.com/sol3/papers.cfm?abstract_id=3041906. Accessed 12 January 2018.
3. Barrdear, J., & Kumhof, M. (2016, July 18). The Macroeconomics of Central Bank Issued Digital Currencies. *Bank of England*. https://www.bankofengland.co.uk/working-paper/2016/the-macroeconomics-of-central-bank-issued-digital-currencies.
4. International Monetary Fund Special Drawing Rights Fact Sheet (IMF). http://www.imf.org/en/About/Factsheets/Sheets/2016/08/01/14/51/Special-Drawing-Right-SDR. Accessed 3 January 2018.
5. Scorer, S. (2017, September 13). Beyond blockchain: What Are the Technology Requirements for a Central Bank Digital Currency? *Bank Underground*. https://bankunderground.co.uk/2017/09/13/beyond-blockchain-what-are-the-technology-requirements-for-a-central-bank-digital-currency/. Accessed 13 January 2018.
6. Critical National Infrastructure (Centre for the Protection of National Infrastructure). https://www.cpni.gov.uk/critical-national-infrastructure-0. Accessed 13 January 2018.
7. Denial of Service (Tech Terms). https://techterms.com/definition/denial_of_service. Accessed 13 January 2018.
8. UK Payment Markets Summary (Payments UK). https://www.paymentsuk.org.uk/sites/default/files/products/report/summary/PUK-UK-Payments-Markets-2017-Summary-AW-Online.pdf. Accessed 13 January 2018.

9. Winston, H. (2014, November 11). The Internet of Things Will Revolutionize the Payment Industry. *Yale Economic Review.* http://www.yaleeconomicreview.org/archives/2204. Accessed 13 January 2018.

10. Settlement Finality Directive (European Commission). https://ec.europa.eu/info/business-economy-euro/banking-and-finance/financial-markets/post-trade-services/settlement-finality_en. Accessed 13 January 2018.

11. Real-Time Gross Settlement (Investopedia). https://www.investopedia.com/terms/r/rtgs.asp. Accessed 13 January 2018.

12. Using Financial Information (UK College of Policing). https://www.app.college.police.uk/app-content/investigations/investigative-strategies/financial-investigation-2/using-financial-information/. Accessed 13 January 2018.

13. Delivery Versus Payment (Investopedia). https://www.investopedia.com/terms/d/dvp.asp. Accessed 13 January 2018.

14. Payment Versus Payment (Hong Kong Monetary Authority). http://www.hkma.gov.hk/gdbook/eng/p/pay_versus_pay.shtml. Accessed 13 January 2018.

15. Barrdear, J., & Kumhof, M. (2016, July 18). The Macroeconomics of Central Bank Issued Digital Currencies. *Bank of England.* https://www.bankofengland.co.uk/working-paper/2016/the-macroeconomics-of-central-bank-issued-digital-currencies. Accessed 3 January 2018.

16. Dalal, D., Yong, S., & Lewis, A. (2017, May 26). The Future Is Here Project Ubin: SGD on Distributed Ledger. *MAS/Deloitte/R3.* http://www.mas.gov.sg/~/media/ProjectUbin/Project%20Ubin%20%20SGD%20on%20Distributed%20Ledger.pdf. Accessed 3 January 2018.

17. MAS and ABS Lead Consortium to Harness blockchain Technology for More Efficient Inter-bank Payments (Monetary Authority of Singapore), 5 October 2017. http://www.mas.gov.sg/News-and-Publications/Media-Releases/2017/MAS-and-ABS-lead-consortium-to-harness-blockchain-technology.aspx. Accessed 13 January 2018.

18. Project Ubin: Central Bank Digital Money Using Distributed Ledger Technology, Monetary Authority of Singapore (MAS), 14 November 2017. http://www.mas.gov.sg/Singapore-Financial-Centre/Smart-Financial-Centre/Project-Ubin.aspx. Accessed 3 January 2018.

19. Engert, W., & Fung, B. S. C. (2017, December 1). Central Bank Digital Currency: Motivations and Implications. *Bank of Canada.* https://www.bankofcanada.ca/wp-content/uploads/2017/11/sdp2017-16.pdf. Accessed 3 January 2018.

20. Lohade, N. (2017, April 24). Dubai Aims to Be a City Built on blockchain. *Wall Street Journal.* https://www.wsj.com/articles/dubai-aims-to-be-a-city-built-on-blockchain-1493086080. Accessed 3 January 2018.

21. Bank of England Research Library. *Bank of England.* https://www.bankofengland.co.uk/research. Accessed 13 January 2018.

22. Milano, A. (2018, February 22). The Next Petro? Iranian Minister Reveals Cryptocurrency Plans. *Coindesk*. https://www.coindesk.com/next-petro-iranian-minister-reveals-cryptocurrency-plans/. Accessed 28 February 2018.

23. O'Leary, R. R. (2017, August 24). Russian Deputy PM Says He Supports a State-Backed Cryptocurrency. *Coindesk*. https://www.coindesk.com/russian-deputy-pm-says-supports-state-backed-cryptocurrency/. Accessed 28 February 2018.

Further Reading

Koning, J. P. (2016, November 15). Fedcoin: A Central Bank-Issued Cryptocurrency. *R3*. http://www.r3cev.com/s/R3-Report-Fedcoin.pdf. Accessed 3 January 2018.

Coppola, F. (2017, December 18). Central Banks Are Considering Their Own Digital Currencies for Global Payments. https://www.americanexpress.com/us/content/foreign-exchange/articles/digital-currencies-by-central-banks-for-global-payments/. Accessed 3 January 2018.

6

Shifting Values in the Connected Economy

As currencies digitise and trade globalises, the world's getting more connected. In this chapter, we consider the macroeconomic impact of this trend, the shift of value that appears to be taking place away from larger organisations towards smaller firms and the implications for banks.

Work, Money and Utility

Traditionally, work has been closely linked to money—the "labour theory of value", first coined by Adam Smith,[1] argues that value of goods reflects the cost of labour needed to produce them and has been espoused by economists in one form or another ever since. Other models argue that value is instead derived with usefulness and scarcity of products—the less there is of something, the more valuable it becomes. But what happens when people start working for no money and there is an almost limitless proliferation of instances of a product? Or what happens when your extended identity starts operating autonomously and earning money without your direct control?

If there are theoretically close to infinite instances of a product, the value of each instance falls, and to use the example of iTunes, the price you pay may mostly be covering the cost of processing the payment and profit to iTunes, with a tiny fractional value going to the recording artist. And the cost of production is, to iTunes, close to zero per unit, as the potential sales are limitless. Conversely, there is a growing number of people producing stuff for nothing—the huge range of open source development software, Wikipedia, all those useful videos on YouTube showing you how to change a recessed light

© The Author(s) 2018
S. Blakstad and R. Allen, *FinTech Revolution*,
https://doi.org/10.1007/978-3-319-76014-8_6

bulb, build decking, prune roses or cut in a skirting board and many more. People all over the world are creating and distributing content for nothing.

Everyone has an agenda and, in many cases, will be distributing their content for nothing in the hope that it will further their profile, sell something else for them, etc., but in many cases, the agenda is more complex than that—it's a genuine desire to share knowledge (and maybe show off a bit), develop skills, gain entry to a community or some other such community-based motivation. It's about developing a network.

Conversely, the direct linkage of work to value is broken when your products do the work for you. The idea of a self-driving car dropping you off at work, then clocking into Uber to go off and earn money from passengers while you're doing something else, may be relatively new, but effectively it's analogous to the YouTube video—now your car, like your social media content, is out there on the network, building your reputation and selling units, without the need for either push from you or pull from your customers.

The Value of Network

Networks have value, and several models have emerged to try to describe that value, but all agree that the value of a network increases exponentially with the number of nodes (people, companies, things) in the network.[2] In our connected economy, it's become easier than ever to build networks and consequently, more networks exist; people and companies are more connected than they have ever been. Some of these networks will be more valuable than others, because of their reach or target group. Individuals may be linked via work, interest groups, friendship groups and family groups, via telephone contacts, working groups, communities of practice, online via Facebook, LinkedIn, Twitter, WhatsApp, newsgroups, dating websites, special interest sites catering to every conceivable interest, pursuit, political activity and so forth.

And these groups often intersect or overlap, meaning that they're a part of a metanetwork, which again is more powerful because of the access to other networks.

This has the important implication that we no longer need formal intermediaries to manage distribution of knowledge; it's disintermediated, in much the same way as disintermediating financial transactions with cryptocurrencies. This changes the dynamics of information distribution significantly; what previously was the preserve of large organisations with deep pockets is now open to anyone who has an interesting or valuable piece of information or product. We're all familiar with viral marketing; the term is incredibly appropriate, not just because it describes the transmission mechanism, but because it can apply to something that's infinitesimally small, in global terms, such as a small provider or a one-man-band with a paintbrush and a phone camera.

As we discuss in detail in Chapter 15, a revolution we're all familiar with is the availability and rapid adoption of online shopping—which includes how companies shop, not just individuals. While this has changed consumer behaviour considerably, with more people buying directly from smaller producers, or from smaller, more conveniently located stores, it also means that specialised firms can sell their services to customers.

Shifting the Value

As we discuss in Chapter 21, this means the balance of value is also shifting. The big organisations with the big budgets no longer have exclusive access to a global clientele; anyone with a web presence can reach them today. Distribution opportunities, that would previously have been impossible to access, are now open equally to organisations via marketplace platforms and informally thanks to web searches, regardless of where the organisation is based or how big they are—profiles are built through quality of content, rather than scale of push. Consumers are free to find what they want, regardless of the size of producer or whether they've got a distribution network. It's easier than ever to manage the marketing and distribution of your product or services. Even so, small businesses still maintain that marketing and distribution are two of the hardest things for them to handle, illustrating that there is further potential to make it easier.

In response to this, there is a growing number of SMEs (mostly on the small to micro side) providing goods and services to relatively small numbers of customers, who have a specific need to fulfil. Ironically, the global downturn and related lay-offs have also led to the growth of this sector, as individuals are either laid off or see opportunities as larger organisations disappear, and choose to set up on their own. People who would in the past have bought most of their goods via larger stores are now able to buy direct from exporters across the globe and interact directly with them. Even locally, we shop more frequently than we did 15 years ago and are more likely to visit smaller, local providers.

For supermarkets, the outcome is that the shift towards building out-of-town hypermarkets is in swift reverse. What's less visible is the parallel shift of customers away from larger providers and towards smaller providers, for specialist software and online services. The Fintech revolution is a clear example of this, with small, lean groups of technical specialists and visionaries creating services and products that solve problems for end customers—and in many cases, those are services traditionally provided by banks. In many other cases, they're services that haven't been provided at all, or which have required complicated, manual solutions, finding and exploiting new markets.

And it's happening in corporations, too. IBM[3] tells us that 80% of employees download their own apps, with or without the company's permission, creating massive shadow IT. We take our personal devices to work, so that we can do work for that company which our locked-down and outdated company-issued apparatus won't support,[4] often via smaller, niche providers.

But there's still a gap between these small providers and their customers—the customer is currently required to find the providers individually, which, with viral marketing, is happening, but it's still complicated. There is a growing number of marketplace platforms aimed at the general public, such as App stores and Amazon, and to specialist customers, and we think the evolution of the multi-sided platform marketplace, thanks to the enhanced opportunities offered by blockchain technology, will be the next big change to the connected economy, providing both producers and consumers with faster access to each other.

Doing It All

Nobody, and no organisation, can do everything well. As we discussed in Chapter 2, banks have traditionally provided a wide range of services ranging from insurance to corporate finance, and managed all the supporting capabilities from sales to technology infrastructure. This model is typical of large companies throughout the twentieth century—with few exceptions, such as advertising and specialist software, larger organisations have preferred to insource services, maintaining control within the organisation. While that looks sensible from a control perspective, it presents firms with two problems: finding the best people to do everything in your organisation and putting your best people on the most important things your organisation does. As Jim Collins discusses in Good to Great,[5] organisations struggle to be good at lots of things simultaneously; he argues that they need to find what he calls their "hedgehog concept"—what is the single thing they can be great at, and focus on being the best at that.

Surprisingly, historically there's been little direct correlation between provision of excellent services and profit for large organisations, especially banks—in fact, a much closer correlation exists between positive corporate culture and profit. So this historical lack of impact of poor service to financial performance has meant that banks and other large organisations haven't been punished for poor customer service—until now.

The combination of ease of access to alternatives and wide distribution of customer-to-customer information shifts the power from the brand to the service. Customers, individually and collectively, are voting with their wallets and taking their business to the providers who can give them the service they need in the format that suits them the best. Smaller and startup banks, offering more focused and more customer friendly products, have started to change customer expectations and demands. While some of these challengers will need to pivot to sustain their business models, the impact of their service approach on banks' customers will be to change what customers demand.

So how can today's universal banks address this? There are two basic approaches being taken today by universal banks: strip down the operating model but keep the universal banking paradigm, or keep the universal banking paradigm and the operating model, but bolt on some cool features via Fintech partnerships. In the first model, banks have recognised that outsourcing supporting services to organisations that do these things best will reduce their risk and operational costs. However, they're still running massively complicated service models and may miss the cost reduction opportunity by outsourcing complex and poorly designed services wholesale, complete with bad metrics and a proliferation of over-customised processes. In the second model, by failing to address structural challenges, banks can't transform at all and are likely to lose customers to emerging competition because their core services are complex, slow and unreliable.

Scale vs Networks

Banks have traditionally survived and thrived because of their scale, and because of their access to limited access services such as payments schemes and central banks. Scale provides them with strong capital base, reputation and brand awareness, all of which are important, especially in financial services. What scale doesn't provide for banks, however, is economies of scale;

unit costs for customer acquisition and management have grown in line with banks' increasing size, due to the ever-increasing complexity of their operations, and the increasing regulatory demands for information to try to understand and monitor this complexity.

Meanwhile, global networks powered by internet, disruptive technologies and the shift in distribution are creating a new, connected economy where smaller, more agile organisations with greater focus and innovative service approaches are syphoning business off the older, larger organisations. This has profound implications for any industry where the industry and large organisations have historically owned and controlled distribution. With that network shifting out of their hands, banks, like other industries, are struggling to address how they will overcome the challenge and maintain their strong position and customer share in the connected economy.

The answer is for banks to become active participants in the connected economy—not by bolting on Fintechs or service providers, but by changing their operating models so that customers continue to benefit from their expertise, experience, knowledge and scale, while becoming full participants in the network by truly partnering with, and giving shared ownership to, other organisations, including Fintechs, who can offer truly differentiated services to their customers. We're starting to see this model emerge with the concept of Banking as a Platform (BaaP), and, rather than competing, incumbent banks are now participating in this movement, to benefit from the network opportunities and build their future as full-service providers, via the network, to their customers.

Conclusion

In this chapter, we've argued that because of the rise of the connected economy, banks are losing their monopoly as sole providers of financial services to customers; customers are increasingly voting with their wallets, and with the rise of new companies providing viable options, the threat to the traditional bank is growing. Operating model changes need to address the fundamentals of how a bank's business is run, and need to take advantage of networks, rather than trying to compete with them or buy them out.

Notes

1. Smith, A. (1776). An Inquiry into the Nature and Causes of the Wealth of Nations. AdamSmith.org.
2. Choudary, S. P. Virality vs. Network Effect (Pipes to Platforms). http://platformed.info/virality-viral-growth-network-effects/. Accessed 7 January 2018.
3. Kang, H. (2016, March 31). Seeing Shadows. *IBM*. https://www.ibm.com/blogs/collaboration-solutions/2016/03/31/seeing-shadows/?cm_mmc=PSocial_Linkedin-_-IBM+Social_IBM+Collaboration+Solutions-_-WW_WW-_-P9LJ4Q_PM2+TTD+IBM+ICS_ov47843&cm_mmca1=000000PY&cm_mmca2=10001237. Accessed 7 January 2018.
4. O'Dea, S. (2015, December 11). Digital Tools for Digital People. https://medium.com/@sharonodea/digital-tools-for-digital-people-b659be16ee1e. Accessed 7 January 2018.
5. Collins, J. (2001). *Good to Great*. William Collins.

7

Leapfrogging Banks in Emerging Markets

With the rise of the connected economy, the financial ecosystem is changing, and much of it has already changed thanks to new ecosystem behaviours and innovative business models.

In this chapter, we discuss the challenges for the 2 billion people who lack access to financial services in developing and developed economies. We examine how developing economies have embraced alternative financial services, in many cases bypassing traditional banks, and how lives and the economy in some countries have been transformed where these services are available. We present how these services can act as a gateway to inclusion in the traditional financial system, and how they are also evolving as a valid alternative. We discuss the challenges of regulation, interoperability and usability and how overcoming these barriers will enable them to scale to supplant traditional banking in developed as well as developing economies.

The Unbanked and Underbanked, and Access to Identity

Unbanked is used as a term to define people who do not have access to banking services, of which there are an estimated 2 billion today,[1] or nearly half the world's adult population. While most unbanked people are in countries classified as "developing", a significant minority live in countries classified as "developed", including around 7% of the US population, although the percentage of unbanked population varies by country—e.g. in

© The Author(s) 2018
S. Blakstad and R. Allen, *FinTech Revolution*,
https://doi.org/10.1007/978-3-319-76014-8_7

the Nordics and parts of Europe, less than 2% of the adult population is unbanked. The number of unbanked people has also fallen rapidly in the last decade, with an additional 700 million gaining access to financial services between 2011 and 2014. However, a large number of countries globally have a majority unbanked population, with up to 98% unbanked (Turkmenistan, 2014 data) being the worst.

Lacking access to a bank account means that you typically have no official history of transactions, no ability to officially validate address or other identity criteria, lack of access to basic services and utilities, property and many jobs. It creates barriers for parents wanting to educate their children, perpetuating low levels of literacy and cross-generational poverty. For businesses, it means no way to receive payments other than cash and no access to credit other than through friends and family or overpriced non-bank lenders. This creates the micro and small business credit ceiling, making it impossible for them to grow and scale. This credit ceiling is keeping millions of micro-entrepreneurs, such as roadside traders and small farmers, in poverty, leaving them open to exploitation.

As we explored in Chapter 2, the other key service banks provide is identity, but getting a bank account in the first place requires some sort of identity documentation. Currently, around a billion people lack access to formal identity documentation, many of whom are also displaced and dispossessed, such as refugees. For many others, a decision to gain formal identity is a day to day economic choice between subsistence existence of investing a week's income in the process of acquiring ID. A lack of formal identity, while being a barrier to access to financial services, also prevents people from proving ownership of resources such as property or land, leaving many of the poorest open to exploitation by corrupt governments and corporations.

Since the 1950s, governments and NGOs have put in place strategies to support small enterprises run by the poorest, with alternative finance institutions such as Microfinance Institutions (MFIs) (some run by NGOs, or by commercial banks and other commercial organisations), financial co-operatives, development banks and low-capital rural banks. These institutions are more lightly regulated than standard banks, and largely focus on giving credit to small and micro-businesses. However, despite their proliferation (an estimated 200 million customers[2]), studies have called into question their effectiveness in lifting people out of poverty,[3] while there are concerns about the divide between urban and relatively underserved rural populations. As the institutions are often small scale, incurring high operational costs, they are widely propped up by government or charity donations, while the high costs are also passed on to clients in the shape of high interest rates, and in many cases augmented by MFIs exploiting the lack of viable alternatives for borrowers. Similarly, savings accounts and other products offered by these type of institutions have been criticised for inefficiency and lack of usability.[4]

Over the last decade, however, several non-bank services have emerged to fill the gap for the unbanked, allowing people access to financial services and identity without the high barriers to entry presented by a traditional bank account.

Alternative Payments and Wallets

Africa has led globally in the adoption of mobile payments without a bank account; in 2014,[5] 12% of sub-Saharan African adults had a mobile money account (mostly in Kenya and Tanzania), of whom half did not have a traditional bank account, and these numbers are rising, largely thanks to the success of M-PESA.

Launched by Safaricom in 2007, M-PESA is a simple money transfer and payments system which allows users to store value in an e-wallet on a SIM card (Pesa is the Swahili word for money). Originally setup as a vehicle to facilitate microfinance, it was soon adopted as a payments tool and relaunched as a remittance and payments service. Kenya was an ideal market for M-PESA—the service was inspired by the practice of Kenyans exchanging mobile credit in lieu of cash, and with a market where only 17% of the population originally had a bank account, growth opportunities were significant. It's estimated that nearly 100% of Kenyans have now used M-PESA, which is an astonishing development in 10 years, but what's even more significant is that it has opened up access to the traditional financial system, with the customer base for one of the national banks growing from half a million to 6 million customers in the same timescale.

Kenya, and Tanzania, where M-PESA launched subsequently, had the right conditions for M-PESA to succeed and grow rapidly—low access to traditional finance and concerns about security for physical cash. The existing network of mobile kiosks provided the facility to exchange to physical money, and although M-PESA was originally launched, and is still run, by Telco operators (Safaricom still operates the East Africa franchise while Vodafone is operating other markets), it now partners with some local banks as well. It's able to run on basic feature phone units, and in areas where people don't have access to private phones, shared phones are used, with each individual having their own SIM card. Anecdotes tell of people sewing SIM cards into their clothes to transport money securely.

M-PESA has now launched in South Africa, Afghanistan, India, Eastern Europe and other markets, with varying degrees of success. While it has had a major impact in East Africa, issues with usability, lack of fungibility and functionality mean it has limited applications; despite the wide adoption, the number of frequent users vs overall users is much lower than comparable figures for standard bank accounts. It operates best in markets where it's a first mover and can establish dominance, accessing the important merchant ecosystem to enhance usefulness.

Launched in 2013 and headquartered in Nairobi, Kenya, BitPesa[6] is a digital currency exchange with operations in several locations including London, Dakar, and Lagos. In 2014, it launched a beta site that allows users to send money to any mobile money wallet within Kenya, and by 2015, it began offering payment to and from seven mobile money wallets and more than 60 banks in Kenya, Nigeria, and Tanzania.

The original aim of BitPesa was to help diasporas transfer money to Africa quickly and cheaply. They accept digital currencies and offer users fiat money in exchange. It allows users to bypass the mammoth wire-transfer companies like MoneyGram and Western Union. This reduces the fees by two-thirds, resulting in savings of about USD 74 million each year. Since the average remittance fee to Africa is about 11.8% by other companies, which is higher than the global average of 8.9%, BitPesa will play a major role in lowering the global cost. Although BitPesa focuses on diaspora, it has also been largely adopted by small and even larger businesses, enabling import and export from African countries, and the remittance of money from abroad.

> BitPesa was the first company in the world to establish a market between African currencies and digital currencies. We lowered the cost of international payments by 75% and reduced the time to settle between currencies from 12 days to less than 2 hours.

Elizabeth Rossiello (Founder & CEO, BitPesa)[7]

The Singapore-based blockchain startup Everex[8] launched in 2016 and focuses on building platforms to conduct cross-border transactions with real time settlements, coupled with blockchain technology for security. It also targets the 3.5-million people around the world who are sending money but are underbanked and unbanked due to the lack of access to modern financial institutions and pay high remittance fees to send money to families back home.

Everex has created cryptocash assets using the Ethereum blockchain. With cryptocash, expats, migrants and international aid organisations can cheaply and efficiently transfer money to any part of the world. Since the global remittance industry still suffers from various challenges, Everex aims to improve this by reducing fees, delays and queues.

Stellar[9] is an open-source protocol connecting payment systems, banks and people to integrate quick, reliable movement of money at almost no cost. With many servers running the Stellar software over the internet, a global value exchange network is created. Stellar is being implemented by several non-profit organizations in the developing world as their financial infrastructure. A good example is the Praekelt Foundation[10] in sub-Saharan Africa. The foundation has integrated it into Vumi, the messaging app to help young girls save money in airtime credit.

Humaniq[11] is focusing on the many people around the world without bank accounts who own mobile phones. With biometric identification built into the app, Humaniq intends to provide secure transactions to these individuals. Humaniq is essentially a mobile wallet you can use to store and transact stores of value, designed to work with universally recognisable symbols instead of words and will work with the cheapest Android smartphones, using face and voice recognition to verify account holders' identity.

This process of bio-identification will enable people without official identification to access crypto financial services, and ultimately the world economy. Transactions conducted on this system will be fully transparent, preventing any use for illegal purposes. Local currencies will be available to use in the app.

Identity

With an estimated 20% of the world's population not having a legal identity, proof of identity is a significant barrier, particularly for refugees, to accessing financial and government services. BanQu has piloted a blockchain-based scheme in the Dadaab refugee camp in Kenya, helping displaced Somalis create economic identities so they can create a long-term, secure economic profile and access financial and government services. Additionally, initiatives such as ID2020 are bringing together technology companies, development agencies, and think tanks to help the one billion individuals without a legal identity.

BanQu[12] is tackling poverty and inequality by allowing those in developing countries such as small farmers to create an economic identity on the blockchain, regardless of how little land or income they might have and regardless of gender. This not only allows them access to credit, but also opens them up to the global economy. Further to this they have a "verifiable identify" in the supply chain allowing better equality as their "identify" will be linked to their product in the blockchain. BanQu is currently running pilots alongside the Dadaab refugee camp pilot; providing end-to-end supply chains for rural farmers and small-plot farmer land mapping, especially for women farmer in Latin America, where lack of land rights and outdated property registries restrict access to finance.

ID2020[13] is a broader initiative, working towards solving the problem of identity exclusion to the over a billion people worldwide through a public–private partnership. It focuses on protecting individuals through the four principles of identity:

- principle 1: Personal identity unique to you
- principle 2: Persistent identity from life to death
- principle 3: Private identity only key-holder can use
- principle 4: Portable identity accessible worldwide

This project was started due to the need for a self-sovereign identity, a concept that says people and businesses should be able to store their own identity data and provide it efficiently without needing to validate it and without relying on a central repository of identity data. It aims to promote legal identities, including birth registration. Companies such as Cisco Systems, PricewaterhouseCoopers, Accenture and Microsoft are all partners in this venture.

What Has This Meant for Real People in Developing Economies?

One of the most significant developments M-PESA has enabled has been the empowerment of many female entrepreneurs[14] to develop their small and micro-business, allowing them to enter the formal economy and significantly rebalancing economic power for those communities. By enabling the vast majority of people to transact, M-PESA has enabled bottom-up, entrepreneur-driven development across whole segments of the population, which in turn has improved their ability to invest in educating their children, with the long-term improvements that result at a population level.

M-PESA is also integrated into other utilities that are changing lives, such as water metering and M-KOPA solar panel hire purchase, allowing the poorest access to clean water and electricity.[15]

While microfinance and top-down investments are important to supporting economic development, bottom-up, community solutions such as M-PESA tend to enable longer-term success, as they aren't reliant on third-party support. And while BitPesa focused on diaspora, it had a significant impact on local businesses too, as the CEO explains, "We've had a lot of companies that have said that they would not be able to stay in the country if we hadn't provided this efficient solution. United Airlines left Nigeria because of payment problems. We want it to be easy for people to do business in Africa".

The other solutions described in this chapter are achieving success in their early days in empowering and including some of the most disadvantaged populations; allowing recipients of aid to receive food directly funded by donations, rather than passing value through many middlemen, means more of the donations reach their intended targets, while projects such as Praekelt. org target young women and girls in areas where they are statistically less likely to have access to financial services. They're supporting people not just through reducing costs and enabling access to financial services—which are foundational to saving, entrepreneurship, access to education and utilities— but also communication between communities, empowering minorities and disadvantaged communities.

Alternative Finance and Banks

There's some disagreement about the long-term impact of these initiatives on the traditional financial system. Having access to M-PESA and creating a financial record has enabled millions of Kenyans to open bank accounts, increasing the banked population from 17% at launch, to over 60% today, an astonishing growth even in the light of the global increase in the last few years. However, there's still a lack of formal banking infrastructure across much of Africa and the developing world, which together with low levels of trust in banks, means that many customers may never choose to open a bank account, if alternative services are available[16] (Fig. 7.1).

Clearly, a major goal of the identity services we've described is to allow individuals to gain access to financial services, which today we equate to banks. As we've discussed, there are many alternative financial services, particularly in developing economies, that are also potential targets for these customers, which may not offer the same advantages and charge higher fees, which were closer and more convenient to use—in particular the MFIs, which are widely used across Africa for short-term loans by micro-entrepreneurs.

Services like BitPesa also offer opportunities for individuals and companies to build up financial records, allowing them access to formal banking services which they may previously have lacked. However, the downside for

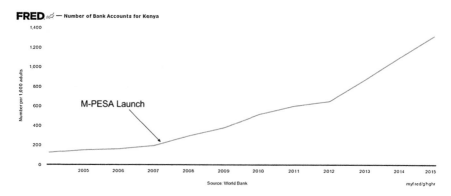

Fig. 7.1 Kenya bank accounts per 1000 of population, 2005–2015[17]

the banks is that these services are cheaper, quicker and more convenient than the services offered by the banks themselves, which may draw customers in the other direction, away from the banks and towards these services as they grow.

The dominance of M-PESA in Kenya and Tanzania, and of other wallet providers in other African countries, has led to some challenges, however: as private companies, the telcos are able to capitalise on the transformational impact they've had on local economies to influence government policy and stifle competition; hence while BitPesa is also a Kenyan company, government regulation, influenced by Safaricom, has, until 2018 lifting of government cryptocurrency constraints, significantly restricted their ability to act in their domestic market. The risk posed by the wallet providers in Africa is that they will stifle further innovation thanks to their market dominance, and, while they have indeed been transformational, these solutions are still first generation—relatively expensive, lacking interoperability and not providing a rich range of financial services.

The other great success story in the wallet space is the rise of the mobile wallet in China and now across South-East Asia. Alipay, WeChat Pay and local providers across the region have rapidly converted users from traditional payments to mobile payments, most using the QR code as a quick, secure transaction tool. The difference with these providers is that they are not yet operating as banks, but integrating with local banks—and in the case of Alipay, have explicitly said that they don't intend to become a bank. What's truly remarkable about these apps is the speed with which they have captured the market. An Alipay executive told us of a recent robbery of three supermarkets in a major city in China, where the robbers found a total of less than USD 10. Travellers to China complain they can't function unless they're in the company of a local, because it's impossible to pay without Alipay or WeChat Pay (China UnionPay is a recent entrant to this market, supported by its massive traditional banking user base). While these companies have completely transformed the payments landscape in China, they haven't yet had a significant impact on inclusion, as they work with the traditional financial system.

They have, however, shown that users are open to banking on mobile applications en masse, with Alipay's 550 million customers testament to this.

Alternative Finance Without Banks

As we've shown, many unbanked people have used local, expensive and inefficient alternatives to banks for many years, and the success of M-PESA demonstrates the opportunity for alternative services to achieve significant market share where existing alternatives to banks are expensive and inefficient. However, M-PESA, as a first-generation mobile payments service, has its drawbacks, and doesn't replace full-service banking, as is demonstrated by the large number of customers who have used it as a gateway to the formal financial system. It lacks interoperability, meaning it's only useful within a closed network, and can't be used with other mobile wallets. Anecdotes tell of people with multiple SIM cards for different wallet providers; hardly practical and possibly connected to the relatively low usage per user for M-PESA.

Emerging services which provide richer customer offerings could, however, start to become a viable alternative to the traditional banks, as they become more sophisticated and user friendly. As we've seen with Alipay, a flexible, user-friendly offering can capture significant market share in a very short space of time—combining this sort of usability with the opportunity of an M-PESA could create a compelling offering which would remove the need for traditional banks, NGOs and government-sponsored schemes, reducing the costs associated with MFIs and the barriers to entry for traditional banks. hiveonline is piloting this approach in several developing countries.

Many of the solutions we've described in this chapter, especially those based on blockchain, could present real alternatives to banks, and they're launching in markets with a significant need; this could mean that, contrary to received wisdom, these countries could simply bypass the traditional banking system and start to prosper thanks to financial inclusion via non-traditional providers.

This, then, will present a challenge to regulators: a payments provider can operate under fairly simple legislation, and relatively light regulation, because they are not holding money on the customer's behalf. An e-money provider may have some more controls, as they are holding money but, as with M-PESA, that money, in digital form, is owned and controlled by the customer; unlike banks, they can't use it for liquidity. And, most importantly, they can't "print money" under fractional reserve rules, so don't run the high default risk that means our banks are so tightly regulated.

As we've discussed in the chapter on Central Bank Digital Currencies, a significant move towards alternative providers in developed economies could present a risk to the traditional financial industry, because of disruption to these reserves. But if what these providers are replacing is nothing, or the already lightly regulated alternative providers, it doesn't appear to pose much of a risk to traditional banks in these economies. The case for light regulation will still be strong, allowing these services to grow and mature, and fill the vacuum, but will also require governments and regulators to welcome more competition for the existing wallet providers.

This will be good news for those providers, but very good news indeed for the populations they serve, who will gain access to flexible, full-service finance without the need to overcome the high barriers presented by traditional banks.

But for traditional banks elsewhere, it presents a risk. As we've seen with M-PESA, taking success from Kenya doesn't mean it'll land with equal success in other parts of the world, so there's no guarantee a cookie-cutter approach will work. However, as these services get more useful, cheaper and more flexible, the banks will need to decide whether they should be participating in this market, or letting it push them aside.

Conclusion

Alternative financial services for the unbanked have been around for a while; they have, to date, been expensive and inefficient, poorly controlled and subject to government top-ups. With the rise of M-PESA, a template for alternative financial services that are relatively cheap and useful has demonstrated that (almost) universal financial inclusion is possible, even in developing countries, with relatively basic technology.

Financial and identity inclusion has made a significant difference to disadvantaged groups such as refugees and particularly women micro-entrepreneurs, enabling them to build identity and financial records and break out of poverty. They create cross-generational improvements by increasing access to education, and enabling communities to collaborate.

The new generation of Bitcoin-enabled services for the financially excluded present the opportunity to offer rich remittance, identity and money management services for the unbanked; while in their early stages today, results so far have been good and there's growing adoption. These next generation services could be the answer to filling the gap for the unbanked across developing countries everywhere, and reduce reliance on traditional banking services as the answer to financial inclusion.

Regulatory barriers can be low for these new businesses, allowing them to compete and grow, but requires government support for further innovation beyond today's wallet providers; while this is great news for the unbanked in developing economies, it could also present a threat to financial services institutions in more developed parts of the world, particularly those with a significant unbanked population, such as the USA, where 20% of the populations of Miami and Detroit are unbanked, according to statistics.[18]

Notes

1. Global Findex Database. *World Bank*. http://www.worldbank.org/en/programs/globalfindex. Accessed 1 January 2018.
2. Financial Inclusion. *CGAP*. http://www.cgap.org/topics/financial-inclusion. Accessed 1 January 2018.
3. Donou-Adonsou, F., & Sylwester, K. (2016, June). Financial Development and Poverty Reduction in Developing Countries: New Evidence from Banks and Microfinance Institutions. *Review of Development Finance, 6*, 1 (Science Direct). https://www.sciencedirect.com/science/article/pii/S1879933715300920. Accessed 1 January 2018.
4. Access to Financial Services in Developing Countries. *Rabobank*, September 2005. https://economie.rabobank.com/PageFiles/3584/access_tcm64-75165.pdf. Accessed 1 January 2018.
5. World Bank Infographic. *Findex*, 2015. http://www.worldbank.org/content/dam/Worldbank/Research/GlobalFindex/Findex_Infographic_Regional_SSA.jpg.
6. BitPesa Home page. https://www.bitpesa.co/. Accessed 1 January 2018.
7. Rossiello, E. (2017, September 6). Interview. *Leaders League*. http://www.leadersleague.com/en/news/elizabeth-rossiello-bitpesa-we-have-lowered-the-cost-of-international-payments-by-75. Accessed 1 January 2018.
8. Everex Homepage. https://www.everex.io/. Accessed 1 January 2018.
9. Stellar Homepage. https://www.stellar.org/. Accessed 1 January 2018.

10. Praekelt Homepage. https://www.praekelt.org/. Accessed 1 January 2018.

11. HumanIQ Homepage. https://humaniq.com/. Accessed 1 January 2018.

12. BanQu Homepage. http://www.banquapp.com/. Accessed 1 January 2018.

13. ID202 Homepage. http://id2020.org/. Accessed 1 January 2018.

14. White, D. (2012, Spring). The Social and Economic Impact of M-PESA on the Lives of Women in the Fishing Industry on Lake Victoria. *SIT Library*. http://digitalcollections.sit.edu/isp_collection/1246/. Accessed 1 January 2018.

15. Stahl, L. (2015, November 22). The Future of Money. *CBSN*. https://www.cbsnews.com/news/future-of-money-kenya-M-PESA-60-minutes/. Accessed 1 January 2018.

16. Murray, K. (2017, June 9). Africa, the Unbanked Continent. *Elixirr*. https://www.elixirr.com/2017/06/africa-the-unbanked-continent/. Accessed 1 January 2018.

17. Kenya Bank Accounts per 1000 population, FRED Economic Data, 2015. https://fred.stlouisfed.org/series/DDAI01KEA642NWDB. Accessed 1 January 2018.

18. Most Unbanked Places in America, 2009, CFED.org. http://seetekcorp.com/img/Most_Unbanked_Places_in_America.pdf. Accessed 1 January 2018.

The Un-bank, Part III
Fintech for Financial Inclusion *Building the Future*

In the previous two sections, we explored first, how the world of finance is changing towards a new, ecosystem economy and how this presents both challenges and opportunities for banks, but more importantly, great opportunities for the unbanked. We explored the developments that are likely to drive future finance for all customers, and how the smaller entity, as part of the ecosystem, is becoming more important and powerful. We described how alternative finance is already emerging as a powerful tool for new players in the ecosystem economy, although the technology has been relatively immature, but is now poised to mature and support a fundamental rebalancing of financial services.

In this section, we describe the new models that will drive the development of that new economy, with a focus on the areas where the revolution is the most extreme, i.e. the developing economies of the world. We show how these models will help accelerate efforts to reach the UN's Global Sustainable Development Goals, by addressing some of the big challenges of provenance, corruption and traceability that have presented barriers. Communities of small businesses are a key element of this, and we show how technology and new service models can help to drive development through alternative financing and removing barriers in some of the world's most needy communities.

8

Alternative Wealth: The Cow in Your Pocket

As we have discussed throughout this section, blockchain technology innovations offer a lot more than just cryptocurrencies; in fact, they can provide a whole range of new opportunities that are nothing to do with digital money. In this chapter, we discuss how blockchain technology, through tokenisation of physical assets and behaviours, enables the creation of new types of community currency, which can be used to shape, support and bind global and local communities.

We present how this can support value chain provenance, and how it can guarantee origin of goods and behaviours of actors in a system. We show how new asset-based tokens will change our relationship with currency and securities, as they become transactable and it becomes possible to hold a portfolio of assets without participating in traditional capital markets or banking. Finally, we show how these new asset types are being used, combining both tokenised assets with the blockchain benefits of being trusted, faster, more transparent and far more efficient than traditional supply chains.

Behaviours and Things as Money

As we discussed in Chapter 4, there are many types of money, and our concepts of money and our relationship with value are changing, due to evolving technology and the way we transact. As we've shown, value systems exist today to support networks of people exchanging value for particular things or particular reasons—for example, reward points, local currencies and securities of various types.

© The Author(s) 2018
S. Blakstad and R. Allen, *FinTech Revolution*,
https://doi.org/10.1007/978-3-319-76014-8_8

Your reward point supplier gives you value for visiting a particular shop or using an airline, while a local currency can only be obtained or spent in a certain locality—these are examples of a behaviour-linked value system; you are rewarded for certain behaviours and value returns in the shape of goods and services, provided by the community or organisation that issues the unit of value. Securities such as futures and even equity and bonds are value systems based on assets, the asset being the underlying commodity or company.

We described how many blockchain-based companies are now issuing Initial Coin Offerings (ICOs) to raise capital for their startup via a token system. Some of these tokens are linked to an underlying asset; either the company itself or a value system it has invented. For example, SolarCoin[1] and Solara[2] are tokens linked to solar energy production and reward producers for producing solar energy. In the case of Solara, the tokens are verifiably linked to the actual energy production of a particular solar panel, via a process termed Proof of Fusion, enabling the very photons striking the panel to be tokenised before being adulterated or intermediated by less green processes that could corrupt the purity of the feed into the respective smart meter (see Fig. 8.1).

Solar and renewable energy token issuance is seeing a surge; it is linked to both an asset (energy) and a behaviour (clean production) that also represents a rapidly growing construction/build phase for the underlying assets. This is popular because of the rising number of investors wanting to know that their money is supporting clean and green businesses, but who also

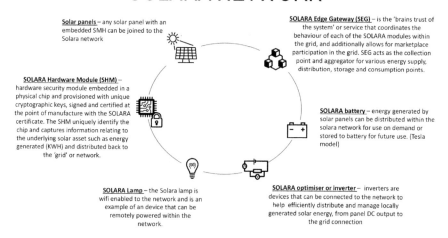

SOLARA NETWORK

Solar panels – any solar panel with an embedded SMH can be joined to the Solara network

SOLARA Edge Gateway (SEG) – is the 'brains trust of the system' or service that coordinates the behaviour of each of the SOLARA modules within the grid, and additionally allows for marketplace participation in the grid. SEG acts as the collection point and aggregator for various energy supply, distribution, storage and consumption points.

SOLARA Hardware Module (SHM) – hardware security module embedded in a physical chip and provisioned with unique cryptographic keys, signed and certified at the point of manufacture with the SOLARA certificate. The SHM uniquely identify the chip and captures information relating to the underlying solar asset such as energy generated (KWH) and distributed back to the 'grid' or network.

SOLARA battery – energy generated by solar panels can be distributed within the solara network for use on demand or stored to battery for future use. (Tesla model)

SOLARA Lamp – the Solara lamp is wifi enabled to the network and is an example of a device that can be remotely powered within the network.

SOLARA optimiser or inverter – inverters are devices that can be connected to the network to help efficiently distribute and manage locally generated solar energy, from panel DC output to the grid connection

Fig. 8.1 The Solara Network (*Source* Solara whitepaper[3])

want a reliable asset which won't deteriorate in value—in fact, the falling price of solar energy may impact some of the issuance, depending on the token economics of the particular system, but at least purchasers know that there is something real underpinning it, and which can be exchanged for other types of value. In the case of a Solara, there is a direct relationship between the energy output and the token, which is encoded into the rules governing the creation of new value tokens.

In this way, purchasers can be confident that the token or coin represents a valid asset that has been generated in the agreed way, meeting the asset and behaviour criteria. If the process for its generation is trusted, then the token is trusted and that is the basis for trust relationships within the ecosystem. The token can then be exchanged for other goods and services and, like the Central Bank Digital Currencies we described, can, if desired, be programmed to only be transactable in certain circumstances, for example for other sustainably produced goods or within a certain community.

For communities with shared values, this represents an opportunity to link behaviour and particular types of goods and services within a value ecosystem, analogous to a local currency, but with more fungibility, or a green milestone linked tiered credit scheme, but without the administration.

Tokens issued against green energy validate that the source of the energy was green and can then be used in the production of new types of derivative or synthetic financial products. They can also be included in green bonds and Green ETFs for which there is massive demand. However, any asset can be tokenised and carry validations of how the asset was produced or where it originated; for example, gold or precious metals being mined in an ethical way, or cows being raised in farms meeting animal husbandry or organic standards.

Tokenised Assets in Value Chains

Associating tokens with assets isn't just a useful way of guaranteeing transactable value. It is also a way of tracking the asset through a supply chain, which can help by assuring purchasers of the origin of the asset, or how it has been processed along the way. This has great significance for goods that are today subject to fraud and corruption, especially food, which has been the subject of many scandals in the last few years. Some examples of these problems are:

Meat, such as beef: a very high profile set of cases in 2013 highlighted the difficulty of establishing the origins of, and the scale of adulteration of, meat in processed products.[4] Processed products included mislabelled horsemeat (including registered riding horses, whose microchips were found in the investigation), pig and offal, while goat was being mis-sold as lamb. The scandal involved a complicated supply chain of abattoirs, packagers, processors and reprocessors, and while some major actors were identified, as the investigation progressed it became clear that adulteration of meat in cheap processed meat products was widespread and deeply embedded into the industry.

There are several groups already using blockchain technology to trace food origin, such as UK startup Provenance,[5] which traces meat back to the origin—the farmer, the location and, if you want to know, the cow it came from. This tracking follows the meat through the supply chain via a variety of IoT and physical tracking approaches to follow the product through the process.

Food safety has also hit the headlines in recent years, notably the melamine milk adulteration scandal in China in 2008, which killed several babies and made 300,000 ill.[6] The crisis raised awareness in China on the risks of food adulteration, and since then, many other scandals have come to light; the old paper-based supply chain management, as in Europe, was subject to fraud, and the financial rewards for passing off substandard or adulterated food were enormous. Fraud costs are reported to cost the global food industry an estimated $US40 billion annually.[7] PwC research found that 39% of food companies said it was easy to fake their products and 42% believed there is no method for detecting fraud, beyond standard food checks.

Spurred by the need to create a safe, reliable alternative to the supply chain problems, a number of alliances have formed to address it. Alibaba with PwC, Australia Post, Blackmores and Fonterra, has been building a food trust framework and blockchain-based solution.[8] Meanwhile, Walmart, IBM and Tsinghua University have been trialling blockchain to track Chinese food supplies, including milk, with great success.[9]

Blockchain can also help to identify sources of bacterial or other infection, tackling problems such as salmonella in the food supply, which have historically been very difficult to pinpoint.[10]

As well as horsemeat, Provenance have also been working on ethical supply chains, using the same technology on the seafood industry, which is currently littered with illegal practices and human rights abuses.[11] Fishing as an industry is also challenged by the need to manage stocks sustainably, and this approach can be used to ensure sustainable stocks are being fished, as we discuss later in Chapter 11.

Alongside sustainability and tackling of modern-day slavery, blockchain can be used to ensure fair trade for the supply chain from producers to payments. Startup bext360[12] is combining the technology with AI and smart booths to ensure fair prices for coffee producers (predominantly women) in Africa, following successful trials in the Americas.[13] The AI integration both grades the coffee and uses facial recognition for the grower, ensuring payments reach the right person and that they are given a fair price for their produce.

Similar combinations of biometric recognition and blockchain have been used for humanitarian goods distribution, as we expand on in Green Fintech.

These examples of blockchain use cases are all reducing inefficiency, corruption and fraud, helping small producers and consumers to be confident that their goods travel through the supply chain unadulterated and ensuring that they are compensated appropriately. By supporting value chain provenance, these systems are guaranteeing origin of goods and the behaviours of actors in a system and by extension building trust—the core value proposition of blockchains. It is not clear whether the implementation of these systems actually tokenise the physical asset before tracking its passage down the supply chain or whether they use other beneficial properties of the blockchain such as its immutability, security, shared data between all participants and transparency.

However, one can imagine such a system, where physical assets are represented by digital tokens—for example, a cow as a coin. That CowCoin can then be passed from farmer to abattoir to distributor to supermarket down the supply chain—usually in return for payments flowing in the reverse direction. Like money, CowCoin has value, is divisible (post-abattoir) and can be used in transactions. Although the token is as unique as Daisy the cow was, it is also fungible in that equal value CowCoins can be considered to be equivalent and can therefore be spent in the same way.

These blockchain systems can be employed to program CowCoin to behave in specific ways under specific conditions, perhaps automatically changing state if certain prerequisites are met (if becomes unsuitable for consumption if temperature conditions move outside programmed tolerances, for example). By recording, immutably, the real-world conditions that affect the asset, with data sourced via "trusted oracles", i.e. deterministic data feeds from trusted sources, the token itself can exactly represent the physical product with which it is associated and the transitions and changes in state during the journey from field to fork. This can even represent the division into multiple parts, or assembly with other tokens into a group representing a new thing (a pie), and ultimately the destruction of the token as it leaves the ecosystem to be consumed.

Given a system such as this, an end consumer should be able to scan a product in a supermarket (or observe it through their augmented reality headset) and see exactly where that product comes from, together with fact-based assurance of sustainability, or whatever other trust categorisation that is important to the consumer.

The challenge with such a system is maintaining the link between the physical thing and the token representing it. Even with barcodes stamped on the products, QR codes, RFID tags, even secret transmitters in the lining of luxury goods, we cannot get away from a certain level of inspection, human or robot, to provide assurance that that link has been maintained throughout.

This does not mean that every beefburger needs to have its barcode scanned at every handover point in the supply chain, which would not be practical economically; that trade-off means that there will always be some uncertainty about whether the goods have been tampered with—for example, the shipping container taking a different route and being delayed; or the grain being commingled with grain from an unusual source. This is not a new problem for industries employing long value chains and one for which blockchains are not the silver bullet. That said, technology solutions such as those used in the value chains described above: AI, IoT, drones and other "smart" systems, are being used to reduce the uncertainty and risk to within tolerance.

There are many good white papers on supply chain use cases for blockchain; here are some recommendations:

1. Trust in trade: Toward stronger supply chains, IBM[14]
2. The paper trail of a shipping container, IBM[15]
3. When two chains combine - Supply chain meets blockchain, Deloitte[16]
4. The Benefits of Blockchain to Supply Chain Networks, IBM Watson Customer Engagement[17]

New Asset Classes, New Wealth

The cow analogy works to a point; beyond that, consider other types of non-currency or security asset that can be owned. Gold, property, land titles, water rights, carbon credits and vintage cars are all candidates! All these can be tokenised and, as long as parties to a transaction involving them trust that the owner of the token representing the thing, actually owns the thing, and that transferring ownership of the token does the same for the thing, with legal protection, there's no reason why these tokenised assets shouldn't be treated in a similar way to a currency.

These asset tracking tokens have transactable value within their own eco-system, and as they become more widely used, are likely also to become units of currency that can be transacted outside of that supply chain, and used as a store of wealth. This enables communities to use and transact with value associated with assets and behaviours that are meaningful for them. As an example, consider cultures which traditionally measure wealth in heads of cattle.[18] Livestock Wealth is a crowdfunding platform that uses traditional technology entirely in tune with the cultural memory of its African customers that associate cattle with wealth. Combining this use case with the tokenisation of cows could be a powerful next step to make these assets more fungible and accessible. CowCoin, in this example, would provide a more granular asset for these investors that could be traded in marketplaces and potentially even have innovative derivatives and synthetics built on top of it.

This example can be extended to any community or culture with strong ethical values that they wish to perpetuate throughout the community, and with technology being global, communities that are now widespread diasporas have ways to maintain cultural ties even though the community may be distributed.

Gold, also, is an asset that is ideal for tokenisation. There are cultures, India for example, that just love gold and can't get enough of it. However, other than looking good as jewellery and being a pretty good store of value, it is a difficult thing to use as an alternative form of money. If, however, one stored it with a trusted vault provider which then issued digital tokens against the deposit, the token could be stored in a digital wallet or be transferred to other wallets or even used in payment for goods, then it becomes very useful.

This kind of innovation could potentially change entire developing economies that are wealthy in terms of precious metals but are otherwise impoverished and bound to the US dollar as a reserve currency. For example, In Indonesia, the lease for Grasberg mine, the largest gold mine globally, reverts to the nation in 2019. A state-issued IndGoldToken (our term, not a real thing), a parallel currency fully controlled by Indonesia and backed against the Grasberg reserve gold, would allow Indonesia to fully leverage Grasberg and provide the Indonesian Government with a natural hedge against loans benchmarked to gold.

This could also lower capital costs; with IndGoldToken, the Indonesian Government would avoid exposure to US government monetary policy and a foreign currency. Interest rates on IndGoldToken loans to the Indonesian Government should be lower than equivalent USD debt issues as there is no inflation component. Savings in comparison with raising funds via 10–30 year bonds in USD could be significant. Banks could manage sovereign risk for loans to the Indonesian Government in IndGoldToken by using Grasberg equity or income streams as collateral and/or syndicating loans. A system such as this has been proposed by Australian startup, Soveren.[19]

At the other end of the spectrum, the alluvial gold found by villagers artisan mining in Papua New Guinea could similarly be tokenised (again given a trusted vault to store the stuff in) and distributed into marketplaces globally, without the current problem of intermediaries taking a cut and leaving the villagers with a tiny fraction of the real value of their natural resource.[20]

So, once an asset is tokenised and available to its owner to use in the same way we use digital money, then other money-like systems and interactions can be built which employ the new asset type—account balances, payments, exchange, securitisation, pooling, lending—anything that the individual and her community consider as having value and with which they want to transact.

This has particular implications for the world's unbanked and also indigenous populations. These communities may not be traditionally wealthy (i.e. rich with fiat currency) and have little or no access to the banking infrastructures that the rest of the world take for granted. What they often do have is alternative forms of wealth.

- Land titles
- Water rights
- Renewable energy assets, solar, etc.
- Carbon credits
- Grants and rewards for green and sustainable community projects.

These new types of wealth, once tokenised, can be stored in digital wallets on mobile phones, used in payment, loaned or used to secure lines of credit—all familiar banking concepts, but based on a new community-based financial services paradigm. By extension, these asset-based currencies will also change our relationship with securities, as it becomes possible to hold a portfolio of transactable assets without participating in traditional capital markets.

The only time a bank needs to be involved is when there is a need to exchange into fiat currency. And as the ecosystem grows and includes many different actor types, as with traditional money systems, it would reach a point of self-sufficiency, like a digital bartering community where fiat is not even necessary.

Conclusion

In this chapter, we've shown how blockchain is already being used both to tokenise assets and to create confidence and security in asset-based supply chains; we've presented a wide range of examples where this is already being used to improve food standards and save lives. We've speculated how a new type of asset and behaviour-based security, such as a solar energy token, can enable communities to transact with a currency system that guarantees support of their value system.

We've shown how the supply chain blockchain security and value-based tokenisation of assets have the opportunity to converge, to create asset-based currencies which will enable communities rich in natural resources to benefit from these assets within those communities, rather than being subject to exploitation because of the need to interact with traditional currencies and many intermediaries.

The Cow in your Pocket is just one form of alternative wealth that could present a shift of value from Old World, country-based fiats towards community assets, and the rebalancing of wealth towards disadvantaged and exploited communities globally. It also represents one of the key changes from a global financial ecosystem based primarily on fiat currencies, towards one based on transactable assets. We're helping to support this movement at hiveonline, and as we've shown above, we're not alone. Your dollar will soon be rubbing shoulders with Daisy, gold and solar photon-generated cryptograms.

Notes

1. SolarCoin Homepage. https://solarcoin.org/en/node/6. Accessed 10 January 2018.
2. Solara Homepage. http://www.solara.io/. Accessed 10 January 2018.
3. Solara Homepage. http://www.solara.io/. Accessed 10 January 2018.
4. Lawrence, F. (2017, July 26). Horsemeat Trial Shines Light on Key Part of International Fraud. *The Guardian*. https://www.theguardian.com/uk-news/2017/jul/26/horsemeat-trial-shines-light-international-fraud. Accessed 10 January 2018.
5. Provenance Homepage. https://www.provenance.org/. Accessed 10 January 2018, a UK Company; Coleman, L. (2017, August 3). Farmers Cooperative Uses Blockchain to Trace Meat Through Supply Chain. *CCN*. https://www.ccn.com/farmers-cooperative-uses-blockchain-to-trace-meat-through-supply-chain/. Accessed 10 January 2018.

6. The 2008 Milk Scandal Revisited. https://www.forbes.com/sites/yanzhong-huang/2014/07/16/the-2008-milk-scandal-revisited. Accessed 10 January 2018.
7. Measuring and Managing Trust in Your Food, PwC. https://www.pwc.com/gx/en/services/food-supply-integrity-services/publications.html. Accessed 10 January 2018.
8. Alibaba, PwC, Blackmores, AusPost Team Blockchain Initiative. https://which-50.com/alibaba-pwc-blackmores-auspost-team-blockchain-initiative/. Accessed January 2018.
9. Parker, L. (2016, October 22). Walmart, IBM and Tsinghua University to Use a Blockchain for Food Supply Chain Tracking in China. *Brave New Coin*. https://bravenewcoin.com/news/walmart-ibm-and-tsinghua-university-to-use-a-blockchain-for-food-supply-chain-tracking-in-china/. Accessed 10 January 2018.
10. Aitken, R. (2017, August 2). IBM Forges Blockchain Collaboration With Nestlé & Walmart in Global Food Safety. *Forbes*. https://www.forbes.com/sites/rogeraitken/2017/08/22/ibm-forges-blockchain-collaboration-with-nestle-walmart-for-global-food-safety/#6ebbb193d361. Accessed 10 January 2018.
11. Levitt, T. (2016, September 7). Blockchain Technology Trialled to Tackle Slavery in the Fishing Industry. *The Guardian*. https://www.theguardian.com/sustainable-business/2016/sep/07/blockchain-fish-slavery-free-seafood-sustainable-technology; Coleman, L. (2016, September 8). Blockchain Technology to Help Fight Slavery in the Fishing Industry. *CCN*. https://www.ccn.com/blockchain-technology-help-fight-slavery-fishing-industry/. Accessed 10 January 2018.
12. Bext360 Homepage. http://www.bext360.com/. Accessed 10 January 2018.
13. Clancy, H. (2017, April 12). Can This Start-Up Use Blockchain to Brew Up More Sustainable Coffee? *GreenBiz*. https://www.greenbiz.com/article/can-start-up-use-blockchain-brew-more-sustainable-coffee. Accessed 10 January 2018.
14. Lubowe, D., & McDermott, B. (2016). Trust in Trade: Toward Stronger Supply Chain. IBM, September 2016. https://public.dhe.ibm.com/common/ssi/ecm/gb/en/gbe03771usen/GBE03771USEN.PDF. Accessed 12 January 2018.
15. The Paper Trail of a Shipping Container (IBM). https://public.dhe.ibm.com/common/ssi/ecm/xi/en/xi912347usen/XI912347USEN.PDF. Accessed 12 January 2018.
16. Kohe, L. et al. (2017). When Two Chains Combine—Supply Chain Meets Blockchain. Deloitte. https://www2.deloitte.com/content/dam/Deloitte/us/Documents/strategy/us-cons-supply-chain-meets-blockchain.pdf. Accessed 12 January 2018.

17. The Benefits of Blockchain to Supply Chain Networks, IBM Watson Customer Engagement (IBM), March 2017. https://www-01.ibm.com/software/commerce/offers/pdfs/Blockchain_3-15-2017.pdf. Accessed 12 January 2018.

18. Tsele, L. (2016, January 21). Crowd-Farming Platform Wants to Launch African Wealth into the Mainstream. *SME South Africa*. https://www.smesouthafrica.co.za/16346/Livestock-Wealth-Bridging-tradition-and-technology/. Accessed 10 January 2018.

19. Soveren Homepage. http://www.soveren.co/. Accessed 10 January 2018.

20. Small Scale Gold Mining and Marketing in Papua New Guinea, Professor Surek Bordia, Professor and Head Department of Mining Engineering PNG University of Technology Lae, Papua New Guinea (Utah University). https://pharmacy.utah.edu/ICBG/pdf/WebResources/ForestBiodiversity/New-Guinea-Gold-mining.pdf. Accessed 12 January 2018.

9

New Standard Models for Banking

The disruption arising from changing customer behaviour and use of technology has come later to banking than to most other industries. Banking, as we've observed, is a very conservative industry, and even Challenger Banks and Fintechs are largely constrained by conservative approaches, engendered by regulation and the need for security and stability. We believe this need for security and stability will never go away—after all, customers will always want to know that their money is safe—but we are seeing new ways to protect and guarantee emerge, arising both from new paradigms in financial services and from reduced confidence in sovereign currencies. In parallel, new digital or crypto currencies are emerging, first from non-traditional issuers (Bitcoin, Ethereum, et al.), from consortia of incumbent banks and, as we discussed in Chapter 5, fairly soon from central banks themselves, exploiting blockchain technology and trust-based authentication rather than traditional intermediaries.

In this chapter, we explore how traditional banking operating models are struggling, and describe the emerging models for banks that are being adopted both by incumbents and by challengers, together with some of the opportunities and challenges these new models present. It's important to bear in mind that this is still a relatively new industry development and, like every other major disruption, early adopters and leading-edge pioneers are more likely to get it wrong than right. We believe some will succeed, but today there is limited evidence to indicate who that will be.

For the purpose of this chapter, we have segmented the different models as follows; however, in reality there is a spectrum and no clear boundaries between these models:

© The Author(s) 2018
S. Blakstad and R. Allen, *FinTech Revolution*,
https://doi.org/10.1007/978-3-319-76014-8_9

- Traditional banking
- Challenger banking
- Ecosystem banking

Traditional Banking: Over-Diversification and Complexity

When we use "Traditional" to describe a banking model, we're describing a model that has actually arisen relatively recently. Before the emergence of Universal Banks, following changes to regulation which allowed banks to conduct retail, transaction and investment banking, banks were one or the other, but for the sake of simplicity, we'll use the word "Traditional" to describe the combined, universal bank model.

Traditional banks share the following characteristics:

- Full-service model, including retail, commercial, wholesale, capital markets, wealth management and in most cases insurance services offered through third parties
- Captive supporting services—banking operations, technology, finance, HR, risk management, etc., managed internally within the bank
- Captive data centres where core customer and account data reside on bank-owned mainframes
- Self-developed front-end applications and apps (web front ends, mobile apps, etc.)
- Branches and contact centres
- ATMs, cards and (increasingly) contactless and mobile payments
- Organisationally siloed, divided by business line
- Geographically siloed by country
- Deep hierarchies with businesses structured according to function (e.g. retail banking operations)
- Heavily controlled via performance metrics linked to units (products sold, time taken to respond, etc.)
- Request-driven, product-centred service models (Fig. 9.1)

It's also important to note the drivers that have shaped banks like this—first, deregulation led to the opportunity to merge previously separated banking models; then, following collapses, scandals and backlash after the financial crisis in 2008/2009, heavy regulation and the need to demonstrate control became dominant. The combination of the land grab culture which followed

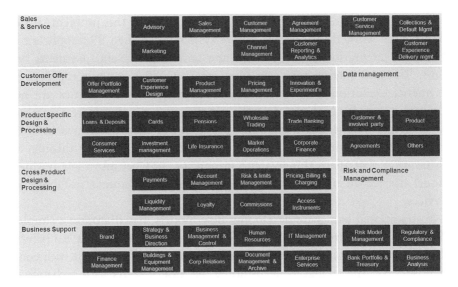

Fig. 9.1 Full-service capability model for traditional banks

deregulation, and then reputational risk, fines and censure imposed by more rigorous legislation, has further enforced the existing command and control culture we described in Chapter 1, creating a culture where decision making is associated with authority and seniority, and where ownership is equated with security. Because senior leaders are held accountable for the outcome of decisions, they feel it is safer to control those decisions personally, rather than delegating them to people who have the opportunity to acquire and use specialised knowledge pertinent to the subject. Instead, decision making is highly centralised and hierarchical, leading to decision support industries within banks and massive bottlenecks in senior managers' diaries.

The belief that diversity of products is central to (especially corporate) customers' experience, based on the desire to be central to customer relationships, and the need to offer every flavour of customer experience, is in many ways a contradictory driver, which together with the need for control has led to banks becoming both excessively complex and almost entirely self-built and run. This complexity is further increased as most universal banks today have formed through years of merger and acquisition, often integrating multiple systems and processes rather than replacing the redundant legacy systems on merger.

Universal banks have recognised that this complexity presents a risk. It has become impossible for them to understand their own risk profile and the management of very complex, and usually ageing legacy infrastructure is both costly and risky. To give an idea of the scale of this problem, a programme we worked on to replace core systems identified 992 applications that were integration points for the new core banking and payments systems. The new payments system was replacing 80 payments capture, 25 payments execution and 40 settlements systems. These statistics are not unusual. Large banks have, over the years, invested more in remediation, system replacement and integration programmes than they have invested in developing customer experience or innovation research—not through an assumption that these things aren't important, but because their business model has led to unsustainable complexity and consequent instability of services.

So traditional banks are developing new models, based around a simpler, more customer-centric view of the world, but implementing this is a painful challenge, and we have not yet seen any universal bank address it with complete success. The change is deep-rooted, because it starts with a change to culture and assumptions about customers which are still based in the "old" world and, in many cases, this has been impossible to effect.

Challenger Banks: Facing Problems of Maturity and Experience

In contrast, Challenger Banks are largely being built ground-up, unhampered by the baggage of the universal banks and their inherited complexities. However, they face challenges of their own, and while there is no "typical" model for a Challenger Bank, most share the following characteristics:

- Focused on limited customer segment/offering—nearly all are aimed at Retail customers, offering accounts and cards—although there is an emerging number supporting the SME sector, see below
- Heavy use of technology as a customer differentiator
- Small and agile
- Use of Fintechs and other service providers to support customer offering
- Third-party payments infrastructure
- Self-developed core banking system (the "full stack" model) or traditional core banking managed by a third party
- No physical branches—although some use existing retail outlets, e.g. Supermarket Banks
- Untested business model/high risk for investors

- Low maturity in regulatory and compliance management

Although challengers make good use of technology, most are effectively following a reasonably traditional model, i.e. offering traditional products to traditional customers, albeit with appealing interfaces and clever apps. The challenger model we see most commonly is built by an organisation buying in expertise from traditional banks, or being founded by individuals emerging from traditional banks to inject banking expertise, together with technical specialists who build the "innovative" software on which the new bank is founded. If we look at the full-stackers, Starling, Mondo, etc., there is a strong rationale for building their own core systems, but at the risk of creating the same challenge of in-house legacy currently being remediated (very expensively) by the incumbents.

While in-house solutions can be attractive as differentiators, their uniqueness becomes a problem as systems age and need upgrading; knowledge is held in a small number of individuals, and this creates a risk, while documentation may not be as rigorous as that provided for standard systems from large vendors. On the other hand, buying in a third-party core system (as Atom has done) can create challenges to agility and real-time service provisioning. OakNorth, the first UK Challenger Bank to declare an operating profit, may be the first of many to go for cloud-based third-party core banking, which may address this challenge.

Ecosystem Banks: Collaborative, Customer-Centric Services

A third generation of banks are now offering what we call the Ecosystem model, where the service layer is the USP and the bank is effectively a marketplace for services offered by third-party providers, together with core banking services offered by the bank or via its partners. While the examples of this model are limited, the approach is gathering some momentum and we expect to see more emerging.

Ecosystem banks are characterised by:

- SME/Entrepreneur target market
- Low number of "captive" technology-based services
- Offering a variety of loosely interconnected service providers
- Heavy reliance on partnership with Fintechs
- Distributed business model

- A "full service" approach—some services offered fall outside traditional financial services
- Small, agile core team
- Business/customer service focused rather than tech focused

These banks superficially look very much like the other Challenger Banks, but their focus is different; their customers are entrepreneurs and SMEs with complex financial management needs, and the extension beyond traditional banking services into financial management of services within the customer's "business as usual" (BAU) operations represents a significant shift of focus from traditional banking. These banks regard their USP as offering service management at the core, rather than financial services, acknowledging that the financial needs of customers extend beyond traditional product-based banking. We anticipate that this model will become one of the new standards.

The Evolution of Banking Infrastructure

One of the key challenges facing new banks and incumbents alike, is the significant cost associated with maintenance of infrastructure supporting core banking and transaction processing, which is still largely held on mainframe systems. Mainframes have the advantage of security, high availability and stability, which has made them the default for critical banking applications. Mainframes are very expensive for banks to maintain. Specialist (and increasingly rare) legacy skills need to be procured and retained; complex organisations have developed over years to manage and remediate them; and the cost of changing these systems to accommodate the consumer expectations of customer centricity and instant gratification is prohibitive. Also, unless very well managed, mainframes usually carry more redundancy than required. Maintaining failover is part of this, and managing potential peaks in usage is a significant driver, but the long lifecycle of mainframes also means that planning must be done with uncertain forecast usage information, which leads to greater redundancy. Mainframes are now increasingly being used for virtualisation, which can reduce this redundancy, but the cost of physical hardware maintenance remains.

While most banks are now using some cloud services, they are hampered by perceived and real regulatory constraints which keep them using the traditional stack. So, in addition to the mainframe cost, all banks must manage the question of how much physical hardware to maintain in the shape of midrange and micros. While not as significant as the cost of maintaining mainframe, these still represent a significant investment. One bank we worked at boasted that they had more developers than Microsoft and more storage than Google (this was some time ago!)—neither is a claim that any bank should be proud to make, given that they are neither development houses, search engines nor cloud service providers. The shift now is towards alternative infrastructure provisioning in a bid to reduce costs. Of course, with Google moving into the Financial Services sector, the quote may come full circle.

As we mentioned above, some are now exploring banking as a cloud-based service (BaaS), rather than the traditional mainframe-based approach. AliBaba[1] has launched its own BaaS platform, providing full-service core banking, KYC and many other services, supporting a number of Chinese banks and now reaching out to global markets. ThoughtMachine, a startup with several Google brains behind it, has also moved into this space, claiming to revolutionise banking by doing all core services seamlessly. While these platforms may not yet be fully mature, this trend is accelerating, and we can expect more players to enter it, replacing the traditional core banking players who provide on-site services to banks.

Traditional banks have needed to own and maintain data on their own infrastructure, because of regulatory requirements and public perception of security, not to mention their own desire to "own" and control critical data. Many regulators still require banks to hold key data, such as customer data and account data, on their own internal systems, which limits the ability of banks to evolve into using these more flexible services. This is changing as regulations evolve, and we are seeing a move towards growing acceptance of cloud-based services as regulators acknowledge that resilience and security can be managed effectively in this paradigm and the benefits of cloud, in terms of availability and reliability, are equivalent to owned systems. Today's cloud-based services can be more secure than traditional mainframe/data centre services—the shredding of encrypted data to multiple data centres and strong authentication being a key element.

However, in the interim and while both cloud security and regulations evolve, alternatives to public cloud are available in the shape of third-party providers providing their own captive data centre setups (hybrid cloud), and a number of these are already supporting many Challenger Banks and other financial institutions with software and platforms as a service (SaaS and PaaS). BaaS providers can offer tiers of service, from client site support and configuration for installations to fully managed and hosted services. Several specialist banks support other banks with payments or core banking systems, again to varying degrees. So, while regulatory drivers are an important factor in shaping how banks choose to design their operating models, the opportunities and options available are significant, and this is why we have seen the evolution of a wide variety of models; the main limitation is how the bank chooses to position itself.

Key to which model any bank—challenger or incumbent—selects for itself, is where it wants to play and what differentiates it. As discussed elsewhere, banking products per se are not differentiators, but banks have the choice of how to position themselves. For example, ING has stated very clearly that it is a technology house—it prides itself on its IT, develops in-house, and makes all its senior managers learn coding. Consequently, it has been able to support adoption of continuous delivery in technology (DevOps), giving it a competitive advantage over rivals who are slower to market with new technology and products. ING has enthusiastically embraced the new financial ecosystem, partnering with some of the more useful fintechs which support its customer needs beyond traditional services. Conversely, a bank that regards itself as a service house would focus on customer journeys, customer experience led service design, support full lifecycle customer management, and is unlikely to have an equivalent level of maturity in technical services management.

Where does this leave the universal bank? Our view is that traditional banks are currently over-diversified, and that they need to choose what sort of bank they want to become. As we discussed in Chapter 2, many alternative service providers are already emerging, and the cost of operations in a world where these services present cheaper competition is one where focus will be increasingly important to survival. As Jim Collins famously described in *Good to Great*, they need to identify the thing they do best and become the best at doing it—the "Hedgehog concept".[2] We believe that no bank is able to be great in the whole portfolio of activities it tries to manage, from IT to customer service and from Retail to Capital Markets. The evidence supports it—we have tried and failed to identify one bank that does it "all" well, despite significant research. And the reason becomes obvious when you ask your organisation a simple question, "Where do you put your smartest people?"

Understanding your focus also helps you to understand which services and elements of services you want to own and manage closely, versus which ones you feel comfortable outsourcing or buying in via partner arrangements. This is covered in more detail in Chapter 23.

There is no clear distinction between the new standard models; rather, there is a sliding scale in two dimensions—operating model being one and scale/complexity being the other. We have, for the reasons discussed, assumed that the standard "Traditional" model is no longer sustainable and have here presented alternative evolutionary directions for banks—both incumbent and challenger:

1. The infrastructure provider
2. The Supermarket Bank
3. The service bank with encapsulated IT
4. The Second Bank

The Infrastructure Provider—Technology Is Our Strength

A model that we see many traditional banks moving towards, is the bank leveraging its scale, infrastructure and technology operating strength to evolve as a centre of banking processing not just for its own customers, but for other, incumbent or emerging, financial services providers. Some of these are pure technology support organisations—for example, FiServ offers hosted BaaS to banks; some have evolved from being technology providers to obtaining banking licences enabling them to hold accounts and manage payments scheme relationships on behalf of their customers, while others are evolving from traditional universal banks into this space. The USP for these organisations is their technology, their robustness and their agility in providing services to third-party financial services customers.

There is also a small but significant number of incumbent universal banks, such as RBS,[3] currently serving this market, offering banking technology services to other smaller financial organisations as an extension of the agency banking model. Our observation is that universal banks offering these core infrastructure and banking services to other institutions are, effectively, multiple organisations running with different heartbeats, values and cultures. On the one hand, their IT service organisations run efficient sales, implementation and distribution networks akin to technology service providers, while their banking services supporting their own customers may run on more relationship-based, "traditional" banking values. The IT organisations supporting these traditional bank divisions are segmented from the IT service organisations at the expense of the native organisations' businesses.

A good example of the challenge of operating supplier infrastructure alongside "normal" banking services comes from when one of us was implementing a new core banking system into one of these banks; finding it impossible to get on the workstack to integrate with the in-house payments systems, in order to meet deadlines we had to "buy" payments services from the much more efficient, 12 week contract-to-live agency banking payments service offered by the same bank to external customers, to meet our own deadlines! Obviously, this wasn't a sustainable solution for that core system, so effectively we were forced to integrate twice, with our own payments systems, by the relative inefficiency of the in-house IT machine. This anecdote illustrates how native IT services can suffer if banks try to provide both IT services and internal IT—again, how do you answer the question "where do we put our smartest people?"—in this case, the answer was firmly "in the revenue generating IT division", at the expense of the IT underpinning the bank's own customers' services.

This is why we believe, while there is definitely a niche for payments and account management services offered by banks to other institutions, especially as the Challenger market grows, the suppliers that will be successful in this sector will be those that firmly place themselves in the "we're an IT company" corner, rather than trying to do it all. ING is an exception, in that they have badged themselves as an ecosystem IT company and in many ways, are moving into the fifth category we describe in this chapter; we will be watching them with interest.

This is also an opportunity niche for Fintechs evolving towards a more full-service banking technology model, and a variety of these have started to emerge, particularly from the old core banking technology sector. These organisations may lack much of the banking know-how embedded in the incumbents and may focus less on important considerations such as risk and regulation when integrating their services, which could present a risk for customers from less mature sectors, who as startups, themselves may lack this knowledge. Alongside these players, there is an evolving trend for providers offering BaaS[4] (usually without needing a banking licence) to be cloud-based, offering security guarantees but in ways not fully compliant with regulations.

However, it will also be very interesting to observe how these organisations progress as the maturity of the sector evolves. While BaaS and agency banking are well established in the industry, the emergence of Fintechs into this space and the evolution of traditional banks towards this model are both shaping the future of this area of banking in unpredictable ways. We're interested to understand how this will affect the traditional banks who have offered a full-service model, in competition with the technology specific offerings emerging today.

The Supermarket Bank—We've Got Customers, Why Not?

Several organisations (not just supermarkets) are capitalising on their customer base to increase their offering by including banking or financial services, using their scale, their established reputation and their customer numbers to develop a business case. Mostly, the offerings of these banks are limited to retail and small business banking with cards and insurance boltons, although we have also seen growing diversification of services.

What we find interesting about these banks is that they're not trying to offer a significantly different service model to traditional banks; rather, they are trying to capture existing market from traditional customers by giving them a similar, or sometimes, cut-down, model to the traditional banks, but using the power of their brand or, simply, *not* being an incumbent, to attract customers. The driver is clear; traditional banks are getting a hammering from governments, regulators, the press and pressure groups, so setting up an alternative is attractive at the moment, and customers are moving despite the relative lack of difference.

This trend is a very important stepping stone on the journey to the ecosystem bank; while the Supermarket Bank offers basic retail services, with no desire to enter capital markets, they are a perfect example of how extending service offerings to customers who previously associated the organisation with a different, but related, core service, and want an alternative to the big banks, can work seamlessly.

However, like full-stack service banks, the Supermarket Bank model is usually relatively traditional in approach and limited in market potential. These new banks are hiring old bankers, assuming that the guys from Lloyds or RBS will have the expertise they need. While this is definitely true as far as existing industry, core service, risk and compliance knowledge is concerned, this also brings in inherited assumptions about bank organisational and service structures, which has the potential to paralyse fledgling banks or at least to significantly clip their wings. The challenge of balancing traditional bank knowledge with new-bank innovative thinking is a difficult one; regulations are restrictive, and deliberately ambiguously phrased so that interpreting them is a skilled and complex business, so it's natural for new players to be cautious, but this can also impede their ability to create a truly differentiated offering.

Key questions remain to be answered before this sector can mature completely; one is, are the businesses entering this market diversifying too much and can they cope? As with banks over-diversifying by embracing insurance as well as banking, high street banking as well as capital markets, the culture and heartbeat of goods retail and other business sectors is very different from banking culture and heartbeat; these new banks require a different organisation with different values, and managing operations across such diverse businesses is likely to prove challenging. A very small number of organisations, with global reach and the financial base to create completely distinct businesses, may be successful, although even the Googles of this world may struggle in creating global business models for a new sector, where so many incumbents have failed.

Another question, which applies to all full-stackers, is how sustainable is the business model, especially now in our low, zero or negative-interest world? Retail banking and cards have always been low-margin businesses, and while economies of efficient operation can be built into these new banks more easily than into the incumbents, they lack the scale to support a large, operations-hungry and low-margin business, while going through the expensive process of acquiring new customers. While the Supermarket Banks are typically investing in vendor-supplied core systems, they're still building their total operation, usually including integration of core banking systems, in-house, at massive expense both from an initial investment perspective and in maintenance.

For global businesses such as Google and Amazon, the landscape is challenging. Current regulations require such organisations to hold licences for each territory and to comply with local regulations there, which is complex. There is currently no such thing as a global, or internet, banking licence; regulators and central banks are siloed by geography in a manner incompatible with the world we actually live in today and much of this is tied into the currency question. As regulations evolve, they may or may not provision for these mega-monopolies, but given trends in regulation, where the priority in most cases is to protect the consumer by encouraging smaller entrants, it may be a long time before global consensus is reached. As we've seen, that hasn't stopped the big platforms moving into the financial services space, with Facebook talking about issuing its own currency and multiple instances of payment and bank-style services.

The Service Bank with Encapsulated IT—Build Your Own Bank

As discussed above, there is a growing number of "full-stack" Challenger Banks offering core services to a clearly defined customer base, usually with attractive and differentiating front-end apps and offering a variety of instant or near-instant, omnichannel services. These banks are often put together by ex-bankers, frustrated with their original organisations, who still carry preconceived ideas about how banks should operate, which influence their operating model design and their choice of technology strategies. Starling's Anne Boden clearly articulates[5] the rationale for building core banking from scratch—you can alter it more easily, encounter fewer barriers to providing more real-time services, and a smooth customer experience, which are strong rationales; however, the challenge is that you are building legacy—introducing your in-house developed technology at any level means that you are, in perpetuity, responsible for every aspect of maintaining, redesigning and upgrading it; effectively you're forcing yourself into the Bank as Infrastructure bracket, without the scale, history or solid capital base of the incumbents.

Clearly, maintaining evolving solutions using modern technology is definitely not as challenging as maintaining systems written in Cobol or Assembler, and banks such as Starling can benefit from learnings from other banks, which is where an experienced CEO like Boden is critical to success, but we anticipate the same problems are likely to arise over time; as banks scale, investment in growth overshadows investment in maintenance, and your once-state-of-the-art systems eventually become buried in a soup of patched-on workarounds and integrations with acquisition organisation systems.

This, then, makes any change expensive and complex, which means more patches, workarounds and partial integrations, until you reach the point we have seen in every single incumbent bank we've worked in; the legacy system is out of date, the documentation hasn't kept up, the infrastructure is a spaghetti of magnificent complexity and your core systems are on their last legs. The support team is a shrinking and ageing set of key SMEs who become a critical point of failure as their numbers diminish, and eventually nobody in the bank really understands how the systems work. Replacing them is expensive, complex and only solves part of the problem, because you've still got the spaghetti to sort out. Every bank that we've seen replace its legacy systems has opted to buy in vendor-supplied software, rather than trying to build its own again, based on their experience with legacy. We also think that there are alternative approaches to providing integrated customer experience, flexibility and real-time services, as we discuss below.

If that sounds dystopian and over-dramatic, you haven't been close enough to the heart of the core systems and surrounding applications in a typical incumbent! While the legacy problem is addressed by the full-stack visibility Anne describes in her blog, this model isn't easy to sustain once an organisation scales.

So, while we understand the philosophy, it has surprised us that so many of the new banks are based on operating models which involve building in-house core systems. We believe these banks, Challenger or no, are effectively replicating the old model; after all, every one of today's universal banks started out as a more specialised, customer sector focused bank, that built its own core systems.

However, these banks do offer some interesting differentiators—in how they support customers and the nature of their offering; they are more likely to include "life management" apps, which extend beyond the traditional transaction account, payments, cards and mortgages offering of the traditional retail bank. This is, in turn, changing customers' expectations of what a bank can offer, which in turn is putting pressure on other challengers and incumbents alike. Boden's decision to focus on a narrow (but large) customer segment with her offering is also a strategically sensible approach, as we've discussed above, and marks Starling as a likely survivor.

As with the Supermarket Banks, we see a lot of challengers entering this space who don't clearly articulate how their business model will generate a profit. The rise of a large number of Challenger Banks in already crowded markets such as the UK also leads us to assume that most of them will fail, purely because there are not enough customers to go around. However, if they are successful in changing customer expectations and behaviour, even those that fail will have made their mark.

The Second Bank—Our Focus Is Customer Service

Other emerging challengers are positioning themselves deliberately as "second banks", explicitly offering a partial banking service either in the retail or (more rarely) the business support space, with differentiating products which are their primary focus, on top of some banking services.

Not mutually exclusive to our definition of full-stack Challengers, this model is emerging alongside the full-stackers, with critical operating model differences but little fundamental difference of philosophy. Banks building in this fourth model are focused on the differentiator they can offer to the market through their customer journeys and the services that underpin them, often linked to clever Fintech apps and appealing interfaces. These banks rely on both incumbent and, increasingly, emerging Fintech and infrastructure BaaS providers to underpin their service model with both core financial services and, to a lesser extent, the niche apps which can support their chosen offering. They share the targeted market philosophy of the full-stackers but with less of the baggage of trying to build full traditional banking models. In common with both supermarket and full-stackers, there are also significant concerns about the viability of their business models; however, operating costs are generally lower due to the more distributed risk of their operating model and the reduced need to invest in infrastructure.

As with the full-stackers, the provision of life management apps has the potential to significantly change customer behaviour and expectations, regardless of the success or failure of individual organisations in this sector. For example, Swedish bank Resurs[6] provides a wallet app for organising loyalty cards and vouchers for Swedish retailers. While this is still relatively niche, it's an example of a growing number of organisations explicitly aimed at the second bank market, never intending to capture the full portfolio of a customer's financial needs. As the service portfolios offered by these "second banks" grow, they will encroach on the portfolio of traditional bank offerings, unless those offerings are equally attractive to customers. Traditional banks, being slower to market than these more agile startups, face the choice of speeding up their product development cycles, reducing their market share, or partnering with these new competitors.

These four models are different from each other, but they have one common feature: they are all based on the traditional bank model—either as a subset of the service, or as a smaller, leaner, more agile version of the full service; using new technology and delivery channels but with mostly traditional operating models.

The fifth, emerging model of banking partially breaks this paradigm, and we believe is a key component to the future of financial services. The model is evolving and, like all new paradigms, will probably pivot significantly before it's proved in any direction, but we believe it will both support sustainable customer outcomes by leveraging traditional and emerging banking paradigms, and provide a platform that is sufficiently agile to adapt to new customer and market directions as they evolve.

The Ecosystem Bank—We're Part of How Your Business Runs

We discussed ecosystems in the first chapter. To us, the term means the breaking down of barriers between banks and their suppliers, banks and customers, and between customers and suppliers; it is about the distinction between organisations becoming less relevant and the diminishing need for full ownership of services. It is about the growth of trust- and consensus-based transfer of value, removing intermediaries to allow value chains to operate independently of central institutions like banks and governments.

So, if we are removing the intermediaries, where does that leave banks? This is the challenge that is worrying the traditional banks the most; PSD2, driving Open Banking APIs and applications of blockchain such as smart contracts and cryptocurrencies, threaten their central cost models, reducing the stickiness of their offering for customers in both retail and corporate offerings, as we discussed in Chapter 2. Banks can choose to continue to play in the old paradigm, but a combination of threat from more agile challengers and Fintechs moving into this space and the reduction of margin resulting from this competition means the opportunity to use their scale in a different way may be easier to monetise and sustain.

The ecosystem bank, fundamentally isn't really what we think of as a bank. Yes, it offers financial services—accounts, loans, payments, all the usual things—but the key thing it offers beyond traditional banks is its multi-sided platform networking, the ability to connect many to many across the network between customers, service providers and financial services including, importantly, disintermediated services where the bank is not part of the value chain at all. The bank's margin comes from customers subscribing to integrated full-service applications such as supply chain and accounting, whereas the Fintech providers pay a proportion of their transaction fees, in exchange for access to the bank's wider customer base. The bank itself only provides very core services (possibly even buying payments and core banking as BaaS), using partners to support the wide variety of services needed by its customers and using its knowledge, customer relationships and reach as key differentiators.

To achieve this, operating models must be completely rewritten. We believe that all banks will need to change their operating models and pricing models with the emergence of open data and customer ownership of data, so this challenge is not unique to new types of banks, but with a specific focus on disintermediated services, revenue models need to focus on other value adds, and therefore the service model becomes a key differentiator. This isn't any more straightforward than building traditional banking services, and risky because of the use of emerging technology and some ambiguity about the bank's purpose. It's important for these banks to be focused on market sector because, due to the extensible potential of the operating model, it could quickly become unfocused, so we believe this model is likely to give rise to a number of regionally focused organisations, sharing market sector and partnering with each other via their networks (Fig. 9.2).

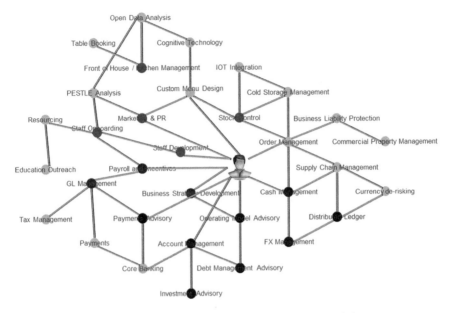

Open Data Analysis

Table Booking   Cognitive Technology

Front of House / Kitchen Management   IOT Integration

PESTLE Analysis   Custom Menu Design   Cold Storage Management

Resourcing   Market & PR   Stock Control   Business Liability Protection

Staff Onboarding   Order Management   Commercial Property Management

Staff Development

Education Outreach   Payroll and Incentives   Supply Chain Management

GL Management

Business Strategy Development   Cash Management   Currency de-risking

Tax Management   Payment Advisory   Operating Model Advisory   Distributed Ledger

Payments   Account Management   FX Management

Core Banking   Debt Management Advisory

Investment Advisory

Fig. 9.2 Multi-sided platform ecosystem bank operating model

Blockchain/Crypto-Technology and Digital Assets

The fundamental principles of what banks are and what are they for is changing rapidly; these ecosystem banks will, we believe, come into their own as the technology supporting them becomes more accepted by the global financial community and, in particular, by regulators. Financial institutions and technology organisations, along with central banks are exploring the implications of some of the current technology-related megatrends—digital assets and cryptotechnology such as cryptocurrencies and smart contracts, in particular—and building a view of how to /how much to control them. These trends are driven by consumer adoption and the innovative and imaginative startup sector that is flourishing in San Francisco, London, the Nordics, Tel Aviv, Singapore and elsewhere. An ecosystem bank enables these new Fintech players to flourish, giving their customers what they want along with unprecedented choice and individualisation. If a customer wants to switch between the financial services offered, then it should be the easiest thing possible—a truly free market driven by demand and quality of service. For its part, the ecosystem bank, or more accurately the financial services platform, provides the resilience, trust, and scale that is required.

Since about 2015, we have seen blockchain technology on the trajectory from experimental to mainstream and we believe that this, or something like it, will underpin the ecosystem banks of the future. It is clear that there will never be a single blockchain technology, but rather the components that form distributed ledger technology will be developed in ways that suit specific use cases. Standards can inhibit and constrain innovation, but they will emerge from the work of the various companies and alliances in the blockchain space (e.g. R3, Hyperledger, Hashgraph, Blockstream, Multichain, Bloq, Chain, Consensys, etc.). Ultimately, progress will be dependent on the adoption of standards and inter-ledger protocols that allow these blockchains to securely and privately inter-communicate. Only then will we establish the conditions for exponential growth through network effect. Also, the resolution of issues around how one's digital identity is combined with blockchain technology will release many the current inhibitors on the evolution of blockchain generally and for financial service applications in particular. The fundamental disparity between boundary-based jurisdictional currency regulations and the boundary-free nature of cryptocurrencies is a big challenge to address for banks and regulators, but possibly bigger is how to manage security and authentication in disintermediated transactions. As we've seen from well-publicised setbacks to Ethereum,[7] such as the DAO, and other high-profile challenges such as the growing number of exchange and wallet hacks,[8] we're not there yet, but we believe the opportunity for ecosystem banks is here already, with growing application of these technologies accelerating.

Startups, Incumbents and the New Models

Banking, like many other industries before, is going through a hype curve driven by disruption, new applications of technology, changing attitudes to data, hyper-availability and changing customer expectations. Like other industries, many of the incumbents will probably not survive, while some will pivot and thrive, possibly even dominate. Most of today's startups will not exist in the years to come; like the dot.com boom, early entrants don't necessarily have first mover advantage, and later entrants will have the benefit of opportunities to learn from the mistakes of earlier entrants. Who will end up dominating is anyone's guess, but we can forecast with some level of confidence is that the dominant players will not look like banks today, and probably not much like the early Challengers.

As during the dot.com boom, there's a lot of investment capital available for Fintechs and Challenger Banks today; VCs are falling all over themselves to offer funding, banks are building their own accelerators, and crowdfunding is giving everyone the opportunity to get involved. Many of these are putting money into business models with four or five-year break-even horizons in an uncertain competitive landscape and, in many cases, that break-even will never be reached. All startups suffer from scale challenges and typically those that grow too quickly, or without sufficient focus, are the ones that fail the fastest. Conventional wisdom says that startups should focus on a small market to succeed and avoid being out-competed in their early months and years, but how can a global multi-sided platform or ecosystem bank restrict their markets? Is BaaS sustainable and how will it impact competition? And when central banks actually start issuing cryptocurrencies, will the cryptobanks get there first, undercutting them?

Conclusion: The Future Looks Horizontal

Ecosystem banking models are evolutionary stages towards what financial services will look like in the future, but all these models will need to mature in parallel with the evolution of the ecosystem itself as a core customer and partner enabler, before stability is achieved. Wherever banks move themselves in this landscape, the universal model looks unsustainable, and we believe banks will either initiate their own focus towards one or other of these models, or be forced in that direction as regulations and market forces change—as is happening right now with regulations such as PSD2 and GDPR in Europe. Whatever happens, the distinction between bank, Fintech, service provider and customer is blurring and may eventually disappear from a customer perspective as more services migrate to multi-entity, cloud-based value chains, where the existence of an entity as a bank, a service provider, a source of funds or a Fintech, becomes indistinguishable and therefore irrelevant to the customer.

Does this mean the death of banking? No, but it does mean that banks need to learn to win through others winning, collaboratively, rather than through the old "I win you lose" paradigm. This will be good for the customer, good for service providers, and eventually good for banks, but will require a significant shift in mindset.

Notes

1. Alibaba's Digital Bank Comes Online to Serve "The Little Guys" in China, 25 June 2015. https://techcrunch.com/2015/06/25/alibaba-digital-bank-mybank/. Accessed 27 December 2017.
2. Collins, J. (2001). *Good to Great*. William Collins.https://www.mindtools.com/pages/article/hedgehog-concept.htm.
3. RBS Agency Banking Website. https://www.business.rbs.co.uk/business/turnover-2m-or-over/cards-and-payments/making-and-accepting-payments/Indirect-Access-to-UK-Payments-System.html. Accessed 28 December 2017.
4. Thought Machine. https://www.thoughtmachine.net/. Accessed 28 December 2017.
5. Boden, A. (2015, September 20). https://www.linkedin.com/pulse/what-sort-bank-you-anne-boden/?trk=prof-post. Accessed 27 December 2017.
6. Resurs Bank Homepage. https://www.resursbank.se/loyo/#humany-topp-5-widget-loyo=%2F. Accessed 27 December 2017.
7. Madeira, A. (2017, September 28). The DAO Hack, Soft Fork and the Hard Fork. https://www.cryptocompare.com/coins/guides/the-dao-the-hack-the-soft-fork-and-the-hard-fork/. Accessed 28 December 2018.
8. Detrixhe, J. (2017, December 19). Bitcoin Exchange Files for Bankruptcy After Hack. *Quartz*. https://qz.com/1160573/bitcoin-exchange-youbit-files-for-bankruptcy-in-south-korea-after-latest-hack/?utm_medium=social. Accessed 28 December 2017.

10

The Money Revolution: Recycling Value to Drive Sustainability

The shape of finance and how businesses are being funded have already seen some fundamental changes, but this is only the beginning. We're starting to see the same sort of paradigm changes in finance and money, as those that hit print media when the internet came along. Just like popularly held perceptions of books and news media over the last two decades, our concept of what money is and how it's invested are being challenged. In this chapter, we explore the impact of these changes on how money is moving around in the system and what this means for small and micro-businesses, particularly in developing economies.

Where Does Money Come from?

Money is a token system designed to make exchange of value easier than barter systems; money represents a universally accepted value which can be exchanged in fixed or variable amounts for goods or services. Much early money was made of precious metals such as gold and was in effect a token/barter system in itself, where precious metal was the agreed standard unit of value, and these were then superseded by more symbolic tokens such as paper money and coins with limited inherent value.

Historically, however, most currencies were still underpinned by a relationship with precious metal, usually gold, with central banks issuing currency notes based on a "gold reserve" or a store of gold which could be exchanged for the notes and coins, on request. This led to nations storing

© The Author(s) 2018
S. Blakstad and R. Allen, *FinTech Revolution*,
https://doi.org/10.1007/978-3-319-76014-8_10

large gold reserves, especially Great Britain, which, thanks to its empire, amassed significant gold reserves and became the dominant currency of the nineteenth-century world. The gold reserve system survived into the twentieth century, when the limited supply of gold and the diminishing dominance of the UK pound resulted in countries adopting increasingly protectionist monetary policies, including deflation, impacting international exchange rates. This was hugely exacerbated following the First World War, when the war debt of most developed economies created a downward spiral in currency availability, production and employment that led to the global depression of the 1930s and eventually to the Second World War.

Bretton Woods

In response, the major economies met to agree international monetary policy, culminating in a 1944 meeting of the world's dominant economic powers at Bretton Woods. The resulting Bretton Woods agreements[1] among other things reversed exchange volatility between those countries by agreeing to pin currencies to the US dollar, which in turn was pinned to the gold standard. These agreements also resulted in the formation of several international bodies, such as the IMF and eventually the World Bank, as well as underpinning modern international trade for the subsequent decades. Following World War II, the US dollar was easily identifiable as the dominant global currency and other countries, particularly the UK, were significantly weakened by their war debt, and under the Marshall Plan, this indebtedness to the USA was further extended.

As economies recovered, however, the relative stability of exchange rates played into the hands of speculators, and as non-central bank currency investments and exchanges grew with the increasing scale and power of the international banks, while the gold supply again failed to accelerate in line with exponential growth in global production and trade, it became apparent that the gold standard was no longer tenable, and it was formally abandoned by the USA in 1971. The gold standard has been blamed for everything from depressions to wars and since 1971 has effectively been replaced by the dollar standard for most developed nations, with the dollar still the default "safe" currency used in local and international commerce within countries with less stable economies.

The modern global monetary system is therefore no longer based on gold or on any other identifiable asset. Bretton Woods functioned based on the assumption that the then dominant economic powers would retain a level of stability in relationship to each other and the global economy, while allowing for development, but was underpinned by the assumption that the state as a monetary authority underpins all currency and currency exchanges. Money as a token functions where the authority responsible for issuing the money is trusted to retain its value against the value of goods and other currencies. Consequently, most trusted money is issued by government-controlled central banks, which effectively means that the value of the currency is directly linked to the trust in the government and its ability to manage the economy well.

Modern Currencies

As we described in Chapter 5, central banks control the amount of money in a country's financial system directly through issuance of currency which is valid for paying taxes and indirectly through controlling how much of that currency other banks can issue in debt. Hence, while licensed banks can "print money", there are limits on how much they can release into the system, and requirements to retain sufficient liquidity to provide for disasters, so it's effectively controlled by the central bank and ultimately by the government of the country. Because this type of money (sovereign currency) is so intrinsically linked with the risk of the country's economic policy, there's a popular perception that it's in some way guaranteed by the government, and while this isn't actually the case, the close coupling of currency and monetary policy means that there is a de facto relationship.

Consequently, currencies associated with high-risk states face more volatility and lower value than currencies associated with strong states. Events such as change in economic policy, depressions and wars impact the value of currencies, but even the anticipation of change is enough to impact their value—the markets don't like uncertainty, as any financial professional will tell you—so as well as real risks, the value of currency is often strongly impacted by market perceptions, which may prove to be valid or not, at a later stage. To avoid this kind of volatility between close trading partners, some currencies are "pegged" to other currencies, for example the Euro or Dollar, which increases their stability. However, this can also lead to more volatility when circumstances change, for example the unpegging of the Swiss Franc from the Euro in 2015, which caused a massive leap in its value (Fig. 10.1).

Sovereign currency is usually regarded by populations as safe and stable, but its perceived stability is in fact something of an illusion—most currencies don't survive that long, the average life being 27 years according to Chris Mack,[2] who also points out that:

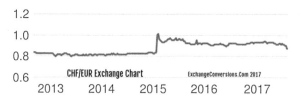

Fig. 10.1 CHF/EUR exchange chart

According to a study of 775 fiat [i.e. currency declared by a government to be legal tender, but is not backed by a physical commodity] *currencies by DollarDaze.org, there is no historical precedence for a fiat currency that has succeeded in holding its value. 20 percent failed through hyperinflation, 21 percent were destroyed by war, 12 percent destroyed by independence, 24 percent were monetarily reformed, and 23 percent are still in circulation approaching one of the other outcomes.*

While some phenomena, such as inflation, are a natural result of growth, it's important to recognise that sovereign currencies aren't as stable or as permanent as they may seem. Local currencies are another type of (usually physical) cash, which are designed to support local economies and are usually pinned to national fiats, but with restrictions about where they can be spent based on collaboration of local traders; they usually can't be used to pay taxes, unlike national currencies. Local currencies are usually even more short-lived than national currencies, due to their lack of fungibility, although some long-running schemes such as the Ithaca HOUR[3] lasted for several decades and are now moving into the digital age.

Digital Money

Digital cash has been around for some time in various forms; it's a long time since everyone used cash for everything and most money circulating in the system (around 95%) is electronic rather than in the shape of notes, even in countries where cash use is high. This has traditionally resided in banks, although the last few decades have seen the rise of non-bank held digital money, either where a provider issues an equivalent to an amount of fiat currency (e.g. as an e-wallet/payment card) or their own currency, such as Frequent Flyer or other loyalty points. In the case of loyalty points, the value of the points is associated with the value of the services offered by that company, although in the case of Frequent Flyer and many other loyalty schemes, multiple companies have collaborated, so that the points can be spent on multiple airlines or outlets. However, this type of digital cash, although it has been in circulation for a long time, is still so fragmented that it's not convenient for normal transactional use outside of the issuer(s).

Much digital cash transfer today is in real time gross settlements, as discussed in the chapter on Central Bank Digital Currencies, which is the mass transactions between organisations or settlements between organisations and banks/central banks.

Over the last decade, as we've discussed, we've also seen the emergence of cryptocurrencies, starting with Bitcoin, which was first described in 2008 and started circulating the following year. In contrast to fiat currencies such as sovereign currencies, Bitcoin and many other cryptocurrencies are not underpinned by central banks, governments or any form of underlying asset. These cryptocurrencies are popular largely because they aren't dependent on any central authority, and because of the ability to transact without traditional KYC and validation controls, which we discuss elsewhere. However, because they're not underpinned by a state's economic policy or an underlying asset, their value is volatile as it is driven purely by the market, which is heavily influenced by events and predictions. Other cryptocurrencies, such as SolarCoin, are underpinned by assets (renewable energy is a popular one), and as we've already discussed, we will soon see the emergence of central bank issued cryptocurrencies, or CBDCs, to bring the benefits of cryptocurrency together with the stability of sovereign fiat, which in itself presents many challenges, as we discussed in Chapter 4. Here's a useful taxonomy of different types of money, from the Bank for International Settlements (BIS)[4] (Fig. 10.2).

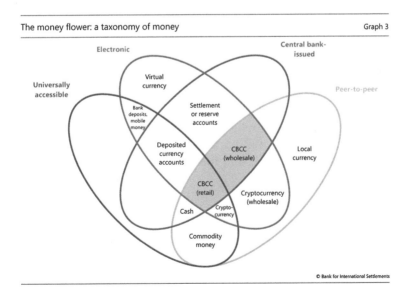

Fig. 10.2   Different types of money

Money Going into the System

Money is today essential for nearly every type of transactional activity; access to nearly every type of goods or service is via a financial transaction where the good or service is exchanged for money. It's convenient, because it represents a commonly agreed standard for valuation, and it's easy to use. Prices for goods and services can be set and easily communicated in a value system understood by sellers and purchasers. Consequently, it's also essential to support the growth of businesses, as money is needed to buy things before they can be converted into goods or services for sale—in exchange for more money.

Prices are fixed by the business selling the good or service; however, how much money people are prepared to exchange for things, including services, may vary over time depending on factors including availability, quality, fashion and so on. Supplier businesses will base prices on a combination of the cost of providing the good or service, and the price consumers are willing to pay for it; however, the price it's sold for may not reflect the cost of production. In many cases, goods are sold at a much greater cost than the cost of manufacturing and distribution, for example where an item has a high value because of fashion, such as the iPhone. In others, businesses may choose to provide services or goods at a loss, for example Uber, which is pursuing a policy of undercutting local suppliers in order to strangle the competition, in anticipation that reduced competition will enable it to raise prices in the future.

Money is put into the business system by investors and banks, with the ultimate goal of making more money; this may be a simple investment in or loan to a company that then makes some money and returns the investment or loan. The difference between investments and loans is that investments are buying a piece of the company (equity), whereas the loan just buys a promise to pay back the loan (debt). However, both types of money going into the system are designed to produce more of the goods or service, for a return of (it's hoped) more money. In theory, the amount of money a company is worth (value) is based on how much it will gain from producing goods or services in the future, and therefore, how much money the investor or lender will get back.

Money Staying Out of the System

As we discussed briefly in Chapter 3, the relationship between equity and debt capital, and production is, however, not straightforward. In addition to simple movements of money to pay for production, it is also possible to bet against movements in the value of companies, debt, goods and money through various financial instruments, interest rates or currencies. This is because the future is uncertain, and valuations of companies or goods are, at best, an educated guess, while the relative value of different currencies and interest rates fluctuates.

Companies may do better, or worse than their forecasts, while many other factors can affect the price of goods—poor weather can lead to scarcity of crops; wars or natural disasters can impact production of goods and the value of currency; and any kind of uncertainty in the markets has a negative impact on nearly everything (except the price of gold). Financial markets have evolved to gamble on the movement of prices, including at the second and third degree via derivatives, which were originally created to manage risk in international trade, but now are traded as assets in their own right—you can buy a derivative that's in turn structured based on someone's bet about what will happen to a portfolio of equities, which in turn may reflect the value of real companies.

Company valuations, in turn, often don't reflect the likely returns of a company and may be high or low for lots of reasons unrelated to their forecast profits. Fashion and FOMO (fear of missing out) artificially inflate some types of company or individual companies, particularly in areas where there are a lot of highly visible successes, such as Silicon Valley, or as exemplified by the dot.com boom. Other businesses by contrast, particularly novel business models, are generally undervalued as investors don't want to invest time understanding them and more likely than not, deciding against the investment anyway, such as AirBnB, which was famously assessed by Y-Combinator incubator as "a terrible idea".[5] While investors take risks in comparison with lenders, even they have a need to minimise risk and expect to make money at a portfolio level; luckily for AirBnB, Y-Combinator thought the founders were worth taking a risk on.

This means that for equity or corporate bond (debt investment) derivatives, in addition to gambling on the returns of a portfolio of companies, you are just as likely to be gambling on the expected impact of reputation, fashion and availability on the valuation of companies, even if you never expect that company to return profits directly to you, or at all. There are many well-publicised examples of companies being valued at millions or even billions of dollars, which have never been profitable and whose ability to return a positive return on investment (ROI) is unclear; where valuations are based on either an assumption that something that popular must make money at some point or, more realistically, that a large global platform like Google or Amazon will acquire it for vast sums—which does often happen.

Structured financial products are designed to make it easy to participate in these gambles, without the money necessarily going anywhere near the underlying company's books. Derivatives are complex products, based on the performance of a number of underlying financial products, which may be equity, or bonds, commodities, futures, etc., designed to hedge across a number of products or markets to reduce risk. Debt structured products and the opacity caused by their complex structures were widely blamed for the 2008 financial crisis, where investors buying structured products had no visibility of what they were investing in. Which is fine as long as the underlying product keeps performing, but as we saw, defaults brought the whole house of cards down (Fig. 10.3).

So a significant amount of value now resides in money markets, rather than in actual companies, and the function this money performs is making more money. It's impossible to know how much exactly, but it's estimated that total global derivatives are valued at around a quadrillion USD, as opposed to between 80 and 90 trillion in money and 70 trillion in stock markets globally. So, over ten times the global money supply is tied up in speculation on movements of value.

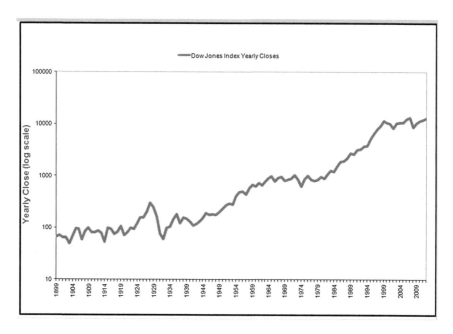

Fig. 10.3 Dow long range trend (*Source* Observations: observation and notes. bnlogspot.com)

Investment Inequality and SMEs

Much of the value of speculation is derived through changing prices and values, which in the capitalist system historically has tended towards the positive thanks to continued growth, positive interest rates and reduction in the number of people in poverty; the global amount of value created keeps getting bigger. For investors, this means over time, a continuous growth trend and positive incentives to keep investing in companies, commodities, securities and derivatives. The positive impact of this is that cash is available for companies to grow; however, there is a downside. Not every company can participate in this liquidity opportunity, as nearly all investments are in listed companies—that is, companies with the scale and history to have its securities accepted onto a stock exchange. We also discuss the downside of continuous growth in a limited resource world in the chapter on capital markets.

Globally, 99% of companies fall into the "Small and medium sized enterprise" or SME category, meaning they have fewer than 250 employees. The EU average SME size is 4.1 employees, meaning that the overwhelming majority don't have the scale to list, and in developing economies, the figure is even lower. However, SMEs employ more than half of the workforce in developed economies and the vast majority in developing economies, where they employ up to 60% of the workforce. Yet, over half of these (an estimated 70% in developing economies) don't even have access to basic bank loans, let alone sophisticated financial products. The global credit gap for SMEs is estimated by the World Bank[6] at USD 2.6 trillion.

This creates a highly polarised economic environment, where most of the world's investment capital is concentrated in a tiny minority of companies, supporting less than half of the workforce. The rewards for senior leadership of these companies keep growing, again creating massive economic disparity between the leaders of listed companies, and both the smaller companies and the workforces of the larger companies. So, while globally there's a trend for the number of people in poverty and financial exclusion to reduce, there's a parallel trend for the gap between the wealthy and the poor to increase,[7] leading to social problems in developed economies and deprivation for large numbers of people in developing economies (Fig. 10.4).

The financial system is stacked against SMEs, with multiple barriers to entry—first, the lack of formal listing means they're not in a position to issue securities. Shareholder investment in non-listed companies is typically limited to small amounts from friends and family, except in the rare cases of companies (usually technology based) that attract venture capital funding (less than .05%). They find it harder than large organisations to prove credit or trading history, because of lower volumes, meaning that bank loans are more expensive if they're available at all—over half of them don't have any access to credit, and many micro-businesses are unbanked. Even where there is willingness to invest, for example through crowdfunding or microfinance, the administration of multiple small loans to large numbers of tiny enterprises is complicated and costly, meaning that they're a poor choice for investors.

And small businesses are a risky investment: many fail. But of the SMEs that fail (which is actually less than half, in the first two years), many fail because of challenges with cash flow and a lack of access to capital. As the World Bank and other NGOs have found, early investment in small companies can get them over the hump of building a business and lead to ultimate success, especially for micro-businesses in developing economies run by people, disproportionately women, who are unable to access traditional financial services. One of the startling results of the exceptional success of M-PESA, as we've already discussed, is the huge growth in numbers of female entrepreneurs now able to run successful businesses, purely through access to a basic transaction history that allows them to break through the credit ceiling.

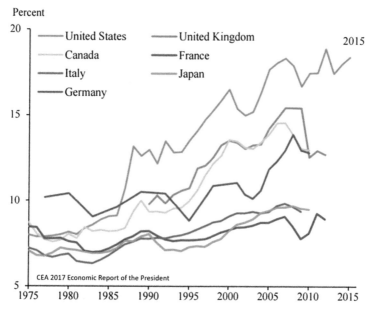

Fig. 10.4 Share of income earned by top 1%, 1975–2015 (*Source* World Wealth and Income Database)

Money Going Back into the System

But things are beginning to change. A combination of growing awareness of investment opportunities, opportunities presented by evolving technology, growing social responsibility in investors and the desire to experiment with non-traditional investments has led to a growing alternative investment market for SMEs in developed and developing economies.

Crowdfunding and Microfinance

Crowdfunding is a growing, although still niche, investment approach where entrepreneurs, usually at the idea/pre-seed stage, raise capital via online platforms to support early stage or growth stages in their business. While most commonly used in developed economies, entrepreneurs in developing economies are also increasingly taking advantage of the opportunities offered by these platforms, although the barriers to entry can prove challenging. A 2015 report[8] for the World Bank highlighted the top challenges for African entrepreneurs seeking crowdfunding, highlighting that it isn't suitable for every business, entrepreneurs are expected to bring a large network of potential investors with them, and that it's a time-consuming and difficult activity. The same points apply to entrepreneurs seeking crowdfunding in developed economies; those with a tangible and significantly different product are more able to raise money than service providers or more traditional types of business.

Crowdfunding is usually run on an equity basis, so entrepreneurs are selling parts of their business to the investors in the form of shares. This means that there's a lot of paperwork and due diligence involved, which is handled by the crowdfunding platform, but it also comes at a cost, with entrepreneurs handing over around 10% of capital raised, and legal obligations which can prevent entrepreneurs from some countries participating.

From an investor perspective, crowdfunding can be a risky activity, especially to the many small investors involved, who will select investments without relevant investment knowledge. Large investors also participate in crowdfunding; however, the majority are smaller and likely to be inexperienced.

Microfinance, by contrast, is the lending of small amounts of money as debt capital to micro-businesses and SMEs who wouldn't normally have access to financing, usually organised by NGOs, governments or consortia of corporations, which again can be facilitated by technology platforms. See Chapter 12 for more details.

ICOs

Initial Coin Offerings, or ICOs, and Token sales have been with us for a few years, with pioneering offerings from 2013 (MasterCoin was the first in 2013; Ethereum raised funds via a Token sale in 2014), but 2017 has seen an explosion in ICOs, fuelled by the relative ease of creating a new token on Ethereum and the skyrocketing value in Bitcoin and Ethereum coins, meaning that early investors have a significant amount of crypto to invest in new projects. Token sales are effectively a type of crowdfunding capital raise, where blockchain firms issue their token in exchange for other crypto-currencies, such as Bitcoin or Ethereum, or fiat. It is a mechanism for raising money, with the money usually being raised to support development of the platform.

Unlike traditional stock offerings, ICOs have to date been unregulated in traditional capital markets, although regulators are starting to classify them as securities in some markets, and this trend is likely to continue. Founders of startups employing the ICO approach go to great lengths to categorise theirs as a utility token rather than a security token, but with different rules in different jurisdictions it is often difficult to be entirely sure. For a token to be classed as a security brings with it a raft of laws to which the company must comply—as well as the investors and any exchanges seeking to list the token. At the time of writing, it is unclear how this will play out, but we are starting to see ICOs being stopped by regulators if they appear to be sell-ing unregistered securities or managed investment schemes. If it looks like a duck and quacks like a duck …

As a booming but, up to 2018, largely unregulated phenomenon, ICOs have seen a high level of scams, fraud and opportunism, with an estimated 10% (possibly higher) resulting in phishing or Ponzi schemes, so greater regulation is welcomed. Only with formal security regulation will ICOs be more widely accepted as standard investment instruments by the wider investment commu-nity. However, this has not worried a new community of crypto day traders drawn to the long bull run in 2017; the demand for new tokens and alt-coins by crypto day traders and "pump and dump" groups has been enormous.

ICOs or token sales offer a window into an alternative investment future, as we've discussed in the context of capital markets, and a mechanism for alternative forms of value to start reaching the mainstream. Many 2017 ICOs were launched on the basis of little more than a sketchy white paper, but once the phenomenon crests the hype curve and becomes accepted into wider investment culture, it's likely they will start to open up a much wider range of opportunities for investors and entrepreneurs, especially as more types of business start using cryptocurrency as a means of value transfer. Anecdotally, we have heard that over 80% of funds provided by Silicon Valley venture capital firms was directed towards ICOs in 2017—easy money for startups who previously had to produce detailed Information Memoranda and jump through hoops for VCs.

Alternative Money Providers

Necessity being the mother of invention, alternative solutions tend to arise where traditional financial services aren't supporting large numbers of people, as described in Chapter 7.

Although M-PESA enabled many people to leapfrog the traditional finance system in Kenya and other markets, it's a relatively low-tech solution which now faces competition from more sophisticated remittance services in other countries, but it illustrates how the right technology, available at the right time, giving access to basic financial services, can transform millions of lives and enable populations to be successful without the need for external intervention.

Alternatives to Capital Markets

As we discussed in greater detail in Chapter 3, traditional capital markets, while still massively dominant, are now complemented by alternative investments, powered by alternative exchanges and now, thanks to the rise of tokenisation and blockchain technology, alternative approaches to securitisation. Although it's early in the evolution of these vehicles, we can see applications of this technology enabling a parallel capital markets economy, characterised by transparency and low administration costs, with significantly less need for brokers or human intervention in structuring and executing instruments.

In such a scenario, a primary tokenised asset class could be issued and owned by community members, above which sits a securitised set of primary investment products based on the direct owners' tokens, also managed through contracts and digitised tokens, but at a level of abstraction away from the direct ownership layer, to be traded on open markets. This enables long-term investment by funds such as pension funds and other large investors with full transparency of the underlying assets, as well as putting money back into the hands of the community. Using smart contract and blockchain technology, a virtual SPV would issue the securities, initially in partnership with local banks or asset managers but eventually without the need for intervention, as assets and transactions can all be managed with automated execution rules.

It would also be possible to create a full derivative layer, which would allow full trading on open global markets; however, eventually we anticipate the need for derivatives would dilute, as through tokenisation and the sophisticated marketplaces it's possible to create through smart contracts and tokenised ownership, it would be possible to hedge across a portfolio of asset classes without the need to create derivatives. We envisage as tokenisation grows, so will the two-layer securitisation model, potentially creating the opportunity for a market in balanced derivatives while the technology matures, but longer term simplifying how capital markets work.

Such a model could tokenise a wide class of assets, with value pinned to those assets or to a globally stable compound index, to avoid FX risk and fully utilise the global nature of cryptocurrency, without creating a currency with the volatility of free-floating cryptocurrencies such as Bitcoin. This would ensure that investment in businesses could be made in multiple countries with relatively low risk. Security coupon rates could also be pinned to this asset or index to ensure parity with actual value.

Looking forward, as governments start issuing sovereign cryptocurrency, traditional money markets and exchanges are likely to also become disrupted, creating opportunities for cryptocurrency-based assets and securities to enter standard portfolios. We see this as the ideal opportunity to expand to green SME investment, supported by the same marketplace, securitisation and capital markets logic.

Community Investment

Marketplace applications of blockchain technology and Artificial Intelligence also present opportunities for local and global business communities to cross-invest in a self-sustaining ecosystem, which can survive beyond the availability of top-down overseas investment. As we explore in SME Microfinance, blockchain and smart contract technology offer opportunities to automate administration and enhance provenance, helping global communities to collaborate in novel ways, including community investment at a global level.

Conclusion

Money is today an essential part of how we operate and particularly how businesses operate. But because of the way that money has been traditionally structured, the availability of money to different sizes of business is distributed in a way that has led to gross inequality between large and small players, and between developed and developing economies. Too much money is tied up in the business of making more money, instead of promoting actual growth, while the entrepreneurs employing more than half of the world's workforce, who are also those most in need of money to grow and succeed, are missing out.

The nature of money is changing, and with it, approaches to financing, which are already making huge differences in developing economies and enabling entrepreneurs to be more successful. Through further technical developments, we also have the opportunity to revolutionise the way capital markets and global investment communities work, opening up opportunities for the billions of unbanked and underserved micro-businesses globally.

Notes

1. Creation of the Bretton Woods System, Federal Reserve, 22 November 2013. https://www.federalreservehistory.org/essays/bretton_woods_created. Accessed 27 December 2017.
2. Mack, C. (2011, January 24). Is This Time Different for the Dollar and Precious Metals? Seeking Alpha. https://seekingalpha.com/article/248299-is-this-time-different-for-the-dollar-and-precious-metals. Accessed 27 December 2017.
3. Dolphin, B. (2015, July 22). Ithaca NY Launches its Own Digital Currency to Boost Local Economy. *CoinTelegraph*. https://cointelegraph.com/news/ithaca-ny-launches-its-own-digital-currency-to-boost-local-economy. Accessed 4 January 2018.
4. Bech, M. L., & Garratt, R. (2017, September 17). Central Bank Cryptocurrencies—The Money Flower—A Taxonomy of Money. Bank for International Settlements. https://www.bis.org/publ/qtrpdf/r_qt1709f.htm. Accessed 4 January 2018.
5. Kuria, J. (2017, June 1). https://blog.ycombinator.com/paul-buchheit-on-lessons-learned-from-investing-in-200-startups/. Accessed 27 December 2017.
6. Small and Medium Enterprises (SME) Finance, World Bank. http://www.worldbank.org/en/topic/smefinance. Accessed 27 December 2017.
7. Economic Report of the President, White House, January 2017. https://obamawhitehouse.archives.gov/sites/default/files/docs/2017_economic_report_of_president.pdf. Accessed 27 December 2017.
8. Crowdfunding in Emerging Markets: Lessons from East African Startups. InfoDev/World Bank, 1 December 2015. http://www.infodev.org/CrowdfundingAfrica. Accessed 7 January 2018.

11

Green Fintech

We've discussed the ways that technology, customer behaviours and service standards for banking are shifting into the new financial ecosystem. In this chapter, we provide a broad overview, together with some examples, of how these emerging technologies can help provide solutions in support of the UN's Sustainable Development Goals. The UN and many other NGOs, together with investors, researchers and technology companies, are converging to start building solutions to some of the thorniest problems in this area.

The SDGs and the UNEP Inquiry into the Financial System We Need

The 2015 Paris Climate agreement between global leaders marked a change to the global sustainability agenda—agreement between all the key economies on what we need to do to reverse the damage that anthropogenic global warming is doing to our planet. In September 2015, the 17 Sustainable Development Goals[1] (SDGs) for 2030 were identified. In support of achieving these objectives, the United Nations Environment Programme (UNEP) set up an inquiry into Sustainable Finance, working with government groups (Fig. 11.1).

In December 2016, the UNEP Inquiry published their Fintech and Sustainable Development[2] Report, which laid out recommendations for how developments in Financial Technology (Fintech) can help to address a broad range of the 2030 objectives through increased financial inclusion, community empowerment and financial support for sustainable infrastructure.

© The Author(s) 2018
S. Blakstad and R. Allen, *FinTech Revolution*,
https://doi.org/10.1007/978-3-319-76014-8_11

Fig. 11.1 The global goals for sustainable development

Fintech Sustainability Opportunities

How can Fintech help sustainability? There are a huge number of potential applications but some of the key ones are using distributed ledger technology (blockchain), smart contracts and cryptocurrencies to remove corruption and inefficiencies. Applications include:

- Food trust and supply chain traceability: by proving where and when crops, fish or meat come from, it's possible to ensure sustainable supply. Corruption in supply chains is endemic, and a decentralised, incorruptible, transparent record reduces opportunities for fraud, and ensures producers get a fair price for their produce, meaning producers aren't forced into short-term decision making by unscrupulous middlemen.
- Reputation systems to build trust: when communities can trust each other, they can work together to make sustainable decisions. While this works in small communities, it breaks down where people are not personally known to each other, and population growth, together with the move to cities, means that more and more people live in communities where we don't know each other. Blockchains can help build open reputation systems, helping community members to see guarantees and audit trails, to create trust without having to know each other personally.
- Fractional ownership of assets: Fintech can help communities to own resources in common, such as agricultural equipment or green energy sources, removing intermediaries and helping sustainable decision making.

Community ownership of shared resources can also turn individuals into both producers and consumers (prosumers), trading surplus from their own solar panels or windmill directly with other community members without having to sell to a national grid.

- Improved identity applications through traceability of use/ownership: especially in developing economies, people often lack formal documentation giving them access to resources such as water sources or land, which are critical to their survival. Fintech applications can use other information sources such as interactions, to build behavioural identities that can be used without needing a formal intermediary such as a bank or government to validate.
- Disaster prediction and management: combined with predictive sciences such as weather tech, Fintech can help communities plan for and remediate natural and anthropogenic disasters, both by ensuring the right people are in place and by ensuring full provenance of supply chains.
- Traceability of investment and tracking of development funds: technologies such as blockchain and cryptocurrencies can be applied to more traditional investment activity supporting sustainable resources, and with their superior traceability, ensure full provenance of the whole investment portfolio so that investors have confidence their money is being used on sustainable investments.

Use Cases for Sustainable Development Fintechs

Some of these solutions are already in the early stages of production, with pilots and young businesses springing up as the opportunities arise. Tokenisation of renewable energy is probably the most mature, with communities able to support development of green energy facilities by transacting tokenised green energy, or carbon offset via carbon credits, while blockchain technology, combined with biometrics, first used by the UN to track aid distribution[3] to Syrian refugees in a large pilot in 2017. Along with other technology providers, we've also been lucky enough to have worked with UNEP, NGOs, commercial organisations and various government groups to help develop pilot solutions in some of these areas. So, while the technology is emerging, and the use cases are maturing, NGOs and investors are already participating in these scenarios.

Below, we explain in more detail how the technology supports both top-down and bottom-up solutions.

Top-Down Solutions

Much of the sustainability agenda requires injections of cash from investors, donors or governments, to progress. While there has been significant investment globally and this has led to a lot of sustainability projects being built, as well as the "greening" of existing industries, the success of initiatives varies between different geographies and industries. In many cases, it is challenging to get green projects initiated because of currency volatility, lack of transparency or lack of clarity about investments, while in many countries, the risk of corruption deters investors.

Fintech solutions using technologies such as Internet of Things (IoT), Artificial Intelligence (AI) and blockchain can help by reducing this risk, creating audit trails, collecting and analysing data and creating greater transparency. Our first worked example describes how using a blockchain can reduce the risk of corruption and volatility in a complex overseas donation scenario, and similar approaches are being taken to investment, as discussed in Chapter 13. By increasing investor or donor confidence in allocating money to countries or industries where transparency and corruption have been concerns, these top-down solutions can expand the scope of overseas investment and aid significantly, while reducing corruption and administration costs.

Example: Foreign Aid Pipeline Management Over Blockchain

An example of foreign aid management using a blockchain has been achieved, with UNDP running the first successful pilot in 2017 with 10,000 Syrian refugees. The solution we describe here is more holistic but shares many characteristics, including the use of technology.

Background

Aid for disaster relief and longer-term development programmes attracts significant investment from governments, businesses and private individuals, but faces a huge logistical and reputational challenge. Typical aid donation scenarios involve a donation in one currency, which is converted to a second currency by the global NGO distributing the aid, then another currency in-country and possibly further conversions as global distributors are used to support the emergency.

Aid is also traditionally subject to significant "leakage", with funds and goods diverted to corrupt officials or, commonly, local people taking advantage and selling goods on the open market. Donations to aid funds may lose around 30% to multiple FX and transaction charges and poor terms from banks, while administration is high, and as it is very hard to trace funds, there are corruption and fraud opportunities.

Aid payouts often take place in challenging circumstances; recipients of aid are likely to be displaced, lacking access to formal identity or traditional financial services and vulnerable to exploitation. Recipients of aid in the form of food or other transactable goods are also known to sell these on, so there's always room for abuse; however, reducing the interim stages such as merchants responsible for distribution, and ensuring end recipients benefit directly from the aid, is critical to reducing leakage.

Blockchain technology offers an opportunity to add transparency and confidence to donation pipelines, by creating an end to end audit trail of each transaction together with non-traditional identification techniques to ensure the correct recipients are benefitting, even if they lack formal identity or bank accounts. The combination of blockchain technology with layered business logic further ensures that confirmation, payments and other events can be tied to firm evidence that desired objectives have been achieved, as well as offering the opportunity to solicit additional evidence and assurance where required.

Self-executing contract technology also offers an opportunity to automate much of the administration underpinning administration of overseas aid donations, including distribution to multiple suppliers and individuals, and the management of financial transactions.

We describe a hybrid solution where a technology platform, incorporating a blockchain and automatically executing contracts, supports traditional actors in the aid lifecycle by reducing administration and increasing transparency. We anticipate this will result in reduced challenges associated with setting up, donating to and administering aid campaigns, so that the leakages, overhead and bottlenecks presented by bureaucracy and lack of confidence typical to aid campaigns in more challenging economies can be overcome.

The Solution

The system can capture predetermined recipients of aid, such as medicines suppliers, individuals in need of support and local workers, provide full transparency of financial interactions and the criteria validating the flow of value end to end, together with a reputation management system that evaluates the quality of performance. The measurement and reputation system is based on criteria relevant to the particular aid situation, combined with authentication such as biometrics which can be managed outside traditional KYC scenarios, while the underlying cryptocurrency provides the full traceability of transactions via blockchain technology.

Cash Flow in Aid Pipeline Example

The system is based on self-executing contracts underpinning the aid campaign, which can be set up to execute based on the provision of evidence in the form of information such as iris recognition for individuals, or documents such as invoices for suppliers, that are measured by the system against the agreed criteria. For example, in an AIDS treatment scenario, a local NGO may set up a campaign guaranteeing funds are allocated to supporting a hospital system, suppliers of medicine, and to the individuals concerned. Once set up and agreed with the global NGO managing the campaign, this information is written to the blockchain as a transparent and immutable record (Fig. 11.2).

Recipients can then "cash out" the aid by triggering the self-executing contracts—for an end recipient, this may be in the form of food provided by a merchant involved in the scheme, validated by biometric identity recognition, for example, as with the pilot run by UNDP with Syrian refugees, where on submission of evidence that the goods have been provisioned to the individuals, the system pays out to the local merchant in local currency. Alternatively, a global supplier such as a pharmaceutical company provides evidence that a certain number of units of medicine have been supplied, and is paid in USD, or a local hospital pays their workers' wallets, based on

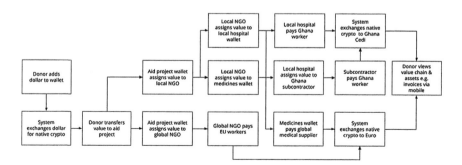

Fig. 11.2 Flow of cash in blockchain aid scenario

timesheets. These events trigger positive feedback and will typically execute payments, but can also trigger press releases, or other transfers of assets. This ensures that pre-agreed criteria are met, reducing ambiguity and the risk of fraud and providing confidence for donors and NGOs alike.

The system also manages the transfer of value (via a native cryptocurrency or one that is pegged to a fiat currency), which can be created based on input of USD, for example, and released as local currency, minimising exchange risk and providing full traceability for every transaction. The advantage of using cryptocurrency, in addition to reducing currency risk, is that every point of exchange for any unit of currency is recorded in a block of transactions that can be accessed by any party to the agreement, which allows full audits and confidence that funds are being used appropriately.

The reputation management system evaluates the quality of any completed campaigns, assessing how well conditions have been met and the quality of assets received in evidence. Donors and NGOs can then see how well their campaigns are performing based on factual, like for like evaluations.

Benefits

This platform addresses the major risks associated with aid pipelines today, i.e. reduced exchange and transaction costs, and "leakage" or diversion of funds by corrupt entities and individuals, because the money is fully traceable and can only be cashed out by predetermined people or classes of people. This in turn gives increased transparency and confidence for donors and clarity of purpose for local and global NGOs. The administration traditionally associated with managing aid pipelines is also significantly reduced compared to standard approaches.

Bottom-up Solutions

While top-down investment and donations are critical to supporting sustainable development, long-term growth is best achieved by solutions enabling communities to support themselves. We cover some of the opportunities in Chapters 10 and 12. Here, we present an example of how such a bottom-up solution can work to support community growth without the need for top-down intervention.

As above, this is one example of a solution, and similar applications of technology can be applied to achieve the outcomes described above and in other chapters.

Circular Economy Platform

Just like international investments, circular economies also face challenges of provenance, benchmarking, measurement and managing interactions, which can be addressed through applications of blockchain and self-executing smart contract technology.

Background

A successful circular economy can function very well in a small, close-knit community, however when running at scale they require technology to support the management of peer-to-peer transactions, or to support interaction with central or distributed intermediaries. Obvious examples of this are platforms like Airbnb or Uber, where peer-to-peer transactions are managed via a platform, and the ability for customers to transact directly with producers has had a transformational effect on how these sectors of the economy work.

Such platforms can facilitate B2C distribution and interaction, however when measuring more qualitative elements such as behaviours and exchange of non-financial assets, emerging technologies present significant benefits of traceability, provenance, disintermediation and transparency. As we discussed in the Cow in your Pocket, blockchain can support supply chain integrity in many ways:

- Traceability: blockchain transactions and self-executing contracts offer a full lifecycle audit of value for asset exchange, together with restrictions on destinations for exchanges of value, so customers can be confident where their money is going.
- Provenance: blockchain records demonstrate the full lifecycle of an asset, which can be a digital representation of a physical asset, service or agreement. This can also include evidence relevant to sustainability such as location of origin, chemical composition and species identification (for food), so customers have confidence they're buying what they intend to buy.
- Disintermediation: self-executing contracts managed through business logic peer to peer remove the need for the traditional third party to intervene in managing transactions. Through automatically executing

contracts, complex business rules, such as those applying to irregular supply and demand in circular economies, can be encoded so that the need for administration and central intermediaries is significantly reduced or removed, taking much of the challenge and cost out of running circular economies.

- Transparency: parties to the contract, which can be all members of a community, can have full visibility of all agreements and execution, meaning that communities can be self-policing, removing the need for third-party auditing.

Furthermore, the use of internal cryptocurrency linked to certain types of activity can encourage a circular economy to promote sustainable behaviours, if used to transact for selected goods and services, which is extremely relevant to circular economy activities. This is an extension of the typical e-wallet use we are familiar with e.g. Espresso House phone app, into a wider and richer marketplace economy.

Solution

The solution is based on self-executing contracts and e-wallets, where assets and cryptocurrency can be transacted seamlessly over the platform via a simple mobile interface. Communities using these contracts and e-wallets would be able to manage complex supply and consumption loops without the need for a central intermediary. In combination with IoT devices such as sensors, stock and distribution can be controlled and partially managed through automation, avoiding the usual challenges of complex supply and demand variations. Additionally, using blockchain technology, we can ensure that community members are only transacting within the circular economy, by guaranteeing the origin of goods and services and allowing transactions only with nominated persons or classes of people.

Because most circular economy initiatives are focused on outcomes rather than technology, this platform is delivered as a bundled package that can easily be configured and modified by less technical startups to meet multiple business model needs, for example integration with IoT devices to monitor supply chains, energy monitoring and AI technology where needed. As the self-executing contracts and payments interface is delivered over mobile, we extend our reach to communities with lower exposure to technology, supporting maximum community engagement, while offering sophisticated solutions.

By creating a base platform for multiple circular economy applications, the door opens for interoperability and interaction between an ecosystem of circular economies across the country and potentially globally.

Native cryptocurrency can either be pinned to local fiat or bespoke internal "GreenCoin", or alternatively associated with a particular asset central to the circular economy in question (e.g. "SustainableFishCoin").

Below we present two examples of how this platform can be used to support sustainable marketplaces.

Circular Economy Example: Community Farming and Urban Greening

Summary

Growing urbanisation, rising food costs and inequality are leading to malnutrition in urban poor populations, even in developed economies. Meanwhile, more food is being imported as cities expand over farmland. While governments are promoting urban farming, the scale and volumes of produce people are able to grow in gardens or open spaces falls far below a practical solution to supply urban populations with produce.

The circular economy marketplace, combined with green and Agritech, provides a solution to these challenges in the shape of a pioneering example of holistic community-based farming and greening, with a positive impact on disadvantaged SMEs and community segments alike.

Background/the Problem

The division between rich and poor is growing, while the population of underprivileged and underserved individuals is increasing in developed economies, where certain sectors, such as immigrants, suffer from disproportionately high unemployment levels. Access to fresh fruit and vegetables is particularly limited for poorer populations in developed economies, with many poorer regions in the USA designated "food deserts" because of the lack of access to fresh produce.

Many countries that have the climate for growing vegetables and fruit are importing large quantities, because the economics of rural farming don't attract sufficient numbers of producers; this in turn leads to higher costs of produce which in turn, impacts the urban poor.

Given the high level of imports and the cost of fruit and vegetables, targeting urban greening and fruit/vegetable production in urban areas benefits urban communities by reducing food costs and carbon footprints. In addition to the core marketplace system, developments in urban greening, both social and thanks to Agritech present solutions for creating a multi-layered food circle:

- Vertical farms are aiming to bring food production back to cities, reduce carbon emissions and water usage and address the growing challenge of feeding the world's ballooning urban population. Vertical farms minimise the need for energy, water and pesticides.
- Low-tech urban farms can be created on any open space or roof, as Copenhagen has shown in the last few years after dictating that any new roof with less than 30% slope has to be greened. Schools, communities and neighbourhoods support urban farms across the city, and this can also be achieved in other urban neighbourhoods, with appropriate organisation. While these don't produce enough volume to be a primary food source, they help communities form an emotional connection with growing food.
- Integral to urban agriculture is the introduction of bees to the urban environment. Copenhagen and Stockholm have also demonstrated it's possible to sustain a large population of bees alongside a greener urban environment, and we can learn from their experience while contributing to a reversal of the global decline in bee numbers.
- Public fridges or People's fridges, placed in strategic locations, can accept unsold food from retailers or private individuals, making it available for others to take.
- Autonomous vehicles for distribution as these become commonly available.
- Home management including cold storage management: as smart fridges emerge, we plan to integrate these into the supply chain removing friction from the ordering and purchasing process. Using the self-executing contract logic, this will enable consortia of domestic and commercial cold storage appliances, including People's fridges, to collaborate on goods ordering and distribution management.

The Solution

The solution is an integrated, community-based holistic combination of the core circular economy platform with vertical farming and urban agriculture, supporting a local food circle, delivered by a consortium of local businesses. Because of the scale of this solution, it is likely to be contracted by the government or municipality. Large circular economy initiatives like this are also a key tool in boosting local small business economy and non-traditional employment, firstly building infrastructure and then operating facilities such as urban farms, beehives and vertical farms (Fig. 11.3).

The solution includes sending waste to biomass energy sources, with internal cost allocation via the cryptocurrency. Large producers such as vertical farms sell their produce directly over the platform to small and large consumers, including commercial or domestic cold storage units, distributed via traditional or automated distribution networks (or simply picked up at the source). Small producers such as households create self-executing contracts over the system, which can be bid for by consumers including automated cold storage facilities, without the need for intervention. Prosumers can therefore transact directly with each other and with commercial consumers, forming a core part of the food distribution circle, and reducing the need for intermediaries and associated overhead costs.

Thanks to the cryptocurrency and contract logic, provenance is clear to consumers and distribution can be controlled to local markets as much as

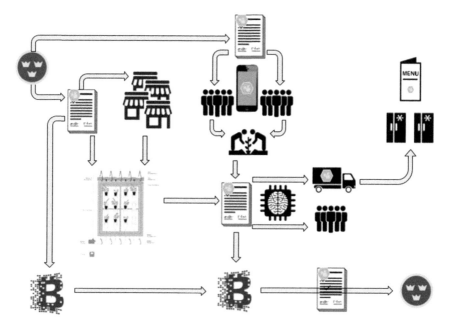

Fig. 11.3 Urban agriculture on blockchain

desired. Opportunities for interaction with other circular or marketplace economies built on the platform also exist, with the option to transact directly with these circular or marketplace economies in cryptocurrency, maintaining the full provenance and integrity of the supply chain across multiple types of marketplace.

The platform supports rich reporting to such authorities, which allows the government or municipality the ability to monitor performance closely, based on the non-financial metrics such as volume of food distributed, number of unemployed people contracted to work or distribution of fresh food in food deserts.

This type of circular economy also provides a rich opportunity for education, again creating opportunities for employment in local urban populations.

Sustainable Marketplace Creation Example: Sustainable Fisheries

While core circular economy applications such as the food circle empower communities to sustainable behaviours, other types of marketplace application can also support sustainability, in particular where scarcity is threatening populations such as fish.

Background/the Problem

With global fish consumption doubling over the last 30 years, 1 in 12 people now depend on fisheries for their livelihoods and around 3 billion rely on fish as a primary source of animal protein. Despite this, 64% of fisheries are now overfished and more than 90% of all fisheries have no effective data management in place. Because locating fish catches is challenging, even with GPS trackers, and once in the supply chain, fish are difficult to trace, validating sustainability is extremely difficult to impossible, and subject to widespread fraud.

Meanwhile, quotas force edible bycatch to be regularly discarded, leading to waste and missed opportunities for additional cheap food sources and increasing the relative cost and footprint of fish that do make it to the table. As with meat and other food produce, the supply chain is opaque and subject to fraud; however, fishing is unique in that it is forced to harvest large amounts of edible food which is discarded, because of quotas designed to protect the environment.

Technology Opportunities

For the catch through to plate supply chain, there are multiple technology solutions which can be integrated with the core circular marketplace platform to address the fraud and provenance challenges.

- Fish recognition technology such as Fishface, currently piloting in Indonesia, can identify species based on a mobile camera shot. This software validates the species of the catch and can record multiple species.
- Cameras, designed to be incorporated in fishing nets, trace the time and origin of the catch together with GPS recording.
- IOT integration with blockchain[4] to tag fish once caught.
- Machine Learning (ML) can support both recognition applications such as the fish categorisation software, and matching applications supporting asset allocation such as the recipe allocation to specific types of fish.

Additional future opportunities include IoT integration of autonomous vehicles into supply chains, which can be integrated into the supply chain at a later stage, IoT warehouse management and sorting, full integration into national cryptocurrency and further downstream applications of ML such as customised pricing and market-based storage management for caterers.

The Solution

The solution is a multi-layer aggregation of these technologies with the core circular economy platform of self-executing contracts, wallets, payments and behavioural reputation system, delivered over smartphones. Tailored cryptocurrency such as SustainableFishCoin or a standardised currency pinned to the local fiat can be used within the system to transact (Fig. 11.4).

When a catch is made, in-net camera records catch and fishers scan fish. The fish identification software then categorises and "counts" the fish, and the platform logs the fish types, location and timing of catch and fisher tags fish. The platform then writes a hash record to the public blockchain identifying the origin of catch, and this is repeated for each box of fish. The platform creates a self-executing contract for core catch, demonstrating sustainability, which follows the fish through the distribution chain.

The platform identifies relevant recipes for bycatch and writes the self-executing contract bundling recipes with species/numbers. It identifies relevant processors and catering outlets with access to distribution centre and

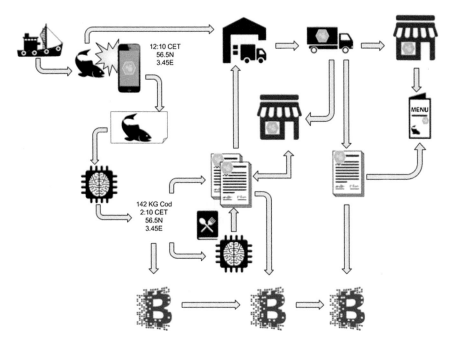

Fig. 11.4 Sustainable fishing on blockchain

alerts them with opportunity, prices and recipe options. Catering outfits and processors bid for bycatch, and the contract makes allocations without the need for a retailer.

The fish is then landed at distribution centre, where it is sorted semi-automatically according to the contract terms (the target is eventually for full IoT automation). The sorting is recorded onto blockchain, tracing forward movement of fish through the supply chain via IoT tags.

For processors and catering outlets picking up bycatch, payment is made over the platform (if using digital or crypto currency) or can be made through standard payments channels, while for the main catch, purchasers are alerted directly and offered the opportunity to place orders via central contract; any residual is assigned via business rules to the distributor and the allocation recorded to the blockchain.

The distribution pickup is recorded on the blockchain including full provenance and contract details, destinations of all allocations. At the central distribution centre, the residual main catch is tagged, and redistribution also recorded on blockchain, and this continues for any number of intermediate transactions. At the point of delivery, the transfer to primary retailer (catering, processor or retail) is recorded, and provenance can be displayed (on menu, restaurant bill, packaging, price display, etc.) as required, with the certification for sustainability, including, if required, where the fish was caught.

Conclusion

In this chapter, we've described how Fintech can support many of the UN's Sustainable Development Goals, and drilled into examples of how top-down and bottom-up solutions can be created using these technologies. We describe the technologies such as cryptocurrencies, tokenisation, blockchain, IoT and AI in greater detail in other chapters.

While many of these examples are in development and some of the technology is still evolving, it is key to note that the technology for all of these solutions exists today, and in many cases, is already in use. We anticipate that these Fintech solutions, and solutions like these, will become dominant in how capital markets and marketplace economies operate within the next few years. This should be good news for the planet, and for economies, at the same time.

Fintech solutions, and particularly those based on blockchain, can help to accelerate the implementation of the UN's Sustainability Development Goals. We need both top-down solutions such as creative approaches to investment, including alternative approaches to investment products, crowd-funding platforms and aid pipeline management, while bottom-up solutions include community-based platforms, circular economy and solutions that leapfrog traditional financial services.

The technology is evolving, but there are existing precedents such as M-PESA that demonstrate the impact that alternative financial solutions can have in supporting sustainability in developing economies. Sustainability challenges apply to developed as well as developing economies, and they can all benefit from these solutions.

Notes

1. UN.org, Sustainable Development Goals, United Nations. http://www.un.org/sustainabledevelopment/sustainable-development-goals/. Accessed 27 December 2017.
2. Castilla-Rubio, R., & Zadek. (2016, December). Fintech and Sustainable Development: Assessing the Implications. http://unepinquiry.org/publication/Fintech-and-sustainable-development-assessing-the-implications/. Accessed 27 December 2017.

3. United Nations Sends Aid to 10,000 Syrian Refugees Using Ethereum Blockchain. *Coindesk.com*, 13 June 2017. https://www.coindesk.com/united-nations-sends-aid-to-10000-syrian-refugees-using-ethereum-blockchain/. Accessed 27 December 2017.
4. Hyperledger Sawtooth Enterprise Blockchain Examples. https://01.org/sawtooth/seafood.html. Accessed 13 January 2018.

12

SME Microfinance, Fractional Ownership and Crowdfunding

Expanding on some of the UN's priorities, in this chapter we explore the challenges facing communities of small businesses globally, including the financing challenges they face, and discuss how emerging technology solutions, platform solutions and behavioural reputation systems can help them re-establish community cohesion and their economic power. This is an opportunity for developing economies, where many people are poorly served by the financial system and exploited as a result, but also in developed economies where there's a real opportunity to rebalance the power of individuals and small businesses.

An effect of this empowerment will be to encourage communities to make more sustainable choices about how their environments are managed; community ownership will allow longer-term and more community-focused decisions to be made, while practical applications of fractional ownership and cryptocurrency rewards for sustainable energy production will reduce need for fossil fuels and costs.

SMEs and Communities

Most businesses aren't big businesses, while nearly everyone today is the member of multiple communities. However, banks haven't traditionally made much money out of most people, or out of most businesses. The big bucks come from doing things for big businesses, whether it's wholesale banking—cash management, merchant banking, equipment financing, etc., or capital markets, where banks can charge a high fee because of volume, and offer discounts.

© The Author(s) 2018
S. Blakstad and R. Allen, *FinTech Revolution*,
https://doi.org/10.1007/978-3-319-76014-8_12

Banking for SMEs

Small businesses traditionally haven't been that profitable for banks, because they're messy and complicated, and don't have much money, so it doesn't make financial sense to offer them services equivalent to those offered to big corporations. So, while banks provide services to small businesses, it's not in their interest to tailor these services, and the high cost of administration is passed on to customers, making SME loans expensive. Because SMEs are relatively risky and difficult to evaluate, barriers to financing are high and the burden of proof is on the SME if they need to borrow, which has the effect of excluding many from the opportunity. Most SME finance takes the shape of asset-backed lending such as collateral or invoice finance/factoring, which is administratively arduous and relatively expensive.

Banks are working hard to enhance services to SMEs: automation and partnering with Fintechs have improved the experience for SMEs to an extent, for example by offering basic accounting and invoicing services through third parties, but the range of services offered by banks to these customers, in contrast to the services offered to larger customers, is still extremely limited.

In addition to the disadvantage SMEs suffer as the result of their limited access to finance, they also have limited leverage with customers. Small businesses typically get paid later than large businesses, and the bigger the customer, the later they pay. This creates cash flow challenges for small businesses, who are typically working with small margins, and for whom a late invoice can be a disaster. Unlike larger businesses, they also have to pay suppliers and workers promptly, so they don't have the ability to pass on their customers' delays in paying.

Small businesses also suffer from challenges associated with their scale; premises, equipment and services tend to cost them more proportionately, as they're not able to benefit from scale discounts, and may need to own equipment that's not fully utilised. They spend a disproportionate amount of time on administration, because the reporting requirements don't go away with a small scale, and they're more likely to pay accountants for basic services such as running payroll or "shoebox accounting", not having the scale themselves to have sufficiently skilled persons dedicated to these sorts of functions.

Of course, not all small businesses are struggling and on the point of bankruptcy, but too many suffer from the triple whammy of unpredictable cash flow, disproportionately high administration and inability to borrow because of challenges demonstrating they're trustworthy. Without community support, most small businesses in developed economies only have recourse to the bank for help, which will only lend where there's a high degree of confidence. The global credit gap for SMEs is estimated by the World Bank at USD 2.6 trillion.

And yet, small businesses, as we see from study after study, form the backbone of economies everywhere. Unlike big businesses, they don't benefit from creative accounting, so they're paying more tax. They usually employ people locally and buy from local suppliers, boosting the local economy rather than finding cheap foreign alternatives. Small businesses make up 99% of the world's businesses, and over half of the global workforce is employed by SMEs.

Communities

Communities are a natural human construct, composed of people with similar goals, world view, skills or other characteristic—religious, political affiliation, etc. Traditionally, your community would be defined by your geography, probably in combination with some of these characteristics, and those communities would have been limited by your proximity to meeting places. In the 1980s, we would have identified with communities associated with a local pub, perhaps a choir, and a workplace, for example.

If we consider communities in history, for much of the time people didn't move beyond the geography where they were born; businesses were passed from generation to generation and everyone knew everyone else. These sorts of communities knew each other well, so they knew who they could trust, and formed strong identities with the community. Formally organised communities such as guilds were dedicated to particular professions, which were both tightly defined by geography and supported continuity through generations.

Fast-forward to the industrial revolution, when communities were broken up by the migration to towns and the movement of labour to larger production facilities, creating new communities of people with something in common, but no shared history. It's no coincidence that this was also the time when religious, special interest and political communities started to emerge among populations of factory workers, seeking for a "home" with which to identify, where the level of trust was greater than across the wider worker population.

Where there was a great need for support, and a need for social change, organised workers' groups formed unions, and because they shared a common and pressing need, these groups became significant and powerful, ultimately becoming responsible for driving much-needed reforms in working practices. Unions are characterised by a visible commitment in the form of a subscription charge, which is then redistributed to unfortunate workers in times of need. This financial commitment, supported by agreed rules, creates a bond of trust across larger and geographically dispersed communities with common goals.

Unions are a good example of informally formed communities, built from necessity, organising and supporting each other and becoming more formal as a result. Whether your perception of unions is positive or negative, they have undeniably played a critical role in the development of legislation protecting workers, such as the abolition of child labour and the weekend.

Thanks to the proliferation of social media, people can now belong to, and communicate with, a variety of communities, which may be local, national or global. For example, you might run a small construction business, enjoy competitive cycling and belong to a Lutheran church. The chances are you can find an online community that shares each of these interests—you can share questions and knowledge about bricklaying on building.co.uk forum, get involved in helmet debates on cyclingnews.com and yes, there's an online forum for Lutherans as well.

However, these communities are bound by shared interests rather than by causes such as those driving the unions. These forums are great for exchanging views or information (and the odd flame war), but they usually don't provide anything further. Unlike individuals, a small business can't benefit from unions, which are there to protect their workers, including from exploitation by small businesses.

By contrast, communities of large businesses regularly help each other in more concrete ways. Supported by the global banking system, they invest in each other, collaborate to pressurise politicians into changing legislation, or to find creative ways of avoiding taxes, form syndicates and consortia to promote advances in technology or infrastructure, and build investment funds or assets together.

Large businesses can operate in communities because they have plenty of information about each other, so they understand which other corporations will support their cause, because they share common challenges or ideologies. They operate in a space between governments and populations, with obligations to both, but identifying more with each other and with their shareholders. As with the very wealthy, there's more in common between big businesses in different geographies, than there is between big businesses and small businesses, and like the very wealthy, they make full use of their global community.

So, on the one hand there is a community of large corporations, supported with tailored services by the banks, and unions supporting workers, but on the other hand there are many loosely coordinated communities of small businesses, who are relatively underserved and overcharged by the banks, unable to get much practical benefit from their communities.

Why are large corporations able to collaborate, whereas smaller companies aren't? If we consider the historical view, it's clear that the difference is because of the level of trust and commitment. Small businesses don't have access to enough information about each other to know who they can trust, and they can't make a commitment to other small businesses without that trust. That leaves them operating in competition, instead of in cooperation, with each other, which is unlikely to work well at a community level.

The Ecosystem Economy and SMEs

The rise of the ecosystem economy and internet marketplaces, by contrast, should be good news for small businesses. Now services are available in the cloud or online, that traditionally had to be provided by dedicated and expensive service providers. A variety of online accountancy packages are now available, many targeted at small businesses—and banks, as noted above, are starting to partner with them to offer more joined-up services.

The internet also expands markets for small businesses—reaching remote customers is easy, meaning a tiny business can create a global marketplace, without needing any formal distribution network. Finding those customers is, of course, more of a challenge! As we've observed, communities of SMEs can already discuss their common challenges and exchange information with each other over dedicated online forums, which can also help to build relationships between small businesses.

We think, however, that the ecosystem economy, together with emerging technology, offers a lot more than a convenient source of global customers and information to SMEs, and that technology can help build new trust communities which can provide active support and help them.

Community-Based Finance

Many years ago, communities were self-financing. Local merchants lent to local producers, with whom they had a personal relationship. The emergence of large banks has broken this relationship, with standardised lending products and credit risk management, resulting in the exclusion of many smaller businesses from access to capital. Recently, thanks to several platforms supporting peer-to-peer lending and crowdfunding, there are now some opportunities for small, individual investors to choose their investments based on personal criteria and to invest directly into their project of choice.

Micro-businesses in developing economies such as smallholdings and small trading outlets suffer from many challenges achieving scale and sustainability. Many lack access to financial systems because they can't prove credit history, lack formal identity or land ownership documentation, while small producers are often exploited by middle men artificially depressing prices. Peer-to-peer lending enables small loans to some businesses, usually facilitated by NGOs, and while this enables a flow of capital from developed to developing economies, it's inefficient and suffers from high costs such as cross-border transaction fees of up to 12% (for some African countries), while administration costs are high.

Microfinance is one of the largest sources of capital for individual micro-businesses in developing economies, helping them break through the credit barrier to achieve scale but today, as we discussed in Chapter 7, lenders typically combine government or NGO funding with private business, with inefficient, often exploitative and poorly coordinated operations, and costs are prohibitive, with lenders charging up to 500% interest.

With the application of Fintech technology to increase transparency, reduce administration costs and risks, however, this type of peer-to-peer and crowdlending could offer two further potential sources of capital for these micro-businesses, and by extrapolation to SME communities in developed economies: First, unlocking smaller savings into working capital, where these would typically have been held by a bank and used for market-based wealth creation in the large bank model. Given the current imbalance in economic power between the micro-business and the lender, this model is likely to grow first, and we then anticipate there will be a second evolution in microfinance and crowdfunding as the economic impact of these growth opportunities starts to spread, where the businesses themselves reinvest in their own peer community. In addition, delivery track records can be proven based on customer interactions and delivery, which don't need to involve traditional bank-based transactions.

Community-based financing makes sense for a number of reasons—individuals are investing in businesses that they understand and in whom they have a personal stake as a customer or as a community member; the growth of businesses within a community is likely to lead to the creation of wealth in that community and the growth of other businesses; and there's the personal connection. However, we also anticipate that peer-based community financing is likely to lead to communities focusing on longer-term outcomes for that community, rather than short-term profits. This could include focusing further on local markets and sustainable production of crops, rather than short-term profit-driven crops for export, for example.

Trust and Collaboration

Businesses within communities helping each other isn't exactly a novel concept; ever since the earliest communities, small businesses have helped each other and collaborated, and we still see this kind of collaboration in business communities in rural areas, to an extent. But it's largely broken, as we explored earlier in this chapter, by movement of people and urbanisation, where communities are too fluid to build long-term trust relationships and individuals are likely to have loose associations with a number of communities, rather than a solid affiliation with a "home" community.

Research shows that communities which can build trust are more likely to make sustainable decisions about their communities—whether it's environment management, or long-term infrastructure. Small businesses that collaborate also benefit from scale opportunities which may not be available to them as individual businesses, such as larger contracts or tenders for municipalities or large retailers, as well as achieving scale discounts by pooling resources or placing larger stock orders.

Community ownership of resources can also reduce costs for individual businesses, for example fractional ownership of agricultural equipment which is infrequently used, rather than leasing it from a large corporation at marked-up prices. But collaboration on both joint tenders and joint ownership needs commitment of finances, resources and reputation from all parties, which is hard to achieve without long-term trust relationships.

Lacking access to the sort of records that larger businesses can find about each other, small businesses can evaluate each other's trustworthiness either by checking their online reputation, or by going through a formal audit of their credit and other histories. Neither is particularly helpful for building community trust; online reviews may be reliable at scale (although subject to platform biases, as described in Chapter 18), but for smaller businesses the low volume, or total absence, of online reviews makes them unreliable. Formal audits may be more reliable, but the available information is unlikely to provide more than a credit rating, which may not be enough to build trust about behaviour in a collaborative business arrangement.

Banks and governments, which could form a focal point for small business collaboration, tend to present barriers rather than support; although they may be trying to engage more small businesses in community projects, they're typically drowning in administration, which makes the collaboration difficult to achieve, hard to measure and ultimately, not a community effort, as it's still centralised through a recognised trust authority. The trust between businesses in these scenarios only last as long as the relationship with the intermediary is in place, and never really becomes peer to peer.

These are some of the reasons small businesses aren't collaborating more today—in fact, they tell us they'd like to work together more, if they knew who they could trust. Trusting someone to enter into a relationship such as shared ownership or a joint tender doesn't have to be based on historical knowledge—we know from the partnerships in the large business community that richness of information is adequate as a guarantee. The challenge is how to get that rich information, without arduous administration or potentially breaching proprietary information.

Behavioural reputation is an emerging field, combining big data analytics, Artificial Intelligence and social platforms. Profiles are built based on network behaviours, such as interactions with other platform users, telephone calls or text messages, combined with other data such as location and movement, to create a rich and contextual view of how someone behaves. These behaviour profiles have been found to give a greater level of confidence than a credit history for creditworthiness. The data for these systems are easy to collect, and very hard to fabricate, can be systematically analysed and distilled into reputation scoring that's not affected by volume or opinion biases. It can also be applied to individuals and businesses who don't have access to formal credit, or even a bank account, thanks to the types of data that are collected.

At hiveonline, we're using rich behavioural data which include the assets our customers exchange with their customers, and the contracts they use on our platform, to give a highly tailored view of our customers' reliability to different types of customers, including each other. We can show other small businesses that their peers have a good delivery track record and don't default on suppliers, while large customers such as governments will want to know they're ethical employers and pay their taxes. A standard phone-based reputation system can also provide a rich and contextual profile based on number, timing and frequency of communications and location data.

Any type of behavioural system builds up data over time, and the longer it's in place, the better the system, but because they collect a lot of different data points, even early views can provide a rich and accurate picture of trust and reliability for the different types of customers. This has mostly been used to date to address the inclusion agenda, helping micro-businesses leapfrog the credit ceiling and establish formal relationships with financial institutions, but there is also a great opportunity to use these systems to build community trust, either within geographical communities, or globally, thanks to the platform availability.

In effect, a behavioural reputation profile is like an instant relationship history, except that in a traditional relationship it was easier to hide deviant behaviour from your peers! Behavioural reputations can give communities of businesses and individuals the confidence to trust each other far enough to make common financial commitments, which enables them to collaborate and work together as communities.

Provenance, Fractional Ownership and Energy

Blockchain technology brings opportunities to demonstrate provenance and identity to micro-businesses and individuals, and to support alternative ownership paradigms. In addition to trust and identity, provenance plays an important role in empowering smaller producers, both for proof of ownership or other usage rights, and for proof of supply. The ownership of land in developing economies is routinely subject to corruption and seizure by powerful business or authorities, while similarly shared resources such as water can be exploited by big business or authorities at the expense of local producers. As we noted above, smaller producers are also typically exploited by middle men setting low fixed prices, because individual producers don't have access to supply chains at scale.

Blockchain-based provenance can address both of these issues, removing the need for middle men and enabling communities to work collectively to prove ownership of resources or land, and to manage supply chains. Blockchain-based usage and production records are immutable and incontestable, so producers can validate their ownership and access to resources, while setting a fair price for goods and working together with other small producers to sell collectively. This has potential to rebalance supply chains significantly, reducing the opportunity for corruption and ensuring both that suppliers get a fair price, and that consumers have validation that their goods are genuine.

Blockchain-based smart contracts also give communities the opportunity to collectively own assets, which again rebalances the power between small and large businesses, enabling smaller and micro-businesses to exact greater control. Fractional ownership is growing across communities and there are a number of Fintech businesses already supporting this in developing economies. This means that rather than paying a third party for use of, for example, a tractor, communities can collectively own equipment which would be beyond their individual budget, and return value to the community. In addition to having a right to use the equipment, there's also the opportunity for collectively owned assets to be leased to third parties in fallow periods.

This is exciting enough for small producers needing to use agricultural or engineering equipment, but when applied to renewable energy sources, the potential for communities to collectively own sources of power and to profit from their use could have an even greater impact. As well as providing the environment for longer-term goals for sustainable agriculture, the sustainability of energy production makes more sense to communities than short-term for-profit activities. There are several Fintechs exploring how renewable energy sources can both be collectively owned using blockchain technology and return profits to the community, in the same way as other fractionally owned assets.

Applications in Developed Economies

Of course, micro-businesses in developing economies aren't the only under-served communities struggling with unequal relationships to markets, suppliers and sources of finance. If we apply the same principles to small business communities in developed economies, the benefits of peer-to-peer community finance are also obvious—the same principles of knowing your investor apply, while the opportunities for fractional ownership of assets and renewable energy sources are even greater. Communities may be localised, or they may be geographically distributed but form a community based on common business activities or other interests; from a financing perspective this enables very broad communities to become involved in peer-to-peer funding, still confident in their shared knowledge and objectives, even in different geographies.

Provenance and taking corruption out of the supply chain also present a potential to revolutionise trade in developed economies, with significant fraud and corruption still blighting the estimated USD 8 trillion of annual global trade finance and shipping. Blockchain applications and particularly smart contracts bring enormous opportunities in these areas, addressing the very high cost of fraud in trade finance and the inefficiencies of typical supply chains. Meanwhile, fractional ownership of renewable energy production can apply to geographically remote facilities, for example with an inland business having an interest in offshore wave energy production, but still benefiting both from reduced power cost and a return on sale of surplus energy.

Community Marketplaces

SME collaboration and common ownership are both positive ways of interacting with large customers and suppliers, but technology also paves the way for communities to transact and do business within that community, keeping wealth in the community and reducing external dependencies or intermediaries. Community marketplaces have many positive benefits:

- No intermediary "cut"
- Building trust within the community
- Working with local suppliers and customers who you understand
- Opportunity for "prosumers" to emerge—producers who are also consumers—and circular economies
- Reduces transportation costs and environmental impact
- Incentivises producers to make goods suitable for local markets, reducing production and environmental costs
- peer-to-peer transaction opportunity reducing the need for money
- Stimulates local economies

Locally produced and sold agricultural produce can reap all of these benefits. An example is farming communities in parts of the developing economies, today forced to grow cash crops for foreign markets by middle men and lack of local market opportunities. Crops not native to the areas where they're growing require more intervention such as pesticides, and more water, than native crops, while exporting food reduces the local food supply.

Pesticide use in developing economies is a major cause of mortality in people and bee populations, which is of great concern to farmers, as without pollinators, crops will fail. And even when local crops are grown locally, corrupt middle men control markets:

> When Mr Nzabahimana wants to sell food, he simply hawks it around the village or hires a woman to carry it on her head to Rubengera, a tiny market town a few miles away. He does not know in advance what price his crops will fetch. As Africa's fields grow more productive, such thin, fragmented markets are becoming a bigger problem. Too few agricultural buyers reach villages, and the ones that make it can often dictate prices. "The traders have all the information—they pay the farmers what they want."—*Economist*, March 2016[1]

Creating local markets using technology—and delivering the technology over the mobile network—allows producers direct access to markets, taking out the middle men. In the case of rural Africa, this presents great opportunities for keeping production close to populations and for reducing corruption, while in more developed economies, offers potential for urban food circles, as explored in our chapter on Green Fintech.

Clearly, local markets don't have to be about food production; any supplier/consumer relationship can be managed at a local market level, given the appropriate demand, with technology enabling consumers and producers to find each other.

The other type of peer-to-peer marketplace that technology enables is the global marketplace. As mentioned above, producers can now access customers all over the world, and platforms enable them to sell to consumers all over the world, and while the platforms enabling these relationships have historically been crude, they are becoming more sophisticated at matching consumers with producers.

As we discussed in Chapter 11, circular marketplaces can be ring-fenced to the appropriate community using guarantees such as smart contracts and cryptocurrency, offering marketplace opportunities for small and large businesses in local or global communities. The risk is that platforms themselves will become so powerful that they take on the role of the corrupt middle man, forcing producers into certain directions and fixing prices. We are confident that this can be mitigated as marketplaces start using the blockchain, with greater prosumer control of contracts and transactions. We also anticipate that as marketplaces become more specialised to communities and economic circles, emerging technology will allow for the development of an ecosystem of different platforms, sharing opportunities for interoperability and a global marketplace economy which is effectively independent of intermediaries.

Top-Down Financing

If the trajectory of SMEs in developed economies follows the current path, we anticipate that they will start to see a higher success rate and more growth than larger businesses, supported by technology. A natural by-product of this increased prosperity could be the financing of equivalent businesses in less developed economies, supporting growth and building capital at the same time.

We've explored opportunities for communities to collaborate and interoperate, which will help address some of their day-to-day operational and cash flow challenges, but there's still that USD 2.6 trillion funding gap. The Economist article referenced above indicates that only 1% of Rwanda's farmers, where four out of five of the working population is employed in farming, have access to credit. Even with the support of technology reducing corruption and creating market communities, there's a big funding hole before these and other small businesses can start to engage in longer-term growth and planning.

None of these solutions in isolation will replace the need for top-down financing for SMEs in developing economies from traditional investment funds, aid and governments, and as we discuss in the next chapter, technology also presents significant opportunities in unblocking financing for many types of existing investment vehicles. This type of funding will remain critical to supporting growth in developing economies in particular, but in developed economies, SMEs also have a funding problem, as we explored at the beginning of this chapter.

We have seen the emergence of a new class of SME financing instrument, aimed at supporting financing for complex businesses based on reputational and other data; hiveonline, like some other platforms, also supports banks in granting small loans to SMEs by encoding credit rules into the reputation system and contracts, reducing the paperwork and friction for loans. So, while the cost of borrowing for SMEs remains high today, we can see several platforms emerging that will significantly reduce the administration, and therefore the cost to SMEs.

Conclusion

SMEs have always been critical to the global economy. Before large corporations arose, all businesses were SMEs, and today they're still employing the majority of the world's workforce, but their support network has crumbled, while larger businesses build the sort of relationships they used to enjoy. Technology, especially blockchain and platform technology, offers greater market opportunities than ever, and with the injection of more confidence, can help SMEs to work as communities again, either globally or locally.

SME finance is still a challenge and one that must be solved to empower SMEs to succeed; current financial solutions are limited and costly. But global networks bring global opportunities and should allow communities to cross-fertilise not only ideas and advice, but funding and market opportunities. When paired with the other emerging investment opportunities offered by Fintech, we anticipate the shape of financing is likely to move towards a more peer-to-peer approach, where banks and other financial institutions still play an important role, but where increasingly individuals and businesses are able to choose to invest directly in businesses they understand and want to support.

Note

1. A Green Evolution. *The Economist*, 12 March 2016. https://www.economist.com/news/briefing/21694521-farms-africa-are-prospering-last-thanks-persistence-technology-and-decent. Accessed 28 December 2017.

13

International Sustainable Investment

In this chapter, we explore the world of sustainability investment, the scope of the challenge and the barriers faced today. We discuss how growing awareness and technology are working together and how current developments in financial technology will help remove some of the barriers.

The Sustainable Development Goals and Investment

Meeting the UN's 17 Sustainable Development Goals (SDGs) by 2030 is looking challenging. In 2015, nearly every country in the world signed up to the Paris Climate agreement but since then, the USA has announced[1] it will be pulling out, causing a schism in the G20 group of nations and consternation at home and abroad. While many US businesses[2] have confirmed that they will continue to work to achieve these goals, and the vast majority of the rest of the world's countries are still signed up, as the second highest source of CO_2 emissions globally[3] (after China) at over 14% and one of the highest emitters per capita, the domestic policy of the USA directly affects the whole planet. As the largest single contributor to development aid, changes in US policy impacting medical services and women's health also threaten many of the SDGs.

The SDGs set out an ambitious agenda, and even without the withdrawal of US support for some key areas, present a challenging set of targets. Some, such as no. 1 (No Poverty), are further challenged by global events such as climate change and war. While global trends are largely positive in areas such

© The Author(s) 2018
S. Blakstad and R. Allen, *FinTech Revolution*,
https://doi.org/10.1007/978-3-319-76014-8_13

as equality, poverty, education and sanitation, further progress needs significant support, estimated[4] at 2% of world GDP, of which around half needs to come from the private sector. Governments have been broadly supportive, although commitments have been matched unevenly, and private investors are increasingly eager to support the SDGs as the impact of climate change becomes more obvious and the urgency greater.

Several investment strategies and vehicles exist which support sustainable development investment, giving investors confidence that their money is going to sustainable activities. And while these have in the past been regarded as niche, strong track records mean they are now attracting the interest of ordinary investors, because sustainable investments are typically with companies that are run not just sustainably, but well.

Sustainable investment vehicles include:

- Stocks (equity) in green companies: many investors choose to purchase shares in companies engaged in sustainable activity, such as renewable energy or circular economy activities; however, there is also a wide range of opinions about what constitutes a green company: a mining company that invests heavily in community development may be offsetting some of its negative impact by benefiting education or health, or an oil company may be cleaner than other oil companies. Purists would argue that neither of these counts as "green", although there is also an argument for encouraging companies to move towards more sustainable operation in any industry.
- Green bonds are bonds (fixed income products) which are subject to tax exemption, issued by banks or companies that are engaged in sustainable activities; many of these today are issued by construction companies building sustainable buildings, or green energy companies, in developed economies. Along with green bonds there are also climate bonds and impact bonds, which may be issued based on running businesses sustainably. Although green bonds have been successful in limited areas, there is both a growing demand and a large need for sustainability investment which they have not been able to cover.
- Social Impact Bonds (SIBs) are bonds issued by governments on behalf of charities addressing quantifiable social problems. If the charities meet their goals, investors are paid back by the government with an additional bonus. Although they have seen early success, measurement is extremely challenging, and they tend to be highly localised to the countries whose governments issue them.
- Green Foreign Direct Investments (FDIs): these are investments by large companies, usually in developed economies, building or acquiring

businesses in other countries, usually developing economies. Examples include a manufacturer building a factory in a developing economy, or a bank or telco buying into a parallel industry such as a bank or telco in a developing economy. Green FDIs can be difficult to validate in some countries and industries, especially in some of the more needy countries where corruption and government intervention create barriers, and FDIs tend to be concentrated in areas with a strong history of FDIs, such as South-East Asia, leaving other areas relatively neglected.

- Green Exchange Traded Funds (ETFs): these are instruments that mimic an exchange made from a bundle of stocks in green companies—because of the lack of consensus on what defines a sustainable company, the underlying businesses tend to be from a narrow range of "safe" sustainable businesses.

The sustainable investment scene is facing challenges: because of the complexity of proving investments are sustainable, and the lack of consensus over what a green company is, most investment vehicles tend to be focused on companies that would probably be operating in a sustainable way regardless, and on "safe" green targets such as renewable energy. Even within this range, however, investment is not reaching areas where it is most needed, particularly in funding for sustainability infrastructure in developing economies, because of currency volatility and concerns about corruption.

Meanwhile, the demand for green investments is growing worldwide as people become more aware of the impact of climate change and the SDGs. Whereas in the past, investors in green securities were large funds, government controlled or otherwise, with the availability of Green ETFs and opportunities offered by technology such as robo-advisors, members of the general public are becoming increasingly aware of green investment opportunities and choosing to invest in them.

Evolving Perceptions of Sustainable Investment

For many investors, especially in the early days of sustainable investment, green investments were perceived as an alternative to profitable investments; funds wanting to present themselves as ethical would choose them, assuming that they would be less profitable than alternatives but because they wanted the positive association. Governments provided incentives to encourage issuers and investors to participate.

As a result of this perception, early investors in sustainable products tended to be from forward-thinking institutions with a clearly articulated sustainability or green agenda, while other investors overlooked them in favour of more traditional instruments. Subsequently, as ordinary consumers and investors became more articulate about their desire not to support businesses that invested in "dirty" industries, more institutions started to invest in green instruments to gain public approval. Over the last few years, however, there has been a visible shift away from this type of "lip service" investment in many large global corporations. We think this is for a variety of reasons:

- Growing awareness of the visible impact of climate change, including to developed nations
- Greater visibility of environmental scandals thanks to social media
- Some high-profile scandals about FDIs, particularly associated with child labour, unsafe working practices and chemical exposures
- Greater economic rewards from sustainable investments

This has led in turn to high-profile pronouncements from industry leaders about their commitment to the green agenda, which then raises awareness and acceptance. As noted above, most "green" investments are actually safe investments in well-run businesses that will generate positive returns—with some exceptions such as SIBs, which remain more altruistic/risky. Many large corporations now have internal teams dedicated to sustainability and are "walking the talk" in the way they run their own businesses as well as their investment portfolio.

This move into the mainstream and general public perception of sustainable investments provides a positive outlook for sustainable investment instruments. However, there are, as outlined above, challenges to growing the scope of sustainable investment instruments, because of challenges with transparency, categorisation and risk in many economies and industries. As the pool of investors grows, it will be important to increase the availability of instruments, moving from a fringe investment choice to the mainstream. As one contributor described it, "we need to move from the concept of green investment, to this is just how investment works", with all investment in businesses having an element of sustainability provenance.

Barriers to Growth

As described above, there are some challenges to overcome in order to increase the range of investments under the sustainability umbrella. This change is needed because there is an imbalance globally, with some of the most vulnerable countries and industries with the greatest need for reform not attracting desperately needed investment. There is an estimated annual USD 2.5 trillion annual funding gap[5] to achieving the SDGs, with renewable energy alone representing an annual USD 1 trillion gap.

What Do We Mean By Green?

One of the biggest challenges that we've heard discussed at G7 and G20 meetings, and hear repeatedly from investment managers, is that there is no commonly agreed standard for what is meant by sustainable, or green, investments. While some areas are obvious, such as building a renewable energy generation facility, others may be borderline, such as making an existing business more sustainable by reducing its resource usage and installing green roofs without fundamentally changing the nature of the business to be more sustainable—they are still worthwhile things to do and to be encouraged, but potentially subject to reversal. This leads to a lowest common denominator approach being taken to instruments such as ETFs, which play it safe rather than excluding investors because of underlying assets that may not appear sufficiently green.

Government Intervention

In many countries, overseas investors are discouraged from investing by the inappropriate level of involvement of government in investment decisions, particularly when selecting vendors for major infrastructure and industrial projects. While government undoubtedly has an important role to play in these decisions, in many countries there is a perception, usually justified, that decisions are made based on relationships and bribes.

Other Corruption

In addition to governments, other political or corporate interests, military and private influence may also threaten the integrity of investments in many countries, with attractive financial incentives for those who can engineer the awarding of contracts or siphoning off of funds to non-sustainable activities or non-activities. In some countries, corruption is so endemic that outside investment is routinely redirected, meaning funding sustainable enterprises is effectively impossible.

Currency and Economic Risk

Many of the countries which need significant investment also suffer from currency volatility caused by financial instability, wars, corruption or GDP issues. High inflation, liquidity concerns or other volatility makes investment inherently risky, especially where projects will also need to purchase goods or services from additional countries, amplifying the exchange and transaction cost risk.

Offsets

Alongside the core challenge of defining what is meant by green, in some cases businesses are creating sustainable solutions in one area, while reducing sustainability in others. There are many businesses in the energy sector in this position, expanding drilling or fracking, while at the same time investing heavily in renewables, while others may be inherently "brown" industries such as mining, but investing in community projects, education and healthcare. As with the "less green" sustainable initiatives, the question arises whether the positives offset the negative behaviours, and environmentalists and investors are divided on this.

Provenance

A by-product of corruption is that it becomes hard to validate that money is being spent on what the investors intend; companies may claim green credentials for activity that doesn't happen, or conceal negative behaviours, such as pollution, from investors. This creates an understandable reluctance in investors, leaving countries already suffering from corruption and volatility problems, doubly disadvantaged.

All of these challenges can be summarised as:

1. Lack of confidence that money will be invested appropriately
2. Lack of agreement over what investors want to support

It has been assumed that at some point in the future, there will be agreement about what "green" or "sustainable" means; however, this debate has been raging for over 20 years and hasn't been resolved by the SDGs or any of the other milestones that have been put in place beforehand, while the problem of transparency is as old as investments.

UNEP, the G7, the G20 and Fintech

Over the course of 2016–2018, we've seen a growing convergence between the world of sustainable investment and the financial technology solutions that can help address these barriers. The UN Environment Programme's Inquiry into the financial system we need has been researching Fintech opportunities, which it summarised in a report in December 2016, Fintech and Sustainable Development: Assessing the Implications, UNEP has been working with Fintechs over the course of the development of this report and beyond, bringing Fintechs to the table with policy makers from other NGOs and governments to start identifying solutions. What was striking about those meetings to us, as technology people, was the huge gap in understanding about technology opportunities in policy makers. However, as more Fintechs were engaged, and through a variety of workshops and expositions, it became clear that policy makers are keen to engage technology in overcoming these challenges.

One of the themes that have emerged is that there is no clear distinction between what's green, what's sustainable, and what's inclusive; although clearly they're not all the same thing, the edges are so blurred that it is hard to separate one from the others. We also believe that achieving one *requires* the achievement of the others, so it is neither helpful nor easy to separate them. Taken from this perspective, the SDGs are a good place to start when it comes to categorising and measuring sustainability, even if you can't put them all in a single bucket.

In parallel, the growing number of practical implementations of technology in support of the SDGs, and in particular financial technology, has given policy makers confidence that these solutions can be implemented to solve real problems. We're describing a few here, knowing that many others which we haven't yet thought of are likely to emerge before the year is out!

Emerging Fintech Solutions

Solutions to the classification challenge, including definitions for green and climate bonds, have already emerged, thanks to efforts by NGOs and big data analytics. There is a small number of platforms already available, that enable investors to select their investment criteria and see a match, for example if they favour projects supporting gender equality or eradicating poverty, or for emission reductions, so that investments can be tailored to the investor. These solutions enable a wider body of investors to access a wider variety of sustainable investments, increasing the scope of sustainable investments, although provenance and corruption may still be an issue for riskier countries or industries.

Tokenisation of green initiatives using blockchain is also becoming more common, with a variety of initiatives involving tokenisation of renewable energy or carbon offset schemes emerging, enabling community ownership of energy resources, facilitating targeted investments in green projects. While tokenisation in itself is effectively a type of securitisation giving confidence to purchasers that the underlying asset is clean, these tokens are also easier to transact than traditional securities, as they can be traded for other cryptocurrencies, or for fiat currencies via cryptocurrency exchanges.

Meanwhile, robo-advisors are starting to make it easier for normal people to participate directly in green investments, via Exchange Traded Funds (ETFs), and we have already seen the mainstream robo-advisor WealthSimple[6] trading a Green ETF as part of its standard portfolio of products, among others.

In addition, a body of research and some emerging solutions take these trends further, combining blockchain, smart contracts, cryptocurrency and analytics to build investment instruments such as green bonds, or funds, with a high degree of traceability and auditability. hiveonline is engaged with several such initiatives, using blockchain and contract technology to add confidence to investors seeking new sustainable investments where previously some of the barriers described in this chapter have proved to be too great a risk. The case study below demonstrates how the technology can be employed to increase transparency and reduce risk in a green bond scenario, and similar applications are also in development for green FDIs and overseas SME community investment. These applications carry the same benefits of traceability and auditability as the solutions described above.

Case Study: Green Bond Benchmarking and Validation Over Blockchain

This case study describes a green bond platform hiveonline is building to help address the estimated USD 2.5 trillion annual global funding gap for sustainable projects.

Background

Green bonds have attracted positive results with a growing number of investors keen to support them. However, the issuance of green bonds is subject to a complex validation process which disincentivises organisations from issuing them and results in limited availability for investors, with demand outstripping supply. Additionally, because of challenges of validation and auditing, the issuance of green bonds outside of low-risk countries creates further barriers as investors cannot be confident that the outcomes will meet sustainability criteria.

Blockchain technology offers an opportunity to add transparency and confidence to green bonds by defining and measuring criteria associated with sustainability. These have traditionally required significant administrative effort to measure in a transparent and low-administration way. The combination of blockchain technology with business logic, further ensures that confirmation, payments and other events can be tied to firm evidence that sustainability objectives have been achieved, as well as offering the opportunity to solicit additional evidence where required.

Advanced contract technology also offers an opportunity to automate much of the administration underpinning management of investors in green bonds, including terms, rights and the management of financial transactions.

The solution is a hybrid, where a technology platform, enabled by blockchain and automatically executing contracts, supports traditional actors in the green bond lifecycle by reducing administration and increasing transparency. This results in reduced challenges associated with setting up, investing in and administering green bonds, so that the market can expand both to a wider range of issuers and to a broader geographical spread.

The Solution

The system can capture and measure criteria for non-financial achievements, provide full transparency of financial interactions and the assets that they were exchanged for end to end, together with reputation management that evaluates the quality of performance. The measurement and reputation system are based on assets relevant to the achievement of SDGs, while the underlying cryptocurrency provides the full traceability of transactions.

The system is based on contracts underpinning the bond, which can be set up to execute based on the provision of evidence in the form of documents and other digital assets, that are measured by the system against the criteria based on the SDGs. For example, an underwriter may choose to evaluate a bond based on zero emissions, certificates demonstrating renewable energy production facilities or insulation criteria for buildings. Once set up and agreed with the fund, this information is written to the blockchain as a transparent and immutable record.

When the criteria have been achieved, the issuer uploads assets demonstrating that the criteria have been achieved, which triggers positive feedback and can be configured to execute payments, press releases or other transfers of assets. This ensures that pre-agreed criteria are met, reducing ambiguity and the risk of fraud and providing confidence for investors.

The system also manages the transfer of value via cryptocurrency, which can be created based on input of fiat, e.g. USD, and released as local currency (USD or other), minimising exchange risk and providing full traceability for every transaction. The advantage of using cryptocurrency over blockchain, in addition to reducing currency risk, is that every point of exchange for any unit of currency is recorded in a block of transactions that can be accessed by any party to the agreement, which allows full audits and confidence that funds are being used appropriately.

This platform, including setup of the contracts and provision of evidence, is delivered via a simple mobile interface, allowing multiple participants to interact with the contracts including, if required, crowdsourced evidence based on input from independent third parties such as local witnesses.

The reputation management system evaluates the quality of any completed contracts, assessing how well conditions have been met and the quality of assets received in evidence. Investors can then see how well their investments are performing based on factual, like for like evaluations.

Benefits

- Increased transparency and confidence for investors
- Significantly reduced administration around audit and reporting
- Clarity or purpose for issuers and underwriters
- Guarantees for issuers that funds are from reliable sources

With solutions like these, the need for standard definitions of green or sustainable doesn't vanish, but multiple standards can coexist comfortably, as investors have good visibility of what they are investing in, and can choose their risks accordingly.

The Future of Sustainable Investing

Blockchain, Artificial Intelligence (AI), Machine Learning (ML), big data analytics, IoT sensors, behavioural reputation systems and other solutions we don't know about yet can all help to expand the range of investment products and investments available to investors, while reduced administration and transparency open up many more potential investment opportunities. However, this additional transparency has big implications for the way that capital markets run, in that it also facilitates a much more direct relationship between investor and the end recipient of the investment.

We think that this is likely to result in more peer-to-peer investment, particularly across business communities, and a convergence of "green investment" with "investment", as the additional transparency gives greater visibility to investors of exactly what they are funding. While not all investors may choose to go green, most will be uncomfortable participating in unethical or actively dirty investments, especially as green investments perform as well as, or better, than brown ones.

We therefore anticipate the future that our contributor envisaged, where it will be in the interest of all organisations issuing securities to demonstrate sustainability in some form, in order to attract investment.

Beyond this, however, as we observed in Chapter 3, the additional transparency is likely to have an impact on the way that capital markets work; products that today require specialist knowledge can be largely automated, while transparency and the ability to maintain complex portfolios in tokenised forms, is likely to have an impact on the demand for many types of derivative products. We addressed some other potential developments facilitated by blockchain and related technologies in Chapter 10, and together we expect they will start to have far-reaching implications for sustainability investment, as well as the overall impact on capital markets. We don't anticipate an overnight revolution, but the growth of sustainable investments, coupled with the increased transparency available to investors and lowered administration costs, is likely to drive the next evolution in how capital markets work.

Conclusion

A number of investment products are available to support the development of sustainable businesses and infrastructure projects; however, there is still a huge investment gap, particularly in countries where it is hard to demonstrate provenance or where corruption and currency volatility are a challenge. Investors and environmental experts can't agree on the meaning of "green", or what the minimum and maximum criteria will be.

Technology is already helping spread the range of investments, and broaden the range of investors who can participate in green investments. We see the work of Fintechs like hiveonline in building end to end investment systems based on blockchain and AI as a continuation of this trend, and expect to see many more participants emerging with similar products and approaches to investment in the future.

While a solution for the funding gap must, necessarily, be the priority, we can also look to longer-term implications of increasing transparency and rebalancing investments. The future is looking brighter for green infrastructure projects in emerging economies, but it is also going to be an interesting journey for global capital markets. Watch this space.

Notes

1. Shear, M. D. (2017, June 1). Trump Will Withdraw U.S. from Paris Climate Agreement. *New York Times.* https://www.nytimes.com/2017/06/01/climate/trump-paris-climate-agreement.html. Accessed 28 December 2017.
2. Tabuchi, H., & Fountain, H. (2017, June 1). Bucking Trump, These Cities, States and Companies Commit to Paris Accord. https://www.nytimes.com/2017/06/01/climate/american-cities-climate-standards.html. Accessed 28 December 2017.
3. US Environmental Protection Agency, Global Greenhouse Gas Emissions Data, 13 April 2017. https://www.epa.gov/ghgemissions/global-greenhouse-gas-emissions-data. Accessed 28 December 2017 (NB US EPA Sites May Have Been Archived to https://archive.epa.gov/ Following Trump Inspired Restrictions to Information).
4. Funding the SDGs, Guido Schmidt Traub, UNA-UK, 1 March 2016. http://www.sustainablegoals.org.uk/funding-the-sdgs/. Accessed 28 December 2017.
5. Wilson, G. E. R. (2016, July 18). There's a $2.5 Trillion Development Investment Gap. Blended Finance Could Plug It. *World Economic Forum.* https://www.weforum.org/agenda/2016/07/blended-finance-sustainable-development-goals/. Accessed 28 December 2017.
6. WealthSimple Home Page. https://www.wealthsimple.com/en-ca/. Accessed 28 December 2017.

Future Business, Part IV

Services for the Ecosystem Economy
What's Behind It?

In the first half of this book, we explored the evolving world of financial services and how new technologies and business models are helping to drive change, particularly for many of the more underserved and needy people in the world. The models we described, some of them already in production, will form a key part of the new financial ecosystem, but this technology and the related business models haven't evolved in isolation, while organisations are having to radically rethink their structures in the ecosystem age.

In this half, we consider the social and technical drivers of changing customer behaviour and how these are leading to different approaches to services, work and truth. We track the history of how customer interaction with producers has changed, the globalisation of supply and how this has changed our perceptions and expectations. We consider the impact of technology on business models, and how the way people work and interact with information is changing perceptions of value and reward. We examine the evolution of identity for organisations, people and ecosystem, and how reputation providers can no longer be trusted, while proposing some opportunities for Fintech to support changing paradigms.

We describe how the move to the ecosystem economy has changed customer expectations and what this means for businesses, particularly financial services organisations. We then describe how existing organisations can embrace and engage with the ecosystem economy, by adopting a service aligned, capability driven approach which is ecosystem ready.

The final part is devoted to a solution-focused approach that banks and other organisations can adopt towards moving into the ecosystem economy, prepared to build services rather than products, with the agility and customer focus needed to thrive in the ecosystem age.

What's Behind It?

In the next three chapters, we consider the evolution of customer behaviour and expectations that have paved the way for the Fintech revolution. We examine the difference between products and what we actually buy, and what this means for financial services companies trying to solve real world customer problems. We then examine the history of the platform revolution and how this has shaped customer expectations and behaviours towards a less loyal, more demanding consumer.

We describe the common trap of conflating technology with customer solutions and how organisations need to focus on solving customer problems to come up with innovative solutions, avoiding some of the common pitfalls. We show how technology companies avoid them, while banks can fall into the trap, based on top-down strategies aligned to service excellence. Amazon is growing while Barclays is shrinking; we identify some opportunities to learn from their different strategies.

14

Services and Demand

In this chapter, we examine the differences in perception for businesses and consumers, of what it is that they're selling and buying, and why the distinction is important for businesses as they design their service offerings. We discuss how a focus on products has arisen in banks, and why this is contributing to their decline as the competitive environment evolves around them.

Product Thinking

Henry Ford may never have actually said, "*if I'd asked what people want, they'd have said a faster horse*" and it didn't do him much good to ignore the customer in the long run, but he had a point. People think in terms of products, based on their expectations and knowledge of what's available, but they use services. And both products and services are being used to solve a problem.

The Product

When interacting with providers, we usually think in terms of products and exchange of cash for products.

© The Author(s) 2018
S. Blakstad and R. Allen, *FinTech Revolution*,
https://doi.org/10.1007/978-3-319-76014-8_14

What Did You Buy Yesterday?

Ask a typical consumer this question, and the answer you'll get will, 99% of the time, be the name of a product, or products. It could be "chicken, eggs, aubergines, garlic, wine" or "a new lawnmower" or "a mortgage". You name the artefact, physical or otherwise, that was on the till receipt and that you took home with you. The transaction was an exchange of an agreed amount of value, usually fiat currency, for a defined product that's characterised by known and mutually understood characteristics, such as size, quality and longevity.

Suppliers tend to think in terms of products, too. It's an easy shortcut, and it helps to have a tangible thing you can count to measure sales and number of customers. Number of products sold is an easy metric to track, and it's relatively easy to understand the cost of sales, too, which makes for comfortable accounting. That's great if your customer will always keep interacting with your organisation, in the same way, buying the same product to address the same need; the problem only arises when the customer's behaviour changes, and they start addressing that need with a different product or service. Then, your problem is that you won't notice the customer's behaviour changing until it's too late. Let's break it down.

Identifying the Problem

To break down how organisations view products, let's consider the problem we're solving by purchasing it.

Why Did You Buy It?

The answer will be "to cook dinner", "because the old lawn mower broke" or "so we can buy a new house".

At this point, we employ a technique, common to Lean process engineers and toddlers, known as the "five whys". It's about getting to the essence of a problem. The reason it's used in Lean is so that you can understand the problem you're solving, rather than just improving on an existing solution to that problem, in case there's a better solution (NB: in Lean re-engineering, there usually is). The reason toddlers use it is because they're trying to understand the world around them, but don't know how to phrase the questions. In both cases, it's a way of drilling into a problem until you reach a point that looks like a root cause.

So Why?

"Because the Jensens are coming to dinner tonight", "because the grass needs mowing", "because we don't have enough space".

Why?

"We wanted to do something fun and relaxing with them that doesn't cost too much", "we don't like the way the long grass looks", "the furniture collection is getting out of hand".

Why?

"We like the Jensens and want to spend time with them", "we want the garden to look nice", "we really like furniture and find it hard to let go of old pieces when we buy new ones".

We could go further, but don't really need to, you can see that the more you distil the essence of the problem, the wider the scope of potential solutions becomes. So why do we choose the chicken, the lawn mower and the mortgage?

Strategising and Prioritising

It's apparent that each of these "problems" has a number of alternative solutions. In order to reach the conclusions we have, we have made a lot of decisions. We've gone through a thought process, consciously or otherwise, informed by societal norms and our own experience, on how to solve them, and come up with the answer in the shape of solutions we feel confident employing, and can find a product or products to support. And in each case, our product purchase didn't come out of nowhere—in all these examples, we will have gone through a period of negotiation along the way before making the purchase decision, either with ourselves or with family members.

"Let's ask the Jensens round". "OK, shall we take them to the beach?" "No, I thought dinner would be nice" "OK, then. Barbecue?" "Not sure, the weather's not looking that great. Might be nice though". "hmm, you're probably right, let's do something indoors. How about Turkish?" "OK then, sounds good". "I'll pick up some stuff on my way home then. You're cooking".

And so on. We don't notice these negotiations, strategising and prioritising as such because they're just part of normal life; hence when I ask you what you bought yesterday you tell me chicken and wine, whereas what you actually bought was a way of cementing your friendship, and possibly showing off your cooking skills a bit at the same time.

Executing the Transaction

Now let's think about the act of purchasing—the transaction between you and the vendor. How did you buy the chicken? We're assuming you didn't go to the farmer and choose it there? If you're a gardener, you might grow the odd aubergine and a few potatoes, but like us, we expect you went to a shop and bought it.

You drove or cycled there, parked your bike or car in the parking spots provided by the supermarket, walked past the special offers at the door, maybe picked up some cheap strawberries? Then, you went through the gate, found a basket, walked to the relevant aisles, either because you know the layout or by navigating thanks to the supermarket's helpful signs, found the products, chose ones that suited your needs best, checked the sell-by dates, and put them in your basket.

Next, you took your products to the till, put them through the self-checkout or put them on the cashier's conveyer, if you're at the self-checkout, called the cashier over to authenticate you to purchase the wine, maybe chatted with the cashier a bit, packed them up and paid for them. Then, you took them to your car or bike, drove away and took them home.

Supply Chain and Distribution

And how did all that happen? Each item that you bought was produced somewhere, originally on a farm of some sort (we'll include vineyards) then harvested and processed, graded, sorted, packaged and shipped. There were negotiations, probably through a third party, about price to the supplier and cost to the distributor, scheduling, containerising, shipping, sorting, unpacking, redistribution, quality assurance, inventory control, boxing, unboxing and, in the case of the wine, currency exchange, customs, international shipping, etc. Your wine, eggs and chicken will have passed through many hands—human or automated—and many dedicated facilities, before it got to the supermarket.

And then at the supermarket, workers unpack, sort, stack shelves and monitor stock. But those aren't the only workers responsible for your chicken being on the shelf where you chose it—an architect designed that supermarket, many were involved in the construction, design, lighting, sound, smell (yes, they design what you smell) and ambiance, all helping you find what you need while subtly selling the maximum amount of things you didn't know you needed at the same time. The supermarket didn't spring into being independently either, there's an army of management, leadership, legal teams, strategists, planners, designers, buyers, accountants, project managers, HR and the usual corporate machine in the background, deciding what your experience will be like from the moment you drive in. And marketers, advertisers, community managers all ensuring you choose to go there in the first place.

So, although you think you're paying for a chicken, up to 40% of what you pay is actually going towards the service of bringing the chicken to you. The same applies to the lawn mower, and the mortgage. But why is that important? Well, a big part of the reason you chose to buy that lawn mower, that chicken, or that mortgage, is based on the choices that have been made for you by others, including the people who you're paying for that service.

Who Chooses What You Buy?

You may think your purchasing decisions are made completely independently, but leaving out the selection and negotiations you've already gone through to decide on that class of purchase, consider the combination of values, available information and the purchasing options that lead to you buying that individual chicken (Fig. 14.1).

The values that led you to purchase that chicken have been shaped by your experience of the world, which in turn has been shaped by a combination of other influencers (see Chapter 18 for more about this). You understand the quality control and authentication system behind certain brands and how to recognise them, thanks to information and advertising. You've been conditioned to purchase expensive and authentic looking chicken by the horror stories you've read about factory farming, and perhaps you have decided to support ethical farming and are prepared to pay a bit more; maybe you've had the same type of chicken before and liked it, but ultimately when you first bought it, the decision was the result of a combination of information and influences, tapped into by the researchers who work for the shop that brought you that chicken.

Fig. 14.1 Would you buy this chicken?

You didn't get a poulet de Bresse because it was the only thing that will bring the Jensens to your house—you bought it because of a lot of research about the things that people like you will pay a premium for, and many people deciding to manage the logistics of getting it to you in authentic looking packaging.

The Customer Journey

Supermarkets and other large organisations will view your purchase in terms of a customer journey, which may start with your need to make dinner for friends, or perhaps with your decision to buy ethically farmed chicken. Your customer journey will interact with the retailer's at a few points—for example, where they raise your awareness of their ethical standards, or the availability of ethically farmed chicken on their shelves.

There are likely to be multiple contact points before you buy that chicken, including previous experiences of the supermarket, which would inform how they view the customer journey. This would be mapped against the effort of getting the chicken to you, ensuring your chicken purchasing experience is positive. Your customer journey, from the supermarket's perspective, doesn't end when you walk out with your chicken, either; a rigorous CX designer will also consider your experience cooking and eating the chicken as part of the experience.

Designing customer journeys is a great way of analysing and understanding customer behaviour, but there's a catch: when your customer journey is designed around the product, you're trapped in a scenario where there's only one possible outcome from the strategising and prioritising discussion. It doesn't allow for a change in values, lifestyle, or outlook. *It doesn't matter how great your chicken buying experience has been if you decide to become a vegetarian.* Supermarkets are pretty good at this already; they understand that you may change your strategy while in the supermarket, and provide you with plenty of alternatives in case you suddenly decide to cook something different, for example, or even not to cook at all.

Products in Financial Services

Banks and financial service providers, however, aren't so flexible. To date, they haven't really had to be, because customers are tied to a very limited range of products to support their financial needs. If you want to exchange value for something, you almost always have to use money in some format; that money will have been issued by a bank under authority from the central bank. Nearly all payments require a bank account, or a payment vehicle tied to a bank account, especially online. If you want to buy a house, you will need to borrow money, and that borrowing is almost certainly going to be in the shape of a mortgage.

Because of the very limited range of financial products and the lack of viable alternatives, banks and FS providers equate products with services. We've worked in bank after bank where the whole organisation is structured around products—"Transaction Products", "Fixed Income", "Equities", "Mortgages" are all names of departments where people equate serving the customer to selling them products.

So even though banks are becoming much more customer service aware, they are still describing service improvements in terms of access to products: "we'll make it easier to get a bank account", "faster payments", "customised loan products" and still conceptually siloed. This has resulted in two big challenges for banks: first, they find it hard to build a holistic view of their customers, because in many cases, different product departments will have different relationships and data for the same customer, but more importantly, they're not able to flex as customer needs evolve.

Many Fintechs have also been drawn into making improvements to existing FS products, helping the banks get better at delivering the products they already support. There's undoubtedly a need for this, to facilitate the progression of banking services into the digitised age. However, it's also easy for banks to be lulled into a false sense of complacency as their traditional products get digitised; it looks as though the problem has been fixed, whereas in fact, all they've got is a faster horse.

Changes in Customer Behaviour

We cover evolving customer behaviours elsewhere in more details, but it's important to note here the drivers for changing behaviours. One of the biggest drivers for customer behaviour change is the availability of alternative services or products. For example, M-PESA, the African e-money provider, has leapfrogged traditional banks and incidentally moved the population of Kenya from 83% without a bank account, to over 99% using M-PESA in ten years. At some point, you will have stopped buying video cassettes and started buying DVDs, at least until Netflix came along.

Other changes are driven by changing values and awareness, often supported by government incentives—the move to renewable energy and reductions in emissions, for example. Negative perception of incumbent banks has led both millennials and older generations to choose alternative providers. These behavioural changes are more conscious and can reach extremes in whole societies or population groups, often in completely different directions from adjacent societies and population groups (Fig. 14.2).

One of the underlying themes in changing customer behaviours that we explore elsewhere in this section, though, is that customers rarely equate their new behaviour as a change in how they transact with products. In many cases, they don't notice the change at all. Which is something that should worry every organisation conducting customer research in the hope of identifying trends.

Fig. 14.2 Transitional tech

Service Thinking

Where products are the manifestation of a selected strategy, services are the solutions to problems. A service view of a customer journey is in context of the "need" rather than the artefact. This can be helpful for consumers, but it's most useful for suppliers, who may be supporting that need in one way but also want to anticipate other ways as a survival strategy. In this section, we'll break down what that means for our consumers and how many suppliers are already helping themselves.

Customer Needs

In the previous section, we identified three customer needs after our breakdown, which can be expressed as:

We like the Jensens and want to spend time with them

We want the garden to look nice

We really like furniture and find it hard to let go of old pieces when we buy new ones

Customers often won't be very good at articulating their needs at this basic level ("faster horse" is more likely), which is why asking "why?" a few times is a good idea. We could probably go further than this, but in these examples, we're assuming fixed values and societal norms.

Alternate Strategies

We've strategised our way to a meal, cutting the grass and a bigger house in the previous section. But it didn't have to be that way; we could present several equally viable options. Let's think about options for the Jensens:

1. Cook dinner at home
2. Picnic in the park
3. Take the kids to the beach
4. Go to the pub

Or the garden:

1. Keep the grass short
2. Plant meadow flowers
3. Build a patio
4. Dig a pond

Or the furniture:

1. Move to a bigger house
2. Build an extension
3. Value the old furniture and maybe sell it
4. Move the furniture to relatives in need

Strong service design doesn't assume a product-focused strategy, allowing for support in multiple scenarios. For the Jensens, your average supermarket could easily provide help for options 1 through 3, and a decent DIY store would support all four options for the garden. What's more, when you walk into the supermarket or the DIY store, nobody will force you to stick to your original strategy, allowing you to re-evaluate based on a number of factors—perhaps you've checked the weather again, and it's looking better, or they've run out of Bresse chickens.

In contrast, when making financial decisions, customers don't see banks as service providers, but as suppliers of products, largely because *you're expected to know which product you want before you walk into the bank*. They don't expect you to walk in and say, "I think I need more space, but I'm not sure how to approach it"; both you and they have the expectation that you are going to ask for a particular product and you'd better have done your homework. Which is a shame, because that leads to customers buying products that don't fit their needs, and banks failing to identify customer opportunities.

Creating Services

It's clear, when looking at the service from the perspective of the need, that a layer of complexity is involved beyond the simple product transaction perspective, in that the decision about which strategy to pursue can become embedded in the service as a conversation between consumer and provider. While that may look, on the surface, as an additional challenge, it's actually turning around another part of the traditional product-centric storyline to the advantage of the provider.

To illustrate, let's consider a scenario where the strategising hasn't yet happened. We have decided we want to do something with the garden, but we haven't decided what to do yet, or perhaps we can't agree. We might well go to the DIY shop for inspiration, knowing that there will be many options available. We can also talk to an expert there, who can give us suggestions for what we might want to do suited to our budget and time. But we probably don't need to go to the store physically, since they've got all this information and many suggestions on their website anyway.

In the financial services scenario, let's say we go into the bank and tell them we have more furniture than space—ok, that sounds weird, but bear with us—and the CSA talks us through the various options. Now we probably knew that we could get various flavours of mortgage for moving or extensions, but she's also explained to us that they can help with recommendations for valuation firms, with some alternative approaches to savings and investments if we decide to sell our antiques. Not only has that expanded the range of concrete, feasible options for us, it's also retained business for the bank.

To get to this point, we're going to need to retrain our front-line staff from a "cross selling" mentality to a "service" mentality, approaching the customer's problem holistically while identifying how the bank can support them. We also need to align the organisation more around the customer, which is covered in other chapters.

Building Products into the Service

It should now be obvious how we can select products to build into the service, rather than building the service around the products. This may mean a change of product set, and as illustrated above, a change in training and staffing approaches, but it's relatively easy to do. In each of our scenarios, there are options that we can choose whether or not to support, and this decision process will inform which products we need to carry. In the case of the supermarket, we may not want to cater for the "go to the pub" scenario, because "go to the pub" involves a complete service experience which isn't in our core business model. However, "go to the beach" or "picnic at the park" are easy to cater for, as we can supply the goods to support the outing with the city providing the ambiance! (Fig. 14.3)

For the bank, reaching beyond traditional products and into the ecosystem will become more important than simply providing a positive customer

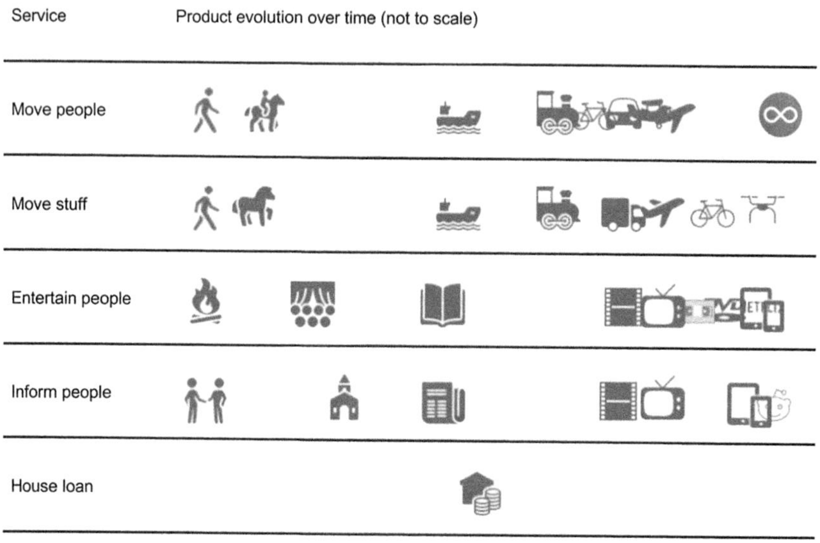

Fig. 14.3 Most services evolve over time as new technology becomes available

experience—as financial services evolve and more providers start capturing customers, it's going to become critical to their survival. As a bank, you may not yet have a relationship with a furniture auctioneer, or a trusted list of local logistics providers, but when auctioneers and logistics providers are selling financial services to your customers, can you afford not to have that relationship? Obviously, you will need to draw boundaries—you don't need to be a pub—but it's advisable to understand where other providers can help you give a more holistic service, and partner with them where it's practical.

And a word about compliance, since it usually rears its head in this discussion. Yes, it is possible to partner with and/or recommend other businesses without breaching the rules, as long as you're transparent about how and why you do it.

With a partnership model, you can select how and when to build alternative products into your core portfolio, but you should also consider which products you need to build into your core portfolio that aren't in there today. To do this, as with all service offerings, it's critical to start with your business strategy and the customer need. We've seen strategy proposals for banks that could be mistaken for a Google results set on "new financial products" or simply "FinTech". As long as you're clear what the customer problem is you're solving, it should be possible to identify which products will fit the need.

Banking for Vegetarians

Sometimes the customer need moves in a direction that doesn't suit your core product set, and you may choose not to change in response. That's ok, as long as you're comfortable losing that market segment, and as long as you are confident it's not going to become a growing trend. As you make these strategy decisions though, it is critical to ensure your decision making is informed by customer needs, rather than by what you can do with existing products, if you want to avoid the Kodak moment when you realise there's no longer a market fit for your product.

As we said above, customers aren't terribly good at recognising the changes in their behaviour, and often don't realise they're using services in a different way, or even that they've switched products. Most market testing involves putting your product in front of a customer in some way and asking them whether they'd use it or prefer it to be different. This is classic putting the cart before the horse, and we think the reason these tests have notoriously poor results is not just because people are bad at predicting what they will do in the future, but because you aren't showing them alternatives. Many times, you won't know what those alternatives are, but you often will.

It's a big challenge for any business to suggest services that aren't part of their own portfolio, or look like anything they do currently, but if those services are the ones your customers will be using, then you need to know.

Going back to the Jensens coming for dinner, we can easily decide on the spur of the moment to go vegetarian, and buy something other than chicken, without taking our custom away from the supermarket. It's a different story for the chicken farmer, though. What happens when more people stop eating chicken? If he's put all his eggs in one basket (pun intended) he's going to lose out, unless he's developed another range with a market that will grow with the low-meat movement—peas and beans, for example.

This is the position banks are in today. They have time to evolve their services to offer a broader range, supporting customers' changing needs and behaviours, but it will require rethinking how their services support customers, and what the customers really need from them, outside of the current narrow range of banking products. Adopting service thinking is the first step on this journey.

Conclusion

In this chapter, we've discussed the difference between products and services, why it's important to think about a service from the perspective of customer need rather than products, and how banks and FS organisations need to respond to changing customer behaviours by adopting service thinking.

Key points:

- Customers are using your products to support a need that may have alternative solutions.
- Understanding the need is key to anticipating changes in customer behaviour.
- Understanding customers' needs helps you build a robust, forward-looking strategy for your business.

Chapters 22–26 discuss how you can design a service aligned organisation.

15

Platform Consumers

In this chapter, we examine the evolution of consumers from retail consumers to platform consumers, as businesses move into the ecosystem and marketplaces emerge to manage B2C and peer-to-peer sales. We observe how platforms have changed customer expectations and behaviours and discuss the impact on businesses, and how their service models have evolved as a result.

Platform Marketplace

The twenty-first century has been characterised by many social, economic and technological developments, but nothing has changed the way customers interact with businesses more than the emergence of platform enabled retail. It has changed the way people buy things, the way they shop for things, their expectations and their behaviours. It has also revolutionised aspects of retail that have led to the emergence of platform giants and opened up markets for retailers in completely new ways.

The platform revolution is ongoing. Retailers, producers and customers are moving into the ecosystem economy, supported and led by more sophisticated and more specialised platforms. While it has made significant changes to the way we work, shop and think about consumption already, many more changes are in store. We explore some of the future state changes in other parts of this section.

© The Author(s) 2018
S. Blakstad and R. Allen, *FinTech Revolution*,
https://doi.org/10.1007/978-3-319-76014-8_15

What's a Platform?

In technical terms, a platform is a technology or set of technologies that supports the running of other technologies. Specifically, in the context of marketplace platforms, a platform is a technology that supports the distribution of content from producers to consumers, or between each other (prosumers), without the need for a dedicated retail outlet. They take various forms—we are all familiar with Facebook, YouTube, LinkedIn, Twitter and other social media platforms, primarily designed for sharing content, and with a business model based on advertising and paid content; others are more obviously dedicated to giving small (and increasingly large) producers access to a wide range of customers, such as eBay and AliBaba. Other platforms are dedicated to specific markets and audiences, such as Uber or AirBnB (rides and rooms) or piecework such as freelancer.com, TaskRabbit or upwork.com.

There are also platforms dedicated to various specialised services, such as payments (PayPal), document sharing (Dropbox), pet sitting, car sharing, bikes, houses, gardening, you name it… and of course, porn. Spotify and Netflix are the best known media sharing platforms which, like Amazon, both sell on their own behalf (Netflix and Amazon are also production companies) and provide a platform for third parties. Crowdfunding and peer-to-peer lending platforms are also applications described elsewhere in our chapters.

The characteristics of a platform described by Sangeet Paul Choudary in Platform Scale[1] are three key conceptual layers: a network/marketplace/community layer, which includes the community of consumers, producers, prosumers and their interactions; the infrastructure layer that manages the interactions and the platform availability, and the data layer, where analytics support the effective functioning of the others.

The key differentiator of a marketplace platform is that it supports consumer/producer/prosumer interactions, so other large commercial web systems don't fall into this category directly, although many large commercial sites do run on some of the big platforms aimed at small and larger businesses, and if you are using a dedicated website for a small business, or even a large one, you may well be interacting with one of these without being aware of it.

A Short History of Marketplace Platforms

The history of online platforms is inextricably linked with the development of two key access facilitators: web browsers and search engines (Fig. 15.1).

Following the development of the world wide web, initially for academic purposes, by Tim Berners-Lee in 1989, the first cross-platform web browser was developed by fellow English mathematician Nicola Pellow[2] in 1991. Technologists slowly started to realise the potential, and by 1994, a few false start platforms were emerging on the world wide web, hampered by poor bandwidth and limited browser capabilities. The milestone browser Netscape Navigator,[3] launched late in 1994, when Mark Zuckerberg turned 10, started to take hold as Amazon launched in the books market in 1995,[4] alongside eBay (originally AuctionWeb[5]).

Netflix started its online DVD service in 1997, the year Larry Page and Sergey Brin were writing their research paper,[6] Amazon went public and Jeff Bezos issued his first famous letter to shareholders.[7] PayPal followed in 1998,[8] while Netscape plummeted from market dominance, as Microsoft pursued an aggressive bundling strategy to get Internet Explorer to market dominance.[9] Thanks to the escalating browser war and growing usage, browsers were improving while infrastructure developments, particularly bandwidth, improved accessibility and usability significantly.

Fig. 15.1 Amazon.com 1997

Towards the end of the 1990s, while organisations like the ones we were working within were moving from intranet and flat websites towards building their own functional commercial sites, Amazon, e-Bay, YouTube and Netflix were paving the way for many more enterprising entrepreneurs to identify the opportunity offered by the internet and increasingly user-friendly functionality, among them Zappos[10] and the Chinese online marketplace AliBaba. By 2000, most schools and businesses in developed economies had access to some form of broadband, although most private users were still on dial-up modems, and governments were prioritising public broadband access, recognising the growing importance of the web in people's lives.

It was then, on the wave of the dot.com boom, that incumbent businesses such as supermarkets and banks started launching their own online sites; Sofie was responsible for building one of the first online wealth managers in 2001, while Walmart, Safeway and Costco all started providing online services. Although banks and large retailers had the advantage of infrastructure and existing customer bases, they were slow to learn the lessons from the early platforms, with Amazon in particular capturing a growing market, partly thanks to its 1999 launch of 1-Click,[11] allowing faster purchases but also thanks to its growing range of products, culminating in the launch of Amazon Marketplace in 2002, where third party sellers can sell via the platform.

With e-Bay, Amazon Marketplace, AliBaba and a growing range of more specialist B2C platforms emerged, fuelled by the early successes and learning from some early failures. In parallel, the acquisition of PayPal by eBay in 2002[12] enabled the development of secure payments over peer-to-peer platforms. This accelerated the development of peer-to-peer marketplace platforms, enabling small payments to be transferred securely without compromising personal payment details.

Amazon Mechanical Turk was the first peer-to-peer service exchange site, launched in 2005, enabling individual producers to sell intelligence-based services via a basic marketplace to buyers at a set price. This is also when YouTube, the peer-to-peer video sharing site, was born, the brainchild of ex-PayPal employees,[13] which rapidly caught on to become one of the fastest growing sites of 2006.

June 2007 saw the release of the first iPhone[14] and shortly afterwards, the rival Android phone was released, providing the first platforms for sharing Apps, allowing for both distribution of phone-enabled apps by existing companies, and the reshaping of the business model for a large part of the games

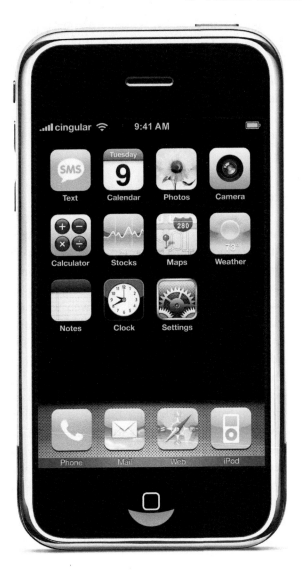

Fig. 15.2 iPhone 1

industry. At the same time, Netflix[15] started offering online streaming for a subscription, alongside Hulu (Fig. 15.2).

Since then, many peer-to-peer marketplaces have been developed, in areas as diverse as education, lending, travel, car sharing, clothes, recreation, venues (we mentioned dog sitting) currency exchange, media and the general commerce, and peer-to-peer service sites.

Founded in 2008, AirBnB was the first marketplace for people to share spaces in their homes, while Uber (2009) was the first to offer rides in people's cars at scale. Both grew in parallel with the skills sharing sites, which have all had a significant impact on supplier behaviour which we discuss below. Peer-to-peer lending has changed the dynamics of a certain class of startup business, while peer-to-peer selling has changed the cost and dynamics of running a retail business. But the biggest impact has been on customer behaviour.

User-Generated Content and Social Platforms

While selling things is always a prime motivator for developing technology, communication is another basic human need that has always exploited new technology as it became available, and online chat rooms existed before browsers were developed, enabling groups of related people to communicate simultaneously, so the move to the world wide web was inevitable. Putting chat rooms and interaction forums on internet sites also enabled people who were interacting with a commercial service to exchange information and commentary, and led to the development of global special interest or general interest groups, hosted by a variety of organisations.

As browser technology developed and it became easier to curate commentary, asking for content from users became more widespread, and "below the line" comments were born, inviting users to comment dynamically on content such as news sites. In contrast to Amazon's product reviews, which were rigorously curated and therefore not dynamic, these online and "below the line" fora encouraged immediate exchange of views. Where sites set up dedicated comments and information exchange fora, many gave birth to broad online communities, and there are today long-running informal communities associated with many news sources, with some well-known regular contributors and, as has been well documented, the rise of the internet troll and flame warrior (Fig. 15.3).

VIEW COMMENTS

Fig. 15.3 Click here

But the real communications revolution happened with the rise of the pure social platform, Facebook being the most successful to date, although many other user-generated content sites such as LinkedIn, Twitter, YouTube, Pinterest, Instagram are also extremely popular, where the interactions and user-generated content are the whole point of the site. These sites allow and encourage the development of relationships between users via a variety of tagging protocols, unrelated to validated purchases (as with Amazon reviews) or a particular subject matter interest. More than any previous forum for exchange of views, these new platforms have created alternative stars, with Facebook, YouTube, Instagram and others providing a platform for exposure for some unlikely new celebrities.[16]

Information over social media has also started to take on a value of its own for platform prosumers, with growing respectability as more establishment and respected figures started to use it as a communications channel—in particular Twitter, which is widely employed by politicians, scientists and media figures to reach a wide audience. Forums such as Medium and Quora invite longer content on specialist subjects, changing how we perceive content and content providers, as we'll explore below.

As the social platform has evolved, there's also been a convergence of chat applications such as Slack, WhatsApp, WeChat and Messenger towards adopting wider and more integrated functionality, starting with file sharing and group chats and developing towards payments and other integration features, and to all extents and purposes these are now also fully fledged social platforms.

The barrier between social and marketplace platform has become more blurred over time; while social platforms have always needed to include a commercial element in the shape of advertising and behavioural data sales to maintain revenue, they are now taking on more service partners and providing more commercial opportunities to their customers, with millions of businesses represented. Payments over social media is an important milestone in this development, and with platforms now seeking banking licenses, it is clear other financial services will follow.

Ecosystem links between a wide variety of sites have increased, partially in a bid to reduce the proliferation of identities, and with the rise of the megaplatforms, now many commercial and social sites can be accessed via, and share data from, social platforms such as Facebook or Twitter. Nearly all commercial marketplace sites offer the option to share comments or content via the social platforms and some are starting to emulate more features of social platforms; the ecosystem is now in your pocket. And, notoriously, it's harvesting information about you, knowing more about you than you know about yourself.

Circular Economy Platforms

As marketplace platforms emerged as a key way of how people did business, 2003 saw the birth of freecycle.com,[17] one of a growing number of platforms dedicated to peer-to-peer exchange between people for no money. In some cases, as with Freecycle, people simply advertise their unwanted things, so that somebody local can pick them up and make use of them instead. Others, such as LETS[18] or the CES (Community Exchange System), are locally based trading systems that use an internal digital currency to reward people in the community for goods or services, which are exchanged peer to peer. These platforms share characteristics with locally issued physical fiat currency (such as the Brixton pound[19]) and are generally managed based on trust and local community values.

These schemes are making use of the internet to expand the concept of circular economies in local areas. More recently, platforms have started to use web technology to exchange alternative units, to encourage green behaviours, such as the startup Bundles,[20] which instead of selling washing machines, sells washes to consumers. This model allows an uber-like sharing economy for household appliances, reduces unnecessary usage and also encourages manufacturers to create longer-lasting machines.

Customer Uptake and Behaviour

The emergence of platforms as part of our everyday lives, combined with smartphone and tablet delivery, has profoundly impacted how we interact with businesses and each other. But as well as behaviour, it's changed our attitudes to information, privacy and identity.

Customers and Marketplaces

It's hard to think back 25 years, and many of us weren't active retail consumers that long ago anyway, so there are a growing number of people who have never experienced anything else. The most obvious impact of platforms is our changing approach to purchasing. In the early and mid-90s, we experienced a global boom in hypermarkets,[21] with retail stores getting larger, selling a wider variety of goods and increasingly building on greenfield or brownfield sites out of town. In cities, large supermarkets dominated, while markets and traditional retailers were shrinking and closing their doors.

Most people drove to the supermarket or hypermarket to do a weekly or fortnightly shop for groceries and household goods.

While in urban Europe, most high streets would have butchers, fishmongers and greengrocers, in other countries and in rural areas, many people would have to drive to one of these, as the supermarkets encroached on traditional businesses. Clothes, books and electronic goods were bought at high street stores, which at the time were becoming increasingly dominated by a limited range of chain stores. Department stores enjoyed a healthy trade.

Many stores catered for specialist tastes, but you didn't get variety—if you lived in a certain area, you might have access to a Chinese supermarket or even several, but other towns would have none. Specialists would exist only in larger cities, often clustered together (Fig. 15.4).

Mobile phones were only just becoming available and not widespread in ordinary populations, so communication between retailers and customers was by telephone or letter. While mail order was common, it was time-con-

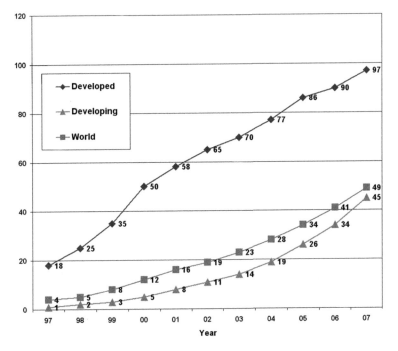

Fig. 15.4 Mobile phone subscribers per 100 inhabitants 1997–2007 distinguished by developed, developing and global world (*Source* Kozuch. (2009). ITU. http://www.itu.int/ITU-D/ict/statistics/ict/graphs/mobile.jpg. Accessed 28 December 2017)

suming, involving choosing items from a catalogue, waiting for the delivery and then sending back any unwanted items, via the post office.

Shops were open at limited times and almost exclusively during the daytime, so most of our shopping was done at the weekend, and particularly on a Saturday. Because of the limited range of shops available, customer stickiness was high, with customers typically visiting a small number of shops regularly for the same type of goods. Visits to city centre shopping centres or specialist stores were logistically challenging because of travel and transportation of goods, so reserved for special occasions or needs. Shopping at either was done at pre-planned times, during the day and concentrated at the weekends. Unplanned needs would see you going to a corner shop, if you had one, which opened for longer hours, but rarely overnight.

Consumer expectations of goods were consequently limited mostly by what was available easily in the same locality, or a short car journey away. While an increasingly wide variety of food was made available thanks to hypermarkets and supermarkets, your choice of books, music, furniture, clothes, electronic items and household goods was limited by what you could buy locally, or via mail order companies that you had gone to the trouble of signing up for (Fig. 15.5).

Most customers also weren't very aware of how reliable the goods they were buying were before purchasing, how they were made or where they came from. It was hard to find independent information about customer satisfaction other than that supplied by manufacturers outside stores, where the interest was in making a sale.

Specialist shopkeepers, whether the butcher, the bookseller, the carpet salesman or specialist staff in department stores, were valuable mines of information for recommendations. Recommendations also spread through word of mouth, but primarily through the media, or through advertising, and it was becoming hard to tell the difference. The first "sex and shopping" novel, Julie Burchill's *Ambition*,[22] published in 1989, saw a pronounced increase in sales of some of the brands mentioned between the pages.

Manufacturers and retailers were also able to manage their image based on what you saw and experienced in their stores. The few ethical retailers, such as the Body Shop (now seen as a pioneer of ethical retail), were regarded as a bit fringe and possibly cranks. Nobody had a clue whether large retailers were paying taxes or employing people ethically, unless it was specifically investigated and published in the media.

Today, the high street is still holding on by its fingernails, and we do still enjoy physically visiting stores, particularly if we're seeking expert advice, but increasingly we shop online, giving us access to an incredibly wide range

Fig. 15.5 USB pet rock

of goods, inducing subscriptions, event tickets and services, many of which we haven't heard of and don't need. This has changed customer behaviour significantly:

- Buy anytime—particularly useful for busy people, now we can shop from our desks at work, while travelling, after hours or at 3 in the morning if we choose. Platforms and online shops allow us to keep adding stuff to our baskets, only paying when we check out or on delivery.
- Buy anywhere—great for those with restrictions to mobility (such as children). We can purchase on transit, at home or while away. We can order

a grocery delivery for a particular time, while on the other side of the planet. And we can buy stuff from anywhere in the world.

- Buy anything—whatever you're looking for, you're more or less guaranteed to find it on the internet.

These aspects have made buying things much more convenient and saved us a lot of time, particularly for mundane purchases such as groceries, or specialist purchases such as sport related products or exotic ingredients, which would otherwise require a special trip. It has also led to the more questionable benefit of:

- Buy in any condition: purchasers can now buy something online while in their pyjamas, while drunk,[23] while depressed, while sick, while fuming over a row (possibly on the internet!) or in any other state, including several that would, 25 years ago, have prevented them entering a shop. While this means that, legally, retailers have to give customers a cooling-off period, many purchasers fail to take advantage of this.

And it has changed our expectations of shopping too. Life used to be a lot simpler:

- Choice—we expect to be able to choose from a wide variety of options, either for the same type of product, such as different varieties of food produce, or different individual products, such as books or music. Although studies have demonstrated that the platformification of book and music sales has tended towards larger sales for a smaller number of titles (see Chapter 18 for the mechanics of this), there's also a much longer "long tail" of low-volume sales for other items.
- Price—we no longer expect a fixed price for a fixed product. Amazon has done more than any other retailer to lead us to expect lower prices, and temporary prices, while the ability to compare multiple instances of the same product with different service options, allows us to customise the service we're buying to some degree, for example guarantee conditions, or different delivery options. Where in the past, the price of goods may have been fixed seasonally, based on popularity and trends, platforms like Uber have taken variable pricing to extremes with their dynamic surge pricing.
- Immediate delivery—Amazon has been a big part of shaping our expectations not just of instant delivery, but also of paying a premium for faster services. The impending drone deliveries will bring down delivery times even more. Other retailers and platforms were early to allow users to

select delivery days and timeslots, responding to customer convenience; the UK retailer Argos was one of the earliest to offer not only same-day, but timed deliveries, at a premium.

- Buy anything—still in development, but we can now buy increasingly expensive and more significant things, alongside cheap and insignificant things, services, experiences and dreams, over platforms—with auto manufacturers now selling cars alongside platforms offering programming, custom-made t-shirts, housework, holidays, paternity tests (yep, really!), gaming and many, many more.
- Information—we expect to know not just product specifications, but information about other customers' experiences, alternative options, etc., at our fingertips.

We expect to be able to pay in a variety of ways, too, and we're becoming increasingly reliant on electronics payments services. Many of these today are linked to our bank accounts, but it's also possible to load money onto an increasing number of services, either through a traditional payment or using electronic money of some sort, now including digital currencies and increasingly, cryptocurrencies such as Bitcoin.

Customers and Information

As well as changing our purchasing behaviour and expectations, platforms have fundamentally changed our interaction with, and expectations about, information. We are now comfortable sharing personal information, and expect others to do the same, with varying degrees of openness, depending on our culture, demographic and the type of information in question.

- The most dramatic change from a commercial perspective is in the availability of, and consumers' willingness to share, information about **products, services and the companies** that supply them; this has resulted in the need for manufacturers and service providers not only to listen to their customers, but also to curate their social profile in a completely new way.
- Of course, social platforms allow global communities to share every other type of **political, social and cultural** commentary they choose, and this is often associated with products, services and the companies that provide them, much more than in previous years. A company's values become an important part of its positioning with consumers.

- This, in turn, is linked to how consumers position **themselves** both in relation to political and social ideologies, and the extent to which they identify with companies and products associated with those ideologies. With consumer awareness, comes a growing trend to associate **consumption with ideology** ("lifestyle choices") which presents both opportunities and headaches for producers.
- We have also seen the rise of products that are basically people—rooted in celebrity endorsement, **platform celebrity** now exists as a valid career choice, and people make a (sometimes very good) living out of endorsing products on the internet, encouraging people to emulate them and creating the growth of online image as a key type of social status indicator in some societies and demographics. It has also led to the rise of social profile being more respected, and valued above, valid expertise.
- And this results in the proliferation of **personal information** being supplied by individuals over social and commercial platforms; personal opinions, experiences (often of products), anecdotes, photographs, trivia and other banalities. And, of course, kittens.

Key to this dynamic is the way that platform reputations are influenced and manipulated. Today's platform reputations are shaped by opinions; these are, and will still be, open to manipulation and influence by scale, intelligent analysis and crowd dynamics such as information bubbles, as we've seen with the Cambridge Analytica election rigging scandals. We describe this in more detail in Chapter 18.

This will be one of the areas that will see the greatest evolution in the next few years, thanks to the growing adoption of emerging technologies such as blockchain, AI and behavioural reputation systems; while the use of data to manipulate and shape opinions is widespread today, the opportunities presented by verifiable data and sophisticated behavioural analysis mean it's now possible to create and use reputations based on facts instead of opinions. Of course, many people do, and probably will continue, to choose information that reinforces their opinion over factual information. How this evolves will shape much of how platforms and commerce interact in the future.

Businesses in the Platform Age

As platforms have influenced customer behaviour, so they've provided both opportunities and challenges for businesses. Transparency (real or perceived) is now a prerequisite, especially for larger businesses with a significant exposure to social opinions, positive or negative, and a need to curate them.

Positioning in relationship to political and social attitudes is now a key part of every business strategy: today, **Tribe beats Product**—it's no longer enough to produce something great, your customers have to identify with people who use your product, or with your organisation. It's also easier for businesses to both gain and lose reputation and credibility through factors beyond their control.

The rise of the megaplatforms is problematic for other large and small businesses. In some cases, commercial platforms can leverage their scale and market value to undercut traditional players, resetting customer expectations with uncompetitively priced offerings to destroy competition, before leaving them in a monopoly position. Amazon is so strong in the book market and is already a market leader in many other sectors, that it can dictate prices to primary producers and secondary sellers. Uber is openly undercutting local taxi services with the stated intention of destroying traditional providers, allowing them to reset prices as a monopoly after competition has vanished (although this strategy is having variable success).

Although many cities and countries are attempting to constrain then, regulations can't keep up with platform economics, and global platforms don't suffer from national restrictions; their scale makes them essential to many national economies and they seem immune to traditional inconveniences suffered by smaller platforms and retailers, such as paying tax or treating workers ethically. The other side of this coin is an opportunity for labour and regulatory paradigms to shift, to both support and benefit from this new economy, but as with all market innovations, regulators struggle to catch up.

However, the opportunities are also significant. Today, businesses of any size don't need a global distribution network, or even advertising, if they can maintain a strong profile on social and commercial platforms through well curated consumer opinion. This means that the focus on holistic, full-stack services is now less important to strong distribution and sales, than a positive and well-curated public image. Smaller businesses can achieve global footprint through creating a tribe, or building association with an existing, powerful tribe. Niche suppliers can build a global audience as scale is no longer about saturation, but cultural reach.

This has a huge implication for small- and medium-sized businesses in developing economies, both for opportunities to interact directly with customers globally, and with global business communities. We're seeing a rise in direct marketing from producers in developing economies, and in parallel, platforms are helping crowdfunding and direct investment for businesses all over the world. As platforms evolve, they will perform an important function in broadening the horizons from small and medium businesses everywhere, but particularly in parts of the world that have to date lacked the opportunity to capitalise on these developments.

Conclusion

Platforms have changed the way consumers behave, how they think about products and services, how they interact with businesses and how they perceive companies, influence, celebrity, information and each other. This has significantly reshaped how businesses need to respond.

However, while significant change has already resulted from platforms, these changes are still at the early stage of evolution. A combination of new technologies and a growing depth of generations that have always lived in the platform economy provides the landscape for the next stage of evolution, into the ecosystem economy.

Notes

1. Choudary, S. P. (2015, September). Platform Scale: How an Emerging Business Model Helps Start-Ups Build Large Empires with Minimum Investment (Platform Thinking Labs). http://platformed.info/platform-stack/.
2. Line Mode Browser (Cern). http://info.cern.ch/hypertext/WWW/LineMode/Browser.html. Accessed 29 December 2017.
3. Sharwood, S. (2014, October 14). Netscape Navigator—The Browser That Started It All—Turns 20. *The Register*. https://www.theregister.co.uk/2014/10/14/netscape_navigator_the_browser_that_started_it_all_turns_20/. Accessed 29 December 2017.
4. Carey, S. (2015, November 25). Amazon 1995 to Now. *Tech World*. https://www.techworld.com/picture-gallery/business/amazon-1995-now-3628914/. Accessed 29 December 2017.
5. AuctionWeb. Later eBay. http://www.computerhistory.org/revolution/the-web/20/392/2342. Accessed 29 December 2017.
6. Brin, S., & L. Page. The Anatomy of a Large-Scale Hypertextual Web Search Engine. Computer Science Department of Stanford University. http://infolab.stanford.edu/~backrub/google.html. Accessed 29 December 2017.
7. Bariso, J. (2017, April 20). This Original Letter from Jeff Bezos to Amazon Shareholders Teaches Some Extraordinary Lessons in Leadership. *Inc.com*. https://www.inc.com/justin-bariso/20-years-ago-amazons-jeff-bezos-sent-an-extraordinary-letter-to-shareholders.html.

8. Mercer, C. (2015, November 25). History of PayPal: The History of the Biggest Online Payment System in the World. *TechWorld*. https://www.tech-world.com/picture-gallery/business/history-of-paypal-1998-now-3630386/. Accessed 29 December 2017.

9. Jones, B. (2015, April 15). Rags to Riches to Rags: The Rise and Fall of Internet Explorer. *Digital Trends*. https://www.digitaltrends.com/computing/the-rise-and-fall-of-internet-explorer/. Accessed 29 December 2017.

10. About Zappos. https://www.zappos.com/c/about-zappos. Accessed 29 December 2017.

11. 1-Click, *Amazon.com* https://www.amazon.com/p/feature/7smbfan9c-84m7rd. Accessed 29 December 2017.

12. Deal, S., Wingfield, N., & Sapsford, J. (2002, July 9). eBay Plans to Buy PayPal In $1.4 Billion. *Wall Street Journal*. https://www.wsj.com/articles/SB1026130187741609120. Accessed 29 December 2017.

13. Fitzpatrick, L. (2010, May 31). Brief History YouTube. *Time Magazine*. http://content.time.com/time/magazine/article/0,9171,1990787,00.html. Accessed 29 December 2017.

14. Titcomb, J. (2017, September 12). How the World Reacted to the First iPhone 10 Years Ago. *Telegraph*. http://www.telegraph.co.uk/technology/2017/01/09/world-reacted-first-iphone-10-years-ago/. Accessed 29 December 2017.

15. Randolph, M. (2017, November 2). A Brief History of Netflix. *CNN Entertainment*. http://edition.cnn.com/2014/07/21/showbiz/gallery/netflix-history/index.html. Accessed 29 December 2017.

16. Holland, J. (October 19). The Couple Paid 200k a Year to Travel. *BBC*. http://www.bbc.com/capital/story/20171019-the-couple-paid-200k-a-year-to-travel. Accessed 29 December 2017.

17. Gunther, M. (2007, August 27). The Amazing Freecycle Story. *Fortune*. http://archive.fortune.com/2007/07/13/magazines/fortune/pluggedin_gunther_freecycle.fortune/index.htm. Accessed 29 December 2017.

18. LetsLinkUK Homepage. http://www.letslinkuk.net/. Accessed 29 December 2017.

19. Brixton Pound Homepage. http://brixtonpound.org/. Accessed 29 December 2017.

20. Bundles Washing Machine Rental Page. https://www.bundles.nl/en/washing-machine-rental/. Accessed 29 December 2017.

21. Ellickson, P. B. (2015, March 15). The Evolution of the Supermarket Industry: From A&P to Walmart*. University of Rochester.

22. Burchill, J. (1989, July). Ambition. *The Bodley Head*.

23. Drunk Online Shopping: Readers' Regrets. *Guardian*, 24 August 2014. https://www.theguardian.com/lifeandstyle/2014/aug/24/drunk-online-shopping-readers-regrets. Accessed 28 December 2017.

16

Technology vs Solution

This chapter will be useful for anyone who thinks that new technology is the answer to their service or operating model problems. We explore how technology has become a shorthand for products or services, and why business and technologists alike have subscribed to this view. We present the arguments for why this is a costly way of papering over problems in operating models or services, how adding technology to a complex organisation or process can reduce efficiency and service levels, and why a solution focus can help organisations avoid falling into this trap.

Technology as a Product

It's very, very easy to equate technology with a product or service, and as we'll explore below, technology terminology or brand names is often used as a shortcut for describing a service, particularly within organisations. If you're working in a large business, instead of creating an employee record, you enter HR data into the employee database or worse, Oracle or SAP. Instead of onboarding a customer, you run them through the KYC (Know Your Customer) system and enter them into the CRM (Customer Relationship Management) system. This leads to a world where people don't talk about what they're doing in terms of why they're doing it, which, in our experience, prevents them from thinking about why they're doing it. Activities become focused on systems, rather than on outcomes, leading to impaired ability to prioritise or problem solve.

© The Author(s) 2018
S. Blakstad and R. Allen, *FinTech Revolution*,
https://doi.org/10.1007/978-3-319-76014-8_16

This spills into our normal lives as well, to a lesser extent; we're tied by habit and semantics to activities centring around technology and the delivery of technology. We don't search, we Google; we don't watch shows, we go on Netflix, we don't vacuum clean, we Hoover. As we describe in Chapter 14, focusing on the product takes away the ability to understand the problem we're trying to solve, which can lead to poor decisions, although it's reasonable to say that we do make a conscious choice about which show to watch!

Calling a Spade a Bully Tools

So why do we do this? It's partly to do with branding; people will generally use the name of technology as a shortcut for describing the service it provides. We do this with everyday technology—Hoovers, Sellotape (or Scotch Tape if you're American), Nespresso, Biro, Google, Post-its, etc. The chances are our actual interaction with these brands doesn't reflect our use of these names; sure, we all use Google and everyone's aware of the monopolistic nature of the world's most successful search engine, but chances are your vacuum cleaner isn't made by Hoover, your tape isn't made by Sellotape (or Scotch) and your Crocs aren't Crocs.

So, in day-to-day experience, although we use these words to name household technology made by other manufacturers, we're not actually confusing the two; it's used as a semantic shortcut which is commonly understood, usually in place of a longer and more complex phrase that would describe its function.

While this usage may be irritating for the manufacturer, it will, in purchases where we make a conscious choice, favour that manufacturer, although for many generic appliances, we also supply our own criteria and, in the case of something cheap and disposable such as sticky tape or ballpoint pens, have little or no awareness of brands when making purchasing decisions.

When we come to technology services in complex organisations though, we're not dealing with single products that fulfil our needs as part of a simple service. Technology, either generic or more commonly, referred to by its brand name, is frequently used as a shortcut to describe a service. This is partly due to the same cue-recognition phenomenon in our homes; we call products by the name we see on the screen when we log in. However, it's more pervasive than this, when our IT departments and our businesses are also talking about, and thinking about, technology in lieu of services.

In our experience, when we're running large transformation programmes for banks, many of the projects are named after the technology we're buying, either generically or by the product name, rather than the service we're implementing. There are several reasons for this:

- The technology is one of the most expensive elements of a large project, so one of the main concerns of the people setting and agreeing the budget for the project is buying the technology. This focus leads to them talking about the technology synonymously with the project.
- A decision about which technology to buy is usually one of the earliest decisions made on the project, often before a project team has been formed.
- The technology is easy to identify and tangible, whereas the objectives of the project are probably less well defined (this shouldn't be the case, but it often is).
- Implementing the project will often involve working directly with the manufacturer, so the project becomes identified with the manufacturer.

Consequently, we've worked on projects called "Flexcube", "Windows 98", "Microsoft Dynamics" and other product names, as well as "Deposits Liquidity Engine", "New Payments Platform", "Core Banking Platform", and others describing the nature of the system, rather than the purpose of the programme.

Further, people in business and technology alike become familiar with the systems they use and associate the success of their service with the technology. We've worked with many business and technology leaders, who favour a particular system or manufacturer because of a successful implementation of that system in another organisation, which can lead to disappointment when the technology doesn't deliver the expected benefits in the new organisation.

Of course, much of the technology branding focus is also to do with sales and marketing; it's in the interests of technology companies to say their products and services can cover a wide range of services; it justifies the cost, and in many cases, the technology companies genuinely think their product *does* supply everything that the organisation needs to run that service, because of their own focus and bias towards technical components.

Counterintuitively, technology people are generally better at separating services from products than business people are, because they have a greater understanding of what's involved. However, within the world of technology, there are also strongly held beliefs and affiliations which may be based on selective information, or even a partial understanding of the technology involved, which can lead to bias and factionalism within technology departments. We've seen this in particular where technology governance is weak, and in technology departments with lower overall skills and continuous education than average.

So Why Is This a Problem?

Equating technology or brand names with services may, as with your household vacuum cleaner, not really be much of a problem in everyday life, even if it does give you an unconscious bias towards that manufacturer. But in organisations, it creates a risky scenario where solutions become equated with technology.

Problems Arising from Confusing Technology with Solutions

We've identified five broad problem areas that this approach creates in organisations:

- First, it creates a **tunnel vision** approach to problem solving, that assumes existing technology needs to be replaced with new, equivalent technology when services fail, or that the requirement for new services equates to the requirement for new technology. We've seen a lot of this in banking over the past 20 years, with banks first slapping web-enabled front ends on top of legacy systems, then apps, and now bots and AI. While this may create cute interfaces, they're increasingly struggling to create the agility customers expect, because of the complexity and age of legacy systems.
- Next, it stops people identifying **why problems arise**, as they assume a failure in the service to be a failure in the technology. This is a particularly expensive problem for organisations, as they often rely on multiple systems and manual processes to support a single service; pinpointing a technology component leads to the assumption that fixing that component will resolve whatever the problem is, while ignoring the challenges created by processes, responsibilities, organisational structure and all the things that actually cause most problems in services.

- Then, there's the **"sunk cost" fallacy**; a focus on technical solutions to problems tends towards heavy investment in technical solutions, which in turn creates a strong psychological barrier to assessing their utility objectively. Since you've spent so much on the technology, the rationale goes, you should continue investing in technology to fix any problems.
- Next, a build-up of technology solutions leads inevitably to **massive system complexity**, particularly when different technologies are owned by different parts of the organisation. While every organisation we've worked in has tried to simplify its IT infrastructure, it's actually really hard to decouple services from complex technology, meaning that even when services are retired, or systems replaced, you're often left with legacy systems that do one thing (or that nobody's really sure of their function, but it's too risky to switch it off). This has led to system complexity in many organisations, that to the outside eye would look simply unbelievable.
- Lastly, it's really **expensive**; often simple, non-technical or low-tech solutions solve problems much better than complex systems do, but because of the problems above, the natural drift is towards adding systems, rather than reducing them. This in turn leads to growing maintenance costs and ever higher cost of replacing legacy, as the integration of any new system becomes more and more complex.

Of these, the biggest problem is that it prevents you from really understanding your organisation's weak spots, which in most cases are the structure of the business, culture and communication, rather than systems or technology.

How Does This Impact Organisations?

The main impact to organisations from this technology focus is overspending on technology and difficulty in achieving strategic business objectives.

A good example comes from the late noughties, and our re-engineering experience; when asking teams for examples of how they'd simplified processes, more often than not the answer would be, they'd built a system to automate a crap process. In one memorable case, the proudly displayed solution was a new system that had been commissioned to reconcile data issues *introduced by three other systems*, which nobody had thought of fixing at source.

In other examples, we've seen many, many cases where banks implement shiny new payments, core banking, CRM or ERP systems at great expense, but fail to address structural problems with their organisation, poor processes, communication deserts and capability issues. Programme and business leaders are usually aware of the importance of end to end flows and processes, but because of the way programmes are funded and sponsored, often don't have access to some of the critical elements that are needed for the new system to deliver services successfully to the customers.

Worse, in some organisations, planning and budgeting is done with too much reliance on vendor teams and not enough expertise from experienced integrators, so the needed resources and budget were never made available. In either case, large technology programmes usually hit major integration challenges as they're running in massively complex organisations, with all the parts moving simultaneously as other programmes run in parallel, so programme and business leaders have to jettison scope and particularly integration scope, in order to get programmes over the line.

This creates a "head down" approach to just getting the job done, which may lead to some incremental improvements and often fixes burning platform issues with legacy systems, but usually fails to deliver the full benefits that were cited when the programme was commissioned.

Of course, banks and other large organisations are aware that complexity is a problem, but again the technology focus causes challenges with this. When a senior banking professional thinks of the complexity of his bank, he thinks of this.

Mortgage System in Retail Bank

...and it's really quite natural to blame technology complexity on, well, technology. But what drives technology complexity, is actually the organisational, communications and process complexity that banks have built; replacing technology can't address these problems, when the problem is actually this (Fig. 16.1).

... in one of the banks we've worked in, there was at one point 16 layers of hierarchy between the CEO and the people on the ground. With organisations this complex, it's impossible to keep technology simple (Fig. 16.2).

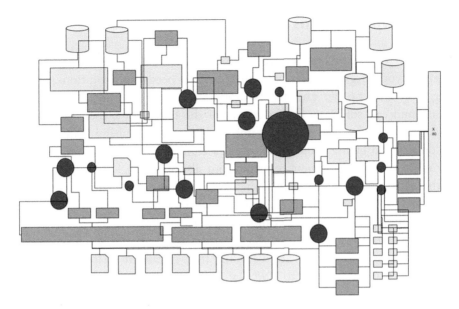

Fig. 16.1   Mortgage system in retail bank

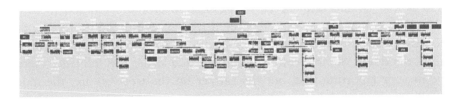

Fig. 16.2   Bank organisational structure

Solution Focus

Thinking about your services as solutions to customers' problems instead of manifestations of technology can help you to identify what customers need more easily, as we describe in Chapter 14, and at the same time help you to abstract from your systems view to thinking about the outcomes of your activities. Customers will always experience the outcomes, and although they may interface with the technology, they're not aware of, or interested in, how it works. That doesn't mean you shouldn't care how the technology works, but thinking about your services from a customer's perspective, helps to view them as results and outputs, rather than as technology systems.

Words, Words, Words

How you describe your services and customer relationships is pivotal in shaping your organisation's view of customer needs and solutions. If you organise your people and teams around products and technology solutions, and call solutions by the names of the technology, then that shapes their view of what they are there for. Conversely, organising teams around solutions, and giving projects solution-based names, not only sends a strong signal to teams about their priorities, but also helps to focus on outcomes rather than technologies. Although this may seem trivial, taken to its logical conclusion it will impact how you structure your organisation, which we describe in practical terms later in this section.

As with products vs services, the key question to ask when naming a unit or project, is "why?" Why are we doing this, and what strategic goal does it support? Then it's easy to find the name and relate it to the customer outcome, but it can also teach you some important lessons about where to refocus your organisation. For example, "reconciliation" is not a customer outcome and we're pretty confident it's not built into your strategy, either.

So as leaders, and influencers, it's possible to promote solution focus in your organisation, but as ever, the key drivers of culture and direction are the senior leaders of the organisation—almost without exception, culture is driven top down. So how you communicate as a leader will influence everyone in your reporting line, but the further up the tree you are, the more influential your words become.

Leadership Rhetoric

Examining the words of senior leaders, we can see a huge variance in tone and approach, from truly solution aligned, to technology focused, to … well, make up your own mind. We present them here.

Jeff Bezos of Amazon wrote about this at length in his 2016 letter to shareholders,[1] where he describes solution focus as "Day 1 thinking"; it's worth noting that he doesn't even *mention* technology until about halfway through his thousand-odd word letter, and only then in the context as technology services they're selling to customers as an IT producer, rather than technology channels or other enablers:

> Staying in Day 1 requires you to experiment patiently, accept failures, plant seeds, protect saplings, and double down when you see customer delight. A customer-obsessed culture best creates the conditions where all of that can

happen [...] There are many advantages to a customer-centric approach, but here's the big one: customers are always beautifully, wonderfully dissatisfied, even when they report being happy and business is great. Even when they don't yet know it, customers want something better, and your desire to delight customers will drive you to invent on their behalf. No customer ever asked Amazon to create the Prime membership program, but it sure turns out they wanted it, and I could give you many such examples

[In Day 2], you stop looking at outcomes and just make sure you're doing the process right. Gulp. It's not that rare to hear a junior leader defend a bad outcome with something like, 'Well, we followed the process, [...] A more experienced leader will use it as an opportunity to investigate and improve the process.'

By contrast, are the shareholder letters and manifestos from banks. ING's Ralph Hamers in his CEO letter to shareholders[2] in their annual report focuses on how technology can help customer experiences; from his opening remarks:

...But the competitive landscape for banks is changing. The pace of digitalisation is increasing, and this is changing customer expectations. We will accelerate our transformation, creating an integrated digital platform to cater to all our customers' financial needs and provide new and relevant offers to enhance the customer experience.

... while he does also mention social responsibility and talks a lot about customer experience, and clearly is driving ING towards becoming an ecosystem player, the order and focus of his points positions ING very firmly as a technology-focused bank. NB we are absolutely aligned on his comments about the changing competitive environment and the move into the ecosystem, which most bank CEOs are still failing to acknowledge, and we cover ING more in other sections.

Meanwhile, failing to explain a position in either customer focus or technology, Barclays' Chairman's letter to shareholders from John McFarlane, in their 2016 annual report[3] instead focuses almost exclusively on their restructure and return to profitability. Here's his summary:

Today the Group is smaller, safer, more focused, less leveraged, better capitalised and highly liquid, with the customer at the centre of the business. The sale of Africa, the settlement of legacy conduct matters and the exit of Non-Core will improve this significantly going forward.

… although he repeatedly mentions they're "putting customers at the heart of the business", it's trotted out as a parenthetical catchphrase, without saying how, and there is no mention of customer ecosystem or community concerns—the community first gets a mention on page 97 of the report.

Leadership rhetoric like this is incredibly influential in shaping culture; it directs not only shareholders, but every employee who reads it, into the core thought processes of their leaders. Bezos' letter is clearly aimed primarily at his team, but also crafted to clearly state to shareholders openly how he wants his team to operate. Hamers' lays out a strong focus for future engagement with the ecosystem via technology, presenting the technology as a means to the end of customer service. McFarlane's, by contrast, appears to be written directly to the shareholders and to ignore the existence of employees and customers alike. We encourage you to read all three, to understand the different perspectives of these three organisations, bearing in mind they will be directly competing for customers when Amazon move further into financial services.

Despite the very different history, there's one striking similarity between the Barclays and Amazon rhetoric, which is its consistency. Jeff Bezos has been issuing an annual letter every year since Amazon started trading, and the tone is still the same—in fact, he regularly re-issues the 1997 letter with his annual reports, alongside the new one. Barclays, which has been around a lot longer, also continues to focus on its shareholders, as it has done historically. Barclays at 2017 has a market cap of USD 45.4 billion,[4] and 119,300 employees, down from nearly 150,000 10 years ago, having been in business for over a century. Like most banks, it's focusing on reducing overhead and simplifying structure, as it feels the pinch. The tone of the letter is at a marked contrast to Barclays' stated aim to innovate, and the money it is putting behind innovation, which is likely to lead to confusion for the people setting those agendas when priorities are questioned.

By contrast, Amazon, with a market cap of 569 billion,[5] has 341,400, up from 20,700 ten years ago, and has been trading for just over 20 years at the time of writing. Obviously, size isn't everything, there's a lot more than rhetoric to leadership, and the comparative fortunes of the two organisations aren't just based on that, but comparing Barclays' report with other, more forward-thinking banks, such as ING or Nordea, is instructive. Similarly, Amazon is far from perfect and has attracted much negative press, particularly around employment practices and tax dealings, but a consistent solution focus seems to be working for them.

Benefits of solution focus like Bezos' are the ability to find non-technical solutions, such as Amazon Prime, to customers' problems, and to allow greater scope for experimentation within the organisation. Many banks are trying to implement an agile, fail-fast culture, but still keeping rigidly to technology-focused budgets and projects, which not only fail to allow for experimentation, but actively direct resources away from innovation, because of the risk of failure. Although there's a huge amount of investment in transformation, while this focuses on technology implementations rather than refocusing on customer solutions, incumbents, and in particular those incumbents who still think they're operating in the same competitive environment as before, will lose the ability to meet customers' needs.

Conclusion

There's a tradition of using the names of technology products or generic terms for technology, in place of the customer solutions they're supporting. This has the effect of shaping how people think and behave when delivering and supporting these solutions. Customers aren't interested in your technology, instead wanting to see positive outcomes. Moving towards a more solution-focused approach helps you to anticipate and solve customer problems, while a system and technology focus can lead to excessive complexity, massive costs, and only incremental improvements.

The language you use about solutions not only shapes the way your teams think about solutions and customer outcomes, it can also help you to structure your organisations in a more customer-focused way. We've presented illustrations of different leadership rhetoric, and how this is likely to shape the direction of those organisations in very different ways. There's a great opportunity for leaders to rethink how they communicate to their shareholders, their teams and their customers. Businesses that just think about systems will end up building lots of systems, that may not support customer needs or solve problems; Technology is an enabler for solutions, not a solution in itself. Amazon is growing exponentially. Barclays is shrinking.

Notes

1. Bezos, J. P. (2017, April 12). 2016 Letter to Shareholders. https://www.amazon.com/p/feature/z6o9g6sysxur57t. Accessed 28 December 2017.
2. ING Group Annual Report 2016, ING. https://www.ing.com/web/file?uuid=bbbb6628-52ea-4469-8232-2a0d0d60f099&owner=b03bc017-e0db-4b5d-abbf-003b12934429&contentid=39230&elementid=1880975.
3. Barclays PLC Annual Report 2016. https://www.home.barclays/content/dam/barclayspublic/docs/InvestorRelations/AnnualReports/AR2016/Barclays%20PLC%20Annual%20Report%202016.pdf. Accessed 28 December 2017.

4. Barclays Market Cap (Page Updates Dynamically). *MacroTrends.Net*. http://www.macrotrends.net/stocks/charts/BCS/market-cap/barclay-plc-adr-market-cap-history. Accessed 29 December 2017.

5. Amazon Market Cap (Page Updates Dynamically). *MacroTrends.Net*. http://www.macrotrends.net/stocks/charts/AMZN/market-cap/amazon-inc-market-cap-history. Accessed 29 December 2017.

Future Business, Part V

Services for the Ecosystem Economy
What's Going on?

In this section, we consider how social change, fuelled by technology and communications, is changing the nature of work, value, trust, identity and truth. We describe the evolution from the tribal, human-centric model to the ecosystem model, with its own pitfalls added to our own limitations as human animals.

We highlight some challenges where regulators and governments need to look beyond the bordered model and trying to shoe-horn the new world into the old paradigms and consider the multi-party, increasingly global nature of everything from work to news to service delivery, and what this means for businesses.

17

Career as Microservices—Reputation-Based Skill Validation

In other chapters of this section, we will discuss reputation systems, truth, identity and authentication, and how hiveonline's and other truth-based contextualised reputation systems will address this. We've observed a number of applications of similar approaches in fields as diverse as medicine, trade finance and community agriculture in developing economies.

We're confident this approach to reputation will become commonplace, and then standard, because it makes sense. It's based on facts and gives trust consumers, for the first time, the ability to apply the filter of their needs to understanding a counterparty's reliability within the context of what they want from that counterparty, without the skew of opinion-based bias. We believe this will have a profound impact on how organisations operate and interact, and that it will be one of the keys to the ecosystem economy developing successfully.

This is exciting and a bit scary for organisations, but what does it mean for individuals? In this chapter, we examine current trends in reputation-based recruitment, implications for employment and career paths, and where we believe this will take us in the future.

Emerging Labour Models and Associated Challenges

While paid contractors have been around for a while, we've recently seen the emergence of micro-contract based services (the "gig" economy), powered by platforms such as Uber, Airbnb, TaskRabbit[1] or Etsy,[2] which provide a

© The Author(s) 2018
S. Blakstad and R. Allen, *FinTech Revolution*,
https://doi.org/10.1007/978-3-319-76014-8_17

marketplace for interactions between individual providers and their customers for short-term, one-shot exchanges of service and value. This has revolutionised access to services and customers, although as we've seen, the platforms, with business models unimagined by the authors of employment legislation, are subject to controversy and many workers are being paid poorly, are unprotected and lack clarity on their legal status as a result.

The pay problem arises from two sources: firstly, the desire of the platforms to build scale, which is critical for platform survival, by undercutting traditional businesses in the sector. As we've seen with Uber, current low prices are subsidised by the platform's investment capital, apparently with the aim of putting competitors out of business, following which presumably fares will rise. Secondly, market economics will have an impact and the availability of workers in lower-cost countries forces down prices for similar workers in higher-cost countries. The first problem applies more to localised services, and the second more to virtualised services, but both can impact both localised and virtualised services.

The lack of clarity on legal status and lack of protection is more to do with the disparity between employment legislation and emerging service models, although there has always been a disparity between people on permanent employment contracts and those employed through a third party. In most developed economies, a large number of people have provided services as third-party contractors long-term to organisations, in some cases emulating or replacing permanent employees, but governed by different rules regarding employment protection, tax, holiday and sick pay. In some cases, these workers are able to demand higher pay to compensate for their lack of status, and typically professionals such as IT contractors, accountants and engineers are able to command favourable rates because of their skills and a shortage in the marketplace.

However, for less skilled workers, or for those where supply outstrips demand, working in contract conditions has and does depress rates, negatively impacting all but a few—freelance designers, actors and translators have always been relatively low-paid for skilled workers, while the growing numbers of those on "zero hours" contracts—typically in catering, maintenance, logistics, agriculture and construction—are generally low- or unskilled and enjoying few benefits associated with permanent employees, with pay hovering around the minimum wage.

Meanwhile, there's a growing number of people voluntarily delivering value for no financial reward at all—open source software, Wikipedia, YouTube guides, Medium articles—the list is growing. Most contributors (but not all) derive income elsewhere, and in some cases, there's an indirect benefit to them, but for the majority, there's no direct exchange of value that

Fig. 17.1 Dan Pink: Autonomy, Mastery, Purpose

could be measured in tangible terms. This, again, risks forcing down the value of professional services, and creative professions such as music, designers, writers and journalists, in particular, have been hard hit by the proliferation of people providing free content.

We're also now conditioned to expect content, particularly creative content, to be delivered to us for nothing—news, op-eds, YouTube videos, Wikipedia have all got us used to the idea that content is free. Of course, we "pay" via other means on most platforms—advertising being the obvious one, but also by providing data to organisations who can learn about our needs and target us with paid-for content—if you can't see who's paying, you're the product.

But all of this has overturned our perception of, and in some cases the reality of, the traditional association between work and money, or labour and value—the Labour theory of value states that the value of labour is directly associated with demand and availability, which holds water to an extent with the depressing effect on unit value where labour is in high supply but lower demand. However, when quality content such as Wikipedia or the BBC news is available for nothing, this association is overturned not just for those sources, but also for other, less widely distributed sources, with consumers expecting to be given content for free (Fig. 17.1).

Reputation as the New Currency?

Before exploring what can be done with employment conditions to fix the problem for individuals, let's consider what's behind this disruptive behaviour. Why do all these people do stuff for nothing, deliberately disrupting the association of value and labour and potentially undermining their own value in the workplace? Why does a software developer willingly spend his weekend developing open source software or a plumber spend time demonstrating how to fix pipes on YouTube? Why do people write chapters on Medium or release free songs, all of which have taken effort and time?

Part of the explanation can be found in Dan Pink's influential book[3] and RSA Animate short[4] on Drive—if you haven't seen it yet, it is ten minutes well invested. He demonstrates that for work requiring cognitive activity, once the need for money is "off the table", i.e. we have enough to live on, we're less motivated by financial rewards than by our need for autonomy, our sense of purpose and thirst for mastery. Incidentally, that video was made around 2010, before it became apparent that the traditional organisation was evolving into ecosystems, but many of Pink's examples are actually of ecosystem economy behaviours. Somewhere in that combination of mastery and sense of purpose sits another motivator we've talked about a lot, and that is reputation.

Reputation is, in several respects, the transactable element of sense of purpose and mastery. Through demonstrating both, you demonstrate value, and reputation is your reward. Your reputation is strongly associated with the quality and volume of work that you produce, much as in the traditional theory of labour and value, money was. And in traditional career paths, reputation is an important element when seeking career advancement, either by promotion or recruitment by another organisation.

That's not to say that money is completely unimportant to professionals— we see a strong linkage between rewards and status, particularly in hierarchical organisations—and while it's important to distinguish status from performance, status is also likely to enhance reputation, so there's an indirect linkage there too. But, importantly, that assumes that more money equates to excellence, which as we've seen, is starting to be eroded by the proliferation of alternative working models.

Conversely, an area where the research presented by Pink shows a strong link between rewards and performance is straightforward, non-creative work. Obviously, many of today's jobs fall into this category, and a lot of these fall into our "gig" economy and zero-hours contract sectors. While you're likely to be motivated by recognition to excel at something that produces results that can be evaluated against complex criteria, the base unit of recognition for these jobs may be as low as "done" or "not done" (although in nearly every role, in real life some element of skill or mastery is involved). We may be programming next-generation software and laying down tracks for the greater good and our enhanced image, but it seems unlikely that anyone will voluntarily drive a cab, process invoices, build a wall, pick strawberries or empty bins for the sake of peer recognition.

However, reputation is also important in these roles—maybe not our reputation for excellence, but certainly for reliability, consistency of delivery and, in many cases, customer experience. Reputation systems such as Uber's and Airbnb's ratings are designed to fulfil exactly this purpose, with quality criteria applied to counterparties on both sides of the interaction. These gig economy reputation scores become the value criteria by which future customers and suppliers can evaluate their appetite for future transactions with those individuals.

The challenge with these platform reputation systems, as we've explored elsewhere, is that they may not be accurate, partly because they're subjective and partly because they're based on user evaluation, which may take other factors into account, or simply misunderstand the evaluation criteria. With platforms like hiveonline and other fact-based reputation systems addressing this, we are addressing this accuracy challenge. Is there, then, an opportunity to extend formalising fact-based reputation systems to other types of workers?

We think that there could be; using evidence of work done gives current and future employers an unbiased view of employees' effectiveness, whether they're one-off "gig" workers or long-term employees under formal contract. The advantages of this, over traditional evaluation procedures, would be significant for any groups currently impacted by glass ceilings and "mini-me" recruitment mentality. But that doesn't address the employment conditions problem.

Square Peg, Round Hole

It's impossible to obtain accurate statistics about "gig" and zero-hours vs traditional employment because the means of measuring the two aren't the same—consider, for example, a full-time employee who also rents out a room via Airbnb, or drives for Uber on Saturdays—it's estimated that the non-standard sector now represents about a third[5] of the workforce in the USA When one of every three jobs falls outside the "standard", you're not talking about exceptions to the rule, and governments everywhere are recognising the need to regularise conditions for people working in these conditions. But they're struggling, because, like the traditional measurements, trying to apply the same employment conditions as a permanent employee doesn't work.

Alternatively, given the disproportionate rise of non-standard employment, is it time to reconsider how we view employment across the board? Is there an opportunity to combine elements of traditional and non-traditional working arrangements to address the imbalance of rights and income? The reason that the rules are different for contract vs permanent employees is that contract employment is supposed to be short-term and temporary; that's why there are rules about how long you can hire a contractor for before you have to start treating them like a permanent employee. The problem is, that just doesn't work when a third of the workforce are in this "bucket".

Let's think about the assumptions underpinning permanent employment.

- The first assumption is that you work for one organisation exclusively, and that organisation is both responsible for paying you and for paying social fund to the state on your behalf; they're also responsible for funding your days off (sick or vacation in all developed countries other than the USA)—and they have some rights to claim small amounts back from the state on your behalf. All of that works fine when there's a one to one you/employer relationship.
- The second assumption is that you don't move jobs frequently, or at all, which means that the benefits your employer accrues on your behalf, whether that's paid leave, pension or redundancy, can be stored and used at some indefinite point in the future when you need them.
- This is linked to the third assumption, which is that your organisation doesn't really change much over time, so there's little or no need to build alternative or new skills in employees.
- The fourth assumption is that the employee works onsite, in an environment controlled by the employing organisation.

As more organisations move into ecosystem supply chains and partnerships, however, all of these assumptions are challenged. Modern organisations need to adapt frequently to survive, which means changing business models, changing roles and changing legal structures. People change roles and organisations more frequently than ever, and this trend is growing in parallel with the rise of the gig economy.

Conversely, a contractor is assumed to be someone who effectively works for a company owned by themselves and is expected to treat themselves like a permanent employee of that micro-business. That creates a huge burden of administration and responsibility on individuals working in the gig economy, as well as massively increasing administration for tax authorities and governments. Contractors are expected to be the exception—the brain-for-hire that fills in when someone has left, or you can't find a particular skillset easily, rather than a permanent solution.

Will there come a time when the permanent employment contract is dead? Possibly not, but it's already time to regard the micro-job as a normal, standard model in how people are employed today. As things stand, governments are trying to apply old-world rules to new-world employment models, and it's not working. Gig economy workers have limited access to things that permanent employees take for granted—holidays, sick pay, mortgages and training, to name a few, because these things have been designed around the permanent employee model.

Accepting the gig economy as a valid employment model is the first step towards ensuring that workers have rights; trying to lever permanent employment rules on top of it hasn't worked, so it's time to look at it from a different angle. Characteristics of the gig economy are:

- Income will vary over time and is based on results, rather than fixed days per year.
- People work for multiple employers, possibly in different roles and almost certainly for many different customers/stakeholders.
- Hours are not regular and may be greater or less than standard employment in any given week/month/year.
- Places of employment vary and are likely to include more home working than standard employment.

With these standards accepted, it's clear that the traditional view of employment contracts between individuals and employers being closely tied to benefits passed on to employees on behalf of the state is broken. States will need to start directly allocating benefits as detached from employment status, if they are to stop penalising people who don't have a single, regular employment contract with a single employer.

Losing the close coupling between holistic responsibility and employers would also enable governments to rebalance the inequality between companies paying social fund for "proper" employees and the current lack of social fund for "gig" employees. A blanket social fund associated with work paid for at the point where it delivers benefit would also simplify the arrangements for firms providing subcontracted services.

By extension, this also implies that firms should be responsible for employee health and safety while onsite at company premises, regardless of their employment status, rather than the current rules which force employers to take responsibility for safety standards in sites such as employees' home offices, which are both unpopular with employees and virtually impossible to impose.

Universal Benefits—Universal Income?

Linking benefits to earnings, as they are in current employment contracts, becomes meaningless and unworkable where people are earning variable amounts of money from week to week and across different employers. This is the main challenge presented when trying to shoehorn gig economy workers into permanent employment style arrangements with employers. The logical answer if you're separating benefits from jobs is to apply a universal benefit across populations, rather than trying to differentiate them based on income. Not only would this significantly reduce administration costs and complexity, but it would go a long way towards equalising social perception of employees in different types of employment, and improve work/life balance significantly for contract workers. An obvious outcome of removing the link between benefits and employment status, is that everyone, regardless of whether they're employed or not, could be eligible for the benefits.

Similarly, it makes sense to consider whether this could be a precursor to Universal Basic Income (UBI) becoming a reality. We've seen a number of experiments[6] with varying degrees of success being piloted in various countries, in both developed and developing economies. While the unit economics look more achievable in some countries than others, there is a clear opportunity to offset administration and social security costs against a simpler UBI (albeit almost certainly under a different name), and the social benefits in reducing stigma and opening up alternative employment scenarios have been documented. As more positions, in particularly lower-skilled roles, become cheaper to automate and the predicted impact on employment rates across populations starts to bite, the unit economics and social benefits start to make more sense.

However, although this is an interesting and likely eventual outcome, the first step is to focus on benefits associated today with permanent employment; making these universal would be significantly less costly than UBI, partly because in most developed economies, there's an element of state control or direct funding from the state already bundled in the benefits concerned.

Career Paths or Career Portfolios?

One of the challenges to gig economy workers is that career structures are no longer fixed and linear for them, as they have been traditionally for permanent employees. We've also noted, however, that reputation is more and more important in determining career progression, with what you've done becoming more important than tenure, as careers even among permanent employees become more diversified.

We've proposed a potential mechanism for accurately documenting reputation using fact-based reputation systems, and these could be applied to portfolio careers across multiple employers or within a single employer, equally. Fact-based reputation systems don't differentiate between the two, meaning that gig economy and contract workers wouldn't be penalised for working for multiple employers. Fact-based reputation systems also level the playing field for employees working fewer hours, or in more junior positions, which in traditional employment structures may be overlooked in comparison with more senior, more visible positions, leading to an uneven distribution of attention as well as financial rewards.

Meanwhile, we've seen a trend in recruitment where networks such as LinkedIn have enabled employers to extend the traditional "word of mouth" reputation-based recruitment across industries and continents; more frequently, employees are being found and finding roles through recommendations and reputation, as much as through more traditional CV-based matching. Isn't it also time to formalise this into fact-based reputation systems, levelling the playing field for less visible workers?

At hiveonline we'll be enabling this for workers within certain sectors, as we build our reputation system not just for builders, restaurants and farmers, but also for the people who work for them. These fact-based reputation profiles will help employers to understand who's a good fit, as well as their reliability. There's a clear gap in the market here—there's no LinkedIn for builders—so isn't it also time to consider applying similar approaches to support the emerging reputation-based career portfolios we see emerging today?

Conclusion

The emergence of the gig economy has accelerated existing trends towards portfolio careers, highlighting the need for the way people are rewarded to catch up. Trying to shoehorn portfolio careers into traditional employment structures doesn't work, and unfairly penalises the growing population of workers in non-standard employment situations. It's reaching a tipping point where we can no longer treat these employment conditions as aberrational, and there's an opportunity to change the relationship between states, employers and employees to recognise new normals in employment.

Benefits, rewards and reputation can all be managed at a portfolio level, and with emerging fact-based reputation systems we have the opportunity to reduce the unfair penalisation of lower-paid workers with multiple employers, levelling the playing field and improving both working conditions and social acceptance of these now-standard employment models.

Notes

1. TaskRabbit Homepage. https://www.taskrabbit.com/. Accessed 29 December 2017.
2. Etsy Homepage. https://www.etsy.com/. Accessed 29 December 2017.
3. Pink, D. (2009, December). *Drive: The Surprising Truth About What Motivates Us*. Riverhead Books.
4. Pink, D. (2010, April 1). https://www.thersa.org/discover/videos/rsa-animate/2010/04/rsa-animate—drive. Accessed 28 December 2017.
5. Gillespie, P. (2017, May 24). Intuit: Gig Economy is 34% of US Workforce. *CNNMoney*. http://money.cnn.com/2017/05/24/news/economy/gig-economy-intuit/index.html. Accessed 28 December 2017.
6. Lant, K., & Tiozon, E. Universal Basic Income Pilot Programs Around the World. *Futurism*. https://futurism.com/images/universal-basic-income-ubi-pilot-programs-around-the-world/. Accessed 29 December 2017.

Further Reading

Mason, P. (2015). *Postcapitalism*. Allen Lane.
Raworth, K. (2017, March 22). *Doughnut Economics: Seven Ways to Think Like a 21st-Century Economist*. Chelsea Green Publishing.
Thaler, R. H. (2015). *Misbehaving: The Making of Behavioural Economics*. Allen Lane.

18

Plebocracy Bias

Post-truth. Information bubbles. Echo chamber. Confirmation bias. We've all heard a lot about these phenomena recently, but they're not new. Opinion, regardless of whether it's founded on fact, has always influenced apparently impartial decision-makers, often unfairly disadvantaging individuals and organisations. In Chapter 19, we will explore some of the challenges presented by traditional reputation systems and how we can apply emerging technology to addressing the issues.

Reputation systems largely fall into two areas: traditional, fact-based systems such as credit checks or histories held with federal authorities, which give limited, but hard to falsify information about an individual, and increasingly, social reputation systems, which are based on opinion. Historically, social reputation has usually been built on some flavour of fact; however, there have always been individuals able to manipulate opinion and change received facts. While in the past this was limited to smaller groups, the rise of broad communications and media proliferation has opened up the scope of this influence, leading to larger groups, from states to nations, adopting beliefs. Meanwhile, the public's relationship with the truth is becoming confused by the proliferation of opinion and obfuscated by learning algorithms.

This influence on public perception is causing shifts in opinion which impact not only individuals and businesses that may be subject to reputational damage, but how political policy and consequently economies progress, with serious implications for trade and for banks. In this chapter, we look more broadly at the psychological background for confirmation bias, the reason it's impacting more than just those who are already bought in, how this affects global reputation systems and what we can do about it.

Why Is Critical Thinking so Hard?

We'll start with some basics. We all know that your truth isn't our truth, and yet we all know that our own truth is right. We don't notice ourselves not questioning information because it comes from trusted sources, even if experience has told us that those sources sometimes get it wrong. We are so confident in our sources and our opinions that we readily back up our opinions by quoting those sources as authoritative. We know that our information is based on sound research, facts and statistics, even if we haven't seen that research. You know that your information is based on hard evidence and direct experience, even if it's not your experience. And yet our views are completely different; we can't all be right.

People aren't designed to know what's happening on the other side of the world. They're not designed to live in hundred-million person societies and work as a nation; rather, they're wired to bypass rationale when they're told something by someone they trust, based on the assumption that the someone has earned that trust. That's part of the problem.

Man is a herd animal.[1] We're psychologically programmed to work in small units characterised by the hunter-gatherer unit of 5–50 people, which we've existed in for most of our biological history. This unit doesn't preclude learning, but it relies heavily on received wisdom, where the older, more experienced animal passes on learning to the young. People are programmed to believe what their authority figures tell them, because it makes sound sense for survival. Don't eat that red thing. If you see that big brown thing, run. Don't walk on that. We're designed to understand, remember and believe these instructions without context and without explanation, because questioning leads to low survival rates. It makes sense both from a survival perspective and from an efficiency perspective; if we debated absolutely everything, we'd never get through all the information about the world that's out there.[2]

Herd animals live in a world where there's scarce food and competition with other herds for the same resources. Our norms, passed down to us by our tribal elders, also help us to identify who's "in" and who's "out" of the herd. Keeping our herd cohesive also means enforcing the norms we learn; another herd may look and smell like us, but we can tell they're foreign and therefore the enemy, because they hold different beliefs or speak differently from us. Questioning the origins of these norms and beliefs would be counterproductive, because it may leave us more open to accepting the other tribe's world view, which is expensive from an evolutionary perspective. Keeping the herd together guarantees its survival.

So rather than learning to build our own mental view of the world, which would be cumbersome and senselessly resource intensive, we learn to identify who to trust, and take instructions from them. But society has developed, grown and morphed beyond recognition, so your authority figures aren't your tribal leader and Shaman any more; they're people who you have been told are, or who you identify as, authority figures, many of whom don't know who you are and whom you will never meet. This is highly unusual in human evolutionary history.

How Do We Identify Authority Figures?

Our early authority figures are both traditional from an evolutionary perspective and relatively safe: your parents have your best interests at heart and will usually give you positive guidance, which may be full of mystery but of course you trust them completely. Other authority figures in early years are the adults around you and older siblings—again, usually responsible people who have your best interests at heart, sharing values and guidance in much the same way that human tribes have since their early evolution. But as society has developed, things have become more complicated.

The first characteristics of early society formation, regardless of geographical origin, are the maturing of codified faith and of government. These are both human constructs which emerge on the one hand to explain the world and define behavioural norms, and on the other to organise it and define social norms. Government leads to administration, which leads in turn to education, while faith leads to organised religion and facilitated rituals, which requires faith leaders. So, with origins in tribal wise women and Shamans, teachers and faith leaders emerge as society became more organised, and these are the second tier of authority figures most people encounter face to face.

Officially appointed teachers and faith leaders are usually doing things in your best interest, although with an unpublished agenda controlled by their organisation. As a herd animal seeking instructions for good behaviour, man is ideally programmed to subscribe to both, so this works pretty well, with societal norms being more or less consistently communicated.

We learn from our parents, teachers and faith leaders what is acceptable and "normal", based on the rules that they are given by our societal constructs. These norms become hard-coded as we develop and are some of the hardest beliefs for us to change, because of the early and repeated exposure we have to them. It has always been important to social animals to conform to the behaviours of their tribe, and as an intensely social animal, people do this extremely well. And on the whole, that's ok, although it does lead to societies with widely differing world outlooks emerging, whether from village to village or now, from country to country.

As societies scale, they become more complex and governments and faiths evolve, forming subtribes with alternate views even within societies, of what the "correct" form is, which again leads to divisions. Because these are based on pretty hard-coded beliefs which form part of our world views, we defend them strongly as part of how we define the world and, by extension, ourselves. Our tribal instinct kicks in when we meet people with opposing views, reverting to our primal "kill or be killed" instincts where anyone who isn't part of our tribe is, by definition, a threat to be eliminated.

Complex societies with government then build two other subsets designed to control behaviour which are not so positive: military and communications media. Typically, early versions of both are directly controlled by central government (or in some cases by organised religion) although as society matures, communications media usually devolves quickly to civil control, following a short struggle by central authorities to retain control. Armies tend to be more closely controlled by central authorities, largely because of the threat they pose to the central authorities when not closely controlled. However, of these two groups, it's easy to see that in democratic societies, communications media has more direct impact on people by impacting their belief systems through building versions of the truth which are approved by central authorities, so even where communications media is not owned or directly controlled by central authorities, they usually impose standards on communications agencies to ensure the output is controlled in some way.

This control is generally viewed as a negative thing both by the communications agencies and populations, who rightly believe that a tightly controlled media will filter information that they otherwise want to see. So, control of communications agencies tends to be more relaxed in countries that value democracy and participate in free elections, which recently started to include the majority of countries in the world by a narrow margin. Even in democracies, however, politicians have always been aware of, and frightened by, the power of communications media. They represent key authority figures to anyone with access to media sources—perhaps that's why the *BBC* is known popularly as "Auntie"—and are usually introduced well before exposure to other authority figures, so have a disproportionately high level of influence on how we think.

This, then, also explains how we self-select our authority figures from media and politics—largely passed down to us well before we have the opportunity to apply personal judgement to our choices. Consequently, we generally choose not just the politics and religion, but the news sources used by our parents, which in turn were passed on from their parents. Bubble, anyone? We may select to review some other sources as we age, but are most likely to remain loyal to the newspaper or, nowadays, news channel we saw across the kitchen table at breakfast, and to choose other sources that reinforce or to some extent echo the agenda it laid out.

What Does This Mean for Our Modern Reputation Systems?

The proliferation of information disseminated by news sources causes some challenges to our 50-person society brains.

Globalisation

As we said above, people aren't designed to know what's going on in the next village, let alone the other side of the world: it's a question of context. We all view events that are happening globally through a filter of our own experience, our own values and our own beliefs about what should be normal. When we see information about events that are happening elsewhere, we have a choice to empathise/relate by mentally putting ourselves in that situation, or to regard the activity as "other"—belonging to a different tribe with different values. In many ways, the more we see about other societies, the less likely we are to relate or empathise, in stark contrast to how our ancestors would experience other cultures, which would be either by visiting different places, where a more full experience is more likely to result in some empathy, or by meeting individuals from other places on "home turf", where they're again humanised.

We're more likely to see people as "of" rather than "other" if we can see something in them that we already have—the obvious ones being if they look like us or speak the same language. But even if we have this connection and empathy, we're likely to misjudge by plastering our own world view on top of other cultures. This can result in some really odd things happening—firstly, a very skewed view of what happens in other cultures, because we only see reports of unusual events (that's the very nature of news) and that is our only experience of those cultures; secondly, forming ill-informed and often culturally inappropriate assumptions about other cultures, as we apply our own values. Thirdly, we dehumanise people in cultures where we can't or don't want to understand the context, which by extrapolation we sometimes start to apply to other cultures which would otherwise be closer to us, and lastly, we apply the same emotional responses to things that are real and things that are made up—we don't just mean "fake news"; we can also have very real responses to situations and societies that exist only in a film or a book. Consider the response when "War of the Worlds" was first broadcast—although not the mass panic of legend, many listeners were concerned that the aliens were really landing. Meanwhile, many fans of soap operas discuss the lives of the characters with genuine sympathy and concern, ignoring the real beggars in their own streets.

In summary, not only does global media reach cause us to dehumanise other people, we can actually develop *more empathy for fictional characters than for real people* and lose our ability to distinguish fact from fiction.

Saturation

We're now bombarded with information from many more sources than we're designed to experience, i.e. our immediate tribe members and environment. We are all, every day, receiving so many conflicting messages and influences that we can't actually process the information. As is often quoted, an average person in the seventeenth century would have access to as much information in their lifetime as is contained in a day's edition of the *New York Times* popularly attributed to Theodore Roszak. We simply can't process that much information effectively, which leads to us taking even more shortcuts than we are programmed to take. This means we find it harder and harder to apply any kind of critical thinking to information that's reaching us; bear in mind that we're hard-wired to believe what authority figures tell us, without asking questions. So any authority figure (press in this case) is likely to be believed without question—as long as it's one of your selected authority figures, obviously!

Hidden Agenda

While you may choose media for a number of reasons, and usually select ones which agree with elements of your world view, the media, fictional or factual, may be driven by a set of values aiming to find additional buy-in among populations for a number of reasons—and they're not going to tell you what those reasons are. The more remote the source of information, the less likely you are to understand the underlying cultural values or to recognise the agenda driving the content. News sources don't declare their methods and generally assume a local audience with certain cultural values, and they're under pressure to keep wordcount down so usually give a very stripped-down message with no available background. So you may find yourself consuming content that's completely divorced from its context which, again, makes it harder to separate truth from fiction.

That was disturbing when new sources were all push—being controlled by boards and investors with a particular agenda, as they overwhelmingly are. However, with the rise of the internet and in particular social media, we've seen further rapid evolution of how opinions are formed, consumed and internalised by people.

The Rise of Plebocratic Reputation Systems

The proliferation of global media sources has now exploded, and opinion formers are as likely to be individuals as news and media outlets. Microcommunities of opinion formers can give rise to global beliefs with no particular evidence or rationale, other than some citations supporting their assertions which may be completely false—"fake news". This gives us a whole new dimension to dissemination and filtering of information, with impacts unique to the connected information age.

Popular Conspiracy Theories, Rumours and Falsehoods

While there have always been conspiracy theories, these have in the past been relatively isolated to particular special interest communities or political/religious groups; only since the arrival of the information revolution have we seen a new phenomenon, where information with no valid source or attribution is shared so much that it gains traction and validation, often being picked up as valid by genuine news agencies.

Why is this? Surely news agencies should be able to root out fake news? The information age presents two challenges to this: one is that the news gains validation by the critical mass of often quite sane, intelligent people crediting it. The other problem is that it's subject to the same attention-span problem we described above, and with news agencies under increased pressure to reduce staffing and increase output, corners are cut; a story which appears to have backing from respectable sources and which confirms the news organisation's values can appear to be genuine, is reported by the genuine news agency and then gains even more credibility because of this.

Non-news Becoming News

Just as we empathise more with fictional characters than real people in terrible situations outside of our experience, people have always responded more to human interest stories where they can directly relate. The corollary of this is the phenomenon we've seen of "vloggers" attracting huge audiences just because of their ordinariness. See also cat videos, motivational memes, out-of-context quotes from dead actors, etc. Your newsfeeds and, as above, your news outlets, are now flooded with non-news which also has an impact on your values and sympathies, and creates new authority figures for you who, unlike a news outlet, are creating content primarily because they're bored, vain or in it for the money, with no regulation or need to tell the truth.

Spread of Fundamentalism and Other Cranky Belief Systems

Give anywhere the right conditions and a committed enough religious goofball, and they'll develop a cult. But for those cults to become truly widespread takes the internet and a whole load of people who can't apply critical judgement to what they read, or more accurately, don't want to. Fundamentalist Christian America and ISIS are both examples of extremist communities that have been able to spread and consolidate influence thanks to firstly, communication between like-minded communities and secondly, the ability to recruit undecided or just bored/uncritical individuals using the same methods used to spread conspiracy theories.

Misquoting, Misappropriation and Misinterpretation

With information cut to short sound bites and the massive volume of information available, traditional editorial standards have eroded in mainstream press and never arisen at all in popular internet celebrities, who feel free to quote sources at random, use any random picture that looks as though it backs up their point, and misquote/misinterpret quotes they're publishing. Twitter has dragged us to new lows and rapid-fire behaviour, such as that illustrated by Sean Spicer retweeting a satirical tweet about himself with approval, opens up opportunities for ridicule.

Trolling

Exposure to the internet now means exposure to everyone's opinion, and recent studies have shown those people aren't actually sad loners living in their parents' basements, but really ordinary people who feel free to share their less pleasant opinions online. Many of these opinions are divisive, tribal and instinctual, driven by disappointment, hate or depression, often combined with alcohol.

Once written, they're visible for everyone to see and draw in even balanced people to argue, push back and create partisan divisions, reinforcing further the beliefs of the trolls. We've seen an explosion of this as America, starkly divided along (mostly) political lines, screams at each other over the internet every time Trump does something, but it has been around for a while. The obvious negative impact of this is a lot of upset people, but it also leads to reinforcement of the barriers between camps and growth of the links between like-minded people, trolls or otherwise.

Removal of Filters and Barriers

There's traditionally been a curtain between public figures and the rest of the world. Their opinions, speeches and lives are only visible as dictated by themselves, their publicity machine and their speechwriters. Obviously, there have been paparazzi for some time now, and this has also exploded, but what we hadn't had before Twitter was their unfiltered voices. Of course, many still use third parties to curate their accounts, but we can now get direct insights from sources as diverse as Stephen Fry, Stephen Hawking,

Oprah Winfrey, Ellen Degeneres and, oh yeah, Donald Trump. Of course, you can see this as a good thing or a bad thing, but it changes the relationship between authority figures and populations into appearing to be much more direct and intimate, and potentially having greater influence as a result.

All of this leads to significant confusion between what's real, what's validated and what's fake. If trusted news sources are picking up fake news and reporting it as true, even a few glitches will undermine people's trust in their sources and lead them further towards sources that reinforce their own confirmation bias. News sources of all flavours are now saturated with advertising that leads to click-bait of all types, so you can find yourself led from a well-researched, validated source to fake news in a couple of clicks—advertising algorithms track your choice and present you with more of the same. Hence the creation of bubbles.

Plebocracy Bias

Worse, though, is the impact we see on political, and then media rhetoric, caused by these bubbles. While it doesn't uniquely apply to politics, politicians in elected democracies are in a fundamentally unstable position; they can't get anything done unless people vote for them. So, they tend to prioritise getting votes over other qualities such as honesty or doing things they believe in, and it's hard to see how they could behave otherwise. Getting votes means supporting policies which people will vote for, which may mean supporting policies they may not personally believe in, for the sake of votes. While this seems dishonest, it's easy to justify in that a politician can't do anything good at all if they don't get elected. But we won't go down that route. Of course, in some cases, hopefully many, politicians' beliefs match their policies, but it's not necessary or universal. You can apply a similar narrative to popular media figures, who also rely on ratings for their continued career success.

Now, look at this through the lens of popular culture. If politicians or pundits believe they'll be supported for policies and views which are getting a loud airing on social media, as their researchers tell them they will, that means that all of the bias we've just described is directly influencing policy formation. As we've seen, social media is used both to source and to influence opinion by political parties and news outlets. We've seen some dramatic reversals of policy in politicians, media sources and political parties, partly fuelled by politicians influencing media and social media to grow support, either through their own social media teams or, increasingly, through sophisticated orchestrated campaigns exemplified by Cambridge Analytica; but also by fringe or semi-fringe elements tapping into the zeitgeist and getting enormous support because they understand how to tap into people's tribal instincts and fear of outsiders. It's happening all over the world, with outcomes of recent elections in both the UK and USA, as we've seen, reflecting social media sentiment more closely than predictions based on traditional research and, conversely, being subject to manipulation by social media.

So, if politicians change their policies and newspapers change their politics, what does that mean for the rest of us? Clearly, it means the rules will change—at the moment towards protectionism and antiglobalisation, with as yet unknown consequences for banks and the economy as a whole. Deregulation under Trump could be a very good thing for the banks, at least in the short term, but not such a great thing for consumers, while what's going to happen after Brexit is (at the time of writing) anyone's guess. Uncertainty, as we know, is bad for the economy (although good for the price of gold, or is that Bitcoin these days?) However, the effect on people's beliefs and values is even more profound.

People are remarkably adaptable—that's one of their key success factors. We all share a weird combination of optimism bias the belief that things will go right, despite all evidence to the contrary, paranoia the belief that everyone else has a hidden agenda to undermine us, however uninteresting we are and confirmation bias, which allows us to change our beliefs given the right circumstances. It means that, just like politicians, we're all prepared to overturn our beliefs if there's enough pressure to do so. Not evidence—in most cases, a well-reasoned argument is no match for strongly held belief—but, as we see authority figures starting to use different rhetoric, however much we may disagree with it, a primal instinct tells us to believe. What starts as a nagging doubt (paranoia) in our dearly held belief can grow to acceptance of an alternate viewpoint as valid (optimism bias) and, eventually, to our sharing that viewpoint (confirmation bias). As we said at the top, argument doesn't change people's views, but authority figures can, usually slowly but surely. The other thing that changes people's views is personal experience, and with social media, it's becoming easier to conflate someone else's personal experience, whether told through Twitter or viral memes, with our own, thanks to the same inbuilt survival instincts.

To an extent, this is how societal beliefs and norms have always evolved; free thinkers disagree with received wisdom, some people get angry about it, more people start to notice and then the politicians and media sit up and do something. This is normal and usually benefits society, although feelings, egos and occasionally people get hurt on the way; but what's different is that, nowadays, those free thinkers aren't necessarily tackling real social ills. Thinking about historical populist reversals of policy, for everything from slavery to disenfran-chisement to civil rights, opposition movements had access to, and reasonably clear understanding of, the facts of what they were trying to overturn. Laws were explained, often by written media such as pamphlets or newspapers, or by people who had a good understanding of them, to other influencers.

What's different now is that it's so hard to separate fact from assertion, that many people are wilfully allowing themselves to be led into false correla-tions. The bewilderment in Sweden over Donald Trump's extraordinary 2017 statement about immigrant trouble in Sweden is a great example—Sweden has lots of immigrants, and reported rapes have increased at the same time. That makes it easy to draw the entirely wrong conclusion. In this case, the reporting of rapes has increased because the Swedish tightened up their defi-nition of rape (which now includes what some, including Donald Trump, may describe as "grabbing") and therefore more are reported. In fact, statis-tics show that immigrants tend to commit fewer crimes, so crime statistics are more likely to decrease with higher immigration. Of course, that wasn't reported on Fox News, leading to Trump's erroneous belief—which is now firmly shared by a huge number of his supporters, in the teeth of any evi-dence to the contrary beyond a deliberately misleading media report.

And that is leading to people voting against their own best interests, because they're voting for something which they are told is in their inter-ests, but will ultimately undermine their own position—such as rural Republicans opposing the ACA because it's "Socialist", without considering that the change will impact them directly, or UK pensioners living in Spain voting for Brexit. In most cases, the rhetoric is about "taking back control" from some group that's perceived as a threat (that's the paranoia hard at work), a lazy but effective alternative for facts. The facts are that we're not going to get back control; we never were in control and whoever we vote for, that's not going to change. But it makes a good sound bite.

So, What Can We Do About It?

The solution is both personal and systemic. Personal change may seem hope-less in the onslaught of mass information and apparently endless confusion, but it should be possible for every one of us who is a leader, which is nearly all of us in one capacity or another, to role model behaviours where we ques-tion our own long-held beliefs and to demonstrate that this is a strength. We're always coming across things we long believed to be true and then found out weren't—small things like why you shouldn't put cooked food on the compost heap or whether glass is a liquid (ok, not so small if you're a physicist but relatively unimportant to a Fintech CEO). It's important to be able to apply the same process of critical thinking to the big things too; see new evidence, don't dismiss it out of hand because it doesn't fit your beliefs, evaluate it and, if appropriate, adapt your belief system. But the critical thing here is to evaluate it rationally and scientifically, weighing available evidence, rather than just taking an authority figure's word for it.

In addition, we need to put ourselves in check when we find ourselves telling stories to back up our gut feelings. People are very, very good at this, and clever people are even better; that's why it can be really dangerous to believe someone just because they're clever, and why it's really important to question yourself more if you are! Daniel Kahneman in his seminal book Thinking, Fast and Slow[3] describes the mechanisms behind this, but to summarise, your gut feel about something, which is strongly influenced by your belief systems, tells your brain what to think, and your brain then goes and cherry-picks information to support the position you've chosen to hold. This is confirmation bias in action. Questioning your stories, as well as your beliefs, is a key element of critical thinking.

On a systemic level, as we've said elsewhere, we now have the opportunity to implement reputation systems that are agnostic of opinion and solely based on facts. Technology is available to implement contextualised trust systems for organisations, individuals, governments, you name it. Blockchain and Machine Learning give us a powerful opportunity to build a future where we can trust reputation systems; that doesn't invalidate opinion systems, but let's learn to separate true reputation from opinion; keep your opinions and beliefs to support your identity, but when it comes to evaluating an argument, have access to a source where you know you can find the truth.

Through the role modelling of critical thinking and making it easy to distinguish reputation systems based on fact rather than opinion, we can start to turn the tide away from this apparently inevitable rush towards plebocracy and the serious consequences it could have for our economy, our environment and our society.

Conclusion

We're herd animals struggling to make sense of the society we created, with a combination of unprecedented access to information and primal mechanisms for analysing it. Although tools are available to filter and interpret information, we're hard-wired to believe things, for very sound evolutionary reasons, that may not be founded on fact. The rise of modern platform reputation systems, largely unregulated and with limited curation, has allowed belief systems based on limited or misleading information to take root across the globe.

Addressing this isn't straightforward—it will need both personal commitment and provision of reputation systems based on fact. At hiveonline, we're leading the charge to address the latter; it will take all of us to address the first. That's a personal choice and may be one people choose not to take, but we hope this chapter has helped raise a few questions.

Notes

1. Shpancer, N., Ph.D. (2010, December). You Are a Conformist (That Is, You Are Human). *Psychology Today.* https://www.psychologytoday.com/blog/insight-therapy/201012/you-are-conformist-is-you-are-human. Accessed 29 December 2017.
2. Cialdini, R. (2009, June). *Influence: The Psychology of Persuasion.* Collins Business Essentials.
3. Kahneman, D. (2013, April). *Thinking, Fast and Slow.* Farrar, Straus and Giroux.

Further Reading

Armstrong, K. (2006). *The Great Transformation.* Atlantic Books.
Coates, J. (2012). *The Hour Between Dog and Wolf.* Fourth Estate.
Diamond, J. (1999). *Guns, Germs and Steel.* W. W. Norton & Company.

19

New Approaches to Identity and Authentication

In this chapter, we explore concepts of customer authentication and identity, arguing that in the ecosystem economy we need to take a fresh look at what we mean by a customer, break the traditional human-based paradigm and start adopting more community-based trust systems for validation and authentication.

Background to Customer Authentication and Authorisation

Customer authentication is central to the trust that banks and other service providers maintain on your behalf. They need to know that you are who you say you are for their security, but primarily for yours. Authentication is your guarantee the bank or service isn't going to give away your money, your data or your stuff, without your permission. Authentication processes check your credentials to ensure you're the person who is authorised to access the service in question.

Regulators also require banks and other institutions not only to know who their customers are, but also to ensure they're the right sort of people, to be authorised to use appropriate services. Know your customer (KYC) for banks includes credit checks for the bank's security, and also nationality checks for individuals, background checks for officers of companies and so on, to ensure that the people they're dealing with aren't involved in fraud, terrorism or other criminal activities.

© The Author(s) 2018
S. Blakstad and R. Allen, *FinTech Revolution*,
https://doi.org/10.1007/978-3-319-76014-8_19

Who you are, where you come from and where you live will also affect not just authorisation levels but also how the bank treats you for some jurisdictions—for example, US persons (which is a broad definition covering a lot of different scenarios) are subject to US taxes regardless of where money is earned, and banks everywhere are obliged to withhold certain types of money, such as tax on interest on accounts, for these persons. Some people will also be subject to authorisation restrictions when registered as officers in a business, such as politically important people, who may put the bank at greater risk of exposure to scandal if there's a fraud.

Typically, you will be subject to authorisation and authentication at two distinct points: one, where your relationship with the service provider is initiated, to validate that you're a fit person to have that relationship and who you say you are, and two, when you transact with that service provider, to validate that you're who you say you are. There may also be further checks as the status of your relationship or something about you changes—for example, you may have opened an account a long time ago, but subsequently moved to a country with different tax laws, or become an officer in a business, a politician, etc., which you may not have been when you opened your account in the first place.

As an individual, you have a one-to-one relationship with your bank, your telco or your department store and these organisations see you as an individual human; today, each holds a copy of your personal data and uses this to determine your authorisation levels and to authenticate you. If you have a joint account, one of you will be the primary signatory, again as an individual human and both of you will be subject to validation based on who you are as people. Even if you have a business account or operate on behalf of your organisation, your bank will still authenticate you as an individual, while nearly all authentication systems today are based on validating that the individual accessing the service is definitely who they say they are.

This makes good sense: you can't duplicate, distribute or corrupt the base unit of humanity, the individual person. It does cause some problems associated with individual humans. People forget what they've told the service (favourite pet, anyone?), they forget passwords, they wear chunky rings that confuse hand topography scanners, they get wet and can't work their thumbprint authentication, they change status or location without telling the bank, they get hit on the head, and eventually, they die. But it's still the same base unit and services have developed to accommodate the fallibilities of humans.

The problem it has created today though is that many individuals have a proliferation of identities, with multiple organisations and platforms holding the same, or similar information about them, some of which is likely to be inaccurate or out of date. Multiple profiles mean multiple passwords and multiple points of failure, as well as multiple potential security vulnerabilities, with all these institutions holding raw personal data. Meanwhile, a large number of the world's population, estimated at 1.1 billion, have no formal identity, while for the world's 2 billion unbanked, identity is unreliable and fails to give access to services.

National ID systems are a good example of how to manage individuals' authentication identity more effectively and reducing the risk of human fallibility in remembering passwords, by creating a convenient ID and single sign-on for everything from banking to health to tax payments and land registry—Denmark's CPR number[1] is so ubiquitous you can't join a gym or sign up for electricity without one, and all services are managed with a single identity and single password. However, these are all currently restricted to individual nations and, as we explore below, many individuals have increasingly international profiles, while others fail to qualify for base identification criteria, especially the world's most disadvantaged.

In today's connected economy and the platform world, things are more complicated. There is now a proliferation of instances of personal data maintained by commercial institutions, platforms and communities still using personal data to create analogous identities for the same individual, with varying quality and a growing struggle to maintain data integrity. Individuals may be working in multiple countries or be part of distinct ecosystems in multiple countries, for example within a multinational organisation. And now as people and organisations increasingly become elements of the wider ecosystem, the very definition of identity is becoming less clear.

Who's the Customer?

Who Are You?

We tend to think of our identity as just ourselves, stripped down to our basic humanity, but studies have shown that our concept of ourselves is heavily influenced by the stuff around us—obvious things like job, wealth and status, the tribes we belong to, etc., but also physical things like what we wear, where we live and the things we have. You may identify as "an American", "a scientist", "a Chelsea fan" or "an opera nut", but you probably also identify as "an Apple person", "an Android person" or "a Windows person". You may also identify with brands such as clothing brands and car brands.

And as the things you own become smarter, some of them take on aspects of your identity, including decision making; your personal identity is expanding. This isn't new; hundreds of years ago people were delegating authority to act autonomously on their behalf to things they owned, but in the Middle Ages those things were people. A feudal overlord would have been quite comfortable with having autonomous economically active entities in his portfolio of serfs, because that's what serfs were for.[2] But in the modern age, people (generally) don't own other people, so the concept of the individual human has become much more closely paired with identity and identity management. That's changing now, as the things you own become more autonomous.

Your phone is already a critical part of your identity. You're statistically more likely to be reading this chapter on your phone than any other device, while your route to accessing it was controlled by algorithms designed to feed you personalised news, delivered on your phone. Your decision to buy this book was made by you, but the experience that led you to make that decision was delivered to you on your phone (or, with decreasing likelihood, your PC). Your phone, and information delivered through it, is independently shaping your behaviour. And, in the not too distant future, your car, your fridge and other devices will be going further than this, becoming economically active on your behalf.

It's 2021. Your self-driving car has dropped you off at work, taken the kids to school and then decides which gas station to go to fill itself up, based on relative prices and distance. Perhaps it chooses one that has a carwash because it's a while since it had a shower. Filled up and shiny, it plugs itself into Uber or Lyft and starts earning money, until you need it again. It's doing quite well via Uber, because you don't really go to the office much, after all you're working mostly via AR from your home office, and only go in because it's nice to see people in the flesh occasionally. So the car suggests it's time to rethink your economic strategy—should you be getting a new model that carries more passengers to capitalise on more ride sharing profits or conversely move to a collective ownership or subscription model instead?

The fridge, meanwhile, is trawling the online grocery stores for better quality meat. It knows you don't mind paying a bit more, but it needs to get a supplier who can guarantee decent shelf life, because you have a habit of letting things go off, even when it gives you relevant recipes—some aspects of your behaviour haven't changed that much! It also knows if it clubs together with three of the other fridges in your road, you can get a pretty good quantity discount and it can organise the distribution logistics. It's having a bit of an argument with the thermostat about the underfloor heating though, it's using more power than it forecast in the cooling system and you don't really need it to be that warm, so you will be asked to arbitrate.

These devices are making independent decisions and transactions, on your behalf. Needing a thumbprint or a PIN code to authorise transactions would add friction to your personal ecosystem, which by its very nature only works because you're not intervening at a transactional level. So they have become economically active autonomous extensions of your identity and need some other mechanism for telling the bank, the supermarket, the gas station and Uber that they are part of you. IoT devices are already proving an Achilles' heel for hackers, so security and authentication both need to be robust, without recourse to traditional mechanisms.

Do You Care if Your Customer Is Human?

This leads to an interesting challenge in traditional identity thinking. As we've said above, identity and humanity are currently tightly linked—every transaction that's performed today has to be authorised by a human, either directly as in typical B2C transactions or via a business rule that a real person has approved, such as a direct debit or a bulk ordering system for B2B. But our 2021 learning devices are building their own business rules, independently of you—you haven't told the fridge directly that you're comfortable paying a bit more buying better quality, it's drawn this conclusion from observing your behaviour data. That means, as a retailer, you're providing goods and services based on a decision made by a machine, independently of any explicit business rules or instruction from a human. And as a bank, you're facilitating that transaction with no human authorisation.

At the other end of this equation is the "I'm not a robot" challenge. As machines get smarter, it will become harder and harder to detect machines posing as humans. The two big headaches are in the traditional touchpoints—relationship initiation and transaction authorisation. Current barriers—typically pictures that humans can process and machines find more challenging—will cease to be effective as machines get better at picture recognition, and they're creating additional friction for real people as they get more sophisticated. People will continue to design new checks as machines get more sophisticated, but there will be a tipping point when the additional friction becomes unacceptable for humans.

Banks, in particular, try to deal with this challenge by putting robust barriers to entry into their system, so that only real humans can transact with them and see their data. However, the barriers tend to be at the peripheries of the system, leaving them open to massive attacks once that periphery has been breached. The operating model of most banking online services is still very close to that of the traditional bank with the iron grille and a vault with a big combination lock in the back—they're hard to get through, but once you're in, all the money (or data in this case) is wide open to attack.

Given that it's now possible to apply business rules that can control access and authentication to services and products, while tracking behaviour for known and predictable patterns, banks can learn from platform approaches to matching customers with services or products, to apply appropriate access based on behaviours and apply authentication at the point appropriate to that service. More of this below.

Who Is Trust for?

As we've said above, trust is for the bank, institution or service giving you access to its services, and it's for you. But consumers/customers of trust have different needs, which should lead to different rules for different consumers, although beyond strata of authentication, this is rarely the case today. Here are some examples (Table 19.1).

Looking at these examples, the consumer of trust isn't always that interested in who you are. Yes, if you're the customer opening a bank account or the refugee, some of the guarantees are associated with *who* you are, but if you're a service provider such as a restaurant, or even a small business borrower in the context scenarios we've given, nobody's actually interested in whether you, John Smith, are or are not from a particular country, of a particular age or even what your credit history is; the important question for those trust consumers is, in the *context* in which they are supporting you, are you trustworthy?

The Big Identity Question

Banks have always struggled with the problem of a "single view of the customer". In short, the problem is that individuals can be customers, companies can be customers, and individuals can represent companies, charities, consortia, funds, etc. Organisations are the original distinct ecosystems in this sense: single entities made up of multiple actors, many of whom can represent the organisation. Again, this makes sense in the old world, because there's always a human (or multiple humans) benefitting from the economic

Table 19.1 Trust perspectives

Who's the trust about?	Who's the trust for?	What validation is needed?
Person opening a bank account	The bank, the government, the bank's shareholders, the customer	Prove you're not a bad risk; prove you're not a terrorist; prove you're not a criminal
Refugee entering a country	The government	Prove you're not a terrorist; prove you're in genuine need; prove you're not going to take unfair advantage of benefits
Builder	The customer	Prove you're going to deliver good quality on time; prove you're going to complete the job; prove you're not going to go bankrupt
Restaurant	The customer	Prove you're not going to poison the customer; prove your food is good quality/organic/vegan …
Auditor	The customer; the government/tax authorities	Prove you're competent and qualified; prove you're going to deliver good quality on time
Small business borrower	The bank	Prove you're likely to pay back the money; prove you can probably afford to pay it back

activity of a company (the beneficiaries). There are further complications for banks because they hold several different views of the customer—from a legal entity perspective, from a credit risk perspective, etc., all organised in different hierarchies, which exacerbates the problem.

Because the base unit is a human, though, this creates a fundamental challenge—an individual may be both a person (Retail customer) and a company official (e.g. CFO of a company). As a bank, from a KYC perspective, you might be happy for them to be a Retail customer but less happy about them being a CFO, because they're married to a senior politician and therefore are a person of interest (i.e. potentially subject to corruption, etc.). And that's before you even start looking at the problem of presenting a single view of the bank from the customer's perspective. Today we manage this by granting different levels of authorisation to different individuals—as a departmental manager, I may have authority to sign off EUR 100,000 and as a sales rep, I have a company credit card with a EUR 3000 limit; all of these authorisations need to be associated with individuals, and those individuals authenticated.

As we move into the ecosystem economy, it becomes even harder to maintain a single view of the entity. The top-down hierarchy, still embedded in companies, is becoming less clear as the edges of service, customer relationships, data ownership and data processing, traditionally ring-fenced within organisations, start to crumble. Beneficiaries become members of a distinct ecosystem, benefiting from networks and platforms, more than from direct sales which can be neatly summed and divided into cost of goods sold vs revenues from sales (Fig. 19.1).

By extension, communities have identities as economically active entities. Collectives and community organisations such as football clubs and choirs have been around for centuries, while crowdfunding and fractional ownership are growing the economic clout of communities and moving them closer to mainstream business paradigms. As these communities grow and collaborate further, more ecosystem-based economic entities emerge, with their own capacity for decisions being made by multiple, instead of individual humans, together with opportunities for the application of AI to those decision-making processes. A good example is the Danish banking organisation, SDC, which supplies core banking to its 120 customer-members. Those members collectively make decisions relating to its investment portfolio and in turn fund the portfolio.

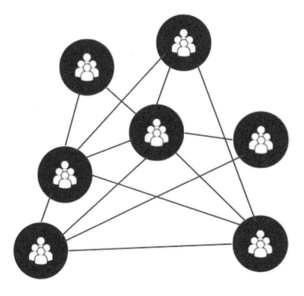

Fig. 19.1 Community ecosystem

A consortium of small builders, who may have met over a trust platform such as hiveonline, will have no central leadership and be managed via the ecosystem platform, where decisions are made by consensus and business rules rather than individuals. For example, they may agree to set up a contract that executes only when seven teams have agreed that they can put the time and sufficient money into a particular project; on execution of the business rule, hiveonline presents evidence to the bank that they're committed and gives the indelible trust record that demonstrates creditworthy behaviour for all members; the bank then decides to grant a loan based on its own business logic and the contract executes the setup of the job with no need for human intervention. This sort of conditional, collective decision making that is traditionally corralled and managed by human representatives, is increasingly being facilitated by platforms and business logic.

The End of Human-Based Identity?

The human-based identity paradigm makes sense only as long as individual humans are the only entities capable of making decisions; regulators will quickly need to decide how to handle this scenario, which equates to extending personal identity beyond humans, to the things that they own or to the broader community, and agreeing protocols for security and authentication that can be used in practice by these things. Once we start developing paradigms of identity as a collective, non-human or distinct ecosystem-based concept, we can also start applying authentication that is more robust, less subject to hacking and more appropriate for the modern era.

To do this, several things need to change. First, how we manage authentication; taking the human out of the equation means using different approaches and technology, and while biometric identification is likely to retain a key position in frictionless identification of a human individual, we think that cryptography will replace passwords and that behaviour signatures will start to replace biometrics, as the distinct ecosystem identity becomes the standard unit. We describe some emerging paradigms supporting this movement below. The fundamental change that's needed, however, is in regulation and how regulators view identity, which in turn is tied up with legal concepts of possession, data protection and in particular, consumer protection. We are already seeing regulators thinking about these identity challenges, but it's very early days.

It's likely that, as with most new paradigms, changes in practice in response to evolving customer needs will outpace the development of the regulations needed to govern them effectively. As with all emerging paradigms, this will leave early adopters exposed to poor practice and almost certainly, a lack of consensus on standards for addressing these concerns. RegTech is likely to lead the debate on many of these challenges, and the answers may be driven more by the available solutions, than by the needs of customers and communities.

Barriers to Entry in the Ecosystem and Platform World

Facebook, LinkedIn and Twitter, the megaplatforms, couldn't go without a mention. They're part of the losing battle to maintain relationships only with humans, and face the same challenges of customer identity as banks, which is already leading to some strange compromises. For example, all have some sort of facility for companies to set up versions of their platform offering as though they were individuals; however, Twitter treats the company as a person, whereas LinkedIn and Facebook treat it as a company, allowing multiple administrators who are real people. None have really nailed what they mean by a company vs a person in the context of the page setup, while regardless of the paradigm, they require page owners to be real people, and spend a lot of money cleaning up the data.

To illustrate, it's still possible for an individual to set up multiple pages—all you need is an online identity, of which most people have several. Consequently, people set up pages on Facebook for their cats, infants, hobbies and so forth, and while Facebook is constantly cleaning up the data, the scale of the challenge is huge. The problem is that your Facebook credentials become an online identity, providing a level of authentication, which can be used to validate that you're a person, even if you aren't, and give access to further online services as though you are a person. We all know someone whose cat has a Facebook page, and as that identity ages, it wields quite a lot of online power. Let's assume you wanted to set up an AirBnB account, which requires both national documentation and an online identity. The sockpuppet Facebook or LinkedIn page you set up 8 years ago gives a strong level of confidence that your fake ID belongs to a genuine person.

As with banks' identity and authentication management, turning the problem round and assuming an online identity does not necessarily equate to a real person, opens up a much more manageable scenario. The fact is that there is no one-to-one relationship between people and online identities, any more than there is between people and bank accounts, or people and mobile phones. Accepting this as a starting point allows us to design authentication and service access to respond to this paradigm, and to apply adoption barriers where they are needed, at the point of service delivery, rather than as an entry point to online identities.

This, then, raises the question of where the barriers to entry to a system should lie; these platforms are fighting a losing battle trying to curate the quality of entrants. Instead, it's time to move away from trying to make the periphery more robust, and rather to apply more robust authentication, in particular, cryptographic keys and behavioural authentication, to restricted services, to demonstrate true trust and use this as a quality filter, accepting that there will always be fake identities, robots and genuine but non-human platform members.

Collective Ownership Identity Challenges

Companies, charities, clubs, residents' associations are all existing examples of communities which have a collective identity but individual officers with particular access rights (usually power of attorney on the bank account, or company-issued credit cards). The trust that goes with this level of access is today tied to the level of trust that company or organisation has in the role that person fulfils.

Then, there are communities with governance, shared goals and a shared trust authentication system operating as single entities in the distinct ecosystem-based identity paradigm. But just like in companies, not all collective ownership systems will be among communities of members with equal trust or transparency. Fractional ownership is a particular challenge, because in many cases, the justification for fractional ownership is the low liquidity of the participants, which in turn means that trust history may be patchy.

Peer-to-peer lending is another example of shared ownership where there may be a mismatch between the due diligence done on the lender and the needs of the receiver. Peer-to-peer lending platforms face challenges of quality curation vs. scale, and while this may be less of a problem for smaller, unregulated businesses, the greater the scale of the platform, the harder it is to manage the KYC on these small investors and the businesses they support.

Distinct Ecosystems as Trust Consumers

We already see examples of distinct ecosystems where there is no individual responsibility for decision making—collectives that require a critical mass of members to approve before an action can be executed, and where there is no single figure of authority with power to press the button. Our collective of builders is a good example of this; but as well as making economic decisions about the priorities or behaviours of the collective, this also extends to decision making about the trust barriers for suppliers to that distinct ecosystem. For fractional ownership or peer-to-peer lending, what are the acceptable criteria and how can this be validated? Traditionally, trust-based systems rely on third-party authorities and brokers, who hold trust evidence for individuals and organisations. But with the availability of platforms and new approaches to behavioural-based trust, is there an opportunity for communities to use trust records without recourse to the traditional means?

We've seen this in action to a large extent with platforms like AirBnB or Uber; in this case, reviews in sufficient volume provide a critical mass giving confidence, although it's not infallible; while a large distribution regresses to the mean, platform reviews are subject to crowd dynamics including plebocracy and early adopter advantage. However, if we can reduce or remove the bias, assuming both supplier and customer have access to a trust-based system that can translate behaviour patterns to scoring for benchmarking and for validation, there's an opportunity to move beyond traditional validation funnels towards a platform-based approach, with communities applying the same criteria they are expected to meet, protected by the protocols that guarantee veracity rather than by historical trust relationships with authoritative entities such as banks.

Borderless Platforms and Regulation

One of the most significant challenges facing regulators is the movement from national to cross-border value systems, such as multinational organisations and more recently, cryptocurrency. Regulations are, with very few exceptions, still defined by extensions of government within territories (national or bloc), and while compromises and workarounds have been developed such as passporting of licences and consensus agreements, even in today's corporate culture, national differences create significant barriers to operating as global entities:

- Socio-economic differences between countries: for most developing countries, ultra-stringent regulations can strangle development, yet more developed countries are rightly wary of doing business because of the opportunities for fraud. Governments and regulators in developing countries struggle to find a balance between policies that allow for growth and restricting opportunities to trade with richer economies.

- Cultural differences between countries/regions: Western regulations in general are geared towards protecting consumers, whereas in APAC and China in particular, regulators take a more economically focused perspective on protecting markets. While these viewpoints are not incompatible (regulators should and do consider both), the different weighting of these considerations can lead to policy differences which may be hard to reconcile.
- Different approaches to taxation: the most obvious of these is the FATCA[3] US tax withholding mentioned above; the USA taxes all US persons, regardless of where they are, whereas many other countries have reciprocal tax arrangements for nationals working abroad, or businesses with foreign branches. While this makes things very complicated for banks and tax authorities, these different approaches are also a significant barrier to true globalisation.

The ugly compromises that have developed are almost all bilateral deals between countries and/or blocs, specific to two or more regulatory regimes—for example, you pay tax in Sweden for the days you work there, while you would get the equivalent break from your Danish payments. Banking regulations in Denmark are more or less the same as elsewhere in the EU, with some sovereign differences, and because you're lucky enough to live and work in a region with a single central bank and more or less united rules, this works pretty well until you need to buy services or set up a legal entity outside the EU, when different regulations apply again.

Currency Without Borders?

The Euro has had some pretty rocky times and bad press,[4] trying to address the single currency/cross-border issue—even with a single central bank[5] and parliament, national economic differences have raised questions of whether cross-border currencies can survive. The US dollar is probably the most successful example of an unofficial global currency, historically valued because of its stability relative to local currencies in many countries and widely used as a reserve currency, but it's achieved this status without official policy to support it. Both local political developments[6] and the rise of cryptocurrencies are now putting that status at risk.

And despite growing acceptance in the mainstream and the emerging trend of central banks to propose issuing their own versions as we discussed above, cryptocurrencies are still subject to significant uncertainty, as they don't fit the traditional, country-based model. Governments and regulators are still unsure whether to treat them as currencies or as something else—tokens, or bonds, which as tradable digital assets, they could equally well be. We think the consensus is likely to move towards the "security" camp for tokens and the "currency" camp for cryptocurrencies, in particular as central banks start issuing sovereign cryptocurrencies, so for practical purposes their cryptos have to be equated with fiat currencies.

But this still doesn't address the cross-border challenge, and one of the reasons Bitcoin's value is so unstable is because of the lack of a single government/nation underpinning it. The value of sovereign fiat currencies is directly associated with the risk of that country defaulting, which is why central bank stability is so critical. Where there is no central bank, there's no guarantee and no stability beyond the collective mood of the market. While central bank-issued cryptos will not be subject to this instability (assuming they're pinned to local fiats), they are also subject to cross-border challenges.

Identity Without Borders

Similar challenges apply when we consider personal and organisational identity. While most people still live in a single country, possibly with occasional travel, and earn money in that same country, things are pretty simple; you pay tax to the local government, which supports you with the services paid for out of those taxes. You follow the local rules as they apply, whether regulatory, tax or social. The same applies to companies, which typically do business in small, local areas.

But that's changing as people and, more significantly, businesses, do work, create value and spend money across multiple countries. From the small supplier selling goods, to the business employing a "gig" economy worker, the internet has broadened the reach of even tiny enterprises and individuals to become truly global. For direct sales, the rules are straightforward, although far from consistent and usually not advantageous to either seller or customer, but for value creation and employment of people overseas, it becomes very complicated very quickly, as regulations are not designed to accommodate an increasingly flexible, global workforce. And it doesn't help the growing number of migrants, particularly those who have fled conflict situations and may have been forced to abandon official records of identity.

Many of the fundamental challenges are rooted in the fact that local services from schools and hospitals, to roads and infrastructure, are paid for by local taxes, so it's reasonable for governments to expect rewards for work produced and people employed in their own jurisdiction, but as these rules create massive additional complexity for individuals and businesses, is there an opportunity to rethink them at a community level, leveraging the broad range of cross-border services to allow business and worker communities to pool their contributions?

That sounds unduly restrictive, because we're still tied to the idea of an individual being synonymous with an identity. But if we accept, as we've said above, that individuals already have multiple identities, it's easier to visualise a scenario where any individual may belong to a number of different identity entities, with different roles. My identity as a parent would be firmly tied to my own family unit, while my identity as an employee of a global enterprise could be more sensibly associated with a community of Danish or Australian architects of global financial enterprises, for example. Similar to the approach of multi-entity distributed computing, this means that only necessary information needs to be exposed at the entity level, rather than every individual having to expose all their details, leading organisations to deal with the consequent complexity.

In effect, we do this today, allowing organisations to treat us as more or less homogeneous groups when it comes to salaries and tax in different jurisdictions. The strength of extending and formalising the community-based approach to communities and distinct ecosystems is that it both reduces complexity and allows for additional richness to be associated with that identity (e.g. certification, regulations) without having to manage these on an individual basis.

Evolving Approaches to Authentication

Most banks still perform their own checks, supported by agencies such as Experian[7] and similar third-party brokers who validate customer information to the banks, which they then hold on record as part of your customer data. This process is expensive and cumbersome, as several data sources need to be consulted for full checks and can lead to long customer on-boarding, especially where the customer is an organisation and checks have to be run against multiple individuals representing the organisation. It's also highly duplicative, as each bank typically gathers and holds the same data about a customer, even if that authentication has already been done by a different bank, with brokers and banks holding customer information on file, at risk of exposure to an attack

Third-party KYC has been available for many years, and while banks have been naturally reluctant to outsource such a critical business process, as the services offered have become more established, many are starting to use these services. The challenge for banks is often integrating these services into their legacy systems used in the customer on-boarding process, which typically spans many systems.

And the challenge for many individuals when facing these checks is that if you're not in the system already, establishing an identity is hard to impossible, meaning that access to financial services and utilities is beyond their reach. This applies to 2 billion of the world's population, adults who are unable to prove their records to sufficient standards and of whom 1.1 billion have no official identity papers such as birth certificates, severely restricting their ability to participate in business and financial activities.

Blockchain-Based Broker Authentication

Moving into the world of distributed ledger-based authentication, things are starting to change. Now broker services can offer cryptographic identity that builds up a profile of the customer,[8] based on traditional authentication data, creating a unique cryptographically encrypted token attesting, for example, whether an individual is creditworthy or meets other criteria. Banks and other interested parties can then compare encrypted data with the broker service's version, and the broker can then confirm with the tokens that the data were correct, without either the broker of the bank exposing the original data.

This has two main impacts—one that the checking only needs to be done once and can be used by multiple service providers, and secondly that the data are not exposed, which will make the customer more comfortable—the #1 worry that customers have when being authenticated is who's seeing their data. This clearly has advantages in protecting personal data and reduces the duplication effort, but still requires banks and other businesses to hold some personal data, with consequent challenges of duplication and deterioration of data quality. There's also the consideration that no encryption method yet invented has outlived the personal data it's protecting, so storage of even encrypted data on a public network is highly inadvisable, which means the trust authorities still need to maintain the personal records.

And it doesn't address the identity/financial inclusion challenge. The transparency and immutability of identification can, however, open up traditional records to individuals who may not have had access to them previously; land ownership recorded on the blockchain is an early use of trust records proving provenance, and the same can be achieved with personal records, supporting many of those without current certification.

Behaviour-Based Personas and Identity

Many Fintechs and telcos are starting to explore the financial inclusion problem with the development of behavioural profiling, typically using mobile phone records to demonstrate that a user is trustworthy. This is an extremely powerful method of identification; with the right algorithm, data such as geographical movements, phone calls, text messages and who your contacts are give a much richer and more accurate confidence score than many traditional methods and are far less open to fraud. Added to this, consider that 80% of the world's population have a mobile phone, including 1 billion of the 2 billion unbanked. Trials with homeless people in the USA (where 11% of the population lack formal identity) are already taking place[9] to provide a combination of identity, authentication and store of value on a blockchain combined with behavioural analysis, which could also help people without identity everywhere.

Behavioural-based identity does present challenges, in much the same way that other personal identification methods do; your behaviour signature is as unique as your thumbprint, so questions of identity protection are extremely relevant and as the technology is emerging, regulations will struggle to keep pace. Behavioural identification of this sort, while extremely appealing to an unbanked person trying to establish trust, is likely to be regarded as personal intrusion to a typical German consumer, for example.

We see the future of behavioural-based identity as one where the consumer, organisation or entity can choose different personae for different purposes, based on different types of behavioural identification data. For example, my "parent" persona, while also needing traditional "I'm a person" validation, could be linked to records of my children's birth, schooling and health, while my "architect" persona, where my status as an individual isn't relevant, would be linked to organisational designs, payments for such and press chapters about the impact on the companies I'd designed, for example. As a member of the architecture consortium, it could also include guild-style peer certifications and community endorsements. Similarly, my organisation can have multiple contextualised distinct ecosystem behaviour signatures based on the customer, government or investor segment relevant to that behaviour—my organisation as a provider of financial services, in collaboration with the partners who support the delivery, for example.

Trust Record vs Review Record (Facts vs Plebocracy)

The first advantage of these behavioural signatures is that they are based on facts. Clearly, a credit history is also based on facts, but when individuals can have a proliferation of bank accounts with different lenders, even credit records aren't as reliable as they were. Compared to other platform-based trust systems, fact-based history can't be swayed by first mover advantage, plebocracy or subjective reviews. When applied to multiple personas, it also has the advantage of using only relevant information, both zeroing in on the context so that users from the same context can be confident, and reducing the need for extraneous, potentially personal identity compromising information to be shared. The third advantage is that with these signatures built out of activities performed, you don't need a trust authority to validate that you're creditworthy; the signature itself shows that your behaviour in context is desirable (Fig. 19.2).

When we also accept that communities, including businesses and distinct ecosystems, build behavioural signatures in exactly the same way as individuals, this also gives us a richer and more context-relevant view of the community's reliability to us as consumers of the community's service. Think about a builder with an impeccable credit history—that tells you he's generally reliable, but does it tell you he delivers and employs trustworthy partners and merchants? And these trust signatures aren't just rel-

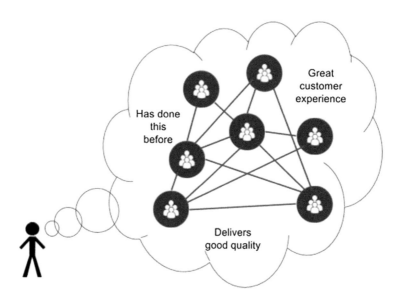

Fig. 19.2 Your trust perspective

evant to you as a consumer of his services, they're also relevant to partner organisations, who can see that he's reliable and a good collaborator for their wider team.

By extension, communities can not only build, but also set parameters for the trust profiles they want to achieve and employ. I can give myself, my workers and collaborators a target and I can specify levels of acceptable behaviour for collaborators, customers and suppliers, creating partnerships only with trusted counterparties. As a collective of builders, as in our example above, we can collaboratively agree to these benchmarks, reducing the typical challenge of one or a small number of individuals being burdened with vetting and selecting suppliers. Taking community-based behavioural signatures as a standard leads to a huge reduction in uncertainty and friction. It also promotes good behaviour; as we've seen with platforms such as AirBnB, the very act of becoming a member means that you're more likely to want good ratings and adjust your behaviour accordingly.

Conclusion

People and organisations are evolving; every entity within an ecosystem may now be part of many distinct ecosystems. Meanwhile, the difference between individuals, organisations and communities is dissolving, as restrictions associated with traditional national boundaries become increasingly burdensome and unrelated to evolving organisations and financial instruments. We need to move away from the old paradigm where the only valid identity belongs to a person, towards accepting and embracing distinct ecosystems as valid entities with identities of their own. People, organisations and the ecosystems that surround them have different, equally valid personas which, when subject to contextual validation, are of use to trust consumers with different objectives.

Traditional authentication protocols are being replaced by emerging opportunities both to apply new approaches to traditional data and to develop behavioural-based trust systems. Behavioural systems are more flexible, more context specific and more reliable than traditional systems. They can be built and used independently of, or in conjunction with, a traditional trust authority, allowing financial inclusion for the unbanked community and a focus on outcomes for trust customers.

Blockchain and cryptography, together with behavioural data, give us the opportunity to create and use different types of signatures as applied to individuals, organisations and communities, moving towards rich context-specific and peer authentication, coupled with factual records and immutability. There's a growing number of platforms taking advantage of this paradigm change, presenting an answer to the challenge of platform bias in the "post-truth" age; however, personal data remain vulnerable regardless of encryption standards.

While technology is creating opportunities, regulations also need to evolve and embrace the changes, accepting that the human-based paradigm is no longer the only version of the truth and that national borders are blurring. We've seen some encouraging developments and eagerly await further changes as behavioural-based identities and validation become mainstream.

Notes

1. Danish CPR System. http://econ.au.dk/the-national-centre-for-register-based-research/danish-registers/the-danish-civil-registration-system-cpr/. Accessed 29 December 2017.
2. Medieval Serfs (Medieval Life and Times). http://www.medieval-life-and-times.info/medieval-life/medieval-serfs.htm. Accessed 29 December 2017.
3. Foreign Account Tax Compliance Act, US Internal Revenue Service. https://www.irs.gov/businesses/corporations/foreign-account-tax-compliance-act-fatca. Accessed 30 December 2017.
4. The Eurozone's Boom Masks Problems That Will Return to Haunt It. *The Economist*, 2 December 2017. https://www.economist.com/news/finance-and-economics/21731822-mismatch-between-its-economic-and-political-institutions-persists-euro. Accessed 30 December 2017.
5. European Central Bank Homepage. https://www.ecb.europa.eu/home/html/index.en.html. Accessed 30 December 2017.
6. Iosebashvili, I. (2017, September 24). US Politics Could Diminish the Dollar's Role as Global Reserve Currency. *Wall Street Journal*. https://www.wsj.com/articles/u-s-politics-could-diminish-dollars-role-as-global-reserve-currency-1506305161. Accessed 30 December 2017.
7. Experian Homepage. http://www.experianplc.com/. Accessed 30 December 2017.
8. Mainelli, M. (2017, March 16). Blockchain Will Help Us Prove Our Identities in a Digital World. *Harvard Business Review*. https://hbr.org/2017/03/blockchain-will-help-us-prove-our-identities-in-a-digital-world. Accessed 30 December 2017.
9. Schiller, B. (2017, December 6). This New blockchain Project Gives Homeless New Yorkers A Digital Identity. *FastCompany*. https://www.fastcompany.com/40500978/this-new-blockchain-project-gives-homeless-new-yorkers-a-digital-identity. Accessed 29 December 2017.

20

Contextualised Trust Solutions

We've covered challenges presented by proliferation of information and modern reputation systems to our understanding of truth, and the challenges of identity and trust, in the previous two chapters. In this chapter, we explain how contextualised trust systems, such as that being built by hiveonline, can address reputation and identity challenges, particularly those associated with truth, for organisations and individuals.

The Need for Contextualised Trust

As we explored in the previous two chapters, we're drowning in information and can't tell what's true or false. Our instincts make us follow authority figures who don't declare their interests and we've seen a rise of anti-truth, with people choosing unvalidated sources over rigour if it supports their value system. Traditional trust authorities provide little context for most needs of trust or identity, while multiple instances of identity records put personal data at risk. Efforts to prevent bots accessing our records are creating increasing friction and may prevent us realising benefits from our IoT devices.

Why do we need to trust individuals and organisations? A transaction with an individual or an organisation means we're handing something over, in exchange for something they're giving us. It could be us handing over services to them in exchange for money, or vice versa. It could be an exchange of non-monetary value on each side, or it could even be a gift, with no

© The Author(s) 2018
S. Blakstad and R. Allen, *FinTech Revolution*,
https://doi.org/10.1007/978-3-319-76014-8_20

reciprocal exchange. The non-monetary value could be a service, goods or a promise of future delivery of some kind of value—monetary, service, goods, etc.

As actors in any of these transactions, we're taking a risk. We're risking that the service or goods won't be delivered; that when it is delivered, it won't be to the quality we expect; that it will be delivered late or not be what we wanted. Every promise carries a risk; contracts with future date deliveries carry an obvious risk, but even if the product is handed over on the spot, do we as the consumer have recourse to support if something goes wrong? Even cash comes with trust challenges—is it genuine and is the counterparty authorised to give it to us? Beyond that, are we participating in criminal activity as part of a money laundering activity by accepting it?

We use traditional, contemporary and primal reputation systems to understand whether the individual or organisation can be trusted. That doesn't form a cast-iron guarantee, but gives us confidence that we're unlikely to be defrauded or be drawn into nefarious value chains (Fig. 20.1).

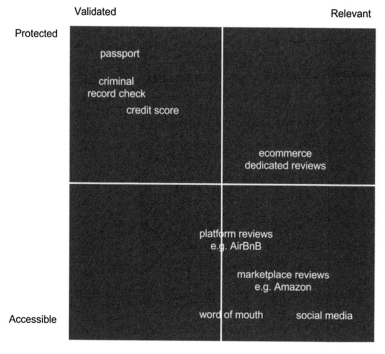

Fig. 20.1   Reputation systems compared

- Traditional reputation systems are based on financial records (e.g. credit history) or fiscal authority records showing we are who we say we are and that we're an ok person (identity cards, criminal records, proof of address, etc.).
- Modern reputation systems, usually platform based, collate reviews and customer feedback, to give us a picture of how other customers or organisations have felt about their experience.
- We also use the original, primal reputation system, word-of-mouth, which is still a powerful, although often flawed system, and as we explore in Chapter 18, has now been hyperinflated and skewed by social platforms.

There's a trade-off in all of these systems between veracity/accessibility and relevance, on a sliding scale where traditional reputation systems are very hard to falsify (although becoming less so), but give us limited relevant information. Social platforms make it incredibly easy to find relevant reputational information, but are subject to multiple biases and largely unvalidated.

The Challenge of Context

It's clear that all these information systems have their advantages and disadvantages. Is it possible to create a system that provides both relevant and validated information? As we said in our chapter on trust and identity, modern technology and in particular blockchain present this opportunity, but first, we need to solve the problem of context.

In the transaction scenarios outlined above, every counterparty may have different needs, and those needs will differ depending on the type of transaction, type of service and other factors such as size and age of supplier, risk appetite of customer and so forth. Here's the trust relevance table from Chapter 19 (Table 20.1).

And we could add a number of other scenarios. But within each of these categories, there are nuances. Let's use the builder, as before (Table 20.2):

… and it varies from country to country, from industry to industry, and from counterparty to counterparty. This is one reason why most contextual reputation systems (i.e. platforms) don't distinguish between the needs of different types of customer; it's just too complicated. You may be

Table 20.1 Trust perspectives

Who's the trust about?	Who's the trust for?	What validation is needed?
Person opening a bank account	The bank; the government; the bank's shareholders; the customer	Prove you're not a bad risk; prove you're not a terrorist; prove you're not a criminal
Refugee entering a country	The government	Prove you're not a terrorist; prove you're not going to take unfair advantage of the country's benefits
Builder	The customer	Prove you're going to deliver good quality on time; prove you're going to complete the job; prove you're not going to go bankrupt
Restaurant	The customer	Prove you're not going to poison the customer; prove your food is good quality
Auditor	The customer; the government/tax authorities	Prove you're competent and qualified; prove you're going to deliver good quality on time
Small business borrower	The bank	Prove you're likely to pay back the money; prove you can probably afford to pay back the money

able to filter reviews for language, and in better cases some other criteria (TripAdvisor[1] is pretty good at this) based on relatively homogenous services, but imagine trying to design those sorts of filters for a marketplace like Amazon. Of course, it already does know quite a lot about you, and filters advertising accordingly, but this is based on what it's observed about *you* rather than things you might want to know about the *merchants*.

The fact that tailored advertising exists demonstrates that it's possible to create learning algorithms based on your behaviour, but it's impossible to apply these sorts of filters to unstructured reviews, at least with the level of intelligence within language recognition software available today. Added to that, given the uneven quality of reviews and their stylistic variability, whether tailoring results on this basis would actually yield useful information is open to question, before one even considers the highly subjective content.

So there are many potential types of information needed, which could be gleaned from your behaviour in much the same way that tailored advertising is today, but the information isn't there to support your needs. Builders just don't put all their documentation on the internet in case someone wants to see it's there; they're not going to display their payroll or tax records either.

Table 20.2 Trust perspectives—builder

Who's the trust about?	Who's the trust for?	What validation is needed?
Builder	Domestic customer wanting new bathroom	Prove you're going to deliver good quality on time; prove you're going to complete the job; prove you have access to relevant suppliers
Builder	Local government wanting new walk-in clinic	Prove you can deliver to scale; prove you've got relevant certifications for previous work; prove you're employing people ethically; prove you're paying tax; prove you have a registered company; prove you've collaborated with architects on similar projects
Builder	Domestic customer wanting garden wall fixed	Prove you'll show up; prove you can do a reasonable quality job and not overcharge
Builder	Employment agency	Prove you're employing people ethically; prove you're paying tax; prove you pay on time; prove you have a registered company
Builder	Larger builder subcontracting to get a big job finished	Prove you have the capacity; prove you'll meet required standards; prove you have a registered company; prove you're paying tax; prove you'll meet required employment standards; prove all your specialists are certified
Builder	Builders' merchant	Prove you'll pay your bills on time
Builder	Labourer	Prove you'll pay wages on time; prove you're giving workers decent working conditions

Conversely, individuals don't usually carry around all of their certificates—criminal record, credit history, etc., but have to retrieve these from trust authorities when required. Most people carry some personal identification, but beyond this, records are hard to access and validate rapidly.

Solutions

There are emerging solutions to the personal identity challenge, such as ID2020, with many academic institutions and industry working on the concept of "self-sovereign identity",[2] where individuals can hold secure, cryptographic keys to their trust authority-held information. This has the advantage of not exposing the information to risk and ageing in the same way, but this still requires initiative from the individual, and as with the traditional trust authority limitations, provides full relevance only within a small range of contexts.

This cryptographic handling of traditional trust authority data, like other solutions we propose, is based on blockchain concepts and cryptography. We think it's a useful tool in a broader toolkit which also has the opportunity to largely disintermediate trust authorities for the majority of customer/business interactions. To frame the solution, let's summarise the problem:

- Different counterparties to transactions have different information needs when validating trust, based on their role, the nature of the transaction and the nature of the value being transacted.
- Suppliers don't routinely publish documentation relevant to the context, because it's cumbersome, confidential or it ages rapidly—usually all three.
- Publishing and maintaining such documentation would require significant effort for a business or even an individual; this behaviour has not become common yet and is unlikely to emerge rapidly as a standard behaviour.
- Proving that contracts have been honoured is even more cumbersome and usually requires additional validation by third parties who may not be available or willing to provide validation.
- Social media reviews aren't easy to filter, and the quality is variable.

But on the solution side, we know this:

- Machine Learning is already advanced enough to identify different customer types and (broadly) their needs.
- Cryptographic key techniques can be used to perform validation with traditional trust authorities without sharing personal data.
- Blockchain and cryptographic technology makes it possible to store records of transactions, digital assets (including dematerialised certificates, etc.), identity attestations and agreements.
- Blockchain records have the advantage of being transparent, immutable, permanent records, but this makes storing personal data (however protected) on a public blockchain inadvisable—can we really be certain that during the course of one's lifetime the cryptographic algorithm will not be cracked?

The challenge is how to capture the link between agreements, payments and digital assets. Some trade finance applications are starting to do this, as we discussed in the first half of this book, by tracking the value chain over a blockchain, storing digital assets to prove transactions and provenance. The same is happening with Agritech applications designed to support communities in developing economies or applied to food safety. We've seen Google announcing[3] it's working on provenance of medical records. Blockchain and smart contract technology, while still maturing, is likely to play a key role in all of these applications.

The platform hiveonline is building will provide full trust records for small businesses, through combining administration solutions already on the market, applying decision logic to contracts and integration with the existing financial system. By integrating contracts and payments, we provide a user-friendly alternative to traditional emails, making it easy for businesses to use and providing a natural platform for exchanging digital assets, which we monitor against commitments to build a fact-based, contextualised trust record, with no effort or administration from the business (Fig. 20.2).

This answers the administration problem by storing the assets on behalf of the business; they exchange the assets through our platform to interact with their customers and staff, reducing friction and effort. With valid and verifiable data underpinning these transactions, we can apply our learning algorithms to which customers of trust need which information, allowing our contextualised trust signatures to grow with changing customer needs.

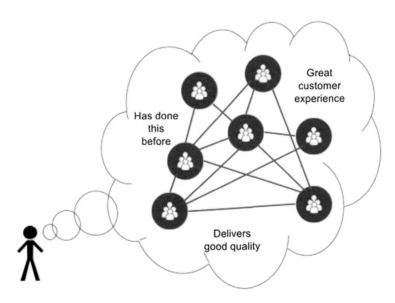

Fig. 20.2 Your trust perspective

Because we're not storing personal information, there's no risk to personal data; the digital assets we store are held separately, while our hash record verifies their existence on the blockchain without revealing any details. This is essentially the same thing that a trade finance application will do, but applied to a B2C situation rather than B2B.

Key to making this work is combining Machine Learning with blockchain, as well as a customer-focused approach (as the Google article points out, this is the non-sexy end of blockchain). The UN identified this opportunity as one of the ways Fintech is going to support both economies and natural ecosystems, by handing trust and control back to the communities. The applications are manifold. While today we face challenges of finding standards with emerging technology, we are taking measures to future-proof our platform using micro-services architecture and we're looking forward to being part of this revolution in trust and identity.

Conclusion

As we've explored in other chapters, identity, trust and truth are increasingly challenging fields. However, as we are seeing with applications from platform monopolies like Google to startups like hiveonline, the opportunities presented by combining Machine Learning with blockchain technology are now giving rise to a growing number of tailored, contextualised, fact-based reputation and trust systems. As these emerge, the confidence gap will be closed, with customers, communities and businesses able to access fact-based information that helps them make the right decisions.

Notes

1. TripAdvisor Homepage. https://www.tripadvisor.com/. Accessed 30 December 2017.
2. Lewis, A. (2017, May 17). A Gentle Introduction to Self-sovereign Identity. Bits on Blocks. https://bitsonblocks.net/2017/05/17/a-gentle-introduction-to-self-sovereign-identity/. Accessed 30 December 2017.
3. Metz, C. (2017, April 11). Google Deepmind's Untrendy blockchain Play to Make the blockchain Actually Useful. *Wired.com*. https://www.wired.com/2017/03/google-deepminds-untrendy-blockchain-play-make-actually-useful/?mbid=nl_31117_p1&CNDID=45271174&utm_content=buffer1e62f&utm_medium=social&utm_source=twitter.com&utm_campaign=buffer. Accessed 30 December 2017.

21

Service Consumers

In this chapter we build on the previous chapters to discuss how customer interaction with services has evolved, how this evolution is impacting customer behaviours and expectations, the complex relationship customers have with service providers regarding data, and what this means for financial service providers today and in the future.

Services and You

We've always used services; as we've discussed elsewhere, services encapsulate products, support, delivery, user experience, inputs, outputs, desires, needs, behaviours and results. Service starts with the identification of a need for something to be different and ends with a changed state, which, if the service has been successful, includes the fulfilment of that need. Traditionally, services were provided to us by ourselves, each other, the community or suppliers. For hunter-gatherers, everything is provided within the community, and for the community—the original prosumers, but in modern society a large proportion of the services we use every day is provided by people and organisations not part of our immediate community, for money or other considerations of value.

Human beings are designed to identify with their community, which creates tribalism, as discussed in the chapter on plebocracy and cognitive bias, because it makes sense for a prosumer society to build and rely on trust. This includes giving credit to community members who render services to

© The Author(s) 2018
S. Blakstad and R. Allen, *FinTech Revolution*,
https://doi.org/10.1007/978-3-319-76014-8_21

us, which is important for community bonding, but can get confused when we receive services from other suppliers. Our instinct is to start trusting the providers of those services, which translates as brand loyalty in today's terms. Of course, with non-tribe providers, we also use our intellectual faculties to evaluate whether we like the services and whether we want to continue the relationship, but there's an element of cognitive bias—post-purchase rationalisation[1]—which we attribute to a service provider we've used, regardless of the quality of the service, based on the fact that we've included that provider into our tribal view, which makes it more likely we'll see the choice and the results positively.

That was reasonably straightforward when services could be attributed clearly to suppliers—we love our parents, who are our first service providers, and most of us remember the brand of our first car, which offered us mobility and independence. As tribal and sensory beings, we identify experiences with people and artefacts, so a single producer offering services through a single channel gains exposure to us, and our loyalty, through the physical artefacts we interact with. That's why using physical branding is very important to service providers who sell us things that aren't associated with physical objects, such as holidays, haircuts or medical treatment. (NB in our experience, hairdressers aren't all that good at branding, but you can usually remember where they were.)

As society has industrialised and products and services have evolved, we are all using multiple service providers we don't know about; the TV is made of components that were manufactured by someone other than your TV manufacturer; you don't know who reared the pigs in your supermarket brand sausages and you're very unlikely to know in which country your T-shirt was made or whether any of those products used slave labour or unethical practices in their value chains. But the supply chain is still controlled by Sony, Tesco or the Gap, so it's relatively easy to identify the primary service provider who controls your customer experience.

Things have got a little more complicated over the last few decades. Companies whitelabel services—banks, for example, provide third-party insurance and mortgage products, with an uneasy relationship when it comes to using the services. Now service experience is getting smoother with better integration and APIs—thanks to apps, Payments Service Providers (PSPs) and the evolving ecosystem economy, we can now use services with no clear visibility of who the core provider is. We use apps on our phones which may be accessing our bank accounts, credit cards, lots of third-party suppliers such as identity providers, or buy things through Amazon which are provided by another retailer.

While the Amazons and the other big platforms are using this ambiguity to capture and cement their portion of the world's tribal identity at the expense of the other providers, brand awareness of non-platform providers is becoming less concrete—you don't know who the providers are behind various apps on your phone—in some cases, you're probably not even sure what the app is called. And we no longer use a single app or a single provider for services; in the old days, you might have used a travel agent to manage a trip, but in the ecosystem we now use a multitude of service providers—Google Maps, booking sites, airlines, insurance, to provide the trip—and these in turn are using third-party suppliers.

Our booking app gives us access to a range of hotels, some of which we have a brand relationship with (that physical thing), but also offers the option to choose alternatives based on price, diluting our brand loyalty. Even though we use a small range of airline apps, these give us access to multiple code-sharing airlines, so we don't know which airline we'll be flying. We have become the travel agent—as we observed in Chapter 6, the customer now owns the customer experience and the concept of an integrated service provided by a single third-party supplier is becoming less satisfying.

There have been many complaints about this movement[2]—as consumers, we're now expected to manage our own experience, taking responsibility directly for booking, supermarket checkout service, finding our own news and entertainment. Service providers no longer take responsibility for end-to-end services, and we don't expect them to; the downside for producers is that with increasing self-reliance, our brand awareness is reduced and brand loyalty is dissolving. That's not a problem for the consumer, but it puts service providers in a new position.

Customer Behaviours

We've said the move of services into the ecosystem isn't a problem for the consumer—and in general, it isn't. Of course, not all customers are equally comfortable with this. There's also a generation divide—one of our grandmothers never got the hang of self-service petrol pumps, for example, while we're mystified by some communications protocols (Snapchat? Just why?). Consumer bodies are concerned that the move into the ecosystem is leaving many consumers behind, especially older consumers,[3] and there's a divide between information workers and those who work with their hands. Providers are seeking to address this by making technology easier to use and more intuitive; IoT devices are helping to provide seamless access to services.

In an idealised digital world, we would all be using technology seamlessly, interacting with technology and the real world frictionlessly without thinking about which is which. This presents two challenges—one, is that everyone's experience and expectations are different—sometimes at a cultural, national or demographic level, but also at an individual level, as all of us are shaped by our unique path through life. This problem can be addressed to an extent by providers creating more intuitive and seamless experiences, but that leads to the second problem: branding. The more seamlessly our customers interact with our services and switch between ours and those provided by someone else, the less they are aware of who's providing those services, and the fewer opportunities we have to create brand loyalty.

Brand loyalty today is being replaced by providers, with experience loyalty. Rather than keeping customers engaged in traditional ways, we're hooked by an emotional attachment to the experience of using the service; it's frictionless and addictive, the natural place we turn to meet a need. That may be the draw of Facebook to check up on friends, Uber to grab a ride, swiping the payment app to get stuff. It's not the brand that keeps bringing us back, and if an alternative provider gave us the same service more seamlessly, we'd start using that pretty fast. In fact, we don't even trust these providers of these apps very much these days. But we still use them.

By reducing friction, apps are making us lazy. We're too lazy to walk around the long way, when we can swipe left instead. Cinemas[4] and restaurants[5] are losing footfall as people consume services at home rather than going out. We don't care that services are harvesting our data or showing us annoying averts, as long as the overall experience makes life easier for us. People in their 20s can't understand how people could have operated before the mobile phone, and small children, presented with a book, attempt to swipe the pages. Parents IM their children in different rooms to tell them dinner's ready, and partners IM each other from either end of a sofa. Low-friction experiences are winning.

The Value of Your Data

One of the key ways of reducing adoption friction is, of course, to make the service free, even though we know, as the saying goes, if you can't see who's paying for the service, the product is you. We use services, knowing we're subject to data harvest and, in some cases, not being too happy about it. Studies have shown that while we're vocal about protecting our data, when tested we'll hand over secrets for relatively low incentives.[6] Service providers understand this balance. They also understand we'll accept a level of inconvenience including advertising and even, in some cases, substandard experiences, in exchange for rich service provisions, easy access and zero cost.

There's also a balance between the friction of adoption and access, versus friction within the experience. As long as your customers can get onboard easily and use services easily, they're likely to come back, even if there's some friction within the service. Providers focus on easy onboarding and integration, encouraging signup through multiple channels to achieve the most important statistics: customer numbers. And that's important not because of unit sales, but because of the data. It started with advertising, but now everyone's behaviour is up for grabs to a multitude of paying customers, including retailers, political groups, other lobbyists, researchers, law enforcement agents and not just your local ones (Fig. 21.1).

Many will be seeking to use the data you provide via their service directly, in a relatively benign way—for example alerting you to a discount as you pass their store, or using past preference data to allocate the sort of hotel room you like: one hotel chain we used extensively used our data to ensure we had plenty of the right sort of teabags in the rooms, for example. Platforms such as Facebook will use your data to feed you more things that are relevant and interesting to you (although this, as we discuss in Chapter 18, is problematic, as it creates information bubbles). Many others, however, will be using your data to draw conclusions from your behaviour to target you with relevant advertising, lobbying and news, with the goal of influencing your future behaviour. This has been covered extensively thanks to scandals about political social engineering,[7] particularly the manipulation of elections,[8] but that hasn't cured us of our addiction to social platforms.

Even when we're aware of our data being harvested and used to manipulate us, our views can differ widely; unlike Sharon, you may be positively impressed that Starbucks has informed you how much you've got left to spend, if you were contemplating a purchase. We're keen on having a surplus of Earl Grey teabags in the room, and it's great that the desk clerk knows our names. We were less impressed when, on turning 50, Facebook started trying to sell us incontinence pads and funeral insurance. Yes, these uses of data may influence our behaviour, but they do it in a straightforward way.

But these are only the above board, obvious uses of our data that we can detect and rationalise easily. Other uses, particularly targeting our fears through selected news coverage to influence political decision making, are not just changing our individual behaviours without our agreement,

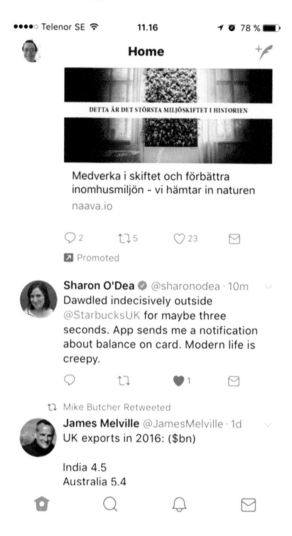

Fig. 21.1   Big bucky's watching you (Twitter)

they're also changing the fate of nations.[9] Our feed is showing us ways of behaving—through online recipes, exercises, self-help and recreation suggestions—that may move the needle on how we behave for better or worse for our health, our wealth, our jobs and our family life. Data users are manipulating our behaviour towards their own ends—which may be benign, but are intrusive, unrequested and undetected.

Of course, one of the key behaviour changes that these platforms have encouraged is our willingness to share data—and many of us share a lot.

Nearly all users of platforms such as Facebook share more information about themselves than they realise, through expressed opinions, clicks, time spent looking at items and "likes". Because of our herd instinct, we're also more likely to start sharing more personal and revealing information, the more we're exposed to our friends sharing theirs, giving the platforms an ever-richer source of data.

The flipside is that we expect our service providers to know about us and, in some cases, can be dissatisfied when they don't understand our preferences. Just like the child who tries to swipe the page of a physical book, our behaviours and expectations are shaped by our service experience. In the 1990s, it was the "Edit/Undo of life" but now we expect services to be customised and expect our service providers to know us, sometimes really well.

What Does This Mean for Service Providers?

As we've discussed, your brand, unless you've reached market saturation, is unlikely to be a big draw to customers today; there's just too much choice and experience is key. Customers may not know where your part of the service starts and ends, and they're unlikely to care too much. Of course, subliminal branding—messaging, values, colour scheme—is still important in helping customers relate a positive experience to our services, but today it's more likely to be a familiarity marker than a positive loyalty draw.

So that leaves service providers with the much more complex question of how to position their service experience, which is even more complex, since many services are now provided by multiple service providers and you don't have full control over the customer experience any more. You have some control over how good your product is, but the key to customers choosing you and not your competitors is the multitude of factors making up your service, which provide the customer experience; not all of these will be in your control.

And for those that are, you need to make many more decisions today about how much you want to use the customer's data to enhance their experience or move them towards new experiences, how much you want to show your hand and, in Sharon's words, how "creepy" it's ok to be. Some, like us, will expect Earl Grey teabags and be disappointed if they're not there. Others will resent all interference or any display of knowledge. Most people are examples of both of these[10]—Sofie hates being addressed by her first name by strangers, yet expects air stewards on frequently used airlines to know who she is. Your demographic may predict how you'll behave in certain situations but it's a rocky road.

As service providers today, then, we not only have to be sensitive to the customer's experience in using our product or service, but also to how well they will expect us to know them. They know, and we know, that we've got a wealth of data about them that can tell us more than they know about themselves. We are complicit in maintaining a fantasy where we're still guessing about their preferences, demographic and behaviours—or are we?

Data Use for Service Provision Is in Its Infancy

Most service providers, despite the data they have, are terrible at using data—really, really terrible. They're so terrible they can't even manage to switch us between services or departments without giving us a new phone number to call and forcing us to give all our credentials and authentication again, even when we're dealing with a different department of the same company (never mind third parties, such as mortgage providers!). A common complaint from corporate customers of banks is that they have to go through KYC with multiple different departments.

Your bank knows you use the same credentials for your business and personal accounts, but can't maintain chat support on your business account because it doesn't work with their login process. Your electricity supplier is also your water supplier, but needs separate details, separate authentication and separate payment for each department. A shop that really, really wants to close a sale with you has to give you a different number to call because the furniture is sold by a different department and there's no way of putting you through. An airline's customer service department berates you by email for trying to ask a question unrelated to post-service care and offers a telephone number in the country where the airline is headquartered, on a different continent to you, as a solution.

None of these scenarios are necessary; all of these organisations have sufficient data about you and sufficiently sophisticated organisations to manage the transmission of information between departments, the intelligent mining of data and a focus on customer support, but they don't. And they don't, because they choose not to. As we will show in the last section of the book, in our chapters about service alignment and architecture, organisations that have a product and department focus are often myopic about customer needs, and incapable of refocusing to support customers. They consequently misuse the enormous amounts of data they have available to them, often using excuses such as customer data protection, but actually protecting their own inefficiencies and investment in maintaining an inadequate and unsupportive status quo.

So, What Does This Mean for Financial Services?

Customers are becoming brand blind and ambivalent about sharing data, but service providers are lagging behind. While we have seen that data can be used to manipulate and influence customer behaviour, this has been applied by the platforms and media outlets to manipulate behaviours into behavioural changes, including political and purchasing behaviours, but service organisations, including financial services organisations, aren't using the data they have effectively to manage their own customers' interactions with their businesses. Of course, it varies, we've used hotels and coffee shops as examples and these organisations are generally a lot better at using data effectively for customer service than banks, but the applications of data as a service provision tool are still in early stages of development.

This should be both scary and reassuring for financial services providers. On the one hand, the platforms, which may be their biggest threat, are too complacent to care very much about whether data are being used well, while their competitors aren't really using it at all. That presents a big opportunity for financial services providers prepared to step into this gap. On the other hand, customers distrust banks, are suspicious of data being used to manipulate their behaviours outside of the social platforms and are also lazy. Understanding this, and being able to project your business objectives beyond sales of products, and into providing services, can help organisations to grasp underserved sectors and leapfrog both platforms and traditional players in the financial services ecosystem.

And, as we've observed throughout the first half of this book, there's an enormous untapped market out there—the world's unbanked and underbanked aren't just sitting ducks waiting for financial providers to come and seize a chunk of their limited incomes; by helping the unbanked and underserved to build wealth, identity and businesses, as we've seen with M-PESA, financial services providers can help them to break out of poverty or the challenges of running small businesses. Today's unbanked could be tomorrow's wealth creators, with a little bit of creative help from financial service providers, if we can design services that help them to flourish.

Conclusion

Service consumers are the customers of the new service ecosystem. They're a mess of contradictions—they don't want to share their data, but they'll sell it for the price of a pizza; they don't care about brand but they're too lazy to use something that's hard work if the alternative is easier, even if it means giving away their data. Despite the scandals surrounding political manipulation by social media, and wide publicity it attracted, people are continuing to use the platforms.

And there's a divide between the sophisticated social media manipulators and service providers, who aren't using the data they already have, to improve services for their existing customers. Some are responding to changing customer behaviours by creating low-friction services, but most are still expecting the customer to navigate their organisations to access services. And that's because they're not thinking like service providers, but sellers of products. The mindset of the organisation needs to move to start thinking like a service provider, to support today's service consumers.

Notes

1. Post Purchase Rationalization. *NLP Notes*. http://nlpnotes.com/post-purchase-rationalization/. Accessed 30 December 2017.
2. Levine, I. S. (2014, September 30). 6 Reasons You Need a Travel Agent. *Forbes*. https://www.forbes.com/sites/nextavenue/2014/09/30/6-reasons-you-need-a-travel-agent/#d7f057929edf.
3. Digital Generation Gap Remains Wide Open as Older Generation Fail to Embrace New Technology. *Nominet*, 25 October 2017. https://www.nominet.uk/digital-generation-gap-remains-wide-open-older-generations-fail-embrace-new-technology/. Accessed 30 December 2017.
4. Elder, R. (2016, September 7). Movie Theater Attendance Is Declining as Cord-Cutting Becomes More Popular. *Business Insider*. http://www.businessinsider.com/movie-theater-attendance-is-declining-as-cord-cutting-becomes-more-popular-2016-9?r=US&IR=T&IR=T. Accessed 30 December 2017.
5. Richter, W. (2017, July 15). Why Restaurants Are in Their Worst Slump Since 2009. *Business Insider*. http://www.businessinsider.com/restaurant-sales-slowdown-reasons-2017-7?r=US&IR=T&IR=T. Accessed 30 December 2017.
6. Wong, M. (2017, August 3). Pizza Over Privacy: Stanford Economist Examines a Paradox of the Digital Age. *Stanford News*. https://news.

stanford.edu/2017/08/03/pizza-privacy-stanford-economist-examines-paradox-digital-age/. Accessed 30 December 2017.

7. Hern, A. (2017, June 19). Facebook and Twitter Are Being Used to Manipulate Public Opinion. *The Guardian*. https://www.theguardian.com/technology/2017/jun/19/social-media-proganda-manipulating-public-opinion-bots-accounts-facebook-twitter. Accessed 30 December 2017.

8. Earle, S. (2017, October 14). Trolls, Bots and Fake News the Mysterious World of Social Media Manipulation. *Newsweek*. http://www.newsweek.com/trolls-bots-and-fake-news-dark-and-mysterious-world-social-media-manipulation-682155. Accessed 30 December 2017.

9. Kuchler, H. (2017, October 31). Facebook Finds Wider Russian Meddling in US Election. *Financial Times*. https://www.ft.com/content/0f228a9e-bdc7-11e7-b8a3-38a6e068f464. Accessed 30 December 2017.

10. Hulls, K. (2015, July 28). Consumer Cultural Differences When It Comes to Online Customer Data. *Celebrus Blog*. http://www.celebrus.com/blog/business/consumer-cultural-differences-when-it-comes-online-customer-data. Accessed 30 December 2017.

Future Business, Part VI
Services for the Ecosystem Economy
Building the Future

We've described the social, technical and information changes that have reshaped customer expectations and the way businesses interact with their customers, their workers and each other. In this final section, we roll our sleeves up and describe some practical steps that existing organisations can take to evolve and embrace the ecosystem economy and start supporting today's service consumers, in both developed and developing economies.

Organisations provide services today, but they're still structured to provide products, which makes helping customers difficult. Worse, they're often structured to provide products for which customers are already finding alternatives. To survive and thrive in the ecosystem economy, organisations need to be structured in ways that align with solving their customers' problems, rather than their own. They need to be organised so that integrating with partners to provide elements of service to their customers is straightforward and agile. And they need to be structured to include new customer segments, in the emerging economies of the world, to help eradicate poverty and move towards an inclusive global economy.

In this section, we change pace to draw on our extensive practical experience and research into organisational design, to offer a template for organisations to follow to prepare themselves for delivering services in the ecosystem age. We describe some practical steps for how banks and other organisations can become service aligned, and the key pillars of capability aligned organisations that they can adopt to move towards the ecosystem. This section will be of most interest to readers considering offering services through their businesses, while giving useful insights to other readers interested in how organisations deliver services.

We have presented this section as a walkthrough of opportunities; for the interested reader, more detailed versions of these chapters, and additional articles on the practice of building service aligned organisations, can be found on our website.

22

Service Alignment

In this chapter, we discuss how banks and other organisations need to evolve away from product focus and towards service alignment, to become fully functional ecosystem players. While we focus on banking transformation, the same considerations apply to large, traditional organisations across many industries, struggling to evolve in rapidly changing competitive environments.

> Only 30% of customers believe they are receiving a personalised customer experience, while 45% of bankers indicate they think they are delivering on that promise
> 48% of banks think they are doing a good job encouraging strong customer loyalty while only 35% of customers agree. (IBM)[1]

But Aren't Banks Service Aligned Already?

Every bank we've ever worked for (and we've worked for twelve of the big ones) cites customer service as their top priority. Banks have become less complacent with the shifts in market and recognise both the strength and value associated with their customer base. Like any other service provider, it's important for banks to provide a positive customer experience.

Banks suffer from a challenge common to utility providers: their product set is pretty undifferentiated. A loan is a loan; a bank account is a bank account. Banks may dress up the product offering by adding incentives and keeping the unit cost as low as possible to ensure pricing is competitive,

© The Author(s) 2018
S. Blakstad and R. Allen, *FinTech Revolution*,
https://doi.org/10.1007/978-3-319-76014-8_22

but fundamentally there's not much in it. That's why banks need a strong reputation to maintain their customer base; but as we've discussed, reputation is no longer something banks can control through actively curating customer perception.

There's been a fundamental shift in customer expectations, as we explored in the previous section. People of all ages expect a more tailored customer experience, as their experience of life teaches them to expect it. Brand loyalty is being diluted, and the Fintechs, alternative finance providers and Challenger Banks are at the gate.

Of course, for the big banks, traditional considerations such as security and tight regulation still go a long way towards the maintenance of a customer base; customers will always put the security of their money at a high priority. But as the challengers and Fintechs learn to work within these paradigms that edge will be lost. And in the absence of differentiated products, brand loyalty or even traditional stickiness caused by inertia, customer experience is becoming the key differentiator in financial services. Customers today want and expect a service that suits them, supports their needs and feels personalised; we need to provide a differentiated service which will make that customer want to come back.

This is tough for traditional banks to achieve; their organisations are built to support standardised activities, to drive down cost and guarantee low risk and regulatory compliance. The customer-facing staff are in a difficult position too: trying their hardest to support the customers with the experience they expect, customer support teams are hampered by the very standardised processes designed to protect those customers. The customers don't understand why things take so long; support staff can't explain and can't help them. Both customers and support staff are frustrated. We usually (staff and customers) blame antiquated technology; older or less flexible technology can look like the root cause of the problem. So banks invest in fixing our technology, but fixing the technology won't make the problem go away.

We also know how important the people element is—service culture is something you need to grow and nurture, role model from the top down, etc. Banks create training, put motivational posters on the walls and build friendly scripts for their staff to use. Service culture is pushed hard down to the customer-facing staff—although it often seems to skip a few layers of management on the way—and again, the staff are left to slug it out with the inflexible processes and frustrated customers, but with a smile on their face.

This undoubtedly has a positive impact on the individual customer encounter with that staff member; it's much better to be told that you'll have to pass another security check if the person telling you is being nice and friendly. But fixing the culture won't make the problem go away either, if the service still isn't meeting the customer's needs. And fixing culture is difficult where the culture you're trying to impose is not supported by people's day-to-day experiences. One of us once had a micromanaging boss who kept saying to her team "be empowered! Why aren't you empowered?" We see a lot of that sort of behaviour when traditional banks impose top-down culture change.

So they fix the processes. They Lean/Six Sigma everything in the operations area, eliminating waste and standardising the end to end process. That takes cost and resources out of the organisation, and eliminates a lot of risk. Clearly, that's critical. A good Lean effort will usually improve service delivery times, but it also forces customer-facing staff into increasingly prescriptive standard processes, which make them even less able to support the customer with any kind of flexibility. They lack empowerment and share the customers' frustration. And the problem is still there, although costs are down.

The problem is built into the organisations.

Service alignment isn't created by imposing culture, and it isn't delivered by process optimisation, although both of these are important elements. The key to building a service aligned organisation is the very shape of the organisation itself, together with governance structures, rules, decision rights, metrics and accountabilities. Before we explore the details though, let's first recap what we mean by a service.

What Do We Mean by Service?

Service is a much-used word and can mean a lot of things to a lot of people. Many organisations equate service with product, as we've discussed, or with process. As we'll show, service may encapsulate products and will always have an element of process, but it's not a one-to-one relationship. At some level, service may also equate to capability but once you drill down, any service will reach into a number of capabilities. A definition of service we find useful, and one that we haven't yet been able to break is:

A Service is a configuration of Capabilities that delivers value to the customer.

We also like to think of a service as **a set of activities with a customer at each end**—note the use of "set of activities" rather than "process" here.

A customer may be a traditional customer, the sort that experiences the services and puts money in the balance sheet. Or it may be an internal customer, drawing on an internal service. Alternatively, a customer may be an external stakeholder of another sort, such as a regulator, a central bank, a payments scheme, a media entity or the shareholders. Fundamentally, services are our way of delivering value from the capabilities provided by our organisation.

Customers consume the results of our services—those may manifest themselves as a combination of products, experiences, rewards and other elements. The whole package will influence how happy the customer is with our organisation and their perception of the products, our staff and our brand. An unhappy customer won't be sweetened by the smiling face, or even the slick delivery of the product, if other elements aren't in place. So in delivering a positive customer experience we need to design the service holistically, and deliver it in a controlled way. Like the best restaurants, every element of the service must be tuned to create the experience we want the customer to have.

What Makes a Service Work?

Services are made up of all the same elements of any other operating model—human, process, technology and so forth, all of which need conscious design to integrate successfully. See the chapter on Service Architecture for further details (Fig. 22.1).

Within each of these elements, further design is required, and these are explored below and in the relevant chapters. For now, let's consider the elements that make up a service.

On the left, we have all the things you normally associate with delivering products and services to customers—the tangibles, things you can draw on a wall. The things on the right are those things that are usually handled separately, by line management, HR and compliance (is Compliance a department or a behaviour?) and rarely consciously designed in conjunction with the hard delivery on the left.

And then the things in the middle—the structures that make up the organisation, and directly shape how the teams behave and interact—are usually left completely up to chance; teams are organised by function, with people with the same skill sets working for someone who is even better at that skill set. Little thought is usually given to putting people with the same *goal* in the same room.

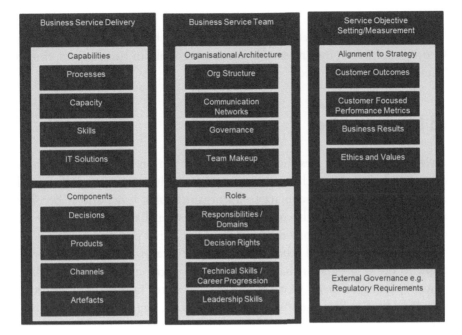

Fig. 22.1 Operating model for services

As we discussed in the first chapter, organisational structure is one of the biggest inhibitors to the delivery of excellent service, closely followed by governance and decision rights. While teams are arranged in silos, they have to formally engage each other (usually with the help of technology), to perform tasks which lose context as they are passed around the organisation. Every time information is passed from one team/system/process to another, not only does that cause work for the team passing the information and that receiving it, but it injects risk and degradation of quality.

The support teams are trying their best to provide what's needed by Sales, but without any visibility of the customer and with their own drivers (which are different to those of Sales), it's not only difficult to support a seamless customer experience, in many cases, it's nearly impossible. The organisational structure designs poor customer experience into itself.

What Is Service Alignment?

Simply put, Service Alignment means aligning the organisation to the service, not the other way around. It sounds simple and obvious. So why isn't everyone doing it? You could argue that nobody's thought of it before, but this is not only naïve; all the evidence is against it, after all Apple,[2] hotel chains[3] and other retail/service organisations have been doing this for years. We think there are other reasons it hasn't taken hold in banking yet, despite the massively pressing need.

No More Empires

Service alignment requires the organisation to run on principles of governance, rather than hierarchies. This is a reasonably easy concept for small teams to absorb, but extrapolate to an organisational level, and it becomes less easy. The people at the top of an organisation have risen through talent, political manipulation, hard work and massive personal sacrifices. As we observed in Chapter 1, they have built their status in the way they were taught to build it—and in banks, that's through the creation of ever larger teams, reporting to them. Once conferred, this status becomes self-enforcing as leaders strive to increase their importance to the organisation by building ever larger teams.

As we also observed, they centralise decision making into themselves, to avoid the risk of losing control. This results in them also being ridiculously busy and difficult to access—in the modern business world, a packed diary has become a status symbol in itself. They are usually making decisions with partial information, which has been filtered and massaged multiple times and passed various other decision-making bodies, before being presented to them in digestible form. Often the wrong decisions are made because the information is partial, or they don't have access to the facts due to their distance from the people who work for them.

And then the execution of their decisions can be partial, misinterpreted and happening too late to have the desired effect, because of assumptions they make about their subordinates, the competing priorities of their subordinates, their partial communication skills and networks, and the time it takes to transmit information up and down the hierarchy. Empires were very effective in establishing autocracy and control in the Old World, but when the organisation becomes too complex to manage top down, they create problems and delays. Unfortunately, we've created a leadership hierarchy that regards empires as a critical status symbol and enabler, so this will take some breaking down.

Service alignment means blurring the old association between leadership and management of large numbers of people, and putting decisions in the hands of the people best qualified to make them. There are roles associated with leadership, but the service aligned organisation is flatter, modular and composed of self-organising teams, managed by governance rather than hierarchies. The challenge with this is that the most fundamental barrier to implementing service alignment in an organisation is the leadership team it has today.

No More Heroes

Closely related to empires is the hero leader culture we have developed—the one guy/girl who can cut through the spaghetti and get things done. We've both made careers of this, so this one's pretty personal to us. However, in the service aligned organisation, there is no role for hero leaders. Partly because service alignment makes heroes of everyone, but also because there's less spaghetti to cut through, and things get done without the heroes being needed. This is a very hard thing for the key talent to absorb and adapt to. After all, what's the point of me if I'm not in there, fixing the crap? Organisations will need to re-educate the key talent to become leaders in devising and developing the governance structures that shape the organisation, as well as applying their subject-matter expert skills to key advisory roles. Putting them into the change teams delivering service alignment is a pretty good start.

The Banks Are Doing Fine—Why Change?

As we've shown in the previous sections, customer behaviour is changing, and there are billions of unserved or underserved customers who banks, or other financial service providers, can help through a change of focus. As we've also shown throughout the book, alternative providers are leapfrogging traditional services. Despite all evidence to the contrary, there's still a significant perception in banking culture that everything's going to continue as it has for the last 200 years or so, and everything's going to be fine. For organisations that are still pulling in a healthy amount of cash and maintaining strong liquidity, this seems like a rational argument. But look at the statistics! 20% of millennials changing their account every year.

If banks don't do something to hedge against the emerging future now, they'll be the guys sitting on the ground, asking "where did everybody go?" Unfortunately, this isn't so obvious to their staff, and particularly middle management; unless they create a burning platform, people will continue to be complacent and present a barrier to change, until it's too late.

The benefit of service alignment is that it presents a solution to current as well as possible future challenges, which makes it an easier sell, but it is really important that the people, and especially the leaders, understand that the status quo is not sustainable. *The competitive environment has already changed.*

So, What Does a Service Aligned Organisation Look like?

As the major subject of this section, we're not going to go into all the details in this chapter. Please see Chapters 23–25 for the details of how to structure the organisation at a macro and micro level. We'll outline the fundamentals here.

A service aligned organisation doesn't look like a triangle. There is no fixed hierarchical structure with more junior people at the bottom and more senior people towards the top. As mentioned above, this doesn't mean no leadership, and it doesn't mean anarchy—if anything, you need more governance in this model than you do in the traditional hierarchical shape. But the service aligned model brings everyone and everything closer to the customer. It does this by literally flattening the organisation, and putting teams of people with different skills together in support of servicing a common goal. Capabilities are still differentiated, but the slant is towards providing services, rather than functions. Nobody should be more than two functions away from the customer, and most people will be closer than that.

Customer service teams are made up of the people who understand every part of what's required by that service. For example, in a typical Retail banking customer service team, you would have both the traditional sales/customer relationship management resources, together with roles that specialise in compliance, operational processes and technology. They are then able to draw down on the back-end capabilities, to provide the support needed by the customer. Front-end teams are largely case managed, able to configure the customer experience at the point of delivery, while back-end capabilities are largely standardised, pre-loading components as much as possible so that delivery is instant or very fast. We expand on this in the next chapter.

In this model, nobody is very far from the customer. The value chain is shortened while maximising flexibility in the customer-facing teams, and the opportunity to standardise and reduce cost in supporting capabilities. The model also enables companies to embed customer experience metrics into every part of the value chain, so that everyone participating has visibility of what good looks like, and can work independently to prioritise their work within their teams, confident that value is being delivered, without having to check. Here's an example of a single instance of service alignment we delivered into a major universal bank a few years ago—an employee onboarding experience.

Case Study: Employee Onboarding

Employee onboarding is a support service, i.e. the customer is internal; however, it's also an important differentiator in the service offering, as employees' experience of joining the organisation will permanently shape their view of it. It's also something that many of us have had negative experiences going through, especially when joining large firms. If companies get it right, it's also an important selling point, as the new recruits will call all their friends and tell them what a great place it is to work—we've seen this in action.

We think this is a universal example, because in most organisations, the responsibilities are distributed, and the service doesn't work very well; in this banks case, over thirty separate functions were responsible for it, and unsurprisingly it never worked. So, we simplified it by pulling together a small support team made up of people from many of those functions, who could work as a team to manage the customer experience, while drawing on the standardised capability teams; the resulting model looks like this (Fig. 22.2):

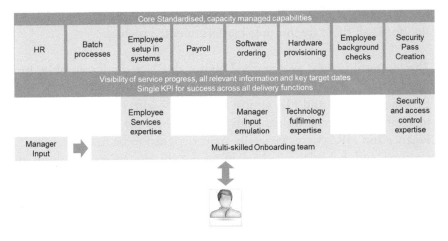

Fig. 22.2 Employee onboarding service aligned example

No service is more than one team away from the end customer (the new employee):

- All capabilities have visibility of the key information (employee start date).
- Core standardised teams are able to prioritise their own workload, instead of being governed by tickets and meaningless KPIs.
- Customer facing teams able to adjust/configure the customer experience by applying their knowledge to each case—e.g. if employee is from overseas, background checks might be prioritised before confirming employee setup and HR processes, to avoid late rejection after the employee has invested in moving.
- While some technology investment was involved, technical changes were minimal compared to organisational and role changes, which made the change cheap to implement.
- All teams share the same metric to measure success—"Can the employee do their job on Day 1?"

In this real-life example, the simple metric "can I do my job on Day 1" moved from 6% success prior to rollout, to 98% success, within two weeks of operation, saving the organisation significant amounts on wasted employee time and, more significantly, making a tangible difference to employees' perception of the organisation as a "great place to work".

And the same model can apply to analogous services, such as customer onboarding, but an important principle to understand is that it can apply to *any* service in the organisation, founded on the capability model described in Chapters 23–25.

But achieving this in a traditional organisation, as we've observed, isn't straightforward; there are multiple barriers to entry, such as:

- The leadership team: as described above, this is a significant shift from Leadership by Numbers, to Leadership by Results.
- Existing Financial and HR setups: to make this effective, companies need to create new organisational units and move people from existing ones. Finance and HR systems generally aren't designed to be flexible.
- Cultural and behavioural changes needed in the teams involved: not everyone will be comfortable working in self-organised teams, and not everyone will be comfortable making decisions. However, people like to learn, and they really like being able to support the customer!
- It sounds too good to be true! This is another very real barrier to even starting.

These barriers can be overcome, as we've discovered. If you'd like to learn more, you can see a longer version of this chapter with some practical guidance on our website.[4]

Conclusion

In this chapter, we've outlined the core rationale for building service aligned organisations, and why it's important to banks and other financial service providers to focus on service to retain and enhance their customer share. We've described what a service is and the building blocks for implementing one. Service alignment isn't an optional extra if you want the business to survive; needs are evolving fast, they're demanding more personalised services and businesses need to respond. But as other organisations like Apple have shown, it's achievable and will have tangible bottom-line benefits.

Notes

1. Banking Redefined (IBM). http://www-935.ibm.com/services/us/gbs/thoughtleadership/bankingredefined/. Accessed 30 December 2017.
2. Gallo, C. (2012, August 30). Apple's Secret Employee Training Manual Reinvents Customer Service in Seven Ways. *Forbes*. https://www.forbes.com/sites/carminegallo/2012/08/30/apples-secret-employee-training-manual-reinvents-customer-service-in-seven-ways/#7d43fba564fd. Accessed 1 January 2018.
3. Blandino, S. (2016, July 25). How the Ritz-Carlton Delivers Exceptional Customer Service. http://stephenblandino.com/2016/07/how-the-ritz-carlton-delivers-exceptional-customer-service.html. Accessed 1 January 2018.
4. Blakstad, S., & Allen, R. (2017, July 23). Service Alignment in Banks (long version with practical guidance). hiveonline. http://www.hivenetwork.online/2016/07/service-alignment-in-banks/. Accessed 1 January 2018.

Further Reading

Blakstad, S. (2013, December). Why Change?
Kingsley, J., Brown, P., & Paterson, S. (2015, July). *The Fear-Free Organization*. Kogan Page.

Laloux, F., & Wilber, K. (2014, February). *Reinventing Organizations*. Nelson Parker.

Robertson, J. B. (2015). *Holacracy, the Revolutionary Management System That Abolishes Hierarchy*. Portfolio Penguin.

23

Case Managed and Core Standardised Capabilities

Instead of trying to standardise end to end processes, which degrades customer experience and artificially maintains parallel processes, keeping key differentiator services flexible allows more standardisation in supporting services, while delivering a fully flexible customer experience.

The service aligned model described in the previous chapter relies on two key types of capability: Case Managed—flexible at the customer-facing edge, and Core Standardised—pre-loaded elements that are instantly available to the customer-facing teams on demand. This chapter describes the two types of capability. With these two simple capability types, organisations can easily flex structure to include third-party providers, partnership-operated services and other ecosystem players, and continuously evolve to meet changing customer needs.

While the two models are superficially completely different, they do share some important characteristics, and in the real world, you will rarely see a single function which is a pure example of only one of the models; on top of most core standardised capability, you would expect to see a thin case managed layer, facing off to internal customers, and within case managed teams, there will almost always be some core standardised elements. Because both models rely on governance structure, roles, accountabilities and decision rights, it's actually very easy to mix and match them like this; however, it does mean that getting the governance right in the first place is critical.

Service alignment is more than just how teams are structured; the organisational architecture and in particular, the capability model, needs to

© The Author(s) 2018
S. Blakstad and R. Allen, *FinTech Revolution*,
https://doi.org/10.1007/978-3-319-76014-8_23

distinguish those services. The capability structure may look something like this in the service aligned universal bank (Fig. 23.1):

But before reaching that level of detail, the basic model for any organisation remains the same: customer interacts with case managed capabilities, which in turn draw down on core standardised. While the customer may also have some direct interaction with some core standardised capabilities (payments spring to mind), even these will have a customised element at the customer-facing edge, so the basic model still holds.

Each of these boxes represents a capability—i.e. a purpose of the organisation, such as "Customer Management" or "Buildings & Equipment Management". Each of these will represent a number of disciplines and roles, potentially spanning large ranges of what would have been different parts of the organisation in the traditional, pyramid organisation. Instead of being managed by a hierarchical triangle structure, capabilities are managed by formal communication networks and governance, agreed by key roles within the relevant parts of the structure and regularly reviewed for relevance.

Within the capabilities, formal roles, domains, accountabilities and decision rights are agreed within the same governance structure, so that everyone is clear about roles—their own, and just as importantly, each others'.

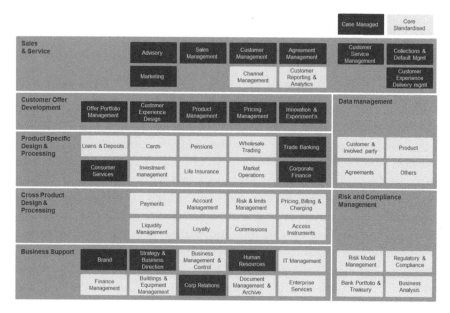

Fig. 23.1 Case Managed vs Core Standardised capability model

The importance of this governance in contrast to traditional hierarchies becomes clear when considering this at an organisational level:

- No supporting function is more than one "team" away from its end customer.
- Teams are not arranged to fit into a specialism-oriented hierarchy, but aligned to delivering customer outcomes.
- Management hierarchies are replaced by governance structures, decoupling seniority from numbers of people managed.
- Each capability has clearly defined and agreed supply links with its donor capabilities—and with its customers, internal or external.
- Each capability has clear visibility of the customer-facing metrics and how they can influence their fulfilment.
- Each capability has the ability to prioritise and manage its workload internally, with formal governance triggers for escalation and rebalancing when problems arise.
- Decision rights, including the ability to dynamically adjust and prioritise workload to support customers, are embedded into the capability.

These important principles maintain the agility of the modular organisation, as well as embedding empowerment and customer-aligned behaviours into the teams. But as we said above, this is where the similarities end. We'll first examine each model and then describe how they interact in practice.

Case Managed, Multi-skilled Teams at the Customer-Facing Edge

Case Management,[1] as the name implies, arose originally from healthcare, where they've been doing it for centuries, and has subsequently been adopted by a huge range of retail and service organisations, either consciously by design, or by evolution. You may already have teams using case management in the organisation, unless you've learned everything—it's equivalent to the old-fashioned model of the bank manager making decisions about his customers on the fly. Let's have a look at the typical case management system from a medical perspective.

Each customer of the system is presented as a unique case. You walk into the doctor's surgery with a pain, or a fever, and the doctor, after some critical first steps (Are you still breathing?) and authentication (Are you who you said you are?), uses her knowledge and experience, through a series of questions, to determine the nature of the malady and the appropriate treatment. She will then recommend a course of treatment or further investigations, depending on whether the problem can be quickly identified. The treatment and further investigations will all be standardised, centrally provided—by the pharmacy, the hospital, etc.—and rigorously governed, but how they are delivered to you will be configured by your medical practitioner, based on her knowledge of you and your case.

Costs are controlled, and standards are maintained by the rigorous standardisation of operating theatre equipment, pharmaceutical production standards, etc., but she is (within standard control limits) completely free to prescribe and agree with you how your ailment should be treated. She will also have access to other specialists in the practice—nurses, administrators, etc.—who can support the configuration of your experience at the point of delivery, without having to pass it on to another team in another building. In larger practices, you will also be able to undergo minor surgery on site and there may be a dispensary.

Other industries have learned from this model—you experience it each time you enter an Apple store. They don't make you wait in line; they work with you as individuals to configure your experience based on your needs and stated wants. Apple consistently generates some of the highest customer loyalty of any brand, despite producing a smaller range of products than any equivalent manufacturer and using cheaper components in its products than its competitors. It's not the multiplicity of products or even the quality of the components that creates the customer experience.

Apple's products are designed with the consumer at the heart, but it's not just that. The Apple experience also extends beyond the store, to when you unpack the product in your home, and this is all part of the configured customer experience. Apple still does all the things in their stores that every other shop does—take your money before handing over goods, validate your credit card—but what happens around these checks is designed with your experience in mind.

So, case management isn't a lack of control—the governance actually has to be more rigorous than in the functionally aligned model—but it embeds the controls into the customer experience in a way that's seamless and appropriate for that customer. Let's consider a banking scenario, with an account-opening example.

A customer walks into a branch—or a virtual branch, if you prefer, wanting to open a new account. Close your eyes and think of that customer.

Ready?

Who is the customer? Is it you? Or someone else? Is he/she/it an individual or an organisation? A boomer opening an account in a new name following a divorce, or a 13-year-old kid opening his first account? A refugee doctor with no identity paperwork? A sole trader or a big corporate? Is it your self-driving car? Maybe you had more than one in mind. Maybe it's a sole trader who's also just got divorced, has a share portfolio and wants to move some funds from abroad?

For each of those cases, the bank is going to need to do the obvious: KYC, credit checks, account-opening procedures, validation of origin of funds, etc. But you wouldn't instinctively treat each of these customers the same. The order in which they do the checks might vary and how robust they are; the risk appetite and potential cross-selling opportunities will vary.

Nowadays we have different account types for many of these customers, and we have as many different procedures, carefully designed around customer segment and profiling, predicted behaviours, etc. But they all want the same thing. And no customer really fits into a predetermined box. However, many types of account the bank thinks up, they'll never really flex to all the different customer needs. Furthermore, many standard processes are imposed in a linear fashion, which means they're asking questions in an illogical sequence, or simply not adjusting based on the answers they get.

For fun, let's do our sole trader who's also just got divorced, has a share portfolio and wants to move some funds from abroad. They go through the application process with someone in the branch (let's call her Julie), who takes their details and passes them through to the processing centre. In the processing centre, Jim puts the details into the system (Jim can't read some of the entries, so he puts some queries in the queue for Julie to pick up later, but he does what he can) and initiates the checks, which are operated by different teams, and the customer waits. Meanwhile, in Sanctions screening, it turns out Julie hasn't asked all the questions they need so they have to contact Julie to get more information from the customer. Julie manages the customer by trying to give him realistic expectations of how long the account will take to set up and answering his questions.

Now, let's picture the scenario differently. The same customer, with the same needs, walks in. Julie walks up the customer and asks what they need. On learning that the customer wants to open an account, Julie performs a triage, adjusting the questions along the way. There's a question about the offshore funds, so she calls Pete over to offer some expert advice.

Pete answers the question, drawing on an online tool for a quick answer, and the customer has the account provided with mobile payments and card issued on the spot. The transaction takes minutes.

So far, so Apple. But what's happening in the background? The key differences in the case managed example are.

- Multi-skilled customer-facing teams available onsite at the point of customer interface to support every aspect of the customer need, not just sales.
- Customer service teams able to adjust workflows in real time based on customer input.
- Customer-facing teams able to draw on core standardised resources, preconfigured to allow for instant access.
- The resulting customer experience is seamless and quick, with controlled customers in the places they belong.

Sounds too good to be true? It isn't, but achieving this model takes careful design and whole operating model change, either at the service level, the capability level or the organisational level (usually all three) and that's not a simple process, or an easy transition. We won't go into details of building a capability here, but you can see the longer version of this chapter, which includes the building blocks, on our website.[2]

Core Standardised, Capacity Managed Capabilities

We tend to avoid using the term Capacity Managed in conversations with stakeholders, because it can confuse people, but the term best describes how these capabilities fundamentally differ from the prevalent internal service model we see in most banks today: the ticket, or request-driven approach. In this approach, nothing happens unless driven by a specific request and only then are teams mobilised to start providing a service. In Capacity Management, service teams anticipate the capacity that will be needed, and front-load that capacity so that it will be available when needed. Just as water or electricity is provisioned, enough is there when you need it, and you use what you need, when you want it. That sounds really simple, and actually, it is.

The underlying assumption is that when you regularly produce large volumes of something, you can predict the need for that something based on past demand. The challenge is that the greater the number of variations of that something there are, the more difficult it is to forecast how many you will need of each variation and the harder it is to manage it as capacity. So, it's also really important to reduce the number of variations as much as possible, unless you are supported by a layer of capacity managed elements. Even service organisations producing essentially similar outputs, with some variation, can be managed in this way, by applying a thin case managed layer within the capacity managed capability (which is a perfectly effective variant of this model, discussed below).

The advantage of this two-layer approach is that, by configuring the capabilities at the point of customer delivery, i.e. the case managed end, whether it's a separate capability or embedded within the capacity managed capability, we can achieve much greater standardisation at the back end by having a very small set of base products, artefacts, resources and core components. For example, if the customer-facing teams are empowered to fix the term of a deposit based on customer requirements, you don't need a three-month, a six-month, a 12-month and an 18-month version. You just need a deposit. The same applies to everything from technology to agreements. So, with little product variation, volumes are much easier to forecast, and it becomes very easy to manage front-loaded capacity.

So what's wrong with using the term "Capacity Managed"? Our experience has told us to shy away from any term that looks as though it might involve doing something "to" people, and most leaders leap on the "capacity" word as related to people, rather than output. So we feel the term core standardised, while not so descriptive, is sufficiently accurate and captures the critical essence of why you're doing this, for leadership consumption.

Like case managed teams, core standardised teams have embedded prioritisation rights and decision rights. This means that they don't need to operate on a ticket-based system; just like the case managed teams, they can and should use visual management techniques to have visibility of the customer metrics in real time and are able to adjust priorities in order to meet the metric for each customer, achieving a much higher hit rate than the usual time-bound targets for ticket closure.

How Does It Work?

Many elements of Core Utility teams are exactly the same as case managed—teams which are self-organising, self-prioritising, can share multiple roles and readjust in real time. Unlike case managed teams, they are also usually their own Communities of Practice, so many of the things you would normally expect not to find in a case managed team, such as skills development, career paths and management mentoring, exist within the home capability for core standardised services.

This has both advantages and challenges; it can lead the Core Utility resources to feel differentiated if not managed effectively, so they need the opportunity to explore additional roles both within and outside the Core Utility capability, if they want to experience how their skill set could be applied to other types of teams, for example. It also means that there's a temptation to centralise all three management roles (Lead Allocation, Lead Link and Pastoral Development) into a single individual. This should be avoided, not just because it will give the capability the tendency to be more inward-looking and hierarchy focused, but also because it creates unnecessary stress in the single leader and the subsequent need to create multiple layers of cascading hierarchy to support them, thus losing many of the advantages of agility and flexibility and making self-governance impossible (Fig. 23.2).

The advantages of this approach to supporting services, on the surface, are the significant cost saving involved (and this should not be ignored, both manpower and capital investment are reduced by around 20–30% by this approach) and

	Case Managed	Core Standardised
Team Structure	Multi-skilled	Single skillset (differing maturity /roles)
Community of Practice	Separate to team, formed of individuals from multiple Case Managed teams	Within one or small number of similar Capabilities sharing the same skillset
Customer Metrics	Determined based on direct service delivered to Customer	Determined based on metrics of supported Case Managed Capabilities
Processes	Case Managed, not standardised – able to flex at the point of customer delivery	Standardised, Lean, little variation, high quality
Work throughput	Forecastable but not predictable, resources need to flex frequently; output configured based on customer need	Predictable with occasional need to flex based on changing demand; standard elements preloaded for later drawdown
Skills Development	Largely within Community of Practice; skills mentoring likely to come from outside home team	Within Core Standardised Capability; skills development likely to come within home team
Lead Allocation role	Responsible for allocating resources to tasks on a daily basis and recommending temporary or longer term role assignments; resources may also be allocated long term by their home CoP	Responsible for allocating resources to their long term roles and short time re-allocation of roles as required
Lead Link role	Represents Capability to wider organisation	
Work prioritisation	Agreed collectively, usually dynamically within the team; final decisions made (if needed) by Lead Allocation role	
Team dynamic	Self-organising, everyone is clear on their decision rights and can recommend changes to roles on the fly, based on visual evidence of priority work	

Fig. 23.2 Case managed vs core standardised similarities and differences

the improved time to market of the output. Quality also goes up considerably, but again this isn't the only benefit. As with case management, the key consideration is the impact on customer experience, which is significant not just because it delivers a better customer outcome, but because of the engagement with that customer outcome, the supporting service staff are now able to experience.

This is partly because the value chain is shorter, so they are closer to the end customer anyway, but also because they are now managing their own throughput based on visible customer satisfaction metrics—not some internally generated "do it in three days or else" metric, but "did the customer get what she wanted? Yes or no? Did we meet the date we promised *as an organisation* to deliver this service and was it to the quality we expect our customers to experience?" It may be hard to imagine the impact that has on the supporting service teams, who usually haven't been anywhere near a customer, let alone understood how what they do benefits them. The effects, I can assure you, are extraordinary.

Here's an example of how this approach can work even on deeply embedded technology.

> **Storage Capability Creation**
>
> About ten years ago, a very large global bank had a problem with delivering storage into its data centres. Not surprising, this was universal before virtualisation and cloud were widely used, and even now in most major banks, it's pretty normal, especially for mainframe and midrange. We have to wait for a need to arise before we commit to spending any money; this kit is expensive, and we need to be really sure we need it before we put our necks on the line and order it. Obviously, nowadays many of us (not all, and not always) have more flexible options for storage, but even if this is the case, we still face this challenge in many service areas. We've chosen this example to demonstrate that it's not just AML or product standardisation that this works on.
>
> In this bank, it took about nine months to get a new server—six if you were very lucky. That's because when you were developing an application, you had to be pretty sure how you wanted that application to be set up before you could even order the storage; the data centre engineers knew they'd have to order bespoke kit for you, so they wouldn't even talk to you before you knew what you wanted.
>
> Then, once you'd got to the point in the development cycle that you had a pretty good idea what configuration and volume you'd need, you could go ahead and order the kit. The engineers would then design it, build a spec and have that signed off as ok from an architectural perspective. Then, they'd build a bill of materials for the vendors, which the vendor would quote on. That quote would then be built into a financial approval process with 55 mandatory approvers.

When it had been approved, the quote had expired because it took longer than a month to get responses from all 55 approvers and go through the layers of meetings (two in EMEA, one in global HQ) for signoff, so you had to get another quote before revalidating and making any necessary adjustments. Eventually, it found its way into the order system, someone would order the kit, and you'd get it delivered (3-month order cycle), and then someone would schedule it for racking, stacking and configuration in the data centre. When you look at that, it's impressive that they even did it in six months—and usually, they didn't, unless you could shout very, very loud.

Multiple attempts had been made over a number of years to fix the ordering system, by introducing new technology for placing tickets, putting in place architectural controls, etc. But none of these helped make it quicker, in fact most of them slowed it down even further. Because the answer was that the root of the problem (time to market) was a misperception of what successful customer outcomes looked like.

The underlying assumption in the system was that the primary objective of the (internal) customers was to have custom builds for everything they were creating. This was proved to be false even before the core standardised service was introduced to replace the old system—orders stopped coming into the team over two months before the new service went live. Because the primary objective wasn't the specialisation, it was getting storage. By moving to a capacity-managed storage service, lead times dropped from nine months to six days and probably could have been driven down further, but it wasn't felt necessary at the time.

So how did it work?

The solution was simple; achieving it was less simple. Instead of the full request-based design, order and build service, we moved to four types of server within each of the core technology families (Unix/Windows)—small, medium, large and very large. These were bought in batches and pre-racked and stacked in advance, with standard operating systems loaded. A small, case managed team was created within the capability to manage incoming orders and apply any operating system configuration needed at the point of delivery.

This team of six consisted of people with project management, engineering design, capacity management and service delivery skills. Embedded in the core standardised capability, they were the only people who weren't hardware engineers of some sort, or data centre support staff, and they identified with the skills communities from which they came, while their primary anchor was in the capability they served. An existing order system was modified to support the new, hugely reduced options available, which made it much easier to learn and use for the team.

Because all the software teams had been holding their orders for the new approach, when it first went live, we were nervous about the backlog, when those two plus months of orders hit the system, but it worked like clockwork and we immediately hit our SLA of six days (or less). There was still the option to order fully customised kit in the case where something special was needed, but this was hardly ever used; the level of configuration that could be applied was more than enough for most purposes. The previous assumption that customisation was needed at every level of hardware built had simply been wrong, even though it had originally been based on experience of how orders came in—but we had never tested our assumptions against customer behaviour, simply what they were telling us.

Immediate benefits delivered by this change were:

- Time to market reduction from nine months to six days.
- 32% cost saving on data centre supplier and service management.
- Reduced errors and greater environmental stability due to simpler architecture and more standardised builds.
- Greater transparency and traceability made incident management much simpler (and less needed).
- 72% reduction in number of infrastructure project managers needed.
- Reduced staff attrition.
- Faster onboarding of staff due to reduced learning needs.
- Reduction in cost of approvals process (which had been running at about $3.500 per request in man hours).
- Greater transparency for Total Cost of Ownership, as data centre rate cards were completely standardised.

Of course, implementing this new approach was not without challenges. The main difficulty to overcome was persuading infrastructure management and Financial Control to invest upfront, rather than waiting for the tickets to come in before making an investment decision. Analysis was needed to support the business case for making a change that is so counter-intuitive. But a key learning was that, by examining the actual customer need, we could identify and separate the case managed and core standardised elements, leading to all those benefits

Conclusion

In this chapter, we have described the two basic building blocks of the service aligned organisation: the case managed capability and the core standardised capability. We've given you a comparison table to understand the similarities and differences and briefly discussed the relationship between Communities of Practice/Centres of Excellence and the case managed/core standardised model within service aligned organisations.

We have included a case study of the core standardised model, demonstrating how by lifting customisation into case management, businesses can achieve extraordinary improvements to customer experience factors such as time to market and to organisational targets such as cost and headcount.

Case managed and core standardised are two superficially very different types of capability needed to deliver full-service alignment; they share important common elements such as internal self-management and key governance constructs. Fundamental to service alignment, enabling case managed capabilities to configure the customer experience at the point of delivery supports radically standardised product and supporting services in the core standardised capacity. With these elements in place, organisations can deliver truly excellent customer service and turn on a pin to integrate with other players in the ecosystem or develop new services.

Notes

1. Case Management (IBM). https://www.ibm.com/analytics/case-management. Accessed 30 December 2017.
2. Blakstad, S., & Allen, R. (2016, July 23). Case Managed and Core Standardised Capabilities (full version). hiveonline. http://www.hive-network.online/2016/07/case-managed-and-core-standardised-capabilities/. Accessed 30 December 2017.

24

Communities of Practice and Centres of Excellence

This chapter describes a way to manage skills development in any organisation in the ecosystem, but in particular within the service aligned organisation. It expands on the theme of devolving decision rights and control to expert groups, covered in the previous chapter. As with the other chapters in this section, you can find an expanded version with some practical steps and a road map on our website.[1]

Building any kind of business requires people with skills and guidance for them on how to apply those skills. Organisations have traditionally arranged themselves along functional lines, with people sharing skills in the same organisational unit or units. However, as organisations grow, this model breaks, with pockets of skills forming in parallel functions across different areas of the organisation. Banks have multiple teams supporting lending, doing process mapping, building technology, etc., and often these teams aren't in communication with each other. Assumptions about common practice lead to fragmentation, with teams thinking they're following a standard, but actually operating quite differently.

The people who really know their stuff aren't listened to, not used effectively and become frustrated and disenfranchised because they're being told to follow standards designed by someone else who doesn't understand their customer and their day-to-day experience of delivering value in the business. But, as Steve Jobs said, "It doesn't make sense to hire smart people and then tell them what to do; we hire smart people so they can tell us what to do". And in the service aligned organisation, people are even more distributed, as

© The Author(s) 2018
S. Blakstad and R. Allen, *FinTech Revolution*,
https://doi.org/10.1007/978-3-319-76014-8_24

the very essence of multi-skilled teams includes having a limited number of people with any given skill set in any one team.

In the service aligned organisation, as in any ecosystem built of small units, we also break the traditional model of a leader managing and mentoring people within their own skill/experience domain. Not only are the holders of lead roles not usually responsible for line management of their teams, their domain expertise may also be very far removed from the skill set of many or most of the people working in their unit. So not only do they not have official responsibility for developing their people, they will probably be unable to do so from a skills perspective.

Clearly, this risks people with specialist skills or knowledge becoming isolated, and their skills being diverted and not following common practices. Service alignment also presents the challenge of people developing new skills and taking on new roles, where they will primarily pick up skills from team colleagues, but also need to keep abreast of developments in the area, and separate learned behaviours which are supportive of common practice from those idiosyncratic to individual role holders. It is also likely that all people with roles involving a particular skill set will need to develop those skills and surpass previous practices, as industry best practice evolves.

Even in traditionally aligned organisations, all people with common skill sets benefit from learning from each other—both within and outside the organisation. There are also clear benefits for people with common skill sets to pool methods and frameworks; the experience they deliver will be consistent, regardless of where they sit in the organisation, and they can benefit from sharing ideas, effort and learnings. The traditional approach is to offer training in skills, which is a legitimate way to develop skill sets, but still risks leaving people isolated and unable to compare problems and develop solutions with others with similar sills.

Of the three leadership domains in the service aligned organisation, Communities of Practice are the easiest to design, largely because they fill a gap and people are keen to participate. But they still need a kick-start, and this chapter describes how to build such communities.

There is also a sliding scale between Communities of Practice and Centres of Excellence; the one being more informal and self-evolving, while Centres of Excellence equate to capabilities and tend to be more formally structured, with allocation of tasks being controlled within the community. This chapter also discusses how to build CoEs and the benefits of each type of model.

What Is a Community of Practice?

Loosely defined, a Community of Practice is a group of people with the same skill set and tasks within an organisation or an ecosystem. So the sales people would have one, while the risk people who sit in their teams would belong to a distinct community, even though they sit in the same capability supporting Lending in their day-to-day work. CoPs and Centres of Excellence are both arranged by skill, rather than purpose, although a centre of excellence is likely to equate to a purpose and therefore a capability within the business model.

A CoP would also include people at all levels of skill development, from the most senior to the most junior, the critical thing being the sharing of common skill sets, so it may include people with a variety of different roles, but who are either progressing along, or dipping into, a common skills development trajectory. In service aligned organisations you would find more Communities of Practice supporting the case managed capabilities, with Centres of Excellence concentrated in core standardised capabilities, while in traditional organisations, Centres of Excellence are able to leverage scale and consistency to support delivery of services across the organisation.

At the more informal end of the scale, or across an ecosystem, a loose community of practice would usually include common frameworks, a charter and knowledge sharing. At the other end of the scale, a centre of excellence will also include formal career paths, a common plan, workforce management and a strategy. In practice, most CoPs will fall somewhere in between these two extremes, with the level of centralisation and formal control depending on the type of capability and the need for centralisation.

So for example, an Infrastructure Build team is very likely to be arranged as a centre of excellence, with the team co-located and controlled centrally, with some individuals being allocated to projects or case managed teams as needed but running under a single plan, largely supporting a core standardised capability building hardware. The sales people, at the other end of the scale, will look to their community to support their skills development and tooling, but will be formally aligned to their case managed capabilities and their local teams for day-to-day work allocation.

So why is this useful? We think Steve Jobs was spot on with this. You've hired a load of people for their skills and experience, then you get some external or internal function to design how they use those skills, often at great cost, and at the same time seed disenfranchisement and frustration in the teams on the ground. We present here an elegant solution to both the cost and the enfranchisement challenge, while at the same time using the embedded knowledge in the organisation most effectively.

That's not to say CoPs won't use external help—they may decide they need training, or support to build frameworks, which they either haven't got the knowledge or the bandwidth to develop internally, and that works with the model, plus they will be more accepting of any resulting framework or training programme because it is something they've initiated.

Benefits of Communities of Practice include:

- Common standards developed by the experts—i.e. the people who were hired because of their knowledge.
- Cross-fertilisation of knowledge within the team.
- Development of toolsets, approaches and frameworks by people who really understand how the organisation works.
- Feeling of belonging and value within the community, addressing potential isolation issues.
- Agreement on how "things should be done around here" by the people who do them and ownership of standards, tools and methods.
- Mentoring and support for community members by people who can understand the challenges they are facing.
- Links to relate CoPs.
- Significantly reduced reliance on HR and centralised functions to support training and personal growth (Fig. 24.1).

So, Isn't This All a Bit Touchy-Feely for a Bank?

Actually, no. Communities of Practice give the bank concrete and very measurable benefits. Critically, they are a pivotal part of supporting the governance building, which is important in traditional organisations but fundamental to service aligned organisations in the ecosystem. They become the glue between individual teams aligned to particular services and the underlying standards they need to adopt and support.

If we think about large organisations as opposed to franchises, they have some unusual, but not unique challenges. They are big, and federated, and different standards naturally evolve within the teams supporting the user experience and configuring it at the point of customer delivery. This may be ok for an organisation supporting, say, community nursing.[2] After all, in

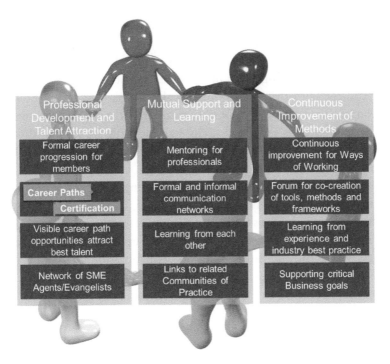

Fig. 24.1 Communities of practice

these small, self-organising teams, the only important customer experience is that delivered one-to-one by the nurse in question, and the configuration of capabilities by that individual nurse is the only important customer experience that customer will have. So variability is not only desirable, it's completely practical.

Something we've seen from the more ecosystem-based organisational strategies, while many are excellent at addressing the "how teams work" aspect, is that many either don't formally address, or don't need to address, the consistency question; a large corporation can adopt and benefit from consistent practices across the communities, whereas self-organising teams generally don't, where teams are closely aligned to a consistent customer base. They use training and knowledge sharing, which is positive, but there's an underlying assumption that self-organising teams will have the right skill sets and knowledge, or buy them from somewhere else, and that some variability of customer experience between customer sets is acceptable and probably desirable.

While this is true for professional skills such as nursing and architecture, there is a need to align skills and behaviours more closely within larger organisations, not just to provide consistent customer experiences, but also, in many cases more importantly, consistent employee experiences. This is especially true of banks, where customers are likely to have multiple relationship managers dealing with all their needs, interfacing via a lot of different channels, with teams of people (or things that pretend to be people). Their relationship needs to be consistent on all of these channels, to create a seamless experience, as they may be interacting with a bot via online channels, switching to specialist humans for additional needs or specialist services, in the course of a single encounter.

Not only are paying customers experiencing multiple instances of organisation in terms of brand and product, via many different delivery points—channels, branches, business centres. Regulators and consumer protection bodies, payments schemes and governments are also expecting common standards, while the increasing need for collaboration with Fintechs and competitors will also mean banks need to be joined up with the ecosystem. So it's not simple, and we should assume there will be a need both to develop common standards internally and to communicate and collaborate with these standards across the wider ecosystem.

Within an organisation, the need for consistency is also significant in teams coordinating all the core standardised activities, but also in more federated internal support teams, who will again be interfacing with the same internal customers, whether receiving organisation teams or supporting teams such as technology delivery. In this case, the consistency of approach reduces risk and the need to learn repeatedly.

Communities of Practice can also play an important role in allocating resources to case managed capabilities—and, in some cases, supporting core standardised capabilities with either long-term or short-term specialist support. As repositories of accumulated knowledge and skills development, they should also be represented within decision-making bodies.

Centres of Excellence

At the other end of the community scale, a centre of excellence is a formally organised community of people with the same skill set, who probably also fulfil the skills element of a single capability. CoEs don't exist in truly Agile organisations, but they do exist in service aligned organisations and in banks, where elements such as hardware and data centres still (for now) present the challenges of physical centralisation and interface with the wider business, while other activities such as customer due diligence processing may still involve large teams processing information with predictable inputs and outputs.

A centre of excellence is effectively analogous to a core standardised capability. There may be many good reasons for organisations to manage their own Centres of Excellence rather than buying in services; however, for many organisations and especially banks, it makes more sense to buy in these services, rather than investing in the infrastructure and organisation to support them internally, if they're not key differentiators for the business model.

The key identifiers by which you would recognise a centre of excellence as opposed to a community of practice are:

- Composed of people with a narrow range of skills supporting a single purpose of the organisation, rather than contributing to a composite purpose supported by multiple skill sets.
- Usually arranged in the traditional skills-aligned way under one "roof", either virtually or physically.
- Manages skills development within the capability.
- Leaders usually responsible for both skills development and work allocation.
- Procedures are streamlined and very standardised, with little variation.

However, in common with case managed capabilities, these teams are still largely self-organising and self-developing and, like Communities of Practice, will have significant autonomy in prioritisation of work, development of skill sets and allocation of tasks within the teams. NB in service aligned organisations, you will almost always have a thin service layer overlaying large Centres of Excellence, as discussed in the previous chapter but for the sake of argument we'll treat the whole unit as a single entity.

Community of Practice or Centre of Excellence?

The major differences between CoPs and CoEs are listed below. In essence, if someone is working in a-case managed capability, they probably belong to a CoP as well. If they're working in a core standardised capability, the home capability is also the CoE.

However, as we've said, it's not usually that straightforward, in the same way that the case managed vs core standardised model isn't really that pure—albeit a very good guide. Capabilities and communities will operate best under different levels of autonomy and management, depending on what they're for, how big they are, and the level of central interaction that best fits their purpose. In a typical business like a bank, some obvious elements fit neatly into core standardised:

- IT Environments Management
- Reporting
- Financial Control.

Where you would expect centralised or federated units, effectively doing one thing (each); others that are clearly case managed/Agile:

- Customer Management
- Business Strategy
- IT Solutions Development.

Where you would need CoPs to support the individual skill sets, such as risk management, product management, financial management, business analysis, project management, solution development, process modelling, development skills and unit testing; while others still have elements both of Centres of Excellence and of CoPs:

- Business Architecture will be heavily centralised in planning, but syndicated into Agile teams to support development.
- Deployment heavily centralised in planning and execution, but seeded into the individual business units to support the release of new technology in detail.

As with the case managed/core standardised model, it's not as simple as putting every area into one bucket; it's also worth noting that the model that works today is likely to evolve and change, so it needs governance to support regular reviews and the ability to flex over time to support changing customer needs.

Conclusion

In this chapter, we've described what a community of practice is, the benefits of building them and why they're important not just in a service aligned organisation, but in any large organisation.

We've also presented the outlines of a centre of excellence and how this differs from a community of practice; together with the case managed/core standardised capabilities, these four concepts form the heart of the organisational construct in the service aligned organisation. We've illustrated how the lines are blurred and there is a sliding scale between CoPs and CoEs, and that the governance structure needs to be carefully designed to manage this effectively.

Notes

1. Blakstad, S., & Allen, R. (2016, July 23). Communities of Practice and Centres of Excellence. hiveonline. http://www.hivenetwork.online/2016/07/communities-of-practice-and-centres-of-excellence/. Accessed 1 January 2018.
2. Holmgren, M., & Betz, A. (2016, April 17). Buurtzorg Moves Beyond Nursing. *Enlivening Edge*. http://www.enliveningedge.org/organizations/buurtzorg-moves-beyond-nursing/. Accessed 1 January 2018.

25

Service Architecture

In this chapter, we discuss some core principles behind and practical steps towards developing a Service Architecture and how it sits alongside the other chapters in this section, with particular reference to Service Alignment. This chapter briefly describes how the concept of service fits into the constructs of service aligned organisations, and focuses primarily on how to arrange services as a Service Architecture (or Ecosystem) both within and beyond the organisation.

What Is a Service?

A Service is the value you provide to the customers; it's why the customers choose you and not somebody else to achieve their outcomes. At the heart of the service model must lie the questions, "What does the customer need from us?" and "Why would they choose us?"

In Chapter 14, we described the difference between a product and a service. The example of Haier shows why it's important to think of services, rather than products.

> Washing machines and potato farming.
>
> Haier,[1] the Chinese electronics manufacturer, offer a good example—one of their ranges (washing machines) are pretty standardised in the West, but they have chosen to take a different approach; responding to the needs of the Chinese customer. When complaints came through that their machine was clogging when farmers washed potatoes in it before taking them to market,

© The Author(s) 2018
S. Blakstad and R. Allen, *FinTech Revolution*,
https://doi.org/10.1007/978-3-319-76014-8_25

> another manufacturer would have told them to stop washing potatoes in it—after all, it's for clothes, not potatoes! That's the organisation dictating how the customer uses their product.
>
> Haier instead designed a model that *can wash both clothes and potatoes*. They offer another line coated in plastic to avoid rusting, based on the large number of customers who place their washing machine outside the house, and others that can operate at sub-zero temperatures. This is putting the customer's needs at the heart of the service, rather than telling the customer how to use the product.

Contrast Haier's approach with a senior banker, who recently explained to us the reason it took corporate customers six months to open an account, was that the customers were using the process wrongly. When thinking about services, we find it helpful to abstract as far away from the product as possible and think instead in terms of customer results. Like Haier, this means that you don't suffer from being constrained by what the product can do, or how you as an organisation think of the product.

When building a service architecture, it also helps to think in terms of customer needs and customer outcomes, rather than products, although there is a relationship and you will need to develop and deliver products to support the service architecture, but this step should come after you have decided which needs you are supporting, so throughout this chapter we assume product development is an outcome of the service design process.

As a reminder, in technical terms, a Service is a configuration of Capabilities that delivers value to the customer. In this chapter, we first demonstrate the relationship between services, processes, capabilities and organisation, how service architecture works from a governance perspective, and how to go about designing it, at a holistic level, although all of these topics are covered in more detail by other chapters. Let's have another look at our Operating Model abstract to put this in context (Fig. 25.1).

At first glance, it's clear that a Service has all the same elements of a capability or an organisation. That doesn't mean it's the same as either of those things, though. What it does mean is that it can, and usually does, include all of the same elements. Which makes sense, when you consider that a service is a Configuration of one or more Capabilities—i.e. it delivers value to the customer via delivering certain elements of that or those Capabilities in a way designed to support that customer's needs. Organisationally, it will be drawing on many parts of the organisation, or several organisations, which support those capabilities and again, all have these elements. But that doesn't help to define what we mean by a Service.

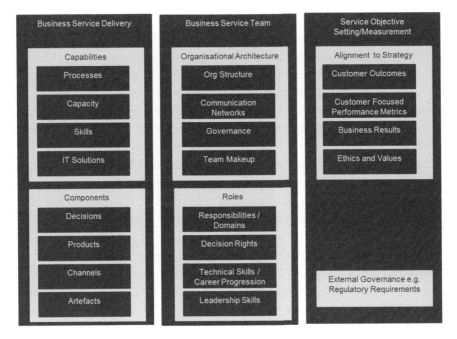

Fig. 25.1 Operating model for services

Services, Processes and Capabilities

Services, processes and capabilities have a lot of things in common: they are all organisationally agnostic, i.e. exist across organisational structures and may reach outside the organisation; they all require many elements of the Operating Model elements (although processes have fewer than either Capabilities or Services). It is therefore common for organisations to be confused about what is a process vs. what is a service vs. what is a capability, so we'll offer a comparison here:

- A **Capability** is a purpose of the organisation, which can encapsulate people, process and technology; it's what the organisation does.
- A **Service** is a configuration of capabilities, which delivers value to the customer.
- A **Process** is a predetermined set of activities and decision points, that is performed in a predictable way, with any given set of inputs resulting in a predictable set of outputs.

NB, a *case managed* process is a special type of process that meets the above conditions, but with so many potential variations that these are usually not captured in a traditional end-to-end process view.

NB: Service, in this context, has some parallels with, but is not directly analogous to, the IT Service definition embedded in BAIN, TOGAF and other architectural models. That doesn't mean it subsumes the IT Service definition, and when building full service aligned organisations, it's important to maintain the distinction, as IT services in architectural terms form an important component and shouldn't be confused with the service aligned service concept, which is broader and applicable to full customer service delivery.

Beyond these broad distinctions, the nesting of definitions can be confusing. Processes will often sit within capabilities and services, but may also flow across capabilities and support multiple services. Capabilities are likely to support multiple services and processes, while also encapsulating other capabilities and processes.

As services configure many capabilities, processes may draw on many capabilities, and capabilities will themselves encapsulate both sub capabilities and processes, the picture is not simple, but it's important to be familiar with the different definitions as we expand on the topic.

Service Model vs Capability Map

The organisation's service model is the representation of how services provided by the business to its customers, internal and external, supports the full range of customer outcomes that deliver the organisation's service objectives. Typically, as with Capabilities, there will be a number of views and layers depending on the audience and information needs. As a whole, you should be able to test the service model against the service objectives to identify any gaps and any services that are superfluous. It also helps to identify which capabilities are supporting your services, and how any modification of those services or development of new services will require changes to capabilities. While the capability map as a standalone artefact supports decisions about which capabilities to standardise/centralise/offshore/outsource and how to prioritise development of capabilities, the service model in addition is a bridge between strategy and the capabilities that support the services, which further supports decision making about capability development and prioritisation.

The service model is also in constant dialogue with strategy and in particular with strategy changes driven by changing customer needs. How do strategic changes impact the service model, and where are the opportunities in the service model that might translate into strategic opportunities?

For example, my strategy might be to build a USP in supporting small businesses in the catering industry, so my service model would include things like helping customers with all the usual business banking services in that sector, such as employee lifecycle support, revenue management support, supplier management support, and so forth. So, I would need to ensure I have capabilities that can provide payroll, cash management, supply chain management, accounting advisory, etc. But I might also want to differentiate my business by supplying services to that customer segment that gives them a unique reason to choose me, over another bank, because I understand their business and the challenges they face.

So as part of my supply chain management, for example, I might also provide some additional capabilities useful to businesses dealing with a variety of suppliers of short life goods, such as fresh ingredients, which could be parameterised to support their more complex supply chains, or one that supports tip management. Acknowledging that many small restaurants are owner-run, I might create configurations of my channel offerings that are more intuitive to people working with food and kitchen hardware than to somebody sitting at a desk all day.

This service model, then, will tell me what I want to offer via my services to the customers. I can then overlay it on my capability map and identify whether the current capabilities support it, or whether there's a need or an opportunity to evolve, change, or create new capabilities. Building on that example and those capabilities:

Service: **Employee Lifecycle Support**
Selected Capabilities configured by the service:

- Employee management

  - Employee selection and onboarding
  - Performance management
  - Career management
  - Employee offboarding.

- Payroll

  - Payroll
  - Tip reconciliation and allocation
  - Pensions administration.

- Cash management

  - Cash pooling and booking
  - Tip pooling.

Service: Supplier Management
Selected Capabilities configured by the service:

- Transfer of value management

  - Payments
  - Cash management.

- Supply chain management

  - Balance sheet management
  - Supplier scoring
  - Inventory control management
  - Cold room order manager.

In this example, the bank is not making any money directly from every one of the extras you supply, and it shouldn't try to! These are loss leaders—the cold room order manager is something we've partnered with a Fintech to provide, and the tip pooling and allocation system may be something we developed in-house, which don't offer any direct financial return to us—but they are part of the service ecosystem we offer, and distinguish our lifecycle service as one with the customer at the heart.

These are examples of the service ecosystem in action; they are also the things that create customer stickiness in the non-traditional world; the customers have quickly become accustomed to these aspects of your service, and to lose them would create a negative experience for the customers' staff and suppliers. The same cannot be said if they switch mortgages.

As discussed elsewhere, it's not enough trying to think on behalf of your customers, although sometimes you may have great and important insights on how you can support them based on your better understanding of your organisation's capabilities and how they can be configured differently to provide more useful services—think Henry Ford's faster horse—but it's also critical to engage with the customer and understand their behaviours, to come up with these insights in a way that really supports their business or personal needs.

Here are some examples of service models in traditional and non-traditional banks.

Traditional Retail Bank Service Architecture

In the traditional banking model, services are product related and triggered by interaction between the Bank and the Customer, usually initiated by the customer: There is a clear delineation between the bank as an entity and the customer as an entity (Fig. 25.2).

In this model, there are a variety of organisationally agnostic services which support the customer's needs. While these are largely driven or triggered by customer requests, the sequencing and interaction of services are well understood, and, in some cases, one will lead to another. Customer-facing staff delivering the service can anticipate the customer's needs and offer additional services accordingly, and there is an interaction between certain services across service families which can be predicted—for example, bereavement account closure can link to insurance payout services. However, while there's a sequence of likely events, there's also flexibility in this model, allowing customer-facing staff to flex their conversations and the way the service is offered, depending on the customer's needs. See case managed vs core standardised for further details of how this model works.

The benefit of this model is that it offers familiarity, while allowing for a capability-based operating model, so that banks can continue to offer customers traditional services and products which are familiar to them, while adopting more effective ways of working and a more personalised experience

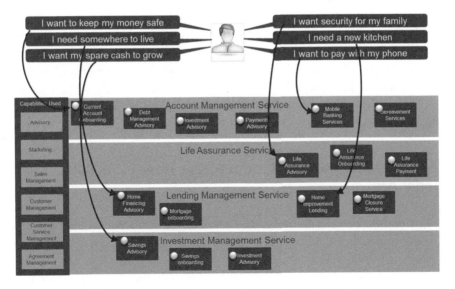

Fig. 25.2 Retail bank service architecture (domestic customer)

for the customer. It works well as a model for segment-specific banks with a clear limit to the service offering they want to expose to their customers. It also works well as an interim state towards offering a wider service model with more tight integration with customers and less clear divisions, as in the ecosystem model.

As the Service Architecture evolves, another key benefit is identifying gaps, synergies and the opportunity to evolve the supporting capabilities. While mapping capabilities give a great opportunity to identify core utilities, opportunities for consolidation and outsourcing, as well as gaps, the service view also adds the dimension of identifying further gaps, and superfluous capabilities, and to prioritise change based on customer needs.

It's important to note that while Service Architecture can look superficially a lot like a capability model or a customer journey, it both contains different information and gives different opportunities for decision making to both of those very important artefacts.

Ecosystem Small Business Bank Service Architecture

In the Ecosystem service architecture, the distinction between customer and bank or customer and supplier becomes deliberately blurred. As well as supporting the customer's traditional banking requirements, the bank is also supporting the business (or personal) goals of the customer beyond those services, and supporting partner organisations in providing services to their customers via their ecosystem. The customer also helps the bank to evolve its thinking, as it, too, learns and grows based on the support offered by the bank and partner services. The strength of this model is both its flexibility and that it offers symbiotic opportunities to the customer and partner organisations alike—and the partner organisations are likely to be customers too, and have their own ecosystem service architecture view of the bank (Fig. 25.3).

Key Differences of This Model to the Traditional Bank Model Are:

- Not request driven; many services are integrated and/or triggered by the ecosystem rather than by a request from the customer directly; for example, in this illustration, the cold storage and stock control system interacts with the menu planning system, data from customers, broader data anal-

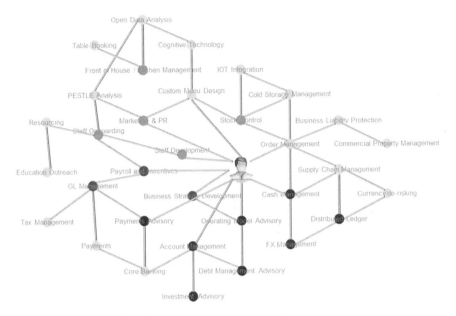

Fig. 25.3 Ecosystem bank service architecture

ysis and supplier data, to tell the management team which ingredients or dishes are out of stock, going end of life, fashionable/written about externally, popular with their customers, or cheap, which offers the customer the opportunity to design menus and pricing. This then interacts with the order management and cold storage systems, which in turn manage orders, while the order management system interacts with Payments, and services such as Distributed Ledger and Supply Chain Management as needed.

- Microservices based; managed through digital identity authentication, the Internet of Things and an ecosystem of apps, checks and balances are in place to alert humans of any suspicious conditions and invite direction in creative decisions, but otherwise things run smoothly without significant human intervention or the need for requests. Of course, customers can, and probably do, choose to select some but not all of these services, leaving manual or alternative flows in between, but the decision about how much to manage by request versus how much is integrated is in their hands.

- Services are not clearly "captive" or "outsourced"; some are jointly managed (the mid-grey dots), others are partnership (the light grey dots), others managed internally to the organisations involved, but in most cases it's not really important who provides the technology or service element;

they key differentiator is how these add up to support the customer in managing their business. On the whole, organisations will "own" the services core to their USP and partner with other services which are core to other organisations, and key to this model is the bank supporting the small business in becoming part of, and enabling their integration with, this ecosystem, to maximise their own growth potential.

- Note that, in this model, the bank offers both payments services and core banking supported by third-party providers. This is because both those services are managed as core standardised capabilities by third-party providers; the bank's core USP, which doesn't even feature on this customer-centric model example, is in designing and maintaining these ecosystems, applying banking know-how to support customer operations and growth, thereby providing the scaled services you do see; including the Business Model Development advisory which is an offshoot of this USP. See New Standard Models for Banking for more details of this.

The margin for the bank comes from several sources—obvious ones like Payments and account management, plus small but useful margins on scale services that wouldn't otherwise be available to the business. So while, for example, the bank may facilitate the integration of IoT to the ordering system for free, there are opportunities in the value chain to inject reasonable margins, which will grow as the customer's business grows.

In this model, the black dots are services run by the bank, the lightest grey ones those run by the client, the mid-grey ones by partner organisations/ecosystems and the light grey ones bank/client partnerships. We don't key the model because it's supposed to be obvious. But the point is the distinction of who does what becomes less important in this model.

Services and Customer Journeys

As referred to in the narrative for the first Service Architecture model for traditional banks, there's a strong relationship between Services and Customer Journeys, and the same is true of the second example, although it's harder to see (and draw) in the Ecosystem model because of the integrated nature of the ecosystem. You could equate the little buttons in the service element on the traditional model to customer touchpoints (or "moments of truth") on the customer journey. That doesn't mean that services equate to customer journeys, however: a customer journey will detail the instance of a use of a service, rather than the whole service, and may also include multiple services.

A customer journey, while an abstraction, is essentially ephemeral, while a service, although mutable over time, is a static part of your service architecture, embedded in your operating model, and carries all the potential states needed by the customer journeys that might apply to it.

Why Is This Useful?

Thinking about services reminds an organisation why it is in business; it allows it to identify the capabilities that are supporting your customers, and reflect their needs in terms of capabilities that you can then develop to deliver a great customer experience. More usefully, it's also an evolution of the ability to identify which capabilities should be consolidated/outsourced/offshored/removed; it helps you to identify capabilities that may not be core to your perception of your business, but in which you can provide expertise which will support your customers. The development of partnerships and business models is a good example of capabilities that banks usually have, but don't use to support their customers.

When working for one big bank, as a Change person with expertise in setting up banks, Sofie was outsourced to support both startup banks and NGOs that were customers of the bank and who were going through the process of building and executing complex business models—the customers benefitted from her experience, and while the bank made nothing but goodwill from it initially, they indirectly realised the value of her services as a lever for securing long-term customer loyalty, lucrative payments services for the new banks and a lot of good publicity in the business community via the NGOs. The success of these organisations under their new business models also created continued revenue for the bank, as they thrived and grew. This model allows you to optimise the offering to your customers by really thinking about the services you can offer them and, in a coordinated fashion, to benefit both parties.

The ecosystem approach takes this one step further, treating both customer and supplier as business partners, and offering a model where, acting as a partner and intermediary, the bank can support growth in both so that all benefit, directly and indirectly, not just from the expertise of the bank, but also from the services they offer to each other. Central to this is the concept that expertise gained by banks can help other organisations to develop more effective business models, just as when Sofie was being offered as a free commodity by that traditional bank.

hiveonline is taking this approach with its partners, and we're seeing more players in the new financial ecosystem collaborating across traditional banks, Fintechs, NGOs and governments to support customers. This helps open up the opportunities to support traditionally underserved and unbanked customers, as the combination of expertise, networks and service enables us to work on new service opportunities.

Of course, the ecosystem model is much more reliant on service architecture, partly because the scope is more complex, but also because it is much more based on multiple entities rather than captive services. In the ecosystem model, if there is a central entity, it is the customer and the bank is very much part of the wider support system; the challenge in visualising it is not so much that the delineation between customer and bank is not well defined, but in that it's difficult to define where the "edges" of the ecosystem lie; this means that in ecosystem organisations, any view really has to start with a single customer entity, as this allows the focus to identify what is part of that *particular* ecosystem and what's excluded.

As we hope is clear from the example, this makes it much easier to make decisions about where companies want to play, additional services they want to include or exclude, and how they plan to present their service offering to customers. It doesn't make it any easier to identify which services should include outsourced or insourced capabilities; this is a question to address to the capability model, as covered elsewhere. It does, however, provide focus and ideas for where to look for partners to support the ecosystem model further, and help to identify any capability gaps to be addressed.

To identify capabilities they *don't* need or want to develop, the business will have to compile the results of multiple capability analyses against its service models. This will help to identify which common capabilities are critical to supporting the models, which ones they want to keep captive, which ones they may want to outsource, and which ones they want to retire or merge with more useful capabilities.

Both flavours of service model also allow businesses to associate cost and organisational structures supporting those capabilities with the market revenues generated from the customer segment, based on volume and cost of management. The advantage of applying a service view to the ecosystem business model is the ability to analyse services holistically rather than piecemeal, without having to separately account for loss leaders and, to a large extent, reducing the need for ringfencing of innovation costs, as the direct needs of an ecosystem model clearly articulate where the capability gaps are and the business benefits of developing capabilities and services to fill those gaps.

These models also support the ability to identify key marketing and sales generation ideas, as they take you to the heart of the customer need—whether in the traditional or ecosystem model, so businesses are less likely to blunder into focusing on trying to sell the things important to them, rather than the things important to the customer, or into wildly inappropriate advertising that looked like a great idea at the time. They help to keep the customer clearly in focus at all times, and in all decisions.

For the same reason, they are also useful tools to communicate to their workforce and partners where everyone sits in the ecosystem, how they can add value, and get some great ideas for how they could change things to add even further value. We recommend keeping your service models on the walls of the office, many times over the typical motivational posters and empowerment bullshit we see in most corps—"it's all about the customer" is much less effective than a visual that effectively says, "X marks the spot" for both customer and whichever capability to which that department delivers.

But service models aren't a silver bullet, any more than capability models or process architecture are. Service architecture needs to be firmly rooted in business strategy and closely analysed for achievability, ROI, cultural fit and all the usual drivers. It also enriches all these aspects of an organisation and builds understanding from strategists and financiers through to the front line—and beyond, in the ecosystem model—of the value they are adding, thus enabling them to participate in the improvement dialogue.

Service Architecture and Organisational Structures

The service view of an offering, whether traditional or ecosystem, while still an abstraction of that offering, can also help businesses to structure the organisation much more directly than capability models can. Where capability models are fantastic for identifying capabilities businesses need to consolidate or outsource, and are critical to getting the support service architecture right, a service model gives them the ability to make decisions about organisation structure at the customer-facing edge of the organisation. Of course, this also applies to internal service and the organisational design supporting these, but the smart organisation will focus primarily on how best to align its services to its external customers; in nearly every case, this makes internal services easier to organise as well. Organisational considerations are covered in the first three chapters in this section.

When building a broader organisation with Service Architecture at the core, it is also critical to align communication governance to the service model. This can be achieved by comparing how services map to your capabilities and overlaying the governance structure between capabilities against this comparison. If there are governance structures enforcing alignment across capabilities that don't support related services, there may be good reasons, but organisations must understand whether this governance will help or hinder their ability to support customer services; conversely, they will quickly see where there are communication gaps between capabilities supporting the same service. We discuss decision architecture in the next chapter.

Conclusion

In this chapter we have described the core concepts of Service in contrast to capability and process; we've described two contrasting service architecture approaches for old and new world organisations, together with the benefits and approaches recommended for each approach. We've discussed why it's important to have a service architecture and the central role your customers play as organisations build a service catalogue and align the organisation to the services.

Services need to start with the customer—they're the reason for the service. Services should be the starting point for organisational structure; it should be structured around the service and the customer, rather than expecting customers to navigate the organisation. Service architecture helps identify both where organisations need to focus, and where they don't want to focus. It should reach beyond the organisation to understand the customer's needs holistically, and how partner organisations impact the customer experience. Services, processes and capabilities have different focus and drivers; all are needed to build an effective service aligned organisation.

Note

1. Haier homepage. http://www.haier.com/ae/. Accessed 30 December 2017.

26

Decision Architecture

Following on from service architecture and the structures needed to support a service aligned organisation, in this chapter we address the governance implications for organisations in general and the service aligned ecosystem in particular.

What Is Decision Architecture?

Decision logic is a commonly used concept, which has been widely used in technology design, and particularly interface design for customer-facing applications—you encounter it every time you phone up a Interactive Voice Response (IVR) and are invited to select options, sometimes from seemingly endless menus. The concept of decision architecture has also been used in some of these, to streamline the logic for these applications, so that instead of going through a tree structure, you experience a network with logical outcomes being anticipated based on early inputs.

We apply a similar approach to designing organisational governance, by anticipating the decisions that an organisation will need to make and building these likely decision points into an architecture that can be applied to an organisation's capabilities. The advantage of doing this is that we can then design the governance decision-making bodies—committees and so forth, around the decisions they need to make, rather than trying to find existing committees to make a decision or, more commonly, create a new one every time new decisions come up.

© The Author(s) 2018
S. Blakstad and R. Allen, *FinTech Revolution*,
https://doi.org/10.1007/978-3-319-76014-8_26

The Problem with Governance

Appropriate governance is critical to balancing an organisation's ability to control outcomes, with its ability to innovate and respond to changing circumstances. A rigid governance structure, with no flexibility and all decisions flowing up a hierarchy, paralyses decision making and prevents organisations from evolving. Too fluid a governance, and it's impossible to understand who's responsible for making decisions, which leads to no decisions being made. Most organisations fall somewhere in the middle. Unfortunately, governance is often the last thing to be designed holistically, with an organisation's outcomes in full view. There's a good reason for this; governance bodies are closely aligned to accountability, and, as with hierarchical organisation structures, where accountability for decisions rests, the committee naturally sits. This makes sense where organisational design is closely aligned to organisational outcomes but, as we've discussed in the rest of this section, this doesn't apply to most organisations.

Making Decisions with Courage and Conviction

Organisations, as we've discussed, are usually structured around function, and decisions flow up the hierarchy to bodies composed of increasingly broader collections of function, until they reach the executive committee, where decisions are made based on information passed up the organisation through this hierarchy. The bigger the decision, the further it goes up the tree; smaller decisions are made "lower down" in the organisation, by bodies composed of a subset of functions. This has characteristic results:

- Big decisions take a long time to make, because they're passed through successive governance bodies to get to the top of the tree.
- Big decisions are usually made with partial, highly filtered information, that has been doctored as it moves up the tree, meaning decision-makers don't have access to relevant information that would influence the outcome.
- Smaller decisions (often quite big) are often made by decision-making bodies with an organisational skew based on their representation; for example, decisions about technology which impacts end customers are likely to be made in the absence of any customer-facing representatives.
- Decisions are more likely to be made by bodies where the person requesting a particular outcome has a reporting relationship, than by bodies with specific subject matter expertise relevant to the decision.

- Because decision-makers are partially informed and often generalists, rather than skilled in the subject matter under review, the outcome of their decision is likely to be influenced by personal relationships and the position of the person in their reporting line wanting to influence the outcome, rather than by the content.
- Similarly, decisions can be subject to "group-think", where even if individuals have doubts or contrary opinions, they are less confident because of the limited information available, and likely to go with the majority or the most influential person's opinion.
- Once made, decisions may be communicated in a high level and unclear fashion, not specifying who is accountable for implementing them, resulting in slow or no response—even where the decision's clear, without clearly communicated accountability, the implementation becomes "somebody else's problem".

All of this leads to many wrong decisions being made, in good faith, by people who are very smart, committed to making the right decision, and fully prepared to be accountable for the outcome of that decision. Obviously, that doesn't mean *all* decisions are the wrong decision, because the decision-makers do have a broad range of experience and often are the right people to be making those decisions, but in too many cases, not enough of the right people are involved.

But, isn't that what leaders are for—being able to make decisions with partial information defines the job? That's what we have learned as we have progressed through traditional organisations to take up leadership roles, and it's absolutely true. In many cases, leaders must be there on the front line, making educated guesses with courage and conviction, and taking the associated risks.

But what if they're taking educated guesses with courage and conviction, when the information and expertise to make *the right* decision is freely available, within their organisation or within reach? Far from demonstrating leadership, that's allowing bad governance to lead them astray. And too often, the structure of organisations and decision-making bodies forces us into bad governance and making the wrong decisions.

A Question of Trust

In the absence of sufficient relevant information or expertise, organisational hierarchies effectively delegate decisions down the tree, even when that decision is officially taken by the highest body. It's what we call "Fred in the carpark" syndrome. It goes like this: Fred in the carpark wants a decision made, but it's more expensive/impactful than his mandate allows, so he passes it to his manager. His manager reckons it must be ok because she trusts Fred, but it's too big for her, so she passes it up the tree, and so on. Eventually it lands with Group Executive Management, and because everyone in the tree, from Fred's boss upwards, trusts the person recommending the decision to them, the decision is made. So effectively, the executive committee has delegated the decision making to Fred, who's probably the person with the right expertise anyway, so that's all good.

Of course, it could be derailed if Fred's manager, or her manager, or someone else up the tree, has another point of view. While their point of view may well be valid because of their broader viewpoint, it may just be that they don't like Fred's manager, because they have some vested interest or because it conflicts with something completely unrelated that they want to do instead. So Fred's need could be derailed, but he's unlikely to be involved in the discussion about the decision if it's happening two or three layers up the hierarchy; Fred's manager's manager may be in there arguing his case, but without Fred's direct experience and with information that's probably been filtered already, all he really has to support his case is how much he trusts Fred's manager, which won't always win. Again, depending on his relationships and the status of the person with the counter-argument, Fred's need could be dismissed for a variety of other reasons.

And whatever the outcome, all of this takes a lot of time and investment of effort from all the people throughout the hierarchy who've been involved in decision making. In Fred's case, that's a straight lineage through the management hierarchy, but as we know, that decision making usually doesn't happen in isolation; it's probably gone through several committees, where a number of highly paid individuals have reviewed the material in advance, then had a bit of a discussion about Fred's need, in committee.

Here's an example of a decision process with the associated costs.

In a global bank, there was a technology investment sign-off process for any expenditure over $25,000. Any expenditure went through the same process, whether it was for $25,000 or $25,000,000. When we reviewed the process, it turned out to be hugely expensive to run—55 mandatory approvers, five committees, various documents that needed to be originated, lots of negotiations. The whole process was costing around $8000 in people time every time it was run, as well as injecting nearly two months into the process of actually buying something.

When we conducted our review, of all the requests that had been put through in a period of six months, *not one* had been rejected. The cost to the organisation of signing off a $25,000 investment in people hours was about a third again of that expenditure, and more importantly, a two month delay in time to market. We weren't able to measure the cost of chasing the process, but we'd expect this to have taken up plenty of person hours as well.

Let's look at the reasons we use for passing the decisions up the tree:

- Somebody up the hierarchy may be better informed than Fred.
- Somebody up the hierarchy will have a more holistic perspective than Fred.
- Somebody up the hierarchy has more authority to spend money than Fred.
- Somebody up the hierarchy has more authority to change supplier than Fred.
- Somebody up the hierarchy has a cousin who owns a car park surfacing company.

Only two of these are good reasons (clue: the first two). It's true that Fred's perspective may make him underqualified to make the decision, if the implications are beyond his sphere of visibility. But why should his position be linked to his spending ability? We take it as natural that junior people in the organisation shouldn't be allowed to fritter away our P&L, but why not? If there's a decision that falls within Fred's area of expertise and he has the budget and all the information he needs to make that decision, passing it up the tree does nothing but inject cost and time into the process of making the decision. The Ritz-Carlton group[1] knows this and allows every employee a discretionary spend, which has had an incredible impact on efficiency and customer service.

Good governance gives decision rights to the people or bodies most suited to making the decision, and this is where decision architecture comes in. We probably wouldn't want Fred to make a decision about customer strategy, or design the menus for the canteen, but he might be the perfect person to choose the surface when we're rebuilding the car park and a budget has been allocated. What value will an executive committee bring to that decision? Of course, Fred probably won't make that decision in isolation, but the people who need to help him are not his manager and the hierarchy; they might be materials engineers, architects, someone who understands vendor management and maybe whoever's allocated the overall budget for the refurbishment; the people with expertise to inform the decision-making process.

But we can't let Fred make a decision which costs us $40,000! Or can't we? What is the difference between Fred making this decision, and Fred passing this decision up the tree? If he's involved the right expertise in making that decision, passing it up the tree will just inject time and cost to the process. You could also argue that we shouldn't put Fred on the spot and take the risk away from him, by giving him the rights over such an important decision. But if Fred knows his matter, what is the risk? We've already taken the decision to spend the money.

Another argument is that Fred may be incompetent, or be in cahoots with the supplier of the car park surface. This comes back to the trust issue. If we've hired Fred to do the job, we have to assume he's competent to do it. Anyone, at any level of hierarchy or pay, can be incompetent to do a particular task, or be dishonest, and it's up to the organisation to prevent this happening, rather than restricting their ability to perform their roles.

...Within Formalised Structure

But we're not advocating delegating all decisions to the lowest level; this puts us at the risk of entrusting too many decisions, the wrong decisions or too high a volume of decisions to Fred. Trust works both ways and Fred needs the support of the organisation to be able to successfully implement them. Devolving too many decisions to the lowest level also risks those decisions being hampered by the consensus building that typically happens at lower levels.

Cultural differences aside, in most cases paralysing consensus building is the result of a lack of experience, lack of confidence or lack of mandate, and if there's extensive consensus building going on, it's a symptom that Fred has wrong decisions, the wrong mandate or the wrong information. If Fred's going to make an informed and confident decision about the car park surface, he needs to know the boundaries of that decision—that it's in the budget, for example, and criteria for quality; he needs to feel confident that his leadership will support his decision—as they would if they were representing it up the tree, in fact. And he needs to have a clear mandate, telling him who to involve (and who not to involve) to avoid the paralysis of consensus decision making.

Let's say Fred is now asked to make some additional decisions, say about the opening hours of the car park, how frequently it's cleaned, or who can use the car park. These decisions, which may have a much lower cost implication for the organisation than the car park surface, are not encapsulated in the same way; they may depend on a lot of different factors beyond Fred's sphere of experience, although he needs to be consulted. In these decisions, Fred becomes a subject matter expert, but the decision rights, as they affect other individuals not in Fred's organisational capability, need to be taken by someone with a more holistic viewpoint, probably responsible for wider building management, who in turn will need to involve relevant people in the decision making.

So at any level, without clear alignment of expertise and roles to decisions and to different types of decisions, we're likely to be making some of the wrong decisions.

Strategic (Direction Setting) and Execution (Operational) Decisions

We hope that most executive committees aren't regularly making decisions about car park surfacing or opening hours, but when we compare some of the decisions that bubble up to senior governance and to executive teams, they're comparable, especially when the decision involves a lot of money; we confuse the *strategic* decision to spend the money with the *execution* decision about what to spend the money on. Strategy and execution don't just involve decisions about money; they can be about scope, technology or people, for example, and it's sometimes difficult to clearly understand the difference between strategic and execution, so we've created some definitions which explain how we see the difference.

Strategic (direction setting) decisions are likely to need endorsement from a capability independent committee such as a governance body to ensure strategic fit.

- The level at which decisions are made is based on agreed criteria, usually detailed in the governance of the organisation or charters of the decision-making bodies.
- Decisions should be targeted at one decision committee only for each decision, rather than a stack of committees.
- Example: a decision to expand into a new customer segment.

Execution, operational or delivery-focused decisions should be decentralised where possible for timeliness.

- Guidelines are needed for decision ownership and decision level.
- Use a simple scorecard to identify decisions requiring committee-level endorsement; capability teams may act as guides were in doubt.
- Interested parties are kept in the loop by an exception-based process (consent is assumed if not advised otherwise within predefined period).
- Example: a decision to agree metrics for sales staff in a new customer segment.

Clarity

These guidelines will work in most single cases; the art and science of decision architecture is more complex, and we find that in many cases where decisions are going to the wrong, or too many, decision making bodies, the problem is not so much that those decision-making bodies want to micromanage, but that there's a confusion about what's strategic, versus what's executional or operational. We've seen senior committees arguing about, approving and ultimately endorsing, details of reporting processes, while their strategic decisions are being made out of sight by Solution Architecture. SteerCo members dive into the details of how requirements are being built. This isn't usually the fault of the governance committee alone; it takes a whole organisation to build good, or bad, governance. But committees also need to be proactive in not accepting the wrong decisions being brought to their attention, and to do this, they need clarity on what those decisions should be.

You could argue that a strong governance committee would be composed of members that are capable of calling this; but even strong committees are controlled by their governance, and if that governance says they have to sign off decisions pertaining to the subject, with no distinction between strategic and execution decisions, especially in organisations where there's a history of people being penalised for making the wrong decisions, operational decisions will continue to bubble up.

So clarity is an answer; it's not the only answer; structure should precede clarity, but clarity in itself is a pretty good start. Most governance bodies have a charter of some sort, detailing the role and scope of the committee and its members, but few detail what they mean by the decisions this committee should be taking. Even capturing the decisions that the committee should be making today can help a lot (see below for some tips on this) and when this is built into a clear decision architecture, it's also much easier to see where these decisions are reaching the right, or the wrong, decision-making body.

Roles and Encapsulation

In addition to the right governance bodies making the right decisions, strong decision governance also needs clarity of which *roles* are responsible for making which decisions as we discussed earlier in this section. It's not enough just to tell people they should be making decisions, without telling them *which* decisions, what information they should gather before making that decision, and who should be consulted about the decision.

Decision architecture has very close ties with strategic workforce planning, as well as with capability design. Capabilities and Communities of Practice encapsulate roles, which in turn will have decision rights assigned to them. In most cases, broad decision architecture (where the bigger, strategic decisions are made) can be designed around the organisation's capability map, while lower level decision design associated with roles can be done within capabilities, through co-creation by capability communities. Necessarily, there will be a continuous dialogue between these two "layers", which together form the decision architecture of the organisation.

Because many decisions, associated with roles within capabilities, can be made independently of the broader governance structure, it's also possible and, indeed, desirable, to encapsulate these decisions within the capability's governance, rather than exposing this level of decision architecture to the broader organisational decision architecture. As with all other encapsulation, at some point a need may arise to expose the results of these decisions to the wider organisation, and it's therefore important for the organisation to understand that these decisions are made within the capability, but unimportant to understand the details of how that decision is made, or who's making it.

Decision Design, then Governance Design

As we've shown, most governance isn't really designed. It grows as the need for decision bodies arises, sometimes through omission being identified rather than through design, but more often in a planned way, as business units, programmes or initiatives are created. Every organisational unit needs a governance board to make decisions for it, or to ratify decisions. These decision boards are almost always tightly aligned to the organisational hierarchy of the units concerned, with senior people or their representatives on the boards.

While this works pretty well in a small, functionally structured organisation, it almost always translates as extremely complex, bureaucratic layers of governance in larger organisations, where units have responsibility both for their own governance, and towards the wider organisation. It gets worse when those organisations are managing any kind of matrix arrangement, with boards representing both organisational and policy/strategic alignment for different disciplines.

Add to this change programmes, and the matrix gets more complex. One of the fundamental challenges of implementing strategic change is attracting sufficient attention from sponsoring units at a senior level, but effectively what that means is that any organisation in transformation, as most are today, requires its senior managers to sit both on management and transformational bodies, absorbing significant amounts of their time. It also means that decisions are more likely to be passed through layers of decision fora, as accountabilities are unclear and often budget allocation requires authorisation by multiple units. In parallel, senior managers are likely to delegate responsibility for attending these fora to layers within their organisation, effectively removing the senior attention that was needed in the first place and again creating layers of decision making.

Radical though it might sound, we're proposing instead, designing decision fora *based on the decisions that need to be made*, rather than on the organisational hierarchy. Our experience shows that this is likely to meet with some resistance, but in practice creates a more positive experience for the forum members, while expediting decision making. There are potential pitfalls—some of the most significant decision bodies may turn out to be meeting too frequently, if there's not enough material that really needs their attention; agendas tend to get filled for the time available, rather than because of the relevance of the content. Where meetings are too frequent, the removal of irrelevant material may leave the committees with not enough decisions to make. Conversely, it's likely to identify the need for fora which didn't previously exist, where concentrations of decisions are clustering in a decision forum vacuum.

The beauty of analysing decisions prior to designing decision fora is that nothing has to be broken; unfortunately, real life isn't usually like that, so you're almost always working with an existing set of decision-making bodies, with entrenched behaviours and preconceptions. Landing change can be challenging, but having a body of evidence generated by decision analysis is useful to support delivery of the change.

Service Aligned Decision Architecture

When we describe service architecture for service aligned organisations, it looks complicated. As discussed elsewhere, this isn't because it's any more complicated than any other type of organisation—in fact, usually the reverse, but because we've stripped out the hierarchical view, there's a set of commonly used reference points that's entirely absent, and so the organisation needs to be described in terms of capabilities, services and decisions, rather than hierarchies and processes.

Those capabilities, services and decisions also exist in traditional organisations, but we generally don't try to capture them schematically because we have the hierarchies and processes to point to; services, decisions and capabilities are sometimes bolted onto the hierarchy or process diagram (typically a side box to a leader for a governance forum) but usually not captured separately as decision or service architecture, as outlined here and elsewhere in this section.

Decision architecture, like service architecture, for service aligned organisations, can't be pinned to a hierarchy, which can make it harder to know where to start; without a hierarchy, organisations are unlikely to have the same formalised top-down governance fora already in place. But it's usually easier to see the flow of decisions if they're based on service architecture, rather than hierarchies, so it's actually easier to get it right, without the baggage of a hierarchical organisation influencing the thinking.

In the absence of a hierarchy, decision architecture becomes more critical to understanding the organisation and the flow of control within it. It also makes it easier to identify where the most important decisions are being made, and to ensure that the right people are in the right roles to make these decisions.

Decision Architecture in the Ecosystem

As with services, for organisations operating as part of an ecosystem in the connected economy, decision architecture will persist beyond the boundaries of any individual organisation, and be closely associated with the services they support. This means extending decision rights across the organisation to groups and individuals who may be based in other organisations, which can at first look challenging, until we consider that many of the decisions made about our organisations are already being made outside our control; obvious ones like tax and regulation, but also less obvious ones such as how our services are positioned in relation to others by third-party agents, how our competitors position themselves, educational and social norms in the countries in which we operate, and so on.

An ecosystem in which the organisation is an active participant is a microcosm of a competitive environment in which that organisation has more, not less control, over how potential competitors (partners) are interacting with its customers, and therefore it is in the organisation's interest, and theirs, to ensure the decisions are taking place in an agile, decentralised way.

Like microservices technology, this means that there won't be full visibility of the decision-making process for decisions made outside the organisation, and governance needs to be robust to ensure that all parties are comfortable with the way decisions are being made and who's making them for this to work effectively. In general, the closer the decision is to the organisation and the more impact it has on it, the more likely it are to want to be involved with the decision, but this isn't always the right answer; often third parties in the ecosystem, especially those with a closer customer relationship for the service in question, will be both better informed and more able to make effective decisions without its direct input. The organisation may want to establish a right of veto over certain decisions, and just as important is for agreement upfront on which decisions over which it will *not* have a right of veto.

We present the components of decision architecture and some practical steps towards implementation on our website,[2] for readers who are interested in further details.

Conclusion

Through decision architecture, we can ensure the right decisions are being made by the right people, with the right information and in a timely fashion. That's not the only thing that makes an organisation run effectively, but well-designed decision architecture can significantly reduce management overhead, risk, time to decisions and confusion, while clarifying output of decisions and reducing the need for long management meetings.

Notes

1. Toporek, A. (2012, September 27). The Ritz-Carlton's Famous $2000 Rule. *Customers That Stick.* http://customersthatstick.com/blog/customer-loyalty/the-ritz-carltons-famous-2000-rule/. Accessed 7 January 2018.
2. Blakstad, S., & Allen, R. with Reith, T. (2016, September 20). Decision Architecture. hiveonline. http://www.hivenetwork.online/2016/09/decision-architecture. Accessed 7 January 2018.

Index